Judeities

Series Board

James Bernauer

Drucilla Cornell

Thomas R. Flynn

Kevin Hart

Jean-Luc Marion

Adriaan Peperzak

Richard Kearney

Thomas Sheehan

Hent de Vries

Merold Westphal

Edith Wyschogrod

Michael Zimmerman

John D. Caputo, *series editor*

PERSPECTIVES IN
CONTINENTAL
PHILOSOPHY

Edited by
BETTINA BERGO,
JOSEPH COHEN, *and*
RAPHAEL ZAGURY-ORLY

Judeities

Questions for Jacques Derrida

TRANSLATED BY
BETTINA BERGO AND MICHAEL B. SMITH

FORDHAM UNIVERSITY PRESS
New York ■ 2007

Save for Hent de Vries, "The Shibboleth Effect," the essays in this book were originally published in *Judéités: Questions pour Jacques Derrida*, ed. Joseph Cohen and Raphael Zagury-Orly © 2003 Éditions Galilée, 9, rue Linné, 75005 Paris.

Copyright © 2007 Fordham University Press

Library of Congress Cataloging-in-Publication Data

Judéités. English.
   Judeities : questions for Jacques Derrida / edited by Bettina Bergo, Joseph Cohen, and Raphael Zagury-Orly : Translated by Bettina Bergo and Michael B. Smith.
      p. cm.
   Includes bibliographical references.
   ISBN-13: 978-0-8232-2641-2 (alk. paper)
   ISBN-13: 978-0-8232-2642-9 (alk. paper)
   1. Derrida, Jacques—Congresses. 2. Jews—Congresses. I. Bergo, Bettina. II. Cohen, Joseph. III. Zagury-Orly, Raphael. IV. Title.
B2430.D484J8313 2007
194—dc22

                                                          2007019010

All rights reserved. No part of this publication may be reproduced, stored in a retrieval system, or transmitted in any form or by any means—electronic, mechanical, photocopy, recording, or any other—except for brief quotations in printed reviews, without the prior permission of the publisher.

Printed in the United States of America
09 08 07   5 4 3 2 1
First edition

Contents

Translators' Preface — ix

Preface to the French Edition — xi

Abraham, the Other — 1
Jacques Derrida

The Last, the Remnant . . . : (Derrida and Rosenzweig) — 36
Gérard Bensussan

This Stranjew Body — 52
Hélène Cixous

The Story of a Friendship: The Archive and the Question of Palestine — 78
Michal Ben Naftali

Jacques Derrida and Kabbalistic Sources — 111
Moshe Idel

Historicity and *Différance* — 131
Gianni Vattimo

How to Answer the Ethical Question — 142
Jürgen Habermas

A Monster of Faithfulness — 155
Joseph Cohen and Raphael Zagury-Orly

The Shibboleth Effect: On Reading Paul Celan　　　　*175*
　Hent de Vries

The Judeo-Christian　　　　*214*
　Jean-Luc Nancy

Contributors　　　　*235*

Notes　　　　*239*

Translators' Preface

BETTINA BERGO AND MICHAEL B. SMITH

For the English translation, we have preserved the neologism that introduces *Judéités: Questions pour Jacques Derrida*. As Raphael Zagury-Orly and Joseph Cohen, the colloquium organizers, pointed out, *judéités* refers to the multiplicity of ways of being and writing "jewishly," or as a Jew: Judaism and Jewishness, today, in the diversity of their multiple interpretations, languages, nationalities, philosophies, and literatures. *Judeities* unravels identifications, although identification is not itself a simple, or fully conscious, decision. As Derrida argues, being Jewish and Jewish-being entails "being" more and less than Jewish, something outside authentic-inauthentic binaries; in short, an ideal, a critique; above all a question.

The translations in this volume were proofed and edited jointly, as were "Jacques Derrida and Kabbalistic Sources" and "How to Answer the Ethical Question," essays presented to us in an English version. This distinctly enhanced the quality of the work and promoted terminological consistency. Michael B. Smith translated "The Story of a Friendship: The Archive and the Question of Palestine," "Historicity and *Différance*," and "A Monster of Faithfulness." Bettina Bergo translated "The Last, the Remnant . . .: (Derrida and Rosenzweig)" and "The Judeo-Christian." "This Stranjew Body" was translated by Bettina Bergo and Gabriel Malenfant; "Abraham, the Other" was translated by Gil Anidjar.

The essays appear in the order of presentation in the French original, though not all the French essays have been included in this English-language edition. Hent de Vries's "The Shibboleth Effect" is a contribution new to this volume.

Michael Smith would like to thank Xiaojing Zu, assistant librarian of Berry College, for her enthusiastic professional assistance and Bettina Bergo and Helen Tartar for having invited him in on this challenging and important translation project.

Bettina Bergo thanks Philippe Farah, Gabriel Malenfant, and Jocelyne Doyon, University of Montreal, for their linguistic and bibliographic assistance. She thanks Michael Smith for his suggestions and corrections. Both translators thank Helen Tartar sincerely for making this project possible.

Preface to the French Edition

JOSEPH COHEN AND RAPHAEL ZAGURY-ORLY

The international colloquium Judéités: Questions pour Jacques Derrida was held at the Jewish Community Center in Paris on December 3–5, 2000. This volume collects talks presented at that venue.

We have chosen the term *judeity* to express a certain equivocation, an undefinable and undeterminable diversity, that may well constitute the interiority of Judaism today. In other words, judeity, as we evoke it, should in no way be understood as a more "authentic" reformulation of Jewish identity. Here judeity is grasped in all the variety of its interpretations and commentaries, its languages, its nationalities, its politics, philosophies, literatures, and religious currents. The term *judeities*—upon whose plurality we insist—has opened the very possibility of this colloquium. That is the dual possibility of simultaneously questioning what is understood under the term *Judaism* and interrogating the relationship (if there is one) between Jacques Derrida's writing—itself invariably inscribed in the tension of the undefinable—and those multiple judeities.

There thus opened up for us vast and free spaces for questioning, where we could welcome inquiries concerning the political as much as those involving philosophy and religion, aesthetics as much as psychoanalysis and literature. Attentive not to circumscribe an entrenched identity nor to restrain discussion within definite contours, seeking rather to preserve all its aporetic quality and indecision, here academics, philosophers, and writers lend careful ear to the infinite questioning and the relationship (oblique at best) that link "deconstruction" and what we might designate "being-jewish." One of the conditions of this meeting consisted, precisely and in all faithfulness to the philosopher's own approach, in not attempting to go back to some relationship between the writings of Jacques Derrida and judeity that would be originary, named, established, full, and identifiable. With this precaution in mind, the relationship proved to be particularly fertile, as the wealth and heterogeneity of the texts assembled here attest.

The meeting would not have been possible without the support of the Jewish Community Center of Paris. Over and above the Center's wise counsel and hospitality, its director, Raphy Marciano, its president, Edmond Elalouf, and Professor Franklin Rausky sponsored this exceptional meeting: to them we owe exceptional gratitude. We are grateful also to the French Institute of Tel Aviv, the Cultural Services of the French Embassy in Israel, the Embassy of Israel in France, and the French Institute of the Netherlands for their generous support. The success of this event also depended—in great measure—on Karen Taïb, Martine Cohen, Michaël Allal, David Cohen, Myriam Skurnik, Gilbert Neddam, Elisheva Aron, Claude Lanzmann, and Michal Govrin. Finally, we thank Jacques Derrida for his remarkable availability and his capacity for listening throughout this colloquium, and for the numerous questions he raised, which continue to live on in us.

Judeities

Abraham, the Other

JACQUES DERRIDA

"I could think of another Abraham for myself."

This is a citation. "I could think of another Abraham for myself." One could translate it slightly differently. For the word *think*, one could substitute "imagine" or "conceive": "Ich könnte mir einen anderen Abraham denken"; "I could, for myself, aside within myself [*à part en moi*], as for myself, imagine, conceive the fiction of another Abraham."

The sentence comes to us from a brief parable, two short pages, by Kafka.[1] It bears as a title only a name: "Abraham," precisely. "Ich könnte mir einen anderen Abraham denken." And further: "Aber ein anderer Abraham"; "But yet another Abraham."

Perhaps, perhaps then, there would be more than one Abraham. And this is what would have to be *thought* (*denken*). *Perhaps*.

A few weeks ago, in New York, the largest Jewish city in the world, sometimes said to be inhabited by more Jews than Israel itself, Avital Ronell, an American friend and colleague, herself of European and Israeli origins, drew my attention to this apologue or fable of Kafka, which I am about to interpret in my own fashion, still otherwise, and obliquely, elliptically. As brief as it may be, this fiction stages not only another Abraham (*einen anderen Abraham*) but more than one other Abraham, at least two others. It is as if the serial multiplicity of the "more than one [*plus d'un*]" inscribed itself upon the very name of Abraham.² The narrator first says, "I could think of another Abraham for myself," and goes on to evoke a first other, a first second Abraham, in order to say, "I do not see the leap" he would have had to make in order to show himself ready to obey God on Mount Moriah—the word *leap* here confirming what is otherwise well known, namely, that Kafka had read Kierkegaard. The narrator then adds: "But there would be another Abraham [*aber ein anderer Abraham*]." This other other Abraham was ready to respond and answer the call, or to answer to the test of the election, but he was not sure of having been called, not sure that it was he himself and not another. He was not sure that it was he, in fact, who was the elected, and not another. He was afraid of being ridiculous, like someone who, hard of hearing, would come to answer "yes," "here I am," without having been called himself, without having been designated; or who would rush to answer the call addressed to another, like a bad student, for example, who from the back of the class, Kafka says, would think that he heard his own name, whereas the teacher had honored another, having meant to reward only the very best student of the class. True, the end of the parable leaves open another possibility: perhaps the teacher intended to stage a confusing test between the two names, or between the two chosen ones, in order to punish the bad student.

Let us leave here, as an exergue, these other Abrahams. Later on I will sketch one of the interpretations that tempt me most. Yet everything that I will risk here could be understood as an indirect response to Kafka's madness, and a post-script to another reading I have offered elsewhere, in *Donner la mort*,³ of Isaac's binding and, already, of more than one Abraham: multiple and sometimes fictitious Abrahams, from Kierkegaard to Levinas.

I must begin now to expose myself without sheltering myself behind these fictions.

Is this possible?

I do not believe, in any case, that it would be possible or justifiable for me, within me, and in the final analysis, to distinguish today between two stories. I say specifically "in the final analysis," two stories in the final analysis, there where the analytic account would be difficult, and perhaps interminable.

What stories? How to count them and give account of them, or better yet, how to be accountable for them? How, and by what right, can one distinguish, for example, between that which, in my experience, touches *in part* my "being jew [*être juif*]" at its most intimate, its most obscure, its most illegible (however one takes this "being-jew," and later I will in fact complicate the stakes of this expression—one cannot do everything at once) and *in part* that which, let us say, seems to belong in a more legible fashion to my work, the public work of a good or a bad student, which does not necessarily, nor always, bear visible traces of my "being-jew," whether it concerns itself with writing, teaching, ethics, law or politics, or civic behavior, or whether it concerns itself with philosophy or with literature.

And yet tonight I will act for awhile as if these two orders were distinct, to seek to determine later on, here or elsewhere, at least as a disputable hypothesis, the rule of what passes [*ce qui passe*] from one to the other, the rule of what occurs [*ce qui se passe*] between the two, and for which I would have, in sum, to respond.

Yes, it is a matter, once again, of responding. And *yes*, of responding "yes."

Without even naming Abraham, prior to daring to issue a summons toward the immense figure of the patriarch presumed to respond to the calling of his name, "yes, here I am," "I am here," "I am ready," one must know (and this is the first Abrahamic teaching, prior to any other) that if everything begins for us with the response, if everything begins with the "yes" implied in all responses ("yes, I respond," "yes, here I am," even if the response is "no"), then any response, even the most modest, the most mundane, of responses, remains an acquiescence given to some self-presentation. Even if, during the response, in the determined content of a reply, I were to say "no"; even if I were to declare "no, no, and no. I am not here, I will not come, I am leaving, I withdraw, I desert, I'm going to the desert, I am not one of your own nor am I facing you," or "no, I deny, abjure, refuse, disavow, and so on," well then, this "no" will have said "yes," "yes, I am here to speak to you, I am addressing you in order to answer 'no,' here I am to deny, disavow, or refuse."

One can draw quite a few consequences from this paradox and from this prevalence of an originary "yes"; from this precedence that makes the "yes" an undeniable vigilance [*veille*], the inheritance of a place [*lieu*] that cannot be uprooted; from this "yes" that comes up through every "no" on this earth and survives through all the negative modalities of disavowal (but what does it mean, to "disavow"? this will perhaps be my ultimate question), through all the negativities of questioning, doubt, skepticism, critique, and, sometimes, of a particular and hasty interpretation of deconstruction. One can draw consequences, and I have done so more than once, on many occasions and in many places. I will have to reaffirm this, no doubt, during the next few days.

It would thus be, once again, a matter of responding, of answering oneself, in one's name, or for one's name. Of answering-*to* [*de répondre*-à] (to whom? to someone, always, to a few, to everybody [*à tous et à toutes*], to you), of answering-*before*, therefore, and of answering-for (for one's acts and words, for oneself, for one's name; for example, for one's being-jew or not, etc.). In short, it would be a matter of taking responsibility, a responsibility that we know, in advance, exceeds all measure. How to respond? And first of all, how to respond to questions: for example, to these "questions" that have been announced, and addressed to me, on the issues that Joseph Cohen and Raphael Zagury-Orly have so prudently, so daringly, called "judeities [*judéités*]," in the plural? Judeities that would remain, above all, in question.

Early on, and for a long time I have trembled, I still tremble, before the title of this conference (questions addressed to me! and concerning judeities!) and never has the privilege of a conference apparently addressed to me intimidated, worried, or flustered me this much, to the point of leaving me with the feeling that a grave misunderstanding threatened to make me forget how much I feel, and will always feel, out of place in speaking of it; out of place, misplaced, decentered, very far from what could resemble the thing itself or the center of said questions, the multiple questions oriented toward plural judeities and whatever could be implied by this word, *judeities*, in the plural, to which I shall return. Is it really to me, at the back of the class, in the last row, that such questions must be addressed or destined? On the matter of judeity or judaism, the insufficiency, the inadequacy, the failure (all mine, and of which I have not finished speaking) are graver and, I fear, more significant than a simple incompetence, an incompetence and a lack of culture, to which, by the way, I at the same time also confess. But I will have to explain myself, and so I must at least respond, precisely, I must answer for all these faults and failures. I must do so, and I owe it to you [*je le dois, je vous le dois*]; I must answer for them to you, before you, all of you who are here, before those who remarkably honor me by partaking in this experience, assuming its meaning with courage and generosity, while alone I would never have even imagined its possibility. Respond I must, in truth, and I owe this first to my hosts in this place, particularly to Mr. Elalouf and Mr. Marciano;[4] and then to express my anxious gratitude to Joseph Cohen and Raphael Zagury-Orly, who have done so much, who have succeeded in overcoming my doubts and my skepticism, in order to give to this encounter all its opportunities, that is to say, all its risks. I will no doubt speak of risks more than of opportunities, even if I do not believe it possible to separate the two, risk taken and opportunity given [*le risque couru et la chance donnée*], no more here than anywhere else. One can no more dissociate opportunity from risk in the case, for example, of peace negotiations—if, that is, one truly wants peace. For example, in Israel and Palestine.

Here, however, it is about more than one dissociation that I would like to begin by saying a few words. The dissociations I am thinking of are not necessarily threats to the social or communal bond, since a certain rupture, a certain departure, a certain separation, an interruption of the bond, a radical un-binding remains also, I believe, the condition of the social bond as such. I mean that of love. Of living love and of lifelong love of life [*de l'amour à vie de la vie*], the lively and exposed affirmation of life [*de l'affirmation à vif de la vie*]. So it is that evil, risk, as well as opportunity, have to do neither with dissociation nor with its opposite, but with the experience of a dissociation that is at once possible, necessary, *and* impossible. An alternative at once promised and denied.

A few figures of this alternative, of this necessary but impossible dissociation, already present themselves. Three, at least.

First, a dissociation between *persons*, the grammatical marks of the person, and what they indicate of what was still being called until fairly recently the subject—a word I would prefer to restrict to its purely grammatical meaning. I designate in this way the dissociation between the first, second, and third persons, singular and plural, male and female (I, you, he/she, we, you, they [*ils/elles*]): I am jewish, you are jewish, he/she is jewish [*juif(ve)*], you are jewish [*juif(ve)s*], we are Jewish, they are Jewish, and so on. How do these persons translate into each other and is it possible? Can one authorize oneself to move from "you are Jewish" [*tu es juif ou juive*] to a "therefore I am" [*donc je le suis*]?

Second, the dissociation, and therefore the alternative, between *authenticity* and *inauthenticity* (I do not say truth and un-truth): authentic Jew / inauthentic Jew. Can one trust in this distinction, of which, as I will recall, Sartre made a famous and troubled use right after the war?

Third, the dissociation between *judeity* [jewishness] (the word invoked, in the plural, in the title of this conference: *judeities*) and *judaism*. Can one trust in the alternative (e.g., jewishness/judaism),⁵ of which I will recall the letters of nobility conferred on it by Yosef Yerushalmi in his book on Freud's Moses?⁶

But before defending with arguments my doubts regarding the trustworthiness [*fiabilité*] of these *three* distinctions (I/you, I/we, we/you, I-we/they [*ils-elles*], etc.; authentic/inauthentic; jewishness/judaism), allow me to whisper the following, with the tone of a more or less innocent confidence. I hardly dare here—I hardly dared even yesterday—to take the floor, as one says. And no doubt I will only do so to confide in you that which in me, for a long time now, feels—in a place such as this, in a place defined in this way, before a topic so formulated, before the "jewish" thing [*devant la chose "juive"*], at once, precisely, *entrusted*, and *condemned*, to silence [confié—*et* condamné *au mutisme*]. Yes, entrusted as much as condemned. Both entrusted to silence, in the sense that one says entrusted for safekeeping, entrusted to a silence that keeps and guards so long as one keeps and guards it. It is a bit as if a certain way of keeping quiet, of silencing oneself [*une certaine façon de taire ou de se taire*], as if a certain secret had always represented, regarding judaism, regarding jewishness, regarding the condition or the situation of being *jew*, regarding this appellation that I hardly dare, precisely, to call mine—it is as if such silence, a determined silence and not just any silence (for I have never, absolutely never, hidden my jewish descent, and I have always been honored to claim it), as if nonetheless such obstinate reserve had represented a kind of guard, a kind of care-taking, of safekeeping: a silence that one protects and that protects, a secret that perhaps keeps *from* judaism [*garde* du *judaïsme*], but keeps as well a certain jewishness in oneself—here in me.⁷ One knows the profound link—it is not only an etymological one—that can be found between keeping guard and truth [*la garde et la vérité*]. As if—a paradox that I will not stop unfolding and that summarizes all the torment of my life—I had to keep myself from judaism [*me garder du judaïsme*] in order to retain within myself something that I provisionally call jewishness. The phrase, the contradictory injunction, that would thus have ordered my life seemed to say to me, in French: "garde-toi du judaïsme—ou même de la judéité." Keep yourself from it in order to keep some of it, keep yourself from it, guard yourself from being jewish in order to keep yourself jewish or to keep and guard the Jew in you. Guard yourself from and take care of the Jew in you [*prends garde au Juif en toi*]. Watch and watch out [*re-garde*], be vigilant, be watchful, and do not be Jewish at any price. Even if you are alone and the last to be jewish at this price, look twice before claiming a communal, even national or especially state-national, solidarity and before speaking, before taking sides and taking a stand *as a Jew*.

Is all of this authentic? I will return to the abyssal ground of this word *authentic*, which is anything but innocent.

To guard the silence that guards me, such would be the *order*—which I understand almost in the religious sense of a community, or rather a non-community, of a solitude of withdrawal from the world—the order to which I would have been entrusted forever, almost forever, a bit the way one entrusts or commits an orphan, a pupil of I don't know what nation anymore, even less what nation-state, a lost child—but who perhaps still gives way to the obscure weakness of feeling as if a bit chosen for this being in perdition [*cet être en perdition*]. Called, at the risk of a terrifying misunderstanding about the proper name.

This watch [*garde*] over the secret to which I seem to have been entrusted, or this watch over the confided secret, a secret so much larger and so much graver than I—it is as if I had received a mission to be faithful to it, so long as a proper word about it were not given or dictated [*donnée ou ordonnée*] to me, a speech that I would have to invent as much as discover, encounter within myself outside myself [*rencontrer en moi hors de moi*], and defend at all cost. I do not believe, I am not sure, far from it, that the time has come. And I know that were it to come one day, the decision would not be mine, and the certainty would never be secure. A call worthy of that name, a call of the name worthy of the name, must give room to no certainty on the side of the addressee. Failing that, it is not a call.

I was speaking of silence and of mutism, the stubborn silence to which—entrusted to it as I was—I was, so I surmised, condemned. By whom, by what, where and how? Those are my questions. For if trust, if the confidence of having-been-entrusted, through a kind of secret election, though in its essence uncertain, always ready for an apocalyptic or a derisive misunderstanding, an election that above all would not be the election of a people—a counter-election, therefore, the counter-example of election—if, then, I have always, almost always, felt that what has destined, dedicated, and devoted me [*ce qui m'a voué, dévoué, adonné*] to the law of such a silence was the promised chance of a salvation without salvation that came from I don't know where, well then, it is nonetheless the case that I have felt simultaneously, in-dissociably, under house arrest, even denounced, condemned, damned by the same obscure consciousness of election, of fatal choice by which a power, transcendent and without face, was driving me to silence, striking me with muteness as one inflicts an infirmity, a wound or a plague, since birth or *almost* since birth. The silence of which I speak was, then, and still is, both chosen and not chosen, undecidably decided by me without me, by the other in me. At the endless risk of a tragic or laughable misunderstanding.

To be condemned or damned [*condamné ou damné*] is to have to serve a sentence, to repay a damage (*damnum*), a lesion, a fault, a wrong that was committed, or a wrong for which one is a priori indicted, accused ("charged," as one says in English). What fault, what damage, what lesion, what wound? This is perhaps the open question, the question that no more closes than does a scar, and that has always, almost always, haunted my mutism, cutting off my speech, pushing, pushing away, and holding fast to my words on the edge of all language. And here as well, on the edge of what I am tempted to say, I will let myself be guided by a question regarding that question: Why the big enigma, the quasi-universal and ontological thematic of an a priori guilt or responsibility, of an originary debt, a congenital wrong (which one finds everywhere, notably among so-called Christian, anti-Christian, or atheist thinkers, like Kierkegaard or Heidegger)? Why has the universal argument[8] of this singular indictment come for me always, *almost* always, obscurely, as if stuck to the question of my belonging without belonging to jewishness or to judaism? (Again, I leave for later my questions regarding this distinction.)

Tonight, I feel that I will have to avow or disavow this "je ne sais quoi" that has almost always devoted me, entrusted and condemned me, to a "keeping quiet [*se taire*]." I would, at least, have to pretend to break the silence, if only to state one more time—and I will never say it enough—my anxious gratitude to those who have taken the initiative of inventing such a dangerous encounter, one that for me remains still a bit unimaginable. I would be lying, of course, if I claimed that today is the first time that I speak in public of my being—or my *quasi*-being—jew, or of my unbelievable belonging to judaism. I have often ventured this, most of all in the past decade, in numerous places that I will not enumerate. And yet, every time I have done so, I have only *appeared* to do so [*j'ai seulement* paru *le faire*]. In truth, by the detour of more or less calculated ruses, of generally deliberate ellipses, which were intended to be learned [*et qui se voulaient savantes*], by way of a phenomenological play of suspension, quotation marks and parentheses, I avoided doing fully what I was then doing: un-signing what I was signing [*de dé-signer ce que je signais*]. Is there a category for thinking and formalizing this gesture, which consists in avoiding without avoiding, in disavowing the very avowal? I do not know. Will it be called denial, inauthenticity (I will return to this word in a moment), a double game? My feeling is that none of these words is adequate to master the "jewish" example or case of which I speak. But that this problematic must be rethought starting from that case, or from the abyss into which it carries everything, including the value of exemplarity.

During the time that preceded this encounter, and even yesterday, I have asked myself whether I should speak of these questions in a scholarly, philosophical, exegetical, or "deconstructive" manner. Without renouncing doing so later on, for example, during the discussions, and since I have done so elsewhere, it seems preferable to expose myself more crudely, for example, by asking myself, by trying to remind myself, by recalling myself *tout court*, and for that by recalling *myself*, to myself, how the word *jew* (before "judaism" and, most of all, before "jewishness") arrived, how it reached me like an arrival [*comme un arrivant*] or a first arrival, in the language of my childhood, landing in the French language of the Algeria of my first sentences. I will not reach, tonight—the occasion does not lend itself to it—such anamnesis regarding the arrival of "jew" in my language, of this word that remains incredible [*inouï*] to me, deeper and more profound in me than my own name, more elementary and more indelible than any other in the world, than the "yes" from which I started and from which I have said that it is impossible to part or depart, from which everything, in truth, proceeds, closer to my body than an article of clothing, than my body itself.

But we know that with the interrogation of a word, of the history of a word, of our relation to a vocabulary, to the vocation or the convocation of a word [*vocable*], the temptation, the impossible desire, is to identify a *first time*, the occurrence without precedent of an appellation so new and then so unique that it resembles the appearance of a proper name. What was, for me, such an epiphany of the word *jew* in my Algerian childhood?

Answering this kind of question is easier, if not always possible, when dealing with actual proper names identified with persons. In that case, we are guided by a reference, we know *who* is called by the appellation, and misunderstandings concerning that person are improbable. We always believe we know when such and such a name or surname of a person appeared for the first time—most often along with its referent. It is much more difficult, for me truly impossible, when dealing with words—names or not—that are, as one says, *common*: adjectives or common nouns.

Now, there are two appellations about which I have never managed to know, to know anything at all, and most of all to know how they came to me or whether they constituted names, common nouns or proper names. These are, so far as I know, the only two words about which I have relentlessly sought to find out, in the darkness of my memory, where, when, and how their epiphany came to light for me, gave birth for me—as far as I am concerned.

These two appellations, these two words that are neither common nor proper, are not "Daddy" and "Mommy," but *God*—and *Jew*. In "Circumfession," I have alluded at least once to the anxious amnesia that surrounds the first epiphany of the word *Dieu* (in French, for it is in French, of a French word that I always speak). I will therefore not return to it directly, nor will I revisit what I have risked writing, in a less autobiographical mode, regarding the name *God* in numerous texts. But as for the word *jew*, I do not believe I heard it first in my family, nor ever as a neutral designation meant to classify, even less to identify a belonging to a social, ethnic, or religious community. I believe I heard it at school in El Biar, already charged with what, in Latin, one could call an insult [*injure*], *injuria*, in English, *injury*, both an insult, a wound, and an injustice, a denial of right rather than the right to belong to a legitimate group. Before understanding any of it, I received this word like a blow, a denunciation, a de-legitimation prior to any right, prior to any legality. A blow struck [*un coup porté*] against me, but a blow that I would henceforth have to carry and incorporate [*porter, comporter*] forever in the very essence of my most singularly signed and assigned behavior [*comportement*]. It is as if I had to countersign the blow thus struck prior even to any possible memory. This word, this performative address ("Jew," that is, almost inevitably, as if it were readily understood as "dirty Jew!"), this apostrophe was, remains, and carries, older than the claim [*constat*], more archaic than any constative, the figure of a wounding arrow, of a weapon or a projectile that has sunk into your body, once and for all and without the possibility of ever uprooting it. It adheres to your body and pulls it toward itself from within, as would a fishing hook or a harpoon lodged inside you, by way of the cutting and wet edge, the body of each of its letters, *j.e.w*. One can, afterward, assume this word, treat it in a thousand different ways, think it honorable to subscribe to it, to sign and countersign it. But, for me at least, it guards and keeps the mark of this assignation, of this unveiling that denounces, even of this originary accusation, this guilt or responsibility, *granted* dissymmetrically prior to any fault or act. And to speak honorably of this word *jew*—and by honorably, I mean measuring oneself by way of what is worthy of that name or of that adjective in the audible and visible forms of its syllables, in the turbulent life of each of its letters, in the tumultuous movement of its oral pronunciation and of its graphic destiny—the *j* and the *oui* [yes] of *juif*, between the *suis* [am] of *je suis* [I am], *je suis juif* [I am jew], the *juste* [barely, only, just, *or*: righteous, just] of "je suis juste en tant que Juif [as a Jew, I am just *or*: I am only to the extent that I am Jew]," or "je suis juste un Juif [I am just a Jew, no more than a Jew]," or *juste un juste* [only a just person], "rien que juste un Juif juste [nothing but just a just Jew]," "oui, juste un Juif qui jouit à être juste et plus juste que la justice ou que le droit, oui, je suis juste un Juif par ouï-dire qui s'entend à être juste un Juif juste, plus juste que la justice, et qui doit exiger pour le Juif d'être plus juste que la justice, qu'on soit avec lui et qu'il soit pour les autres plus juste, oui que le droit et la justice, etc. [yes, just a Jew who enjoys being just and more just than justice or law, yes, I am barely a Jew by hear-say who has heard of, who understands himself as being, no more than a just Jew, more just than justice, and who must demand for the Jew that he be more just than justice; that one be with him and that he be for the others more just, yes, than law and justice, etc.]." One would have to appeal to a force of poetic invention *and* memory, to a power of invention *like* the boldness of anamnesis. One would need art, or the genius of an archaeologist of the phantasm, the courage of childhood, too, of which I do not feel capable tonight—and which, I fear, neither the setting, the time, nor the space are available to us in such a conference and according to the laws of its genre.

Two brief remarks here, where interminable speeches would be required.

1. *On the one hand*, every time I have had to address seriously, if in a different mode, within the history of philosophy and of onto-theology, for example, in Nietzsche, Heidegger, or Levinas, and in many others as well, this theme of an originary guilt or incrimination, a guilt or a responsibility (*Schuldigsein*, as the Germans can luckily say in one word), the theme of a debt, an indebtedness, a being-indebted, all originary, prior to any contract, prior to contracting anything; well then, every time I have addressed this great philosophical problematic, I would see returning, from the bottomless ground of memory, this experience of dissymmetric assignation of being-jew, coupled immediately with what has become, for me, the immense and the most suspect, the most problematical, resource, one before which anyone, and therefore the Jew among others (I dare not say the Jew par excellence), must remain watchful, on guard, precisely: the cunning resource of *exemplarism*—of which I will no doubt speak again. Here, exemplarism would consist in acknowledging, or claiming to identify, in what one calls the Jew the exemplary figure of a universal structure of the living human, to wit, this being originarily indebted, responsible, guilty. As if election or counter-election consisted in having been chosen as guardian of a truth, a law, an essence, in truth here, of a universal responsibility. The more jewish the Jew [*plus le Juif est juif*], the more he would represent the universality of human responsibility for man, and the more he would have to respond to it, to answer for it. Such exemplarism is a formidable temptation—to which many have surrendered, even Celan. It operates in every modern nationalism, nationalism never having been the claim to particularity or to an irreducible difference but rather a vocation for universal exemplarity, and therefore for a responsibility without limits, for every one and in front of every one, living and dead, a responsibility that is historically incarnated in this difference (one could give a thousand examples; I will not do so, keeping this question, for now, together with that of a thought of election, that of a people or of an individual, there where it communicates with the immense, grave, painful, and terrible question of the state of Israel—yesterday, today, and tomorrow—a question that I intend neither to run from nor precipitously to broach here. I will return to this, then, and no doubt we will discuss it tomorrow night with Claude Lanzmann, and yet again on the following day).

Under the heading of exemplarity, and above all of what I have repeatedly called the counter-example, when I play without playing, in a notebook from 1976 quoted in "Circumfession," at calling myself "the last and the least of the Jews [*le dernier des Juifs*],"⁹ I introduce myself both as the least Jewish, the most unworthy Jew, the last to deserve the title of authentic Jew, and at the same time, because of all this, by reason of a force of rupture that uproots and universalizes the place [*lieu*], the local, the familial, the communal, the national, and so on, he who plays at playing the role of the most Jewish of all, the last and therefore the only survivor fated to assume the legacy of generations, to save the response or responsibility before the assignation, or before the election, always at risk of taking himself for another, something that belongs to the essence of an experience of election; as if the least could do the most, but also as if (you will have noted, no doubt, that I often have recourse to the "as if," and I do so intentionally, without playing, without being facile, because I believe that a certain *perhaps* of the *as if*, the poetical or the literary, in sum, lies at the heart of what I want to entrust to you) —*as if* the one who disavowed the most, and who appeared to betray the dogmas of belonging, be it a belonging to the community, the religion, even to the people, the nation and the state, and so on —*as if* this individual alone represented the last demand, the hyperbolic request of the very thing he appears to betray by perjuring himself. Hence this law that comes upon me, a law that, appearing antinomian, dictated to me, in a precocious and obscure fashion, in a kind of light whose rays are unbending, the hyper-formalized formula of a destiny devoted to the secret—and that is why I play seriously, more and more, with the figure of the marrano: the less you show yourself as jewish, the more and better jew you will be. The more radically you break with a certain dogmatism of the place or of the bond [*du lieu ou du lien*] (communal, national, religious, of the state), the more you will be faithful to the hyperbolic, excessive [*démesurée*] demand, to the *hubris*, perhaps, of a universal and disproportionate responsibility toward the singularity of every other ("every other is wholly other [*tout autre est tout autre*]" is what I responded to Levinas one day, and I will perhaps say later what the hardly controllable stakes of this expression are, an expression that can barely be translated and is perhaps perverse). I speak to myself, then, I address to myself an apostrophe that seems to come to me from the site of a responsibility without limits, that is to say, hyper-ethical, hyper-political, hyper-philosophical, a responsibility the ferment of which—"you understood this immediately," I said to myself—burns at the most irredentist core of what calls itself "jew." Henceforth, one had to grant the terrifying consequence of this superlative antinomy: the least is the most, the least is the paradoxical condition of the most, a certain experience of perjury is the painful and originary enduring of faithfulness. (I have explained this better in *Adieu to Emmanuel Levinas* and elsewhere, as the theme of perjury is among those to which I have stayed the most faithful, and here I would have to speak—as I did one day, by thus entitling a common meditation with Arab and Muslim friends in Rabat—of a "fidélité à plus d'un [faithfulness to more than one, *or*: collective faithfulness]," faithfulness to more than one remaining this impossible and necessary chance that one would have to be "worthy of inheriting [*mériter d'hériter*].") This experience is even more cruel, for I asked myself, and I ask myself still, whether I should not free myself from an unpleasant narcissistic complacency and from this remainder of exemplarism, which would let me believe in some law of hyperbole, in this inversion of hyperbole that, in the end, for the last, makes "the least" into "the most," in this hubris of the law that would still be exemplarily Jewish and would pass through the body, even the circumcised body, of the Jewish man, through the memory of old Abraham, still another, when the covenant named him anew in order to make him the father of nations. From this narcissistic and exemplarist temptation, from this subtle, twisted and difficult [*retorse*], and ego-centered interpretation of election—which can lead, one knows that too, to state nationalism in its most violent forms, even militaristic and colonialist—one also had to free and emancipate oneself through deracination; one even had to oppose this temptation, precisely in the name of the same demand for a universal and hyperbolic justice, a justice that traverses but also exceeds law.

Tomorrow, in a more narrative mode, and no doubt the day after tomorrow, beyond narrative, I shall perhaps try to describe the paradoxical effects of such experiences from my Algerian childhood. I have already spoken of them elsewhere: the constant, general, and virulent anti-Semitism of colonial Algeria, its aggravation, its own overbidding during the war, which preceded and went beyond the politics of Vichy, the loss of French citizenship, the status of indigenous Jew, the exclusion of all Jewish children and teachers from educational institutions without a whisper of protest on the part of the other teachers—at least on the side of the French, since native Algerians sometimes showed more solidarity with the Jews in this ordeal, and so on. In spite of the painful gravity of it, all this was in no way comparable to the tragedy of European Jews or even French Jews, a monstrous tragedy of which we knew nothing and about which later, for this very reason, my compassion and my horrified indignation were and remain such as must move a universal conscience rather than that of a Jew affected in his own kin [*plutôt que celle d'un Juif touché dans les siens*]. Ultimately, the paradoxical effect I wanted to describe schematically is that my suffering as a persecuted young Jew (common enough, after all, and not comparable to those endured in Europe—something that adds to all the reserve and decency that prevent me from speaking of it), this suffering has no doubt killed in me an elementary confidence in any community, in any fusional gregariousness, whatever its nature, and beginning of course with any anti-Semitic herding that alleges ethnic, religious, or national roots and of which my trained vigilance knows how to recognize the signs and decipher the symptoms with a promptness that I would dare call terrifying (I sometimes wonder whether the deciphering of the anti-Semitic symptom, as well as of the entire system of connotations that indissociably accompanies it, was not the first corpus I learned to interpret, as if I only knew how to read—others would say, how to "deconstruct"—because of having first learned to read, to deconstruct even, anti-Semitism). But the same suffering and the same compulsion to decipher the symptom have also, paradoxically and simultaneously, cautioned me against community and communitarianism in general, beginning with reactive solidarity, as fusional and sometimes not less gregarious than what constituted my Jewish environment. As early as the age of ten (the expulsion from school and the highpoint of official and authorized anti-Semitism in Algeria), an obscure feeling took shape in me, at first uncultivated, then more and more reasoned, of interrupted belonging, a relation vexed *from both sides*: from the side of the declared enemy, of course, the anti-Semite, but also from the side of "my own [*du côté des miens*]," if I may say so. I will speak later of what the consequences were for me and for a kind of political philosophy that began to develop wildly in me, and continues to do so, toward all community, toward all Jewish culture, be it Sephardi or above all Ashkenazi; toward the family, the people, and the communal sentiment, whether it be national or state-national. Of course, this anxious vigilance of a stranger within, this insomniac distrust, has not failed to come up in respect to the still exemplary phenomenon that is the state of Israel, and all the kinds of violence that have marked its young history, the very principle and the conditions of its founding as the politics that, in a more or less continuous fashion, have governed its destiny—and still do so. The childhood and adolescence I am evoking here have coincided in time with the beginnings and then the creation of this state, both so singular and so similar to all others, while the Zionist call was resonating loudly in Algeria after the war. Rightly or wrongly, I have never felt the obligation, the ability, or the wisdom to respond to this call, but I will try to say later, in as just, complex, and prudent, as well as honest, a way as possible, the reasons that I have given myself, that I still give myself in my concerned and noncomplacent judgments about the state of Israel. Yesterday, the day before yesterday, and today. Concerned judgments, certainly, numbed by anxiety and compassion, but judgments that refuse complacency and that address themselves *both* to the justice I believe is owed to Israel and its survival, as a matter of course, *and* to the justice that one expects from Israel, and that a Jew, more and better than any other, even before any other, would have the right to hope for from Israel. The day before yesterday and tomorrow.

All that I would like to emphasize for now is the retreat and retrenchment [*retranchement*] of which I speak, a retreat, a caesura that appeared to decide itself, to carve itself within the very wound, within the wound that will not heal [*la blessure non cicatrisable*], that anti-Semitism has left in me, and a retreat outside of all community, including the one that was called my own, a merciless withdrawal that I felt already, and that I still feel, *at once, at the same time*, as less jewish *and* more jewish than the Jew, as scarcely Jewish and as superlatively Jewish as possible, more than Jew [*plus que Juif*], exemplarily Jew, but also hyperbolically Jew, when I was honing its cultivation to the point of mistrusting even the *exemplarist* temptation — not to mention the even more difficult and problematical language of *election*. This overbidding of an excess that never stops, that pursues and persecutes itself, the most becoming incomparably the least, or the other, a superlative more than a comparative — I have found it everywhere; it has found me everywhere, and one could locate a thousand signs in writings and teachings, in arguments that I did not direct — neither in appearance, nor in reality — toward the theme of any jewish question. I will perhaps give some examples in the discussions that will follow.

2. *On the other hand*, something in me was already living the wound and the retreat of which I just spoke — the first event of which I located in the experience of anti-Semitic violence in the French Algeria of the 1940s — already living these as a trauma at once decisive, determining, inaugural, and already secondary, I mean to say already second, already consecutive and assigned by a law, that is to say, by a

nonmemorable and immemorial repetition. I will say nothing of it here, mainly for lack of time, but were I to do so, I would speak of what this retreat would have to do — or not — with the memory without memory of circumcision. The texts I have published, since the 1960s, and not only those that mention it explicitly, such as *Glas*, *The Post Card*, "Shibboleth," or "Circumfession," all consign an indefinitely insomniac vigil over the event called "circumcision," *my* circumcision, the one that took place only once but of which I have attempted to demonstrate that it inscribed repetition from its first act onward. (A friend asked me whether I thought, as I had told her earlier, that this conference risked being a second circumcision for me. I answered her as firmly as imprudently, "no" — a "no" that I leave to your interpretation. Does it mean that a circumcision worthy of that name must take place and cannot but take place once and only once? Or that I have decided to make sure that it does not happen again? Or that circumcision takes place more than once the moment it first takes place [*plus d'une fois dès la première fois*]?)

To remain with the skeletal logic of this destiny or this *destinerrance*, as I sometimes put it, I will only remark that the dissociation, the retreat, and the hyperbole of this overbidding (the more than = the less and other than), this axiomatics of "I am the last and the least of the Jews," far from reassuring me within distinctions and oppositions, has done nothing but render impossible and illegitimate all distinctions and oppositions. On the contrary, this experience has sharpened my reasoned mistrust of borders and oppositional distinctions (whether conceptual or not), and thus has pushed me to elaborate a deconstruction as well as an ethics of decision, an ethics of responsibility, exposed to the endurance of the undecidable, to the law of *my* decision as *decision of the other* in me, dedicated and devoted [*vouée, dévouée*] to aporia, to a not-being-able-to or not-being-obligated-to [*au ne-pas-pouvoir ou au ne-pas-devoir*] trust in an oppositional border between two, for example, between two concepts that are apparently dissociable. The first paradox or the principial aporia has to do with the fact that the experience of dissociation or of a disseminal heterogeneity is the very thing that forbids dissociation from anchoring itself or being lulled into an oppositional distinction, into a decidable border or a reassuring difference.

I come therefore, and finally, to the *three distinctions or alternatives* announced earlier (Jew/jew, authentic/inauthentic, jewishness/judaism), which you can already feel I hold to be untenable.

1. *First.* Before I even come close to the word *jewishness* [*judéité*], to the plural form, and to the differences that announce themselves in it, I will not have been the only one to recall that there is jew and Jew. "Jew"—is that an adjective? Is it a noun? Can one *convert*, that is to say, translate, without remainder a sentence such as *je suis juif*, a proposition in which the adjective *juif* is an attribute thus *attributed* (but attributed by whom, in the first place? and who, here, says "I"?), can one innocently convert such a *je suis juif* into this wholly other sentence, "je suis un Juif," the attributed attribute becoming an assumed name, and demanding of French this time to be capitalized? I note in passing that these questions, in their grammatical form, are mostly troubling in French where the adjective and the name *juif* are homophones, if not homonyms. This is not true in English or in German. We will have to return to this question of the "French Jew." Not to mention that the attribute thus attributed, *juif*, whether adjective or noun, can designate what one calls, in Cartesian and post-Cartesian philosophy, an essential or principal attribute on the one hand, and a secondary attribute or mode, on the other.

Before any other kind of conversion—of this type or any other—there is one, also grammatical in appearance, that I—and I have every reason to assume that any other Jew will have, like me—found *problematical*, even impossible. This is the conversion that would symmetrically turn the proposition *tu es J/juif, vous êtes J/juifs,* or *J/juive(s)* [you are (a) Jew, jewish] (noun or adjective, singular or plural, male or female) into the apparently reciprocal proposition: "donc je suis J/juif, donc nous sommes J/juifs—ou J/juive(s) [therefore I am (a) Jew or Jewish, therefore we are Jews or Jewish (male or female)]."

I have so far spoken only of the first and second persons, but the third persons have no doubt *already* insinuated themselves into the scene or into the waiting room. Let us enjoy this grace period, for who knows what will befall us next.

This reciprocating conversion of the *you* [*du* tu *ou du* vous] into an "I" or a "we" is problematical, even impossible. It is not sufficient that I be told or that I be assigned a "you are (a) jew" in order for me to subscribe and say "yes, then, since you say so, I am (a) jew, *ergo Judaeus sum*—or *judea sum,* and [I am indeed] the Jew or the Jewess that you say or believe that I am." Saying this is not necessarily, it is above all not, to follow, in spite of the temptation, Sartre's *Reflections on the Jewish Question* [translated as *Anti-Semite and Jew*], a book that mattered very much to me, in the 1950s, as we know it continued to matter for the young French Jews of the next generation. It is a book that is, as always, both so intelligent and so naïve, a well-intentioned and generous book, which one must read, even if this is done less now than before, which one must re-read in its "situation" at that time. It is also a book the logic of which—one that Sartre also called, precisely, the "situation"—turns rapidly around this proposition: "The Jew is a man whom other men consider a Jew: that is the simple truth from which we must start."[10] A truth that is a bit simple, indeed. As if it sufficed for the other to tell me "you are jew or a Jew" for me to be born to my alleged identity as a Jew, to what Sartre calls therefore my *situation* as Jew: "Thus the Jew is in the situation of a Jew because he lives in the midst of a society that takes him for a Jew [*pour Juif*]" (72/88). Or yet again:

> What is it, then, that serves to keep a semblance of unity in the jewish community? To reply to this question, we must come back to the idea of *situation*. It is neither their past, their religion, nor their soil that unites the sons of Israel. If they have a common bond, if all of them deserve the name of Jew [*tous les noms de Juif*], it is because they have in common the situation of a Jew, that is, they live in a community which takes them for Jews. (67/81)

And a bit further: "In this sense the democrat is right as against the anti-Semite for it is the anti-Semite who *makes* the Jew"(69/84). It is not that Sartre's axiom holds no truth at all regarding what is called the "situation" (and like others, at the first reading of this book, as a teenager, I believed that I recognized [*reconnaître*] here, gratefully [*avec reconnaissance*], precisely my experience of said situation, while asking myself already why—a question of good sense—it was these particular individuals and not others that society arbitrarily made into Jews), but before speaking a little more about what I find a bit simple, in fact, in an analysis so necessary after all, I will raise what concerns the third person. Sartre always speaks of the Jews in the third person, and he evokes, as we will hear, the emergence of the third person for the jewish child himself.

Yet what will have infinitely complicated the course of my reading of this very French book, from the beginning of the 1950s, is not only the recourse to a distinction then so confident, which came from Heidegger, between authenticity and inauthenticity (authentic jew and inauthentic jew). And I thus approach the second border I had mentioned, the alleged alternative between the authentic and the inauthentic.

2. *Second*. What worried and, in truth, discouraged my confident reading of these *Reflections on the Jewish Question* is first of all the fact that Sartre determines and confidently limits his discourse by asserting that he will restrict his analysis to the Jews of France, even to the French Jew. This limitation logically proceeds from the concept of "situation," which is the guiding thread and the organizing concept of this entire discourse. Sartre writes: "If I wish to know *who* the Jew is, I must first inquire into the situation surrounding him, since he is a being in a situation. I should say that I shall limit my description to the Jews in France for it is the problem of the French Jew that is *our* problem" (60/73).[11] (Some of the pages of this book are dated October 1944 [71/86], prior to the discovery of Auschwitz, and there would be much to say about Sartre's perception then of what had just occurred in Europe—but let us leave that aside). Here, then, one finds excluded from the analysis not only all non-French Jews—following, in sum, a methodological and situational border quite clearly decidable, but terribly and so artificially, conventionally restrictive, unjustifiable, in truth, in such a singular case—but also, and equally out of range [*hors champ*], if I may say so, are all these strange, nonforeign Jews [*tous ces étranges Juifs non-étrangers*] who, like me, if I dare say so, like the Jews of Algeria of my generation, were in a thousand ways, undecidably, neither French nor non-French. And this indecision of the border had to do not only with citizenship, or with the fact that "we" had lost and then found again, between 1940 and 1944, a young citizenship that was granted less than a century earlier by the Crémieux Decree of 1870. This turbulence regarding French citizenship was complicated, in an abyssal manner, for those who were called, during the war and for a large part of my adolescence, "indigenous Jews" of Algeria (I have made this somewhat clear in *Monolingualism of the Other* and in "Circumfession"), regarding religion, language, culture, the very singular sequence of a colonial history whose kind, as I have tried to demonstrate, was unique in the world. I am one of those who feel both French, very French, French through and through (without being certain, I have explained that elsewhere as well, that I could say, like Hannah Arendt about the German language, "French is my only fatherland," even though language, French, in the irredentism of its most untranslatable idiom, is at bottom the passional body of all

my passions, even if this body often devotes itself to silence). French through and through, then, but at the same time one must accommodate this, one must address this dissociation, radically eradicated, cultivating the uprootedness, if I may say so, but without any desire to grow roots elsewhere, in some community or identifiable nation-state. I hope to say this better later, but it is certain that without this experience I would not have had the same access, nor perhaps any access at all, to the ethico-political motifs that have occupied me since long ago around what I have called a "new International," beyond even cosmopolitanism (that is to say, a citizenship of the world, against which I have nothing, of course, on the contrary, only that it still implies, as citizenship, the rootedness of the political and of democracy in a territory and state), or around what I have named the desert in the desert, *khōra*, messianicity without messianism, or the im-possible as the only possible event, for example, in the unconditionality of the gift, of forgiveness, of testimony, of hospitality, and so on. All these motifs are, I hope, coherent, and in any case, they bear affinity with the experience that remains singularly mine, and with a destiny that was sealed from childhood of a little French Jew doubled with a little indigenous Jew of Algeria, an Algeria badly named or over-named [*mal-nommée ou sur-nommée*] French Algeria, being less and less so, and which this child barely knew, in sum, except in time of war, from one war to another, of one war, the other.

I was readying myself to clarify, then, how Sartre, himself speaking of Jews in the third person, was also describing the emergence of the third person in the little French Jew himself, at the origin of the consciousness of the French Jewish child. I will not yet hurry toward the great universal question of the third, which later became for me an essential site of reading, of interpretation, and of debate with Levinas, the thought and memory of whom I do not want to delay saluting here, for a thousand all too obvious reasons. Without insisting upon what Sartre's thought may recall for me, as for many others, of my childhood, it is to argue another question, namely, that of the distinction between authentic Jew and inauthentic Jew, that I will cite a passage from *Reflections on the Jewish Question*. Sartre writes here, in italics, the expression "special name." The name *Jew* is a "special name." For my part, I will emphasize, without further commentary, *together* the third person *and* the trans-generational or genealogical logic *and* the "strange and uncanny [*louche et inquiétant*]"[12] or "murky [*troubles*]" words, which beckon toward what

Freud or Heidegger regularly thematize under the name of *Unheimlichkeit* (the uncanny [*familière étrangeté*] of what is *at once* at home and not at home, intimate and strange, domestic and foreign, as if *unheimlich* meant, in sum, "jew"—both for the anti-Semites and for the philo-Semites, and, above all or finally, for the so-called Jews themselves: but what is a *so-called Jew* [*un* soi-distant Juif]? here, finally, is perhaps my only question). I will finally underscore what Sartre evokes lightly, as if in passing, as if it concerned a pedagogical figure, destined to help better understand, to wit, the allusion to the sexual violence of a primal scene, when the child, or rather, a boy, a "little Jew" rather than a little Jewess, sees his parents making love. It is from this precocious experience, which Sartre successively calls "truth," "discovery," and "revelation," that jewish children feel themselves—here again are Sartre's more or less calculated words—"separated," "cut off [*retranchés*]." Here, then, is a kind of primal scene during which the revelation of a truth cuts and cuts off [*tranche et retranche*], leaving nothing but traces of trouble in identity, the distinction between inside and outside, the at-home and the not-at-home: "someday they [Jewish children] must learn the *truth*: sometimes from the smiles of those who surround them, sometimes from rumor or insult" (75/91). (If I could allow myself to interrupt this citation for a brief remark, I would clarify that, in my case, which I believe to be very common to many jewish children, it was first of all "through insults," through wounding apostrophes that led me to understand that shame can precede the fault and remain foreign to any possible avowal or disavowal. The insult or injury, prior to qualified injustice but like an elementary injustice, the inflicted wound, "injury," was indissociable from the word *jew*, uttered in French or in Arabic, the same word, name or adjective, the same attribute then incomprehensible and keeping, perhaps forever, some kernel of unintelligible darkness [*quelque noyau de nuit inintelligible*], between "jew" and "just," anti-jew and injustice, the same word, *jew*, constituting, as I said, in the cutting and excising experience [*l'expérience tranchante et retranchante*] of the same cruelty, at once the weapon and the wound, the blade of the knife and the wound forever open.)

> The later the *discovery*, the more violent the shock. Suddenly they perceive that others know something about them that they don't know; that people apply to them this *strange and uncanny* term that is not used in their own family. They feel themselves separated, *cut off* from the society of the normal children who

run and play tranquilly and securely around them—those lucky children who have no *special name*. And they return home, they look at their father, they think: "Is he a Jew too?" and their respect for him is poisoned.¹³ How can they fail to keep the marks of this first *revelation* all their life? There have been hundreds of descriptions of the *disturbances* [troubles] which occur in a child when he suddenly *discovers* that his parents have sexual relations. But what must happen to the little Jew when he steals a glance at his parents and thinks: "They are Jews." (75–76/92; Sartre emphasizes only the phrase "special name.")

In what Sartre analyzes as a sociologist or a historian of a particular situation, that of the so-called or alleged, the said Jews, one could easily recognize—I will not do so here—the exemplary weave of a universal structure. I will also neglect, for lack of time, the lexicon of the cutting off [*retranchement*] ("They feel themselves separated, *cut off* from the society of the normal children") and the pedagogy of an Oedipal scenario—Oedipus being here the one who responds to the name of man, as always, but, Sartre would say, here he is a man, the condition of a man without human nature: "a child when he suddenly discovers that his parents have sexual relations." This remark will later be followed by a strange reference to Oedipus' daughter, Sophocles' Antigone, and to the advice given to her by Greek wisdom: "modesty," "silence," "patience" in misfortune, all virtues that, Sartre explains, could lead the inauthentic Jew toward anti-Semitism and masochism (109/132). I will only note the constitutive dissymmetry imposed by the law of what announces to the Jew his own identity or his rapport with himself. The "here I am," the "I am jewish," resonate first of all as the accusative of a heteronomous response to the order or the injunction of the other to whom the "I" of the "I am jewish" is first of all the hostage. "I" is not the first to know that "I am jewish." The path is clear now to go on and conclude that I am always the last [*le dernier*], the last to know. But you will no doubt have recognized in this heteronomous dissymmetry of the hostage that I am [*de l'otage que je suis*], the very traits, the *universal* features that Levinas gives to ethics in general, as metaphysics or first philosophy—and against ontology. There again is posed the great question of an *exemplarist* temptation, and we could be tempted to analyze here a configuration, which is quite French—and generational—a configuration of discourses that are, indeed, different, but all analogous in the attention they direct toward heteronomy and the subjection of the subject to the law of the other. Including Sartre's discourse (and *Reflections on the Jewish Question* is largely dependent on the universal phenomenological ontology, deployed in *Being and Nothingness*, of the gaze of the other upon me), those of Levinas and of Lacan, the genealogy of this configuration would produce a great rhizome rather than a tree. Alongside the jewish question, one would find Husserl, but also a Freud reinterpreted in light of a very mediated reading of Heidegger and Hegel, by way of a certain Kojève, but let us leave this aside. Were I faithful to the thread of affiliation and of heritage, as to the motif of genealogy, which has always worried rather than reassured me, especially when it takes a hurriedly Oedipal form, I would concede the following: for my part, I belong to the generation of the more or less heretical or bastard grandsons of these French fathers and foreign grandfathers, the first infidelity of the grandson consisting, in this familiar yet *unheimlich* landscape of the extended family, in addressing in a manner altogether different from the said fathers or grandfathers, the woman, the question of the woman, of the mother, of the daughter and the sister, and therefore of the brother—with, and above all without, Antigone.

I will dare to claim—and I would not be the first, even if I wish to do so differently tonight—that the alternative between authentic Jew and inauthentic Jew does not hold up under analysis for a second, even as it appears to play such an essential role in *Reflections on the Jewish Question*, providing the book with something like the vein of an argument or that of a taxonomy, omitting for the moment the considerable if now dimmed resonance of this book in the years that followed its publication. It would require no great effort to demonstrate that Sartre himself cannot quite believe in it, this distinction between authentic and inauthentic. In good or bad faith, he finds himself compelled to discredit that alternative with the same gesture that wagers everything on it. One could sustain this with a luxury of arguments, for which I do not have sufficient time. I am referring here to the difficulties Sartre encountered at the time of the book's publication. He admitted one day that some of his jewish friends had asked him to cut the fifty pages concerning the distinction between authentic and inauthentic Jews. This led him to publish separately and at different times "Portrait of the Anti-Semite" and "The Situation of the Jews in France."[14]

Sartre himself could not take this alternative between authentic and inauthentic seriously, because it had to appeal to at least one principle of identity, if I may say so, to an essential being-jew that would be identical to itself, something that seems incompatible with the concepts of "condition" or of "situation." "Authentic" implies, in Greek as in French, the assured power, the mastery of speaking and of being oneself, the sovereign ipseity of one who is sure of oneself and of one's power to be oneself. Authenticity, according to Sartre, would thus consist in *choosing oneself* [à se choisir, à se choisir soi-même], freely, *as jew*, while the concept of situation or of condition excludes such autonomous choice that touches upon the being of the "I am." "Jewish authenticity," Sartre writes,

> consists in choosing oneself *as jew* [emphasized by Sartre, the remark of a phenomenological ontologist that recalls the importance of the "as such," which will be emphasized, as well, later on], that is, in realizing one's Jewish condition. The authentic Jew abandons the myth of the universal man [a proposition that would understandably have shocked many]; he knows himself and wills himself [Sartre was just speaking of "choosing oneself," and this voluntarist, reflexive consciousness, this confidence in the freedom of a *cogito* and in the "self" of "choosing oneself," "knowing oneself," "wanting oneself" has, since then, done much, along with existential psychoanalysis and the notion of an originary project, to take me away from this sympathetic intelligence] into history as a historic and damned creature; he ceases to run away from himself and to be ashamed of his own kind. He understands that society is bad; for the naïve monism of the inauthentic Jew he substitutes a social pluralism. He knows that he is one who stands *apart*, untouchable, scorned, proscribed—and it is *as such* that he asserts his being [*et c'est* comme tel *qu'il se revendique*]. (136–37/166)

Sartre emphasizes again an *as such*, which beckons [*fait signe*], as always, toward the self-identity of sense, of essence, of oneself, toward an ipseity in general. Toward its autonomy. Like the word *authentic* itself. Yet when he must define this self-identity, this self-identity of the Jew, Sartre cannot avoid this apophatic form, this rhetoric, some have said, of "negative theology." Erasing all possible predicates, he transforms the concept of Jew into a non-concept, without any attribute that a Jew could attribute to himself, that is to say, that he could assume or claim. This gesture, to make of the Jew a non-concept, could be interesting, it could lead to a thinking beyond the concept if Sartre did not so much want to convince the Jews authentically to become what they are. Yet following his own reasoning, a Jew, in sum, and an authentic Jew, cannot even speak of himself as a Jew; he cannot define himself, present himself, say "here I am," without misunderstanding. This is because of the following—I quote this passage again:

> What is it, then, that serves to keep a *semblance* of unity [I emphasize *semblance* as I will underscore, in a moment, the word *quasi*] in the Jewish community? To reply to this question, we must come back to the idea of *situation*. It is neither their past, their religion, nor their soil that unites the sons of Israel. If they have a common bond, if all of them deserve the name of Jew, it is because they have in common the situation of a Jew, that is, they live in a community which takes them for Jews. (67/81)

Since they are not jewish in the truth of their being but only taken as such in a "semblance of unity," one could only escape this absurd circle by determining why the community in the midst of which they live takes these particular individuals, rather than others, to be Jews. Sartre, however, does not offer any answer to this question; he even deprives himself of the principle that would enable such an answer, since all the reasons that would be available to non-Jews for calling anyone jew are unacceptable and justly discredited by Sartre.

A. Indeed, *at times* he makes a strange use of the words *jewish race*—words about which it is difficult to decide whether or not he assumes them for his own account (e.g., in the passage where, speaking in the name of the human and protesting against what would be an inhuman measure, Sartre ends up saying that man does not exist). He evokes a politics of forced assimilation and, while protesting, clarifies that:

> It would be necessary to supplement it with a policy of mixed marriages and a rigorous interdiction against Jewish religious practices—in particular, circumcision. I say quite simply: these measures would be inhumane.... No democracy can seek the integration of the Jews at such a cost. Moreover, such a procedure could be advocated only by inauthentic Jews who are prey to a crisis of anti-Semitism; it aims at nothing but [*rien moins que*; I suppose that Sartre wanted to say "nothing less than" (*rien de moins que*)] the liquidation of the Jewish race. It represents an

extreme form of the tendency we have noticed in the democrat, a tendency purely and simply to eradicate [*supprimer*] the Jew for the benefit of *man*. But *man* does not exist. There are Jews, Protestants, Catholics; there are Frenchmen, Englishmen, Germans; there are whites, blacks, yellows. (144–45/174–75)

B. *At other times*, on the contrary, and in order to avoid both affirming and denying some essential and proper feature of jewishness or of judaism, Sartre makes a singular appeal to the value of an "as if" or a "quasi," against which I have nothing, and which I have myself cultivated, if differently and for other ends, but of which one can at least say that it ruins the credit that we are asked to grant to authenticity and to the concept of authenticity. How could Sartre himself believe in it, when he twice uses the small and terrible word *quasi*? "The Jewish community is neither national nor international, neither religious, nor ethnic, nor political: it is a *quasi-historical* community. What makes the Jew is his concrete situation; what unites him to other Jews is the identity of their situations. This quasi-historical body should not be considered a foreign element in society" (145/176).

Even if, in another logic, which was never Sartre's, one were to take seriously this "quasi" in order to draw numerous consequences (something I have attempted to do elsewhere from another point of view and regarding other examples, which I will not evoke here in order not to deviate from my purpose), well then, this Sartrian description of the Jew and of the jewish community, of its "semblance of unity" and of its "quasi" historicity, remains, I would say euphemistically, light [*légère*]. Even more so on the part of a philosopher who claims to concern himself with history, with situation and condition. The concept of history that orients this book is very vaguely Marxist and revolutionary. It leaves out [*hors jeu*] any other approach to historicity (internal and external) of, let us say in order to remain prudent, jewish memory and law. Sartre appears to have acknowledged, at the end of his life, the ignorance—not to say the *méconnaissance*—of tradition, of jewish traditions, to which his book testifies in the days immediately following the war.

In the same stroke, the Jew who is called upon to become authentic, authentically historical, has no choice but to resolve himself to a *quasi-authenticity*. Besides, the definition, this time, of the inauthentic Jew is enough to make all the Jews of the world—the authentic, the inauthentic, and a few others as well—scream, at the moment when

Sartre, in the condescending tone of concession, declares himself ready to accept this inauthentic Jew "as such," in what he calls the "national society":

> We have described objectively, perhaps severely, the traits of the inauthentic Jew. There is not one of them that is opposed to his assimilation *as such* [again, emphasized by Sartre] in the national society. On the contrary [and here is the description of the inauthentic Jew], his rationalism, his critical spirit, his dream of a contractual society and of universal brotherhood, his humanism—all these qualities make him something like [*comme*] an indispensable leaven in that society. (146/176–77)

This figure [*silhouette*] of the inauthentic Jew (rationalism, critical spirit, humanism) in which so many non-Jews and Jews would like to recognize themselves, implies that authentic Jews are, for their part, strangers to rationalism, critical spirit, and humanism. It is understandable that many among them were indignant.

Let us not go further in the direction of edification. My intention here, you understand very well, is not to criticize Sartre. While paying him the homage he deserves, and associating myself with the testimonies of gratitude that many Jews have addressed to him, my concern would rather be to show the essential difficulty that can be found, when facing a certain logic, a powerful logic that is perhaps philosophy itself, in signing (and what one demands of a responsible signature is that it be original and authentic), in underwriting and in countersigning [*à soussigner et à contresigner*] an utterance of the type: "Me, I am jew" (authentic or inauthentic—or quasi-authentic), in knowing and meaning what one appears to be saying. Of this essential difficulty, I want less to indict Sartre's discourse (even if I indeed do find its logic and its rhetoric to be quite fragile) than to testify as well. To say "I am jew," as I do, while knowing and meaning what one says, is very difficult and vertiginous. One can only attempt to think it after having said it, and therefore, in a certain manner, without yet knowing what one does there, the *doing* [*le* faire] preceding the *knowing* [*le* savoir] and remaining, more than ever, heterogeneous to it. What *must not* be done [*ce qu'il* ne faut pas *faire*], and that is the core of my limited reproach to the Sartrian logic, is to pretend to know, to dissemble as if one believed one knew what one said, when one does not know. Here, too, I could deploy these words in another language, and I do so elsewhere, but there is not enough time. If, on the one hand, Sartre implicitly, practically, recognizes that this distinction (authentic/inauthentic) is from the first limited in its pertinence, even untenable, what he does not recognize, on the other hand, is from whence came and toward what the ruin of the distinction is going, wherever it is in use, and in the discourse of the age, first in the Heidegger of *Being and Time*, for whom the question of authenticity was no doubt more originary and more powerful than the question of truth. The ruin of this distinction comes from a bottomless ground [*un fond sans fond*]. And it has incalculable consequences. Some, and I am not one of them, would say that these are disastrous, devastating consequences: affecting the logic of all these discourses, of course; affecting their existential axiomatics, the ethics and the politics they at least seem to call for, but first, affecting the sense of "being-jew," the extent, the very pragmatics of any utterance of self-presentation of the type: "I affirm that I am jewish"; or "here I am, I am a Jew of such and such kind"; or "there is no possible misunderstanding, here is why I call myself, why I am called, me, jew."

What, then, would the undecidable oscillation be, the impossible "either/or" that matters here to me? What is the vacillation that turns the head and produces vertigo, a vertigo one can love or detest, a vertigo through which one can love or hate? It is that the being-jew, the "I am jew [or jewish]," of which one can never decide whether it is or is not authentic, one can either take as a case, an example among others of an originary contamination of the authentic by the inauthentic; or, inversely, one can consider that the experience one calls being-jew, whether it be the so-called or alleged Jew or the other, is exemplarily what deconstructs this distinction, squanders the credit granted to it and with it to so many others—in truth, to all conceptual oppositions. Being-jew would then be something more, something other than the simple lever—strategic or methodological—of a general deconstruction; it would be its very experience, its chance, its threat, its destiny, its seism. It would be its hyper-exemplary experience, ultimately, eschatologically, or perversely exemplary, since it would implicate the credit or, if you prefer, the faith that we would place in exemplarity itself. Hyper-exemplary, more than exemplary, other than exemplary, it would threaten, by the same stroke, with all the philosophical and political consequences you may imagine, its alleged exemplarity itself, its universal responsibility incarnated in the singularity of one alone or of one people, and with this, everything that may reassure itself in the sense of the word *jew* and in the eschatological or messian*ist* (I do not say messian*ic*—we will no doubt come back to this distinction) promises of the covenant, the election, and, consequently, of the people, the nation, not to speak of the modern and philosophical figure of the nation-state, armed as it is with all its attributes from international law, and even well-armed *tout court*. At this point, what I wanted to confide to you, simply and in my name, if I can still say that, is that I insist on saying "I am jew" or "I am a Jew," without ever feeling authorized to clarify whether an "inauthentic" Jew, or, above all, an "authentic" Jew—neither in Sartre's limited and very French sense, nor in the sense that some Jews who are more assured of their belonging, of their memory, their essence or their election might understand, expect, or demand of me. Willing or pretending to be neither an inauthentic Jew, nor an authentic Jew, nor a quasi-authentic Jew, nor an imaginary Jew (although I share much, not everything, of the experience analyzed by Alain Finkielkraut under this title),[15] referring myself to a history that is not the "quasi-history" of which Sartre speaks, in the name of what and by what right can I still call myself jew [or jewish]? And why do I hold onto it, even as I am not even sure of the appellation to which I thus respond, not sure that it is addressed to me, not sure of what I mean, of what I want to mean here [*de ce que je veux vouloir dire là*], be it authentic, inauthentic, or quasi-authentic, beyond all identity, all unity, or all community? Well, I know that I do not know that, and I suspect all those who believe they know of not knowing, even if, in truth, they do know more—I know—much more than I. All I can say is that, at the limit of my public behavior as a citizen and beyond citizenship, at the sharpest but also most exposed limit of my work of writing, of thought, and of teaching (of which, as a matter of rule, I have not spoken until now), I could demonstrate that the logic of this question, of its implications or of its consequences, organizes almost everything. What occurs, what happens to me, what kind of event is it when, responding to the appellation, I insist on presenting myself as a Jew, on saying and on declaring myself [*à dire et à me dire*] "I am jew," neither authentic nor inauthentic nor quasi-authentic, given that I do not know what I mean, that I could criticize, disavow, "deconstruct" everything that I might mean, and that I suspect so many Jews more authorized than I am of not knowing any better than I do? What occurs in this case between *doing* and *knowing*, between *faith* and *knowledge* [*entre* faire *et* savoir, *entre* foi *et* savoir]? And what sense can there be in saying, in affirming, in signing, and in maintaining a "here I am," me a Jew, beyond sense and meaning [*vouloir-dire*]? In saying "here I am," and insisting, given that I know that perhaps I have not been called, and that perhaps I will never know it is not me who has been called. Not yet. Perhaps in a future to come [*avenir*], but not yet. It belongs, perhaps, to the experience of appellation and of responsible response that any certainty regarding the destination, and therefore the election, remains suspended, threatened by doubt, precarious, exposed to the future of a decision of which I am not the masterful and solitary—authentic—subject [*le sujet maître et solitaire—authentique*]. Whoever is certain—as was not, precisely, the other, the second other Abraham of Kafka—whoever believes he detains the certainty of having been, he and he alone, he first, called as the best of the class, transforms and corrupts the terrible and indecisive experience of responsibility and of election into a dogmatic caricature, with the most fearsome consequences that can be imagined in this century, political consequences in particular.

If there is here an experience of undecidability between the authentic, the inauthentic, and the quasi-authentic, well then—once more and as I have tried elsewhere to formulate it in as formalized a manner as possible regarding decision and responsibility in general—this aporetic experience of undecidability or of the impossible, far from being a suspending and paralyzing neutrality, I hold to be the very condition, in truth, the milieu or the ether within which decision, and any responsibility worthy of the name (and perhaps worthy of the name and of the attribute *jew*) must breathe. At the most acute point, the very limit of this experience, all the problems that have tormented me always, almost always, return in order to insist. Not only is the symmetrical distinction between the "you are jew [or jewish]" and the "I am jew [or jewish]" no more given or certain than that between the authentic and the inauthentic; but I can also not credit the proposed alternative, the third, about which I will only say one word before concluding. It is the one supposed to separate, around an indivisible border, judaism and jewishness. Without being able to go deeper here, as one should no doubt, in a proliferation of proposed gaps between judaism, jewishness, judaicity (Albert Memmi), *Judentum*, *Yiddishkeit*, not to speak of Ashkenazi-ness or Sephardic-ness, I will limit myself, given the title of this conference (Judeities) to the one put to work by my friend Yosef Hayim Yerushalmi in his *Freud's Moses*, an admirable book that I have discussed, from another perspective, in *Archive Fever*. The distinction between judaism and jewishness would illustrate, for example, what Freud, speaking of his judaism *via negationis*, apparently said, either in private, or in his preface to the Hebrew edition of *Totem and Taboo*. Acknowledging that he did not know the language of the Holy Scriptures, that he was a stranger to the religion of his fathers and to any national or nationalist ideal, Freud then added more or less the following: If one were to ask this Jew (that is, himself), "'since you have abandoned all these common characteristics of your compatriots, what is left to you that is Jewish?' he would answer: 'A very great deal, and probably its very essence.' He could not now express that essence in words; but some day, no doubt, it will become accessible to the scientific mind."[16] Yerushalmi, too, set his wager on a distinction between *judaism* (culture, religion, a historic, even national or "state national" community, etc.) and *jewishness*, a jewish essence independent of judaism, an essential identity of the being-jew that could interminably survive a judaism that would, for its part, remain finite and terminable (hence the subtitle of Yerushalmi's book: *Judaism Terminable and Interminable*). Yerushalmi thus attributes to minimal jewishness some features about which I have myself asked by what rights they would be reserved in this manner to the Jews (such as, for example, the cult of memory and the openness to hope and to the future [*à l'avenir*]).[17] I imagine the double objection one could address to him from both sides, in order to ruin the very principle of the distinction or at least to limit its relevance, even if one acknowledges it has some such relevance, by pure contextual convenience. Either these minimal features are universal and there is no reason to make them into what is proper to the Jew, save to speculate again on the worrying logic of exemplarity; or, as universal as they are, they will have been announced in a unique and precisely exemplary fashion, by election, in a historical revelation; they would then have to do with writing, with memory or with hope in what one calls judaism. In the logic of both objections, it is no longer possible to separate, in all rigor, these two poles, namely, jewishness and judaism. The memory or the hope that would constitute jewishness seems to be able to emancipate [*affranchir*] itself, indeed, from tradition, from the promise and the election proper to judaism. Yet, whether or not one would have to do so, it will always be possible to re-root the very idea and movement of this emancipation, the desire for this emancipation, in a given of judaism, in the memory of an event that, continuing, as it is, to be threatened by amnesia, would remain a history of the gift of the law and would represent the ultimate guardian of the reference to the jewish phenomenon, to the name or to the attribute "jew," which one continues to inherit in a jewishness that is allegedly without Judaism. This inheritance is uneffaceable, and it endorses even the experience of effacement, of emancipation, of disavowal.

But the oscillation and the undecidability continue, and I would dare say, *must* continue to mark the obscure and uncertain experience of heritage. In any case, I have been unable to put a stop to this experience in me, and it has conditioned the decisions and the responsibilities that have imprinted themselves upon my life. Moreover, it structures the most formalized, the most resistant, the most irreducible logic of all the discourses I believed I had to endorse (I will not impose this demonstration on you tonight), on the subject of writing and the trace, the relations between law, justice, and right, on the subject of what I have called messianicity without messianism, on the subject of the international beyond cosmopolitanism and beyond state or onto-theological sovereignty, on the subject of the democracy to come beyond state-national citizenship, on the subject of spectrality beyond the oppositions life/death or presence/absence, and, most of all, on the subject of *khōra*, as prehistorical place giving (without giving) occasion to any event of anthropo-theological revelation. In all these directions, one could at once and successively accredit two contradictory postulates: on the one hand, it is (from a historical, ethical, political perspective, etc.) the condition that one emancipate oneself from every dogma of revelation and of election; on the other hand, this emancipation can be interpreted as the very content of the revelation or of the election, their very idea. For example, nothing seems more foreign to the God of the Jews and to the history of the law than everything I interpret, even unto its political future to come, under the Greek name of *khōra*, the place, the ahuman and atheological location that opens the place well beyond any negative theology. And yet this manner of interpreting the place can still keep a deep affinity with a certain nomination of the God of the Jews. He is also The Place.

To say that all of this still awaits its interpretation, that this interpretation is not only a hermeneutic or an exegesis, even if such are also necessary, but rather a performative writing and reading, and above all a performative mastery, a hospitality to the event and to the coming occurrence [*arrivance*] of the coming one [*l'arrivant*] (a messianicity without messianism), namely, the to-come [*à-venir*]. The to-come, which is to say, the other, will decide what "jew," "judaism," or "jewishness" will have signified. And although this to-come is not the property of anyone (not the philosophers, the exegetes, the politicians, the military, etc.), it will necessarily depend, as to-come, on an experience of invention that is both prophetic and poetic. The poet-prophets do not always have a name in the Scriptures, and they are not always writers or authors known in the world of religion or in the republic of letters. They can be anyone—and anywhere. They might sometimes be invested, in some situations, with the mission of military generals. There are genius generals, poet-generals, if not prophets, provocative generals, who provoke peace and who sometimes pay for it with their lives. We know one such. On the opposite side of poet-general and just-generals, opposite peace-provoking generals, there are also generals who provoke war. They do, they make others do, or leave for others to do, the worst, without seeing, in their often-shared blindness, that a voluminous appetite for conquistadorlike offensives may dissimulate a death drive and lead, among other crimes, to suicide—theirs and that of their own.

This is why I will always be tempted to think that a Kafka, for example, conjures up more future to come than many others by striking the rock of his fictional writing, and by calling us to this truth (such at least is my interpretation): that anyone responding to the call must continue to doubt, to ask himself whether he has heard right, whether there is no original misunderstanding; whether it was in fact his name that was heard, whether he is the only or the first addressee of the call; whether he is not in the process of substituting himself violently for another; whether the law of substitution, which is also the law of responsibility, does not call for an infinite increase of vigilance and concern. It is possible that I have not been called, me, and it is not even excluded that no one, no One, nobody, ever called any One, any unique one, anybody. The possibility of an originary misunderstanding in destination is not an evil, it is the structure, perhaps the very vocation of any call worthy of that name, of all nomination, of all response and responsibility.

There would be *perhaps* yet another Abraham, not only he who received another name in his old age and, at ninety-nine, at the time of his circumcision, felt, by the blow of a letter, the letter *H* right in the middle of his name; not only he who, later, on Mount Moriah, was called twice by the angel, first "Abraham, Abraham," then, a second time still, from the height of the heavens, as Scripture tells us. There would be perhaps not only Abram, then Abraham, Abraham, twice.

That there should be yet another Abraham: here, then, is the most threatened jewish thought [*la pensée juive la plus menacée*], but also the most vertiginously, the most intimately jewish one that I know to this day.

For you have understood me well: when I say "the most jewish [*la plus juive*]," I also mean "more than jewish [*plus que juive*]." Others would perhaps say "otherwise jewish [*autrement juive*]," even "other than jewish [*autre que juive*]."

The Last, The Remnant . . .

(Derrida and Rosenzweig)

GÉRARD BENSUSSAN

Since I have been asked to make a few introductory remarks for our colloquium, and since it is organized less around a theme, or around some object that we could easily circumscribe, than around questions put to Jacques Derrida—that is, argued and put to him in person—I will start with what he once called his "de facto non-belonging to Jewish culture."[1] Since his work "Shibboleth," and most certainly since his "Circumfession" and *Monolingualism of the Other* (no doubt before this, really since forever, but this is the forever of a non-relation or a without-ground), something turns remarkably around this "fact"—a questioning, ventured in repetition and avoidance, in an insisting, in any case, that we cannot fail to note and that authorizes, by this very "fact," a colloquium like this one, today, in this place.[2]

There is, in Derridean discourse, a "de facto non-belonging" [*non-appartenance de fait*], a sort of immediate and external evidence, like a self-positing, even a self-proclamation or a negative assertion of self. This evidence, passing through the detours and the pitfalls of a long philosophical progression, attests to the singular modality of an *exclusion-on-the-inside* of a relation. This evidence in no way masks the figure of that relation—no more than one could decipher therein the avowal of what is being unmasked. It is not so much a matter of confiding a secret as it is of stating the public notoriety of this secret and of making it speak. This non-belonging is translated, in effect, here and there, by an expression that seems to seal a properly eschatological belonging, a disproportionate belonging, even a belonging drawing from all non-belongings: "I am the last of the Jews."[3] Beyond what one immediately perceives there ("I am the worst of Jews"), but rather, beyond, and from the outset—that is, beyond without sublating [*sans relève*][4] the "worst"—the formula is decided in the developments to which it calls: I am he whose exclusion completes that from which he was excluded, he who in some way, and in his way, guarantees the entire series ("the Jews"), wherein the exclusive-conclusive term or limit takes place; I include myself thus only from outside, at the end of the course, and as this singular gesture ought to be able to justify itself, all the same, by the series from which it omits itself, as it gives itself meaning on the basis of that series in stepping out of it, inclusion from without [*l'inclusion du dehors*] is at the same time, inevitably, an exclusion on the inside [*exclusion au-dedans*].

Excluded-included, inside-outside, such would be the position, then, of the "last of the Jews," a mobile position, as it were, the surveying of an encrypted space, of an architecture made up of secret passages. The logical directions for use of these serial displacements, always at the edge of the series and overflowing it, will consist in a groundless and endless overbidding. It requires this, short of being reabsorbed into the dialectic of what Hegel calls *das Gleichnämige* [the homonymous], or "what has the same name," which [according to Hegel] repelled outward what was rejected, before drawing it back into itself and returning to the same, to the abolished difference.[5] In order simply to function, "the last . . ." must expose itself to the peril of "exemplarism,"[6] and attempt its "inversion"[7]—to use a word from Levinas reading Derrida. Exemplarism, in its remarkable and vicious logic, snatches up anyone who asserts himself in the identity of a presence of self to self. To say "I am Jewish" is to bear witness for those who are not, which corresponds structurally, on the one hand, to the biblical election as the universality of witnessing, and on the other hand, to the witnessing, each time unique, which consists in placing oneself in the word [*la parole*], and through the word, in the position of those who either do not have, or no longer or do not yet have, the word. The identity of the one who says "I am Jewish" in order to say "I am not non-Jewish" thus undoes itself, dislocates itself, from the moment that it identifies itself in a belonging, and by so identifying, levels or planes down the surfeit it contains, the other in its same [*l'autre dans son même*], if you will. In such a case, he who states this is not there [in that identity], or not quite there. What remains then, are the paradoxes or the overbidding of the "the more I say it, the less I am it," or even "the less I say it, the more I am it." The less I coincide with myself, the more I assume something of this election. In any case, one can see clearly that what remains is the "identity trouble" traversing the last of the Jews. That one, then, if he attempts to think the logic of this identity—and with all the subtlety of the *more* in "more than one language," as we find in *Monolingualism of the Other*—obviously neither masters his trouble nor makes himself a master of that identity. The last of the Jews evidently does not constitute himself as a supreme being or as a signifier, commanding the intelligence of all the other signifiers. He is nothing outside the series and its differences. With the name *Jew* and the other names that would be associated with it—starting with that of the "last of the Jews"—it is a matter of trying to think not only the flaw in all identitarian presence but still more what exceeds it positively. More than or less than, not enough or too much, ungraspable, the Judaism of the last of the Jews is impossible. The last of the Jews is the impossible Jew. But what, indeed, could a possible Jew be, if the condition of possibility of the Jew is his impossibility of being-only-Jewish, *the impossibility of a being without remainder or remnant* [reste] what already, long ago, his short essay on Jabès set down, the essay collected in *Writing and Difference*.[8] "Would 'Jew' be the other name for this impossibility of being oneself?"[9] There is therefore no possible Jew, for "Jew" designates what is always more, and other, than the set of its conditions of possibility. One might say an event and, of course, a language event, in language, a name. Of this possibility of the impossible, or of this impossibility as the most proper possibility of being-Jewish, the Jewish tradition itself teaches us, it seems to me, or, in any case (since an extreme prudence is required here), a tradition in the tradition, that by which election is associated with the prophetic notion of the "remnant" [*reste*].

Election bears witness to a surplus in withdrawal, as it were, or a retrenchment or cutting off, or again, a separation of holiness that would exceed by subtracting [*excéderait en soustrayant*]. Election bears witness, which means that it constitutes, by way of the word, that which is absent from all presence, the messiah, say, to put things rapidly. This witnessing word mobilizes the notion of "remnant," *sherit*, for which Isaiah's theology (e.g., Isaiah 4:3 or 10:20–22) already posed the cornerstone. What the prophet calls "the remnant of Israel," which he associates with a germinal surviving group and not with a pure difference, is not the numerical part of a set, which a simple addition or readdition could reestablish as a sum. Its substance is evidently soteriological; that is to say, what remains only takes on its full meaning in a certain type of relation to the messianic event. It organizes and permits us to think ótherwise, non-dialectically, the relations of the whole (which it is not) and the part (which it is not, anymore than it is the whole),[10] or, again, the difference between the empirical and the transcendental. In creating a void there, where the fullness of the world would prevent any event from coming to pass, the remnant thus preserves the very possibility that what it divides, with the implacable edge of prophetism, might be saved. The remnant is the messianic sign of a profound breakdown [*défaillance*], invisibly inscribed in every fullness, in every fulfillment, in every coming. Undialectizable, its resistance to every synchrony, to the present of every manifestation, and to every reality claim expresses the extreme fragility of the messianic, its referral *à-dieu* or *à-venir* [to-god or to-come], at least to an interminable succession of generations, or to a filiality. Isaiah names his elder son with the prophetic name of Shear-Jakouv, meaning "the-remnant-will-return" (7:3). The name of the son is thus the name of an ineluctable *returning*; the inevitable name (against what Hegel believed about the difference between the avoidable name and the necessary concept) of a properly said, assigned to its coming to pass [*son advention*]. The remnant does not even remain; it erases what it designates, referring it to its future [*avenir*] as to a returning [*revenir*]. In the retrenchment of the remainder, the time of witnessing and of the word signifies the void like the space of a coming [*l'espace d'une venue*] and of a welcoming; a welcoming of the Just One to come.[11] This time repeatedly questions or threatens what is substantially fixed in positivity. It puts the present out of joint, anachronically or diachronically, by opening it up, and does the same with the totality by altering it. The Just One to come never stops coming, never stops producing a remnant which, itself, "will return" in the subtractions continuously inflicted upon the fullness of completion [*au plein de l'achèvement*]. The remnant allows us to think at the same time the impossible presence of the present and the future together; the impossibility of the whole, and the coming of the Just One — the return, the repetition, and the uniqueness of a first time. A famous yet enigmatic word from the Talmud makes "despair" the hyper-esperantial condition of the coming [*la condition hyper-espérantielle de la venue*].[12] We may read therein the remainder-effect, inscribed by the tradition, in the very movement of hope. The remainder is a remnant hoping despite everything, against "all hope," and even though nothing remains to be hoped for after enduring disappointing subtractions and the withdrawal of confidence. The remnant bears witness to this nothing, to this hole in the all, with a harbingerlike despair. The witness ceaselessly gives back to time the surplus of a word, or of an alliance renewed, which shall be like its impromptu resending [*relance impromptue*].

The remnant is no doubt just this: what resists in its "remaining" [*restance*] and, thereby, what authorizes an unconditional welcome to the arriving one—who is both unpredictable and unforesayable [*à l'arrivant imprédictible, imprédicible*]. "If the Messiah comes 'today,' the Remainder is ready to welcome him," writes Rosenzweig, conjoining the motifs of the unanticipatable and of the opening.[13]

This is the first, and crucial, appearance of Rosenzweig, who expressly associates the "remnant of Israel" with an unheard-of historical unfolding, which functions by "subtraction," by contraction, and by formation of renewed remnants.[14] This process of narrowing is what accounts for the trans-historic destiny of the "Jewish people." Rosenzweig opposes to this the couple "power" and "expansion," in which he sees the strength of Christianity as much as of the philosophies of history, whose model of universality would aim at obtaining a net outcome thanks to the addition of successive replacements. As for subtraction, it gives us a remainder. And this remainder or remnant bears witness, fundamentally, to the impossibility that the whole and its parts can make up a whole, totalize itself without "remainder," and close itself into a harmonious unity. Between the fulfillment to "unfulfill" and the unfulfillment to fulfill (to borrow Benjamin's messianic terms), the remnant is indeed the prophetic name of a birthing and an interruption, of a beyond to every "goal" in Hegel's sense: it is neither progression, nor self-movement, nor self-engendering. The son names, in effect, through the mouth of the prophet, that which, in the father, can hardly "find itself" in a place where it "corresponds" immediately to itself.[15] It is in this sense that we can say of the "remnant" that it is the name par excellence of the *inadequation to the concept*, whose temporal substrate the messianic recalls with insistence, in distinguishing this world and the world that comes as "ages," whose historic scansions are as irreducible as they are intertwined with each other.

Can we, on the basis of these few brief developments concerning the remnant, attempt to compare it with the *last* [*le rapprochement avec le dernier*]? We have just said that this closeness or proximity gains intelligibility when we establish its relationship to Rosenzweig's *subtraction*. It is instructive to note, in effect, that the cryptic structure of the final term—conclusive/exclusive/inclusive—on the one hand, and growth by subtraction, on the other, enter into each of these two thoughts [the remnant and the final or last], echoing the figure of the non-coincidence of self with self. The one and the other are even in theoretical solidarity by way of their brokenness or their discord. "The Jew is broken."[16] "His identity consists in not being identical to himself."[17] Rosenzweig speaks, for his part, of the radical impossibility for the "Eternal People" to "live in full accord with time,"[18] which results from the extra-historical separation of the Jewish remnant, from the subtraction that causes this remnant to escape from the universal circle of an all-embracing reappropriation—and this, with any possible return. The discord between time and eternity, the Self and the We, the world here and the world to come, sketches an internal division [*entre-écartement*] from inside history, which is the wound of the present world. The gap that the remnant leaves behind contains in itself "the two sides of the frontier" that it traces.[19] There would thus be in Judaism, according to Rosenzweig, a "simultaneous presence" of all "visible divisions,"[20] those that we have just indicated, but also many others (e.g., love/judgment, prophets/kings, literality/allegory, etc.)—and even, in a certain manner, all the other divisions that we might want. In a letter cited in *Of Grammatology*, Roger Laporte evokes the supposed dream of "a single word with which to designate both difference and articulation."[21] For this oneiric word, this impossible word, Rosenzweig proposes a multitude of practical uses: what the word *Jew* says for him is that *difference is the articulation* all the way to the form of a disarticulated ad-jointment [*ajointement désarticulé*].[22] In "carrying the opposition integrally within," in inscribing a "double relation" in "everything produced in it,"[23] Judaism would exclude itself from all territorial delimitations by "including in itself the frontiers," by "attracting" all differences "within its own limits,"[24]—all according to the play of a double mark, interior/exterior: that is, without any reduction to unity, without any derivation based on a unity, and also without sublation [*relève*], obviously, within the unity of a third term.[25] Rosenzweig calls this, in a short text subsequent to *The Star of Redemption*,[26] the Jewish *Binnenpolarität* [between-polarity], a most particular internal polarity. This internal polarity, like the exclusion of something impossible that would assure the possibility of that from which it is excluded (or excludes itself), is a structure that seeks to justify the separation (Jewish, for Rosenzweig, Jewish and beyond, for Derrida) and is what in the separation might be "terrifying" (Hegel), or at least shameful, for dialectical thinking. The eternity liturgically anticipated in Judaism's Holy Year, for example, qualifies for Rosenzweig a time *outside of* time (always to come) and yet also *within* time (to come, as it is in each instant), an out-of-time on the basis of which alone the time-solely-time [*temps-uniquement-temps*] of empires and civilizations is organized according to variable models (mimesis, competition, rivalry, etc.). History would thus escape the form of the teleological idea and of the presence that it implies, even and especially in the deferral to infinity of this presence.

If the two structures (e.g., the internal polarity / the last of . . .) are formally close, this is at least insofar as they are organized around the "remnant," that is, around the *undialectizable* or the *indeconstructible*, that something always at work, which undoes as it does and in order to do. But we can see, also, that the uniqueness, the one of the people-as-one, the *das eine Volk*, carried in Rosenzweig by the all-in-one of the differential polarity, is directed by the schema of an anticipation of redemption. This is so, even if it is always already undone, disappointed, despairing, and led back into the instant. This projective dimension can apparently never find anew, or coincide with, the experience of the strict cut [*coupure stricte*] or of the universal circumcision. It appears capable only of reintegrating the terms of the whole (belonging/non-belonging, or enfranchisement/disenfranchisement) with the broken totality that includes "all" that which excludes itself mutually; that is, "all" those logical exclusions that do not form a set of oppositions (we must not fail to underscore this), but rather the system of an exceeding or an excession [*système d'une excession*]. Totality still haunts, perhaps, the Rosenzweigian text. But it is a totality of such considerable strangeness, it is so reduced, that we hesitate to denote it by this speculative name. It is but the *shadow of a remainder*, a totality totally there in the liturgical anticipation of eternity, as it were. But it is totally fragmented, burst apart between its "there" and the disjointed multiplicity of its fragments. A totality insufficiently clean cut, to be sure. Rosenzweig's philosophy is, in many respects, a philosophy of conversion, that is to say, a philosophy that plays with subtlety and depth on all the harmonics of the root *–version* [*verso*, or side; and *vertere*, to turn or return] (i.e., in-version, sub-version, re-version, etc.). In a thinking of this kind, the last could well become the first. This becoming never comes to pass with the "last of the Jews," certainly, but it is nonetheless always in the process of becoming, always on the point of "turning back around." The last of the Jews—this could only be the last of the last, "the last of the eschatologists,"[27] the line stretched forth toward the Overjew [*Surjuif*]: ultimately, the Christ himself. The question of the totality— posed from the question of its untotalizability—would thus refer back to the question of the "translatableness" or the "untranslatableness" of Judaism into Christianity. In other words, it would refer us back to the question of "becoming" in language, of its particularity and its universality.

From the beginning, that is to say, in the repetition without identity that overdetermines the writing of the tradition, language is taken in its most native movement, under the double mark of translation, of departure and arrival, of the inside and the outside, of the first and the last word. I would like to recall, rapidly, two little maxims, the one Talmudic, the other Midrashic, which comment, each in its own fashion (and, thereby, comment on each other, reciprocally), on the episode of Genesis 9:27, in which Noah gets drunk, strips himself bare, and is seen by Ham, who warns Shem and Japheth: "May God cut Japheth loose [the Hebrew plays here on the assonance of the patronymic and the verb], and may he inhabit the tents of Shem."

The three brothers are the eponymous ancestors of the Greeks (Japheth), the Jews (Shem), and, beyond any precise assignation, the others, all those others of some kind (Ham). Their tormented history is but the history of foreign words, according to the Talmudic interpretations, and of hospitality due to these words, of cruel fraternity and the foreignness of brothers unto each other, with Ham being more foreign still than the Jew/Greek couple, in which he figures as the excluded middle. The welcome might perhaps only be possible at the price of this exclusion and of the elimination [*effacement*] of Ham: "The words of Japheth will be in the tents of Shem."[28]

The words of the Greek tradition thus have to be sheltered in the tents of the Hebraic tradition. The concepts must be included in a vaster domain of reception, one that would permit another use of them [*un exercice autre*], more aerated, one that might be cut loose from the presence of that which only presents itself in the representation of the concepts: "Leave the Hebrew language some space," recommended Luther, drawing a lesson from his own work of translating the Bible into German; take note of the spacing and the open place set forth in this way for the importation of another idiom, notably, that of philosophy. Midrash adds yet another term to this metaphor of transposition, spacing, and play, clarifying it succinctly as the "task of translation": "May the words of the Torah be expressed in the language of Japheth, beneath the tents of Shem."[29]

Here, it is the Greek translation of the Torah, whose necessity is recognized and asserted, that must be placed beneath the Semitic shelter. Nevertheless, the tents are the site no longer of an opening or a reopening but rather of a reframing, of an assignment of address, and of a tightening down. The tents are the figure of the necessity of a return to a nomadic and desertlike truth, which Japheth's language, philosophy, would hardly permit. This is a return possible only in a habitation set back in withdrawal, never in the full winds and great spaces, never in illimitation and pure horizontality.

To speak of the beginning, as we have done, is to attempt to discern a goal or term, starting from which the course or the re-course of the tradition could be engaged. Now in the tradition itself, this beginning is always preceded by a beginning of the beginning, the Torah, which does not even begin in itself since it is, again, *a translation*—but a translation on the basis of a language of departure that was perfectly ungraspable, on the basis of an inaccessible writing of a writer-God. In that way, the status of the Torah as language of arrival will command, according to variable determinations, the whole of rabbinical exegesis as distributed from two opposed principles, albeit disposed in an equal hermeneutic dignity by the Talmud, which refers their paternity explicitly to two great doctors: "The Torah speaks the language of man (Ishmaël). The Torah does not speak the language of man (Akiva)."

The indeterminable nature of this "language" frees it, or ought to free it, from any presentation if not from all presence, the latter thus ruining the former by imposing its own exteriority, its transcendence. If we can maintain judiciously that "Judaism is an atheism with God,"[30] that is also because the absence of a transcendental signified obliges all the signifiers to respond among themselves, to translate each another [*s'entrerépondre, à s'entretraduire*]. Everyone will have observed how much these harmonics resonate throughout the entirety of Derrida's text. Derrida's Jewish secret (i.e., belonging/non-belonging) carries, and is carried by, the secret of language. This is a secret that it is a matter of stealing, or rather, that it suffices to allow—within language—to come to itself, that is, to language. The secret of language is that it speaks: we see clearly that it (the secret) never hides itself, which is the best way for it to preserve itself.

Here, then, is the second entrance of Rosenzweig, who, this time, scoops Heidegger: "Das eigentliche Geheimnis der Sprache: das Wort spricht [The authentic secret of language: the word speaks]."[31] The word speaks: it is not only "spoken," it is also "speaking," and, as speaking, it "is never final."[32] There cannot be a last word. First of all, because there was no first word, but only "a sort of pre-originary guarantee that precedes all other engagements"[33] and that Rosenzweig attempted to theorize in determining what he called origin-words and root-words, like *promise*.[34] To speak is to promise, it is to respond with a "guarantee given before any other event."[35] The simple fact of speaking, of being seized with and by the word, of being always already held to keep it rather than improvising it [*plutôt que de la prendre au vol*], carries with it a wager about the saying, which exposes us to a translation without end in a language of arrival that never comes to arrive: that is the meaning of Rosenzweig's "never final." Always to aim at an arrival, without ever setting forth with a sure departure from a language to be translated—this is the tenuous thread along which each word moves. No, or no more, before-Babels; no, or not yet, an Esperanto: we always speak between the surmounting—itself provisional and ceaselessly threatened—of the absolute confusion (i.e., as many languages as there might be speaking subjects) and the uncertain hope of absolute comprehension (i.e., a single language for all subjects). To speak is thus to be taken up in this élan that goes from an impossible origin (so impossible that the Talmud deliberately confuses it by inscribing the language of the Torah in dissymmetry and the double mark of the "... men / not ... men") in a hoped-for event that has not yet come to pass. This promise of the word (*ver-sprechen*) and of nomination (*verheissen*) has nothing to do with a belief, values, or an intention. Simply, "the promise speaks." We should say, rather, *das Versprechen spricht*; it "calls and assures [*Verheissung*]"[36] and, consequently, "it is not possible to speak outside of this promise."[37]

We may well consider—in this question of knowing what speaking means—that there is a German line, or Judeo-German line, that sets forth from Hamann ("to speak is to translate") and culminates in Rosenzweig and the heuristic he called "the word in the foreground [*parole en avant*]."[38] This heuristic of the "word in the foreground" contrasts with all traditional and historico-critical hermeneutics: it is not a matter, in effect, of starting from the biblical text, Rosenzweig explains, to elucidate retrospectively the conditions of the historical production of its meaning. It is rather a matter of setting that meaning "up front." That is to say, of preceding its historical meaning by the voice or the speech of those future readers-speakers of the *miqra*, the writing that Hebrew calls, precisely, "reading." On this (Judeo-) German line, Derrida would easily take a place, from the "to speak is to translate" to the "to speak is to promise." But he does so in the most singular fashion, out of the Judeo-Maghrebin, or, more precisely, Judeo-Algerian experience of the impossible ownership of language, of a language that one speaks yet which is not one's own; the only language one hears spoken, yet which is nonetheless that of an unassignable other. This maternal language "remains," but not at all in Hannah Arendt's sense of that which remains "set off [*à l'écart*]" from the language of exile, like a spare habitation, a property always and immediately inhabitable, a recoverable authenticity.[39] It is rather *residual* [*en reste*]: in debt and on hold, withdrawn and overdue [*en retrait et en souffrance*]. The experience of language, retraced in *Monolingualism of the Other* from a non-external disenfranchisement, is isomorphic with the experience of the "last of the . . ." An internal, native inhabitation of the French, "forbidden" at the same time as Arabic and Hebrew were, constitutes, in effect, its most particular trait, its most Judeo-Algerian trait. One could, nonetheless, point out that other Jewish groups, in other circumstances, endured similar linguistic trials (e.g., the Jews of Prague, caught between their German "monolanguage" and the impossibility of Czech, Yiddish, or Hebrew).[40] Thus, the Judeo-Franco-Algerian exemplarity, with its originary lack of any maternal language, finds itself radicalized by extension, once come out of self and delivered to its own unfurling. Reinscribed directly into its singularity, directly into its irreplaceability, in the universal structure of a law, this exemplarity signifies the traumatic condition through which we find ourselves assigned to a single language, which we cannot appropriate as our own. The absence or the impossibility of any monolanguage in itself designates an experience caught up in a polymorphous circumcision of speaking [*circoncision polymorphe du parler*], of all speaking, in the cut and the taboo, the separation and the enfranchisement, the alliance by subtraction and the gift of the remnant. We should note in passing that the heritage of the monolanguage, in the universality of what it preserves (the memory of a language never spoken) and promises (the language one does not yet speak, since one never speaks a single language), confuses considerably, by contamination, the conventional distinction between the Sephardi and the Ashkenazi: their respective signifiers managing to find themselves as if untied and attached thereby to unanticipated signifieds.

In Rosenzweig, the movement is slightly different.⁴¹ Language "ties up and divides at the same time," he writes; its "marvel," its "divine nature," as Hegel would say, is that it is path and traveler at the same time. Language dispropriates [*déproprie*] in measuring itself—in an immoderate fashion—against its saying [*à son dire*]. It always exceeds the sign or portent [*présage*] that stimulates it. What is this other than speaking; what is this if not speaking? Spoken language is what expends without a *telos*, in some sense even without thought, that which is always dragged toward its surplus of the unthought [*happé vers ses surplus d'impensé*], that is to say, its promises, that is, the turning back around of something finished (in thought) into a "new beginning" (through the word).⁴² On this ground, the universally dispropriating promise of the word (a theme we underestimate at our own risk in *The Star of Redemption*), Rosenzweig effects a sort of intensive radicalization, by way of Judaism, of this universal structure. If, in many of its aspects, his philosophy is a philosophy of conversion, it is so, curiously enough, by way of *dis-similation*, to borrow Rosenzweig's term, which means that it prefers to change terrain, to pass into something other, rather than reorganizing the sites themselves. According to a figure that would again rejoin that of election-subtraction, of the surplus, of the remnant that does not even remain (but which we would no doubt rediscover, albeit otherwise, in Levinas's theme of exasperation or in Derrida's "supplementarization")—this radicalization through di-version ends by displacing the exemplarist thematic itself. The depropriation, because absolute, is absolutely depropriating when it comes to the "Jewish people."⁴³ The latter possesses no language; rigorously speaking, it cannot have any one language in common, nor, consequently, dispose of that which constitutes, for the "nations," the most living mark of their common enfranchisement: the language that is "proper to them."⁴⁴ Why so, and how is this?

1. The maternal language [of the Jewish people] is, each time, or in any case under many historic circumstances, that of the host that receives them, "the language of its external destiny,"⁴⁵ that is, a language of non-belonging, received but not possessed.

2. The Jewish tongues, Yiddish, Judeo-Spanish [Ladino], and so on, are but contingent parlance, issued from crossings effected on the basis of the Jewish people's wanderings and encounters. They are thus languages of its imposed destinies, or languages received along with the internalization of its external destinies.

3. Hebrew is certainly said to be "its own language," the "Jewish people's."[46] Hebrew is, in effect, a language that qualifies something proprietary [*un propre*], since it governs the liturgical appropriation of the anticipated eternity. But this property can never be appropriated to "daily life" and its parlance. On the contrary, it signifies its own ex-propriety, for it is woven out of death (Hebrew is a sort of "fake" dead language, forever disclaimed, whose "death" must be continuously surmounted in the living dialogue with God[47]), out of *holiness* (the holy language is a language of separation), and out of forgetfulness (the Hebrew language has often to be re-learned by successive generations of eventual speakers, its closure has to be dis-enclosed, its death to be warded off).

All this is so true that, for Rosenzweig, the cut between "Jewish people" . . . "peoples of the world" cuts across an inversion of language/writing, which places Hebrew in a position of surlanguage or sub-language [*de surlangue ou de sous-langue*], or even one of a (translated) discourse of silence. There is an astonishing brief passage in *The Star of Redemption* in which Rosenzweig explains that, for the nations of the world, language is what survives of a lost writing, whereas for the Jewish people writing is what survives out of a language that has escaped any sort of everydayness. What remains of the passage through host languages, through languages issuing from an ephemeral sojourn or settlement, is a non-spoken language that nevertheless is not a "dead language" but something like "a living writing," according to the fine expression Mendelssohn used to signify the enactment of the commandments. Only this writing, this unheard-of thing that would be a language-writing, a writing-language, could liberate "eternity" from its dependency on the historical determinations of existing communities, relative, that is, to the conditions that inscribe it in that time-solely-time [*temps-uniquement-temps*], and thereby defy the oppositions of the infinite and the finite, of interiority and exteriority, of the spirit as living word and the letter as a dead sign. Hebrew is thus the sole language of writing-reading (*miqra*), the only extra-historic language, legible, like every language, in the absence of any empirical subject. Rosenzweig seems to go to the point of saying that it would be legible in the absence of any sign, in the silence and ideality of a liturgical rituality confined to gestures, inscribed in bodies. The sole language capable of anticipating eternity in time—that is, of opening not only the possibility of intersubjective communication, like every language, but above all of freeing the possibility for the intelligibility of an ideal object for a transcendental subject, which is precisely what relates it to writing. Thus defined, Hebrew would be the sole language that is not a monolanguage, the sole non-language language, the last of the languages, because it is the first, in some sense, of all scripts, all writing. The height of depropriation, the height of the proper as well, if you will.

I have neither exhausted (far from it) the examination of the relationship between the two thoughts [of Derrida and Rosenzweig] nor even attempted to follow with any consistency the thread of a Derridean reading of Rosenzweig, inasmuch as we can discern something of this sort. I have simply wanted to suggest a few remarkable consonances, a few intersections, hoping to provoke questions and renewals—and perhaps the beginnings of a commentary by Derrida himself. An expectation all the sharper, all the more concentrated on all these points, in that it was stimulated by the memory of an impressive lecture, given a few years ago in Aix-en-Provence and not yet published, as far as I know: "Entre l'abîme et le volcan, la langue [Between the Abyss and the Volcano, Language]."[48] Derrida chose there to speak of a letter addressed, in December 1926, by Scholem to Rosenzweig, for the latter's birthday. It was entitled "À Propos Our Language: A Confession."[49] Three years after his arrival in Palestine, Scholem expressed the anguish that gripped him when he imagined the strange conspiracy of forces borne by the "actualization" of Hebrew, that is, its secularization by way of the amputation of its messianic and prophetic tip [*sa pointe messianique et prophétique*]. The Hebrew monolanguage, "abased and spectral," the modern Israeli—invoking all too lightly, without paying it the slightest heed, the "names" that represent its hidden power—risks turning fatally against those who speak it otherwise than according to its esperantial vocation, leading them straight toward an "empty future [*avenir vide*]." Fundamentally, Scholem is correcting Rosenzweig. He fears for Hebrew its too considerable identification with its empirical reality, with its graphic and phonic signs, with their immediate distinction. This would detach the language, perhaps forever, from its quasi-transcendental regime as a trace. Derrida proposed a remarkable reading of this apocalyptic tone in Scholem's letter and the thinking on language done by its addressee, Rosenzweig, in which their interrogative parries, with their constrictions and unfoldings, their clarifications and disquietude, are folded into each other. The more the uncontrollable quality of the dynamics contained in the language—here, spoken Hebrew—can be discerned and desacralized (having fallen from its status as a language-writing), the more the chaotic explosion and piling up of catastrophes—whose unfurling seems altogether confirmed by the situation in the Middle East—sanction the linguistic premonition of a universal structure of expropriation, whose experience comes to life in traumatism and violence, injustice and heartbreak—all that to which, precisely, language alone can bear witness, as that from which it will inherit as well, and evermore.

That reflection on Derrida *and* Rosenzweig might have been provoked by the memory of this colloquium, by way of its occurrence and its traces, permits or obliges us to a concluding return to the "I am the last of the Jews," and likewise to "a *confession* à propos language," as to an intimate monstrosity, both irreplaceable and yet substitutable, universalizable by graftings and alterations. Alone, autobiography manages to signify this ambivalence. But that means the autobiography—insofar as it would be a genre of philosophy—of philosophical dialogue, inasmuch as it can weave into the fabric of philosophy motifs foreign to it. To say, "I am Jewish, I am the last of the Jews," "I am Jewish-Algerian-Maghrebin." But also, "I am German though I am not," since I write in a philosophical script. This is to pose, in turn, after the Talmud and Midrash, the crucial question of Jew-Greek in the mode of a presentation that strives to think, while avowing what depropriates [*déproprie*], in a life or in a subject, according to this putting into contradiction of self with self, which Rousseau describes at the beginning of his *Confessions*. Such a writing proceeds necessarily out of that which it does not know. It organizes itself on the basis of the multiple resistances of self-exposition, of its ungraspable others, of its "remnants," which make an autobiography into a heterobiography. The genre thereby determined is thus the complete contrary to some memorial recording of self and one's self-same. The Derridean heterobiography is a modality of philosophy. It runs up against the very obstacle that it obliges us to think. One could show without too much trouble that out of this also doubtless arises Rosenzweig's play on biographemes (e.g., the gaze of the dying one at the Front, the abandonment of the academic career, the conversion and dissimilation, etc.) — and the philosophemes (e.g., death as "something," thinking as "service," Judaism as exteriority, etc.). There is a Jewish fold of language that Derrida and Rosenzweig both share and that shares or apportions them out as well, as we have seen, at least in some of its effects. It is remarkable that these damaged, uneven topographies could give rise, among their readers-surveyors, to motifs, to motions, to emotions of thought, to settings underway, or into motion, of the desire of and for thought. The philosophical tradition requires that we think the thoughts of the thinkers who have preceded us and who, thereby, make us think, and think better, with those thoughts, and thanks to them. Beyond this prerequisite, but that means beyond-within, always and fortunately taken up in Hegel's injunction, there are thoughts that also know how to make themselves loved, to put it rather immodestly, and that, in so doing, let themselves be better *thought*, as well. That of Rosenzweig; that of Derrida.

This Stranjew Body

HÉLÈNE CIXOUS

Antonomasia

He who was born on July 15, 1930—precisely one hundred years after the conquest of Algeria by France; in 1830 colonization begins, interminably; it is still going on in 1930 when he came to life between two deaths, or two cadavers; yesterday was July 14; there were fireworks in Algeria, too, the whole flamboyant artifice, indeed, of French colonization; this July 15, 1930, was it not the first day of an era still indefinable but new, unforeseeable, of wars, repudiations, expulsions, empires, and collapse,

he-who-was-born in El Biar and declared born "French" but not for long, still French while waiting to be expelled [*renvoyé*]—in the place of being "French," being "expelled"—

how to name him, how to define him give him what attributes, call him what, who, how? for no adequate word for this new, unstable, complex, swept-along newcomer [*survenant*]—deported across ends, passing as a crosser of borders, both invisible and marked, the intimate borders, the febrile and obscure ones that beat in the secret depths of the ego [*dans le secret du moi*], police-borders, national-borders, which chew and grind up the undesirables who suddenly become the condemned.

The power of places, the impotence of human consciousness. We have forgotten everything, but eucalyptus-scented El Biar remembers. The grounds the winds the trees are haunted.

The forgetfulness rises so high, it is so well organized.

How to recall, how to bring to mind, the month of July 1830; it is so hot, it was yesterday; how not to recall the surge of the army, the 37,000 men, armed by the ministry of war with a *historical Insight* that permitted the opposition of "truth" to "errors" and promised to the soldiers a victory over the Turks, the Moors, and the others. It is a yesterday well protected by forgetfulness, that evening of July 4, when the army reached the plateau of El Biar and the slopes that dominate the Fort l'Empereur to the west.

When we were little, we took walks there. The bombings were so strong that by July 5 there would be nothing left of the fort, or of the villas with their lovely gardens. It is July 10. "The army has not been camped for forty-eight hours in one of the most beautiful countries in the world, and already that country is devastated," writes the geographical engineer attached to the officer corps. It is July 14. Algiers is in the grip of panic and defeatism. Old General Berthezène ran things well in his time. Do you remember rue Berthezène? And then Ransack Pillage and Plunder fell upon the city like a wave. Some officers think they have never seen anything more hideous, but are afraid to say so. Others fill their pockets so full that next year they manage to buy estates, meadows, and titles in France. Where are we, we Jewish seedlings, during the monstrous sack? Jonas Cixous — that hispano-franco-arabophone hybrid — was he bathed in blood, or in milk? Where are the Safars, the Derridas? A silence answers us. Half of my being, that which lodged on the border between Austria and Germany, was hunted down, deprived of rights, or pogromed; the other half, the hispano-maghrebin, was it on the side of the conquerors or the vanquished? According to my father, we were more Arabic than French, but that's legend. According to Jacques Derrida, we will never know. Among us, not one word and, no doubt, not a trace. We came to the surface, as though nothing had been, in the 1930s. But we need only look: all of Algeria bears military names. We went to the lycée Bugeaud (a field marshal), passing in front of the Place du Gouvernement (Français).

I see that, above, I spoke of "the army."

"The army?" I wrote. — But which army? As though there were only one? What army are you speaking of, when you, H.C., you say "the army"? What side are you speaking from? — And he, Jacques Derrida, my "compatriot"? From what side are we speaking, are we thinking? On what side did we *find* ourselves, always half lost, faltering, we who were crisscrossed by adversary borders, adversary shores, we whose hearts are in no army? We who, in 1830, were absent from these outbreaks, and yet. And yet we who, later on, were the results, the hosts, and the hostages of a blood-soaked history that surpassed us on all sides. We who said *nous* in French. Where in 1830 were we with all that? He, in one Algeria or another, but as what? as who? I, half in Spain still, half in Germany or Slovakia? And thereupon, we arrived, we became, we were declared "French" from one day to the next we were fallen hunted down degraded "French" we received as heritage a memory reddened with a hundred mixed bloods from one moment to the next we were disinherited we have at the depths of our thoughts a memory of apocalyptic dates. Stendhal, in order to tell his story, ascended and descended the ladder of time around the dates of monarchies, the Revolution, the Empire, there was in him the Stendhal of 1789 of 1793 of 1800 of 1803 of 1830—Ah! there it is. Here we might meet up. But we do not meet each other. What were we doing in 1830, what was our thought doing?

In 1830 Stendhal is in Rome, news from Algiers is utterly indifferent to him, nonexistent, the tens of thousands of dead in no way troubled the happiness of my friend. He strolls in San-Pietro in Montorio on the Janiculum Hill the sun shines magnificently. The odors of the mastic trees the color of the rocks, all this reminds me of the shimmering heights of Algiers. A delicious heat reigns on both sides. What a view! He stands on the ruins of Rome. We upon the young vestiges of Fort l'Empereur. He is about to be fifty. Who will read me in a hundred years? he wonders. I will, I say. Seated upon the steps of the world, we will dream an hour or two, of the strange history of men. Of the slaughters. Of the massacres that precede us and accompany us. And without all that blood and all that beauty we would not have been born. We would not have written in French.

The Work of Time: to cover over, to discover, to unearth. More and more hauntings or visitations [*de plus en plus de revenance*] insist in the writings of Jacques Derrida, as though their nature, like old, bombed-out gardens, bombed over and over again, and more often than we knew, were expressed in a voice impossible to ignore.

We are, he from El Biar, me from Clos-Salambier, the children of war, a great one and one that preceded it. We arrive from war, go from war to war. One war silences the war before it. But the dead and the ravished slowly begin to speak.

He himself utters more and more frequently the name *El Biar*, as though it were almost a little his own. "El Biar": the well. A well of bloods. Of knowings. Of tears. Of dreams.

One hundred years, one step, he is born, the family is Jewish. We must also write here the story of the Jews, or more scrupulously, the stories of the Jews, or more precisely of the Jews between communities and the dissident "Jews," of the Jewish Jews [*Juifs juifs*] and the many species of di-Jews and dys-Jews [*dijuifs et déjuifs*], the story of the "Jews" inside outside France and the story of the "Jews" inside outside Algeria, as well as the story of the "Jews inside outside" Morocco and Tunisia, without forgetting the story of the "Jews outside inside" Spain and Portugal; the list is long with all these dissimilar and complicit stories, all of which are differently at work in the mental archivings or the neural, physical, spiritual archivement [*archiverie mentale ou l'archivement nerveux* . . .] of that thought-being ultimately named *Jacques Derrida*. Whole peoples, the effaced, the ruminators, the anguished, the irrepressible, press in on him on each of his sides. Recently we have seen the most nameless the most defiant the most obstinate of these peoples rise in his memory to the surface. He finds himself, finds himself anew, in feint and truth, a *marrano*. An adoption that sits well with his essential way of assenting to the secret, of giving to secrets their incalculable share. *To let himself be overtaken, exceeded*.

As we know, that which at the outset is feigned finishes by becoming true. A marrano truefeint [*un feintvrai marrane*] shakes the foam of his nostalgia toward the faceless names that remain for him from a heritage without origin.[1] The words whisper: Jourdan Jaffa Jackie Jardin

A Desire to Be a Marrano

If one could be a marrano—which is like the desire to become an Indian—this seizes hold of him one morning, a foreign seizure like the one that takes hold of Kafka, that *Wunsch, Indianer zu werden*,² but what is this being-Indian, is it flight feint or word, like that horse's desire, the becoming, the being, the doing, all that is interchangeable, what is a marrano, how can one be one, one must first want, and immediately, astride the stream that feigns being the Jordan, the body quivering with a shudder as though one were astride a real horse, to the point of crossing from one side to the other this stream that seems to be a sea all red, to run faster than desire, faster than possibility up to the moment where one throws off the reins for there are no more reins, to the moment of letting go the bit [*mors*], the dead [*le mort*], yet there never was a bit, death, only the word, the fugue or fury of the body of the soul, bodily seized, enchanted, more and more foreign more and more secret, and one ends by no longer remembering that one has forgotten where one believed one would find oneself, thanks to this all-speed it happens that he substitutes himself, that I substitute itself.

Thus it is on the withers of a dream that he marranates himself. Jewfeint. The dream: to believe oneself the child of a people northis northat in the time of a dream. Norcatholic norjew midjew midsame midindian midhorse. For the dream like the *Mishnah* plays on the force of words.

Engagé

Promised—without having been consulted, worse than an arranged marriage, for in this case the promise that holds him has always taken place prior to the birth of the promise; he wasn't there to hear the sentence or the verdict, nor the oath, promised-and-thus-perjured in advance, prior to himself, promised like Samson to God from his hair to his toes before even having hair, innocent of the trickery of bad good faith, for all this entrapment without beginning or end is the fault of the other who speaks before any word, the so-called God, a pseudonym of a solidity that won't come unstuck. Engaged in the circle of the betrayal, come into the world and at the same time come into the lie, born-lied-to,[3] and this by a family of good faith, from the first instant, with the first scream, divided, betrayed and betrayer obliged to keep the promise to which he was promised without his will—and which, faithful to its fidelity across the whole gallery of structural infidelities, he refrains from rejecting, taking on the faulty condition of the inheritor without espousing it, but recognizing the debt contracted by the predecessors of yesteryear, sharing the bitterness that is not his own the way he speaks that single language that he has without being its possessor—human. Discontinuously. Cleaved slightly, his tensed soul quartered by the two-stroke essence of Time. Having been promised in advance, before himself, he can no longer promise, he can only promise himself to live out the fatality of the inaugural dislocation. To think unflinchingly its incessant torments. To explore its remains folds and hiding-places.

"I never decided anything," he said.

And since the Decision, taken on him, called in French *Circoncision* "I never decided anything," he muses.

Things are decided. For the humble man, whatever his analytic and fore-seeing genius, it is this way: this way. He moves forward in the space where he was thrown, at once earmarked, abandoned, ordered, from the first days to eternity, without knowing, without possessing himself [*sans savoir, sans s'avoir*], knowing only to await that which can still befall him. Philosophical submission. Indocile submission, patient insubordination [*insoumission patiente*].

The word *Jew*, the French word *juif*, this heavy and volatile word, he does not fear it.

Far from a Proust, who picks up the word with tweezers. "Hebraïc," he says of Rachel in "Albertine disparue."⁴

That word, *juif*, like all French words, he receives it, like all the divided divisors of the language.

Double courage: not to be it and not not to be.

Double fear. The courage of fear. His non-avoidance of suffering. He lives *with*. His living is always with. With the word *with* as well: *Apud hoc*. Alongside of. Alongside of himself. We have never seen someone as much inthepresent [*auprésent*]. *Alongside (of nigh-to), with,* adverbs/prepositions that insert the length, infinite length, into proximity. It is the spacing in which the face [*figure*] lodges (itself). Once I came up with the term *passisimplicité* for him. It is thus that he approaches, turns—with his exemplary soul prudence—toward all that lives is to be thought thinks. In the self-restraint passisimplicity. As though he were naturally attentive to what hid in the depths or the reserve of every subject. First, words. He thinks of, advances, to the word.

Liquors

And if the blood were not to stop, he wonders, this would be his first period,

the first period of "Circumfession," the first sentence, one from a genre that he likes, one that comes, that comes to him, for him, over him, that dictates (itself) and lets itself be taken, that he receives and notes, to which he hastens to grant a moved, desiring hospitality,

this is his first outpouring, confession or confidence, and if, once the severing effected, the cut, the ablation, the piercing, the intrusion of a blade, a point, a needle, a stinger that opens the vein, the blood were not to stop,

this would be his first fluster, first anguishing, first pain; he should like not to lose a drop of it and yet lose it all, to go flowing and dissolving himself to the extremity of this red-colored effusion,

to go, to go, to roll on, to flow, the course, the hunt, the exploration of the world, to come to throw himself, without his knowing if where when the blood, the mysterious fascinating liquid will lead him, to what end, what glory, what mouth of hell or philosophy.

In great mourning the Greeks, Homer, the Tragic Poets bent over this rivulet, this fateful torrent, this vital essence, which once shed in the dust has great trouble flowing back, as Aeschylus lamented, Sophocles warned.

If his blood flowing away "abandoned him" signified to him the sentence hidden in the liquid, the Latin word that reminds us that the liquid, the liqueur, the *liquor*,[5] in flowing out leaves us behind it, drops us! *linquit, linquere*: to leave behind, leaves us the victims of a *de-re-linquere* in a dereliction that can threaten at any time—by repeatedly leaving us short of it, lacking our own essence—in *delicto*, in delinquency.

The fast liquid once shed does not flow back. It is over.

And if the blood in flowing away ceased to be *sanguis* to become *cruor* making him feel how much life can from one instant to the next pass from maternal sweetness to cruelty, while the body turns into flesh into meat into cadaver, this is how he/it goes musing and reminiscing, cradled or pierced [*bercé ou percé*] by the secret sense of familiar words, from even before he became a thinking being.

If he has a "childhood memory," it is the one necessary to him— the lost-memory, that of a scene in which he was the tragic hero, the nursling of the goat or the lamb given over to the knife, eyes still incapable of reading the luminous signs, yet the subjectile, the fragile flesh, registers the violent message for the future.

No doubt many Jewish males ancient heroes despite themselves of the scene of the Circumcision will have responded, later on, to the blow delivered before their coming to consciousness to their astonished body, to their impotent member, by a movement of return, by a narcissistic reappropriation of what was inflicted upon them, by an identitary reinterpretation of the circumcision. Not he.

Glory is not there where the scar formed. There remain the trace, the rage, the phantom of pain. Where is glory then for him?

Once again a word from which he has drawn numbers of echoes to form one day one of his most beautiful, most resonant operas, which I antonymed,[6] *Glas*.

Glory once again a resounding, resanguining word.

Glory in a note of milk and death, which sounds a birth and an end, *gloria* says the Latin, *gloria* as in the hymn and as the milk's mark, milk of glory and glory of milk, *klēos* says the Greek, where the flood leads us, if nothing is interposed, if the nurse who busies himself with the blood sample [*prise de sang*], holding the syringe upright, like the ancient dagger, its tip pointing upward, if the nurse, he tells himself, didn't decide, hadn't decided in the Algiers laboratory to remove hastily from the body the dagger of the syringe, if he hadn't quickly bent the arm upward, if he hadn't interrupted the flow by pressing the cotton down on the inside of the elbow, he recalls vaguely, frightened but longing to continue, then the blood could have continued to inundate until he was exhausted, until he was precipitated albeit voluptuously toward what he called, one day: *the glorious appeasement*. A first effusion, a first antonomasia so as not to say, coarsely, dying or death. He could then have tasted "the ravishing calm" that befell Rousseau by the grace of an event both canine and Danish on the famous day where a dog throwing itself with all its legs into his legs was able to *give* him death — without causing him to perish for all that. He would have found himself carried up to the delicious sky. Whole and without remainder at the present moment you remember nothing. One knows neither who I was nor where I am. Nor pain, nor fears, nor worry. And upon all that he would see his blood flowing like you might have seen flowing a rivulet without so much as thinking that this blood might belong to you in any way. Yet the ravishment of Rousseau was refused him. There was the "brutal intervention of the other," the nurse, to cut the course of the blood and suspend the coming of this strange glory, maternal and dangerous, the nurse was there to sever him, deprive him, to stop the bleeding, the man in the (inverse) role of the medical *mohel* pulling, taking, and then intervening, regulating the outflow of the vein. Without his being able to do anything. In this way the brutal other would have cut short the appeasing outflow of the blood [*le sens apaisant du sang*⁷].

Yet in another sense, if the blood were not to stop, washing along in its wake [*charriant dans sa crue*] the superabundance of meanings, times or faiths [*des fois*], believings, insane *savoirs*, it would have become another language for him, the famous language of dreams, one lacking all brakes, without cuts, absolute, would pour forth, and with all speed, the unheard of flood of his thoughts, spreading upon the "paper" (or any sort of support serving the affair called "paper") the superhuman wealth, greater stronger than himself, of his own thought elusive even to him

Would that blood not be like the dark blood of the black ram poured out by the pious hand of Odysseus, and not by the nurse of Algiers, which, once absorbed by the weakened head of Tiresias, restores communication in the throat of the seer and again frees the flood of words that death had drained dry?

That would then be the blood-that-confers-the-word substituted for the blood-that-silences-it. The blood that awakes all the phantoms, whose traces he loved to follow, starting with his first breath. This blood is his source-ink, he dreams of it alone, without its troubling itself over the obstacles of man, transfers the totality of its boiling thought integrally without letting a single drop escape in a text that would have no ends. He will always begrudge those blood samplers for their simulacra of rape, castration, capital punishment, simultaneously effected and annulled. The threat (of *jouissance*, of death) each time falls short. There remains the memory of anguish; there remains the trace of the moment of tragic impotence that is the lot of all prophetic idiots and others condemned to die and pardoned pointblank, who have just time enough to taste mortality, and think they will no longer forget. An invisible or unspeakable kinship ties him to the *pardoned*,⁸ to those banished from existence unsuspectingly.

Let one not tell me that at the age of eight days the child is not present to his own lot. Like the dead, he lives it all and undergoes, but he hasn't the strength at that time to say it. He will say it later on. And one likewise remembers events one has inherited, even if they came to pass in a "before" us. There is no "before" that is not a now. It is always this theme of heritage that haunts him, it is the transgressions that he has not committed and for which he seeks to respond, since they are deposited before his door, it is the name *TA-CHET*,[9] written in large capital letters on one of the last arcades of the port, which seems to welcome with pomp the traveler come from the sea, WHOLESALE WINES, TACHET, and above this, LITHOGRAPHY JOURDAN, the background of his whole life, staged in this way:

LITHOGRAPHY
JOURDAN
WHOLESALE WINES
TACHET

"Tachet," like a spot on the name of his father at work [*à la tâche*]. Over the entire sea-front with its dozens of elegant arcades one sees only these letters, sealing the face of his city of birth.

There lies the first page and the first lithograph, the first and forever indelible frontispiece engraving of his memory and his work, his first day of the new year and the first spot [*tache*] on his pride, traces of which he still spoke, still bitter though in a humorous mood, in *The Frontage-road* [*La Contre-allée*].[10] Arriving sails folded, these words welcome the visitor to beautiful Algiers *la Blanche*. "Stone and Wine," the title of a coarse poem he could have written for the wharfs. TACHET spells on the old photos of his memory the paternal pain and humiliation, it is these words, these names, French and thus foreign, that cannot be dissociated from his thought, it is these thousands of little letters with claws these minute scars on his book of flesh that never cease murmuring and suggesting new seminar themes.

Hostipitality,[11] pardon, perjury,[12] the death sentence, sovereignty, the animal and the slave,[13] all this began its course toward his light from the rue d'Aurelle de Paladine in El Biar then from the lycée Ben Aknoun and thereafter from the lycée Bugeaud, passing by the Place du Gouvernement and before that among the ruins of Algiers bombed in July 1830, where in the streets lay severed children's hands, "childrenshands-torn-off-of-children" as, at another age, in his other country, Thomas Bernhard observed, and before that he tells himself surely there was perhaps in a lost city of Portugal no one will ever know who, one who pronounced the secret words in the secret "already when I took these notes, from 77 to 84," he tells himself ("Circumfession," period 45),[14] blending his voice with the song of four rabbis whose language he does not speak but who speak to him, add to this choir the sound of wings, it is the angel who comes to mix the work of the computer into this memory devoted to effractions, "already" he says, a word without which he would never have written, already from "77 to 84," leaving to the reader the care and the uncertain pleasure of completing the date that he himself cut short: already 1877 or 1784 or indeed in 2177, or however you like.

Nothing is foreign to him, everything remains foreign to him.

Always already. Everydayalready Everything already plays. [*Toujours déjà. Toujourdéjà. Tout joue déjà.*] It has already happened. Already has already happened. He comes to the event that has already happened to him. He comes to the event that is already happening to him

The déjarrivance from Al Djezaïr.[15]

Expelled

Dawn 1940, my father being now the military physician at the Front, I was admitted to the first Paradise. He will call this PaRDeS.

The PaRDeS, second and last paradise, that after which there was nothing more to lose, was the test Garden [*Jardin d'essai*],[16] a Garden where he like me like him, we discovered together all the essays or assays that grow in the ear and in the soul [*tous les essais qui poussent à l'oreille et à l'âme*], test Garden adored literally, with its paths of palm trees, yuccas, bamboo hedges, its *∂*'s and its *c*'s, its *c* [des *c*], its *c'est*'s,[17] for never would we have gone along these paths without feeling ourselves reading and read in the magic symmetry of the forests, running alongside palaces of palms and sounds, walking, my hand in father's, in the midst of French homonymy. I did this on my part, enjoying the verbal coincidences, up to the day when, thorny, there rose up before me a new version *Décès* [Death] of the Garden.[18] A garden of Algiers was the first essay of our literature.[19] But what did we attempt [*essay-ait*] in this garden? We attempted to be. And to survive. And to safeguard. And to give birth. And to see arriving, from behind the fence that looked out over the sea, the sails that promise and threaten.

The first Paradise is in the military Circle in Oran. There are found all the trees from the arid city, there are earth, sand, viscous plants, and animals among which I, at two and a half, crawl about and know. There remain unknowable unknowns, the distant children sovereign on the swings. Over my little worm's head they speak loudly something like another French, they say they long for postage stamps. Is that, then, the entry ticket for children? Those stamps that we receive every day from the whole world 54 rue Philippe just next door, I boast for real, from the universe of the exiles arrive envelopes stamped from Australia, Uruguay, South Africa, Argentina Chile Palestine or Theresienstadt. To obtain a visa I commit myself to bringing, starting tomorrow, all those little papers to the masters of the garden—Liar! you won't bring those a big little blond spits in my face, me black. All Jews are liars.

Am I a Jew? Am I a liar? The world shows its teeth. Pinned in the sand I felt myself chased out of the hoard out of pure reason paradise rotted beneath my belly. In the street I weighed as fast as I could the choice between two dishonors, to bring, not to bring, two possibilities, equally bad. The poisoned sword in my back hampered me. Now you know what exists above you. I chose. I chose one of the two. If that's called choosing. You now know, then, that you are a child liar.

Immediately after, my father excluded from the physicians' guild unscrews the plaque from the face of our house, we condemn you to death by unscrewing the face [*par dévissage du visage*].[20] The great gates of Paradise slowly close again. Their bars mocking the anagram of the trees, rise in iron [*en fer*][21] up to the blue sky. The inside is separated from the outside with the turn of the screw. But if I hadn't been excluded from Paradise, what hell! My father disphysicianed. That day in Algiers the general superintendent of the lycée Ben Aknoun sends little Jackie home to his parents. October 1, 1941, the weather was extremely beautiful. Dishonor devoured the lungs of the one expelled.

We were chased off hunted down broken degraded dishonored. It's an ineffaceable sensation.

In the moment there is only suffering without clarification. If at least one were guilty, one would defend oneself like a fine devil. But this child is innocent. He feels all the more guilty. Guilty of all the wrongs of the world. Guilty and cause of misfortunes and injustices. Guilty of innocence.

Later, he invents philosophy, from the other side. The philosophy of the other side. All his philosophy is referral, suspension, expulsions, *renvoir*,[22] *renvoyagement*, turning suffering back up into the light, expelled from school, yes expelled from every School and vice versa. Differanciation.

And his ethics is accusation, self-accusation, accusation of innocence, an exercise of immunocence . . .

This scene already took place in Dublin, in Prague, in New York, it begins anew each time a very young poet does not see and does not admit that it is completely inadmissible it begins anew.

Beware the perverse logic of exclusion: it's a trap. How readily one feels at home in *exclusion*. To be internal, interned, to dig one's hole in the outside, to make of the outside an inside, that's not his bent he doesn't make exclusion his thing or his own. Always his State of Watchfulness: to undo to unlock, to detect the closures, to exceed exclusion. What is watchfulness? Night work in broad daylight as at midnight the work of the night, to work the night, to cross through it, to haunt it, to inseminate it with dreams and acts to come, to let oneself be haunted inseminated by one's hours in the dark day.

Watchfulness is always embattled. All can still be saved. All can still yet be lost. All may still be lost.

Flights

There are so many of them. Flight into Egypt. Flight out of Egypt. No, I won't enumerate them, I'll flee. He flees. He fled from that moment, in '43, that Jewish school just like the "alliance," I "cut" classes [*séchai*], he says, without telling my parents, for almost a year, he declares: *fuite sèche*, a dead cut, dry secret.[23] Fleeing "the alliance" to go observe "the Allies" lining up before La Lune, Le Sphinx, to make his alliance with words, to create with words, transfigured, the alliance, to make an alliance with the word *alliance*, a magic word like that of the ring of the Niebelungen, which makes him invisible . . .

Fuite humide, damp flight, the eyes flee so much weeping and tears, his own, his own and those of all his beloved Catherines of Siena,[24] "*persone ne perça* mieux à jour [no one better broke through to the light],"[25] he alliterates, allying sounds with letters, "le pourpre de la coupure pure [the deep red of the pure cut]," purpura, *puer* [boy], "the eighth day she said";[26] he says, "which followed His birth, the little pourspout of His body was pierced, at the time of circumcision . . . let us enter into the cellar opened in his flank . . . (where we shall find that blood) while weeping with anguish over the wound of God." Here I stop the hemorrhage. For, of all this, I only want the signifying flow, like him.

The little cask flows [*fût fuit*], leaks. Cask of divine wine. Casks of wines — *Tachet* [stain, spot] . . .

Sent away, expelled, fleeing now one alliance, now into another, he is essentially a fugitive. Yet he suggests, I would like to come back, I would like it to come back. But, as in the famous letter feigned by Albertine in flight,[27] the secret of his desire flees by way of the verbal alliances of the French language: "I would have been only too happy [*trop heureux*] to come back," he says, given over to the play of différance: "I would have been too fearful [*trop peureux*] to come back." We will never know if he comes back if he comes back by force or free will, too happy too fearful; but the homophony only acts to let the secret of happiness, ever frightening, flee.

We shall never know if one day he will have come back, where, when, as whom. The scenarios of his voyages, displacements, and returns are always marked with the seal of the impossible. He will have loved only the impossible, that name for the fiction within fiction.

Shots: "Imagine Him"

Every year, or almost, he begins a book, or a page, with these words: "imagine him" . . .[28] Or again, it's the sentence itself that comes back, here and there, it insists, to the point of striking my eye. It's that he holds to this: "imagine him, and ceaselessly dreaming, see him first kneeling," he says, and whom should we imagine? It's of *himself* that he is speaking, speaking of another,

—here, of [Jean-Michel] Atlan, from the first page and the first line of his text *De la couleur à la lettre* (p. 8), "Kneeling before a single canvas":

"Imagine him, him through the images that he has 'taken.'"

—here, from Athens, he sends us the order to imagine *the photographer at the Acropolis*, whose photograph is given to us to see, the photo of the photographer, the take of the taker of images that he asks us, from far away, from the Acropolis, to imagine. I imagine him returning along or retracing "the steps of the photographer" (what are *the steps* [les pas] of a photographer? Steps [*pas*]? Images? Glances . . . ?)[29] "I will come back," he says. Coming back "on the" (last) "steps of the photographer" that he is, edging along the abyss of his images of himself. On bended knee, seated, a witness,

he edges along voyages crosses flies over paces, *the abyss*

accompanied by *his future disappearance* which watches him and photographs him, films him from this point of lateron [*plustard*] or that afterward that will not leave him,

he grieves Athens *in advance* [he says, of the photograph], of a city owed to death, and two or three times rather than once, according to different temporalities: mourning the Athens of antiquity, archeological or mythological, no doubt, mourning the Athens disappeared that shows in the bodies of its ruins, but also mourning the Athens that he knows, while photographing it, in the present of its instants, will disappear tomorrow, that is already condemned to go out, and whose witnesses (the *Marché de la rue Adrianou*, the *Café Néon d'Omonia*, the *Piano des rues*) have, in effect, disappeared since the "shot"; and finally, third anticipated mourning, he knows that other photographs have captured spectacles that are still visible, today, at the present time, with the release of the book (the *Marché d'Athinas*—*Marché aux viandes* and *Marché aux poissons*) but *shall have* to be destroyed tomorrow.

I am citing here some of the sublime strophes of the great hymn of double mourning that he sings to himself, weeping and regarding himself in proxy,

—the mourning of the photographer himself (a double mourning in his own turn)

—mourning over the site of mourning, *the City* always, always lost.

Once this canticle has been read, you take it up again—replacing Athens with Algiers (as witnesses: the marché de la Lyre, an enormous market says my mother so vast, the marché de Bab-el-Oued, an immense immense market where I went on Sundays with my father he says, and where for reasons unknown one day we no longer went, the market-where-one-no-longer-went, already disappearing, rejoining markets promised to destruction, the Meissonnier market doyourecall of the rue Michelet and the unforgettable cafés promised to oblivion, even the Milkbar shall be put out like the little café, says my mother, I left Omi in the sun on the terrace, the little café whose name I have forgotten at the corner of the rue d'Isly there where there was a (little) statue whose name I have forgotten, and the Tantonville whose name evokes the splendor of the Comtesse de Ségur, the incongruous Tantonville then, all those sites where we went to enjoy and take life-samplings,[30] it's the law, all must die, while we drink a milkshake they are already condemned, like us, they pass,

he thinks, always gloomy, he has a mourning or bereavement in advance of all time, this is why we cherish, trembling, Pompeii the paradigmatic, in the reprieve in which he holes up between two mournings, between two cities.

Then replace Algiers with New York, the World Trade Center, and at the top of it the café Windows on the World

Then reflect as you walk along the abyss,[31] on the sad and marvelous laws of death by anticipation, the laws of mourning in life's midst, those of regret for what one has not yet lost, always those terribly present unreals about which he evokes, each day, in each book the

> three "presences" of disappearance, three phenomena of the "disappeared" being: the first presence *before* the camera shot, the second one *since* the camera shot, the last one much later still, for tomorrow, but it's imminent, *after* the appearance of the

print. But if the imminence of what is thus due to death suspends its term [*suspend l'échéance*], like the *epoch* of every photograph, it signs at the same time its verdict.³² It confirms and seals imminence's ineluctable authority: this shall have to die, notice is in process, the countdown has begun, there is just a delay, the time for a photograph, but from death no one fancies escaping—and nothing shall be saved.

He thinks of the death of Socrates, of the *Phædo*, of the *Crito*. He thinks of the death of Socrates, as also of his own and, conversely, as also of life and philosophy.

How many, the dead over whom he watches!

"Imagine a marrano of French Algeria who would like to pay homage shoulder to shoulder with the polysemic wealth of the French word *veilleuse* [nightlight] . . ."

"Imagine him," he incants, imagine me, yesterdays and tomorrows. An inaugural injunction that commands us to do "the work of mourning" that *he* does not do, imperious words which from the outset cast the process of writing into an abyss-despair [*abyme*].

Strange ways: a demand for imagination (intimation or supplication?) which is a way to take up the counterpoint of the philosophical tradition. This is the imaginary marrano who strives *to imagine* or *to imagine himself* [*s'imaginer*].

The Word *Religion*

—comes back to him (one must reread here those stupefying pages that gather like a herd of animals, rams, sheep, cows, disquieted by their presentiment of sacrifice, in section 35 of "Faith and Knowledge," in which Jacques Derrida recounts in a confidence wrested from himself the incredible return to his consciousness, to his ear, the words *La religion* as a theme for a philosophical get-together on Capri, in the form of a breath, an inspiration, coming from far away, like the envoy of very ancient forces or divinities, resonating he says "from out of an alchemist's cavern" (he or an other?) "at the bottom of which the word was a precipitate." A precipitate in the manner of Stendhal's crystallization? A precipitate [and a hurried departure] among the dead, from above to below, like Elpinor?[33] "As though," he says, "religion, the question of religion were *ce qui arrive à revenir* [that which comes to return]."

To him will return the word, the question, the thing the specter more beautiful than all the great phantoms, "habituated" "to be dead," religion like Gradiva.[34]

And if "she" [Gradiva, *La religion*] comes back to him and comes to him [*revient à lui et lui revient*], this religion that ceases to seem to be dead for one who knows how to receive her enigmatic light, that is because he dares, as alchemist of the verb, to leave her in all her poetic freedom. She comes back to murmur her name to him in his ear, her own name, in his language, and he hears it, they are made to agree about words, she is Latin. *Religion*, he reminds us, is a Latin word that took the whole world between its letters and passed itself into every language.

So I ask him, hesitating over my words, seemingly awkward: "how is 'religion' said, in Jewish, in Hebrew, for Jews . . . ?"—The word *religion* doesn't work, I don't know how it's said. We ought to ask a rabbi, we tell each other. That's how we're Jews, we think, Jews from the caves.[35]

To have faith is not to believe in a God, it is without clutching without support without a word without a name without address (it's Without) without coming back to anyone, without return, it's naked. It is. In that sense, he has faith. He does, he thinks, everything, as though he didn't believe in it—with a belief hooked on as though he would like to believe, as though he would hope to believe one day, despite himself in this sense he doesn't believe, he has faith. One doesn't know that one has faith, one doesn't know to have faith, one doesn't know if, one doesn't know how much, one has faith, one does not have it with a having, one has it with a love extreme, with humility, with infinite weakness, he has this wild confidence. Faith is without fire or site or religion. Without God too. It is the God that saves the child in us. There is no adjective to state what faith makes of us. "*Croyant*" [Believer] is not *foyant* [one with faith]. "To have" the faith is to be had, *foyé* [faithed]. He does not believe and he is not a believer but faith knows him. He is not aware of it. That doesn't matter. She gives him her word. Blown forth from the cavern.

Without Witness

Imagine him, reflective, untamed, his ears alerted, watching while he kneels before the cat so that no one catches him unawares. There is no one. Except the cat. Only then is a dialogue taken up in a tone of a superhuman tenderness.

—You know what I'm doing? he says

—You're doing a cat. Says the cat.

—I'm transgressing, you follow me? Jews don't give the cat their tongue, it's not done.[36] You know that?

—I know it. I follow you.

—Better not say it. Nor the evil nor the good. The good like the evil.

No one will ever know, no one will ever see him so innocent with the cat.

I question my mother:

—What relation do Jews have to animals?

—Jews have nothing to do with them. The animal is impure says my mother, so there's no relation. When there was one it was long ago, in Moses' time, the shepherds were very nice with the animals. On holidays, they didn't work.

And that's all I know about Jews and animals. When we had to consume them we performed a slaughter that allowed them to die without suffering. Moreover we didn't eat blood. Pieces of meat we had to put in salt to take out all the blood.

But never an animal in the house. A dog is really not kosher. It brings forbidden things into the apartment.

—But our Fips?

—In the house, he stays outside. If your father wanted a dog he wasn't acting like a Jew.

Imagine him, before the talus, kneeling before a shoebox, he is not yet thirteen, he has not yet worn the shawl, nor even dreamed of possessing that which will become his own unique object, the unique talus, the tunic, the only one with which he will have made a secret, and almost religious, alliance. Thus it is before the veil that we should see him gazing at the only gods he ever worshipped, those indifferent idols, those animals that dream beyond the sexual difference of an indistinct sex, in the genre masculine feminine. A worm neither naked nor not naked, to which he devotes his care and his life. Imagine him, this silkworm who sets up, between four corners, a hospitality worthy of Noah, he who was seen naked by his youngest son.

The shoecradle of his whole philosophy. He plays the dove that flies off in search of blackberry branches in the El Biar version of regenesis. Mother and son, apprentice to the worm through whom he learns the work and being for death [*l'œuvre et l'être pour la mort*]. My teacher was a *ver sans voile* [worm without veil] and without prudery. That was before the truth.[37]

Stranjew Body

Juiffrançais en souffrance, en sous-France [Frenchjew overdue/in suffering, in sub-France], Frenchphilosojew "I'm monolingual" he repeats, but what does that mean, what language does he speak, he who dislocates tramples pants in "French"; for "judeity," he responds certainly in French he swears perjures promises in French I imagine, it is to the French that he addresses his scenes and his prayers, the *Français* that so French word, with its ç! its c, and all those *ces* which he moreover stresses, playing off the superabundant homonymy of that simple phoneme, who knows where, if left to its music, he would lead us, "I am monolingual" he says the way another would say "I am Jewish" or again "I am Indian." The monolingualism is the air that saves him "the monolingualism in which I breathe" without which I would die. A profession of faith touching on the spirit, the soul, the psyche.

But this is how he appears at his place in a theater featuring the question forever suspended by and for him: "What is substitution?" This time it is his *body* that he extends and offers to the ordeals of the assembled crowd. Or again it is to an assembly of doctors, or to a gathering of psychoanalysts. Unless, or indeed, it might be a matter of a mass, where he raises it, this body, himself, for the prayers of the parishioners, like the host. Suggesting, and perhaps provoking in the flocks the craving to eat, to absorb, the incarnate message.[38] He says:

> Now I begin.
>
> Let us accept this, if you would, as a likely story, if not a fiction, or a fable: *ego sum, I am* here, but I am here a foreign body, a grateful guest, to be sure, but a foreign body that experiences hospitality. Simultaneously, said foreign body attempts to think this experience of hospitality, of hospitality either conditional or unconditional, ready for anything or almost anything. The foreign body wonders in what way and why a culture of hospitality, even of hospitalization, has always been preoccupied by what is called, in a tradition or according to texts that I will evoke later on, substitution.
>
> What then is substitution?
>
> That foreign body, I am it, and I follow it in its footsteps.[39] I am nothing other than a foreign body determined to follow the paths and ruses of a foreign body.
>
> You might then hear the foreign body speak.

In these few lines addressed to those who listen to him, he will have fabulized [*fabulisé*], represented, performed, in a solemn theater, *the* theme of his most ancient and tenacious magic: substitution. All that interests and fools or bluffs him since forever, himself the first one to bluff himself, which does not mean that, knowing that he allays suspicion, structurally, he might ever finish with this game of him and of me. He doesn't portray being, he portrays in a sense the passage, or the change or the replacement [*suppléance*], he portrays himself dissociated, the dissociated one attempts to portray himself in the deed, *in delicto*, in the process of disappearing, like Athens, like Socrates, in a plane, only to reappear once the verdict is pronounced ready to recommence (he does not say recommence, but commence). Once again to have the experience of transubstantiation.

For he is *the last of the Jews*, did he not proclaim it? None other, in one sense of the expression, than the Christ. To speak of that *he* whom he substitutes so often for himself, himself Jacques Derrida, delighting in all the substituting resources of the French language, pronouns, homonyms, amphibologies, of that he [*lui*] who would ever have shone [*lui*] with a glimmer of the nightlamp in his place, we must never lose sight of his way of making French fructify in all directions:

"That foreign body, I am it and I follow it . . ." he says, he, the body. A phrase that he wants us to hear in two ways at once, he repeats, then: I am it and I follow it [*je le suis et je le suis*], making the homonym redundant. I am it as a being and I follow it in pursuing it meticulously. As an existent and as something writing and something written. There he is already more than one and more than two.

To this is added the subterfuge, specifically French, of *anteposition*. To begin a sentence with "that foreign body" (an anteposition permitted by segmented constructions and by the use of the demonstrative pronoun, *that*, which permits the permutation of words: gifts from the French language), to begin with *that*, is immediately for him the chance to make a change from one 'I' to the other. The deictic function designates both the place of the object and the place of the subject. I before "I," that body, he is it. That body, I am it, I who is this body. I who is preceded in advance by that body of which I am the being, the succession, and the hunter—Artaud, his friend, is not far off.[40]

Thus, he recalls, he is that body to begin with, that body as stranger. A foreign body like dust in the eye, like a fishbone in the throat, our eye, my eye. His throat. Foreign body introduced by wounding in hospitality. Wounding body, wounded body [*corps blessant, blessé*], *blessing* and *blessed* as well. Body introduced as wound. *Hoc est meum corpus*. Host [*hostie*] I am, of the same origin, the same equivocal family as the host [*l'hôte*], and the immense hostile and hospitable tribe of which he long spoke, that guardian of the secret of all societies. Hatred love mixed together, friendship war inextricable.

"I am here a foreign body," he says. From the moment there is a here he leaves himself open, finds himself [*s'y découvre*] and declares *body* and *foreign*. There are only heres, moreover, to which he anteposes himself, offers himself, proposes himself, postposes himself a body separated from himself by the movement of thinking, a body that thinks therefore quits itself, divorces, himself.

If *Jésuis juif* [If I-am Jewish, if Jesus Jewish], he might say of himself, by way of a joke, it is as wounded [*blessé*] migod mianimal [half-god, half-animal], a sort of striped beast,[41] speaking French as in fables.

Band of Outsiders

It was then, amidst this chaos, while I sought everywhere to find a bit of water to finish rinsing my hair of its oat milk shampoo, that I went back along the paths where the homes were abandoned and disorderly, that I ran through the buildings behind the homes, it is then that I suddenly saw an immense tiger the color of the setting sun, a tiger of orange-tinted fire, held on a leash by a Moorish Jew scarcely visible coming out in profile from the wall of the dream, giant, long, sheltering his own flames, immediately around me there was a headlong flight of our little non-wild animals the dogs cowering like mice to the left to the right my cat who is nevertheless very large and he too of that honey-rose color seized with trembling wanted to run to hide himself, fur on end, I held him back, I calmed him with my voice, have no fear my darlings, he is not mean, he is not dangerous, he is only immense and beautiful. Vast long like an animate sculpture this tiger stood in his blazing alongside his wall with its blind shutters. Suddenly I understood that all these little lattice doors concealed a zoo, a menagerie, all the animals of the earth had thus been cloistered in my home, except him, who burned in silence with all the fires of the word fire that burned the silence.

The Story of a Friendship

The Archive and the Question of Palestine

MICHAL BEN NAFTALI

Apparently *The Story of a Friendship*, the document Gershom Scholem has left concerning his friendship with Walter Benjamin, is in keeping with the classic conception of an intellectual friendship between two men, both in Scholem's stated intent and in the content he presents: "When I reflect on what it was we had in common after these first encounters, I can cite a few things that are not to be overlooked easily. I can describe them only in general terms as a resoluteness in pursuing our intellectual goals, rejection of our environment—which was basically the German-Jewish assimilated middle class—and a positive attitude toward metaphysics. We were proponents of radical demands."[1]

The author of *The Story of a Friendship* is also the narrator, witness, hero, and archivist. Moreover, these figures share a common name, that of Gershom Scholem, who moves freely from one role to another. Not only is the writer in control of his writing, knowing where he wants to go, but his intimacy as a friend and archivist gives him a hermeneutic privilege. Paul de Man is one among several commentators on Benjamin who rejected the task taken up by Scholem and the messianic reading he imposed upon that work—he "who deliberately tried to make Benjamin say the opposite of what he said for ends of his own." Thus, all the friends assembled here stand opposed to Scholem's hermeneutic presuppositions: Paul de Man and Derrida, Blanchot and Derrida, and Benjamin himself are all guardians of the secret and the threshold, criticizing the ontological and epistemological assertions inherent in a story, and finding the very act of narration to be unethical. "I have never been able to tell a story," Derrida insists at the beginning of his *Memoires* for his friend after his death,[2] memoirs that call into question (as do some of his books) the demarcations behind which Scholem takes shelter: autobiography, fiction, testimony; memoirs that, like *Le toucher—Jean-Luc Nancy* or "Paul de Man's War,"[3] absolutely forbid touching secrets belonging to the deceased and reflect, on several levels, the domains of the *possible* and the legitimate in each of our textual touchings. The melancholic discourse, nourished by the body of the deceased, desiring to preserve, in its avid gesture, the otherness of that body, expresses and performs simultaneously its commitment, its notion of responsibility, and its gratitude. These insistent feelings do not cancel each other out, even at the difficult moment of an unbearable discovery about one's friend's past. Derrida allows no cloud to darken his writings on the work of a friend he first met in 1967, when Paul de Man was directing Cornell University's first program in Europe: "It was then that I first came to know him, to read him, to listen to him, and there arose between us an unfailing friendship that was to be utterly cloudless and that will remain in my life, in me, one of the rarest and most precious rays of light."[4]

This language of light without shadow is remarkable in the writing of deconstruction, which is known for its transgressive, contaminating, and contaminated image—an image that often leads the reader to forget the fundamental experience of a hyperbolic respect and discretion, the indeconstructible holy of holies. It is significant that Derrida quotes Blanchot in *Politics of Friendship*: "Friendship . . . implies the recognition of a common strangeness *which does not allow us to speak of our friends, but only to speak to them*, not to make of them a theme of conversations (or articles), but the movement of understanding in which, speaking to us, they reserve, even in the greatest familiarity, an infinite distance, this fundamental distance out of which that which separates becomes relation."[5]

But the sentence quoted from Paul de Man does not indicate only his resistance to the misinterpretation imposed by Scholem. He also rejects what he sees as a deliberate blasphemy, a blasphemy that seems to him to serve a friend's self-interest. Is he fair or unfair toward Scholem? This judgment raises a negative dimension that haunts this friendship and probably all friendship worthy of the name. That is why the sentence implies the insufficiency that remains in the classical tradition of a spiritual and reciprocal friendship. Thus the sentence calls, in order to modify the thought concerning friendship, for the modernist or existentialist descriptions of an alienation that surfaced in the works (among others) of Proust, Baudelaire, Sartre, and Kafka, in the unsettling fantasy of the castle, or in the fraternity of friends imagined by Breton in his first surrealist manifesto. Perhaps despite Scholem, the complex text he wrote, the tension between the public archives containing letters, diaries, manuscripts, remembered conversations, and details accumulated by others, elements all juxtaposed with disciplined rigor—and the unconscious archives, repressed, polysemic, disrupting the narrative texture, and also the way he has chosen to describe intimacy, to show the hard, even the immoral aspects of his friend, in choosing not to respect Benjamin's love of secrets, to overcome his restrictions and to present them as pathological paranoia—perhaps this text sheds light on a somber, precise aspect of friendship, a kind of friendship that lasts for years, is dynamic, opening itself to changes, jolts, feelings of distance as well as lack. A friendship that opens itself to the ever-shifting disequilibrium between economic and non-economic dimensions, between absolutizing and politicizing, between aura and profanation, that opens itself to the vacillations bound up with the passage from a live presence to correspondence, and that puts in question even the existence of such a state of perfection. For the two phases are implicated in one another, bound by continuity. The intervals are necessary, structuring the relationship in each of its performances, even though in the letters they become even more explicit or blunt.

Scholem wants to tell a story, another story—a desire that transforms the story in such a way as to make it exemplary. In other words, the treatment Scholem gives the concrete story of the friendship, which attempts in vain to solve the mystery of the friend and that of friendship, is essential to revising the speculative philosophy of friendship. The latter does not reflect sufficiently the difficulties of living together—the moral and political conflicts, the changeable nature of friends and their ambivalence toward one another. Nevertheless, the reading of Derrida's texts (and also of Benjamin's, despite their differences) obviously requires a strategy of juxtaposition and amplification, an accumulation of ideas and figures that reiterate differently. Thus, for example, *Memoires* must be read together with "Fors"[6] in order to perceive—in the face of the terminological resemblance—the problematic link between the scenarios of family and of friendship, and in order better to understand the need for an economic position, as expressed in *The Politics of Friendship*: a position that moderates the hyperbolic imperative in hoping for a symmetry, even while perpetuating our dissymmetrical gestures toward the friend. More directly, one must read *Given Time*, the only text I know that, in studying friendship, touches on its negativity, and it may be more than a coincidence that this text does not discuss a concrete friend but displaces its testimony in the direction of a fictive friendship, to be found in one of Baudelaire's narratives.

I would like to displace the testimony and describe the contours of a friendship through another friend of that community, but the time is too short for me to exhaust the points its members have in common—those that materialized during their lives, and those still commented upon and revised: "we know in any case that a spectral response . . . is always possible. There would be neither history nor tradition nor culture without that possibility."[7]

By means of Kafka's "Before the Law," I would like to sketch out the atopical substratum of friendship, the condition of possibility implied in the basic, unadorned encounter between two people, the conditions of possibility for a politics of friendship preceding the drama of proper names. This locus lacks a proper name, yet all that occurs within it is unique and private. Between Scholem and Benjamin, what is involved is a drama prior to that of Palestine, Paris, or Berlin, the Hebraic or the German, Asja Lacis or Brecht. It is a drama that constitutes the background of their debate, their anger, their offenses. The unspoken of all these dramas. It is a question of place, indeed, of finding a place, of being important in the life of the friend—and for Scholem it is a question of finding the precise idiom of friendship: a strong need that he translates into the vain struggle to found a common language, or, in the final analysis, to impose one. Scholem was never devoured by Benjamin in the way he wanted to be, incorporated and digested in the same way as Proust and Kafka, or as he himself sometimes absorbed the images of Benjamin, in order to treat the Kabbalistic conception of language or to critique Jewish theology.[8] I will begin with Kafka, then, far from cities, outside any specific cartography. I will follow a uniquely Kafkaesque view, at once abstract and corporeal, which is perhaps without precedent in approaching the body and the soul of friendship—thus attaining a better understanding of the discussion about place, a discussion deeply related to the exodus of these two friends, Walter and Gershom, who move in and out, who have experienced exclusions and rejections from their bourgeois shelter since childhood: a burden they could not have avoided carrying with them to their encounter.

Because place is the signifier and friendship the signified, it is place that becomes the subject and carries within itself, along with its proper name, all the demands the friend wishes to make concrete. Thus its dimensions become monstrous, without any of the relativizing the two friends are capable of in other, less fateful circumstances. Here it is the place, the locus, that requires, demands, beseeches. "Come to me. Or, don't. Go ahead, *it is possible, but not now*, the hour is not yet, we'll see. *Now I am going to close this door*."[9]

Before the Law

> If, through "the call to die in common through separation," *this* friendship is borne beyond being-in-common, being-common or sharing, beyond all common appurtenance (familial, neighbourhood, national, political, linguistic, and finally generic appurtenance), beyond the social bond itself—if that is possible—then why elect, if only passively, this other with whom I have no relation of this type rather than some other with whom I have none of the sort either? Why would I call this foreigner my friend (for we are speaking of this absolute foreigner, if only the neighbourhood foreigner within my family) and not the other?[10]

What are the basic elements that make up friendship? How is it generated? En route, at the crossroads, at the threshold, by chance.

Kafka published his story "Before the Law" as an independent work in 1915, in a German Jewish newspaper in Prague. By its immense suggestiveness, which is bound up with the relationship between the story and the novel, as well as to its relation to his other writings (his letters, his diaries, his novels, his novellas), this story calls for an inexhaustible reading. In his preface to the American edition of the correspondence between Scholem and Benjamin, Anson Rabinbach insists on the vital role played by Kafka in their friendship. Their philosophical and theological discussions of Judaism's messianic dimension focused, in 1934 and thereafter, on the weight of the Diaspora and of tradition in Kafka's works. Rabinbach notes that Benjamin, because of the bitter conflict that broke out between them on the subject of his attraction to communism, preferred to shift the debate diplomatically, offering a sort of appeasing gesture to redeem their friendship. This argument, accompanied by an analysis of their theses and the resulting controversy, reinforces the metaphysical, mystic, and Judaic direction conspicuous in the commentary on Kafka's work in general, and especially on "Before the Law." Indeed, in their letters it is a dominant orientation, to the point of creating the impression that neither Scholem nor Benjamin is interested in existential or psychoanalytic interpretations, even to the point of denying their validity. But this story does not take place exclusively between a man and the law. It takes place before the law, and in the presence of another man, before him, face to face. He is the one that the man from the country meets, and not the law. Better still, it is only through him that the man from the country encounters the law, the only encounter it is possible to have. There are thus two aspects to the problem raised by this story, which are both parallel and tangential: how to approach the law, and thus how to approach the other, in his tacit, violent, and mute presence. Benjamin, in his essay on Kafka, writes:

> What has been forgotten—and with this insight we stand before another threshold of Kafka's work—is never purely individual. Everything forgotten mingles with what has been forgotten of the prehistoric world, forms countless uncertain and changing compounds, yielding a constant flow of new, strange products. Oblivion is the container from which the inexhaustible intermediate world in Kafka's stories presses toward the light. . . . To Kafka, the world of his ancestors was as unfathomable as the world of realities was important, and we may be sure that, like the totem poles of primitive peoples, the world of ancestors took him down to the animals.[11]

These lines nonetheless indicate a different orientation in his research—more Freudian—which coincides with his aesthetic, historiographic, historiosophic, theological, political, and autobiographical quests (though this disciplinary demarcation is foreign to his writing) for the presence of primitive history in the present. In an earlier radio broadcast, on a collection of stories by Kafka (July 1931), Benjamin notes that beings who come from all social levels are indiscriminately mixed in Kafka, conjoined by a unique sense of organic dread, as well as by a fear of the immemorial, the fear of an unknown culpability: "In your presence I had lost my self-confidence, and in its place had developed a boundless sense of guilt. . . . I could not suddenly change when I was with other people."[12]

Benjamin does not quote these sentences from Kafka's letter to his father, and he does not discuss, by means of that letter, the psychic constraints imposed by the Oedipal scene, according to Kafka, on such affinity, including friendship. But that association is indicated by a bizarre analogy he presents between the ambiguity of Kafka's testament and the speech of the guardian of the law: "Given its background, the directive in which Kafka ordered the destruction of his literary remains is just as unfathomable, to be weighed just as carefully as the answers of the doorkeeper before the law."[13]

The fictive communicative condition of the story and of the guardian's speech is juxtaposed with the objective condition of the friendship between Brod, who read and interpreted the testament, and Kafka. As for that friendship, Benjamin treated it with cynicism and irony, sometimes even with anger, with respect to problems of understanding and to the blasphemously "pietist" writing of the surviving friend, the guardian of the archive, which offends the dignity of the deceased. Reading his sharp criticism of Brod, which tackles the limit between approach and distance, between intimacy and respect, one senses Benjamin's expectations of Scholem, his friend, when he confided his own archive to him.[14]

In "Before the Law," Kafka describes the preontological, spectral conditions of friendship. He forms a sort of a priori, atopical, unconscious, illegible, impersonal, and undated substratum, which can be peopled with any number of concrete stories attached to specific times and places; stories that often attempt in vain to overcome in *praxis*, and especially by a retrospective narrative, a latent substratum that continually regresses: stories like *The Story of a Friendship*, one among many others, on Scholem and Benjamin, Berlin and Jerusalem, Paris and Moscow. Important places, a fateful time, and yet basic elements that are subordinate to the critical determination of law, the past, memory, the archive, fathers, legacy, punishment, guilt. On a few restrained pages Kafka concentrates the pre-ethical condition as if in a laboratory: a neat, ambiguous, extreme picture, containing a rather rich emotional inventory that becomes concrete in the form of gestures, looks, voice, in corporeal aspects that friends hasten to ignore, to mask—sometimes to themselves as well—or to keep inside themselves like a secret, to work them through or dream them all alone. In relation to speculative discourse, Kafka suggests a counter-movement concentrating on a body that is close to another body. He traces a sequence of looks—curious, voyeuristic, clairvoyant, astonished, cruel, demanding, and desperate—that one person exchanges with another, to end up with the simple happiness of dying in the presence of the other, which does not deny, however, the solitude of a being-toward-death. His minimalist style is well suited to induce his readers to reflect on what friends say to each other, on what they destroy through words, on what they can say only at the end, when it is too late, on what they are obliged to whisper or shout in the ear of the other, who is no longer able to listen. And all that, despite the absent presence of the law, or because of its absent presence. "Before the Law" evokes a dramatic face-to-face situation that gives the impression of being immobile and static, despite the fact that it is pregnant with its future: its movement, inertia, rot, old age, waiting, desire, appeasement, rapprochement, revelation. What various philosophical positions name "intellectual friendship," based on values, moral reasoning, and the justice of each friend, is derived from these implacable conditions, from this drama of waiting by two men who find themselves alone, from these rigid limits imposed upon touching, upon availability, from the distance that signifies respect, suspicion, and misunderstanding, a distance that increases desire and nourishes the relationship. Scholem's text, the story he will write, will move between the poles of canonical discourse and Kafkaesque discourse, both in the events he will conscientiously describe and in the gaps his positivist gesture would like to fill in.

On the road, by chance, in a non-place, beneath the open sky, two figures meet: a guardian and a man from the country. It seems that the two men are already well formed, perhaps around mid-life. We cannot be sure. They are not introduced by name (they do not introduce one another) or by any other attributes, whether national, ethnic, or religious, although the guardian does question the man from the country concerning his place of birth. One man is thus identified by his function, and the other by the place he has left behind. Their meeting is entirely arbitrary, anonymous, cold even, and yet strong, fatal, critical; a deep intimacy has been created—for they will spend their time together for years, bear witness to everything, revealing their essence to one another mutually—in the heart of a lack of intimacy. It is a meeting that works like a post-traumatic effect and that enables them—especially the man from the country, for it is he who left to take this trip initially—to take a glance, to catch a glimpse, of an anachronistic and immemorial wound. The flight from the present, the movement of leaving the countryside toward oneself, causes that intensive, unique affinity between the two of them. For the man from the country there is no other guardian than this one, unique and singular. The ultimate quest he is on, which is probably his first mature confrontation with the law of the father, requires someone else, someone who takes on the concrete form of the guardian, his soulmate, even if he fails on both fronts. Kafka struggled within this triangle—father, self, and other (or the square, when a woman is added, even if she is but the work of fantasy)—and the predetermined failure to construct an intersubjective relation, in several places, such as "Letter to His Father" and "The Judgment." There, he keeps friends and lovers at a distance. Moreover, it is the father to whom the dialogue is addressed—written or spoken. In this perspective, if we restrict our concern to the relations between sons who gather before the law, "Before the Law" signifies another option, which is not that of a complete failure.

Is the division of labor between them predetermined? Apparently, the rather explicit hierarchy shown in their designations and conduct toward one another ("The guardian subjects him from time to time to brief interrogations . . . the way great seigneurs do") conveys a sense of alienation. Thus the possibility that it is a question of an affective relationship seems completely absurd. Following Kant, who doubts love can be a valid and stable basis for friendship, Derrida insists in *The Politics of Friendship* on the importance of distance and respect, where distance is a condition of the possibility of respect, and respect a condition of friendship. Not only is the showing of love slight in the story, but the respectful relation develops gradually. The man from the country quickly learns the physical limits he must respect, and slowly, during the course of years, the limits to a voice of one's own. The threshold on which the story develops forms an invisible line between proximity and familiarity. Can it be that the delirium that occurs at the end ("At the end, his vision becomes weak and he can no longer tell whether it is the surrounding light that is failing whether it is just his eyes that have deceived him") precedes the scene and constitutes the meeting itself? In other words, can it be that each one imposes a task on the other, and that the man from the country forms or transforms the other into a representative of the law in order to receive his discipline, as if he asked the other to keep him from being stronger, more able, more knowledgeable than he, even if that estimation has no claim to reality, not even to a psychic reality of the other? Can it be that the other is necessarily the one who frustrates, the one who judges, who amplifies alternately the weakness and the power that is already there? Precisely like the father who has forbidden, directed, determined. From this point of view, the other is immediately the representative of the law, the guardian of the law, while the law is an empty authority, "I am who am," that each can fill for the other. Without the other one cannot touch the law, while without the law one cannot succeed in establishing a relation with the other. It is necessary for the other to be, to interrupt, to intervene, for the law to go into operation, and to leave open the possibility of recognizing the law in what happens between two people. The law that reveals itself outside the law is archaic, neither formal nor institutional. It punishes brutally, more so than any legal authority; it is universal and yet specific, absolute but also historical. It condemns both, and the relation between them. You are my guardian and I am your man from the country, who looks at you, who sees you, and who keeps you, too, my brother. Each gives something precious to the other, something that touches a strategic point in his soul, making him vulnerable. We have taken each other hostage. We have no freedom or sovereignty. It is you who guard my gate; I feel it without knowing it. It is not for nothing that I have gone toward you. Who has power? Who is the master? Everything will happen between us in the heart of happenstance. Look. Both of us are homeless, without family, possessions, or status: no parents, brothers, or wives; not here, at any rate. It seems as if, except for us, there is no one. In the open space the two men inhabit, without locks on the doors, they can experience only one another; they can do nothing but look at each other with precaution and concentration. But no, they are not alone. Their togetherness is haunted and undone by a "that," designated here as the law. An archive, an abyss, an inconceivable void, capricious, energizing and at the same time weakening them, feeding their dialogue and their silence, "that" which has prevented them from time immemorial, and which will prevent them forever, from going inside and building a place to move into. This "that" will leave them outside, taking them into a common obsession that they will live differently, because they do not agree on the way one should react before the law. What is to be done? How should the law be treated? They are thus predestined to remain on the threshold to learn—even some small thing—about its mystery, to dance to the cadence of the flute of the one who constitutes them.

> One night I kept on whimpering for water, not, I am certain, because I was thirsty, but probably partly to be annoying, partly to amuse myself. After several vigorous threats had failed

> to have any effect, you took me out of bed, carried me out onto the *pavlatche*, and left me there alone for a while in my nightshirt, outside the shut door. . . . Even years afterwards I suffered from the tormenting fancy that the huge man, my father, the ultimate authority, would come almost for no reason at all and take me out of bed in the night and carry me out onto the *pavlatche*, and that meant I was a mere nothing for him.[15]

Their voyage together begins badly, very badly.

> There is more friendship, and more nostalgia, in speaking *to* one's enemy—more precisely in begging the other to become one's enemy, than in speaking *of* the friend without addressing him. . . . Even more friendly, more declared and avowed in its friendship would be even the inverted apostrophe: "O enemies! . . ." If there is in this more respect or fear here, it is because this demand for enmity comes from someone who dare not entreat the other to give him friendship: "At least be my enemy!" he then says. Conclusion: if you want a friend, you must wage war on him, and in order to wage war, you must be capable of it, capable of having "a best enemy."[16]

Anything could happen from the moment of the meeting. *Sin coucheth at the door.*[17] They might kill each other. Their communication is unpleasant, manipulative, contrived. Gradually, however, they become conciliatory, when the man from the country ceases to perceive the guardian as a means, a mediator at once transparent and impermeable, and recognizes him as an end. But what exactly does that man want? He seems to be seeking an entry into the law, thus an intimate encounter with his subjectivity and with the inconceivable archive that founds it. For an entry is by definition an entry toward the inside, into a house, into one's own home. He acts intuitively, reflects for a second; therefore it will take the rest of his life, to the very end, to understand that the conflict he asks for is precisely a conflict with his law, his own, exclusively, even if his first gesture already shows that he recognizes he has been predestined to trace out his own pathway, like a man who goes to join his ancestors and meet his God: "Proust's method is actualization, not reflection. He is filled with the insight that none of us has time to live the true dramas of the life that we are destined for. This is what ages us—this and nothing else. The wrinkles and creases in our faces are the registration of the great passions, vices, insights that called on us; but we, the masters, were not home."[18]

The man from the country approaches the guardian, who is standing before the law, which he guards from the outside, amnesiac, his look lost in the distance, as if he questioned by his physical position the function that had been given him, or perhaps as if he had become accustomed to waiting—which is what Benjamin suggests in describing the guardians of the threshold in the *Tiergarten*. (Benjamin is always fascinated by doors, staircases, thresholds, and passages; the messiah in the "Theses on the Philosophy of History" will pass, he stresses, through a narrow *door*). It is obvious, therefore, that the two of them do not resemble one another. It is possible that they are in different phases of their lives. Their position with respect to one another also expresses their attitude before that invisible law, the motivations leading each of them to approach it or flee from it, to observe their past or turn their backs on it, and in doing so to turn their heads toward the future. The man from the country has left everything with determination. Perhaps he fled, or was exiled, perhaps a traitor, perhaps betrayed; perhaps he was persecuted, perhaps he felt that he was. We do not know his motives. Perhaps he is responding to the call of the other? His distance from the country, on the one hand, and from the city, on the other, his distance in relation to work, to the generational continuity, and to production—that distance is probably his only chance, the condition of possibility for his seeing his past directly. By his heroic act of freedom he gives himself a chance to recognize his chains to the point of suffering. He understands very well: if only he finishes his days like that, if only he does not move anymore, or barely moves—for he cannot in fact move before the other—he will approach the truth of things. Just like that, in a process of purification, in recognizing his powerlessness. He will grow old, will become a child again, and finally will die, leaving the law to manipulate him as much as it likes, letting his power dissipate before the law, and at the same time live himself, the other, and creation with all his being. As for the guardian, he has given up or never tried. He fears failure, knowing that he does not have the means to understand and that he is not strong enough or sufficiently well suited to that trajectory. The "magnitude of the subject goes far beyond the scope of my memory and understanding."[19] First and foremost, he guards himself. Such is his particular virtue, to keep a distance that keeps him. But all are implicated in the law, regardless of what attitude they may take up. And fear lurks everywhere. We learn from the guardian that there are also other guardians *each more powerful than the previous one*—psychoanalysts, aestheticians, priests, ascetics. Their proximity to the law is derived from their strength in confronting their weakness, or inversely, they are strong because they are closer to the law. Where does that ambiguous hierarchy come from? Is it professional, existential, or arbitrary? Have these people exposed themselves at the deepest level? But then, to what depths? What price did they pay? We cannot see them. They are all inside. They have lost contact with the outside—the ability and even the will to get out. What does being close to the law mean? Can one go out thus into the outdoors, travel the world? The two friends feel, without speaking a word, that a symbiosis with the law will take them to their deaths. They feel they must be both near and far, keeping their distance before the law, a distance proper to each one, in order to live.

In the beginning, the man from the country hurries. He is in a panic, like someone who has made a difficult decision and must therefore follow through to the end. He wants to enter now, immediately. So he demands permission to be admitted. But the subject of his demand is not the law—something he has not yet recognized—but rather the other. The other before him, the other and himself, the other within himself. So they must recognize each other, slowly, a recognition that will concretize the law for each of them, that will activate the law between them and within the space of possibilities that the law leaves them. I will take a paragraph from Derrida's "Before the Law" and change the word *law* to *friend*:

> The man . . . must therefore refrain from entering. This self-imposed ruling is designed not so much to obey the friend but rather *not to gain access to* the friend, who, in short, has him told or lets him know: Do not come to me, I order you not to come as far as me. It is there, and it is in this that I am the friend and you will accede to my demand without gaining access to me.[20]

"Things" are not starting off well. That is unnecessary. The opening chord, with which we are familiar, is rather the opposite: fascinated, lost. But here the guardian is tense. He warns, advises, and determines. Not yet, it is not yet the right time. He forbids entry by his words, he does not use force; he forbids without preventing.

> "What? Am I supposed to have threatened you? But, look here. I'm so pleased that you've come at last. I say 'at last' because it's already rather late. I can't understand why you've come so late. But it's possible that in the joy of seeing you I have been

speaking at random and you took up my words in the wrong sense. I'll admit ten times over that I said something of the kind, I've made all kinds of threats, anything you like. Only no quarreling, for Heaven's sake! But how could you think of such a thing? How could you hurt me so? Why do you insist on spoiling this brief moment of your presence here? A stranger would be more obliging than you are."

"That I can well believe; that's no great discovery. No stranger could come any nearer to you than I am already by nature. You know that, too, so why all this pathos? If you're only wanting to stage a comedy I'll go away immediately."

"What? You have the impudence to tell me that? You make a little too bold. After all, it's my room you're in. It's my wall you're rubbing your fingers on like mad. My room, my wall! And besides, what you are saying is ridiculous as well as impudent. You say your nature forces you to speak to me like that. Is that so? Your nature forces you? That's kind of your nature. Your nature is mine, and if I feel friendly to you by nature, then you mustn't be anything else."

"Is that friendly?"

"I'm speaking of earlier on."

"Do you know how I'll be later on?"

"I don't know anything."[21]

Now, the door is open, but the relationship begins with the setting of boundaries. Derrida notes the surrealist causality that leads the man from the country to make his decision, after having examined the guardian: "when he looks more closely at the doorkeeper in his furred robe, with his huge, pointed nose and long, thin, Tartar beard, he decides that he had better wait until he gets permission to enter."[22]

It is an odd couple, Derrida remarks. Couples are odd. Even friends are odd, despite the great tradition that rationalizes friendship. A stranger will never understand the odd moment of a fundamental decision that is at the basis of a manifold, at the basis of a chance attraction, subject to the intervention of the law, and yet certain, concrete, precise. The guardian cannot bear the sight of the other guardians. He can bear the sight of the man from the country. He is the only being he is ready, in his avaricious generosity, to host on the threshold, and the immediate act that he carries out is to give him *a stool and let him sit next to the door*. But the mutual gestures are not only attentively economized—far from the an-economical model, they go so far as to engage in a black market economy. The man from the country offers him goods, and of the most precious kind, and the guardian accepts everything. Each accepts what the other is capable of offering. Each does what he can and must do in a system of exchanges that is rather narrow, almost without imagination. "I am only taking this so you don't think you have neglected anything." From that moment on, he remains sitting for days, months, years. This is not comfortable, not necessarily pleasant. But he stays. He wants it to be that way, he prefers it. He is enchained, and it is stronger than he is, like his leaving the country. His desire for the law, mediated by his desire toward the stranger before him, becomes precisely a desire for him, a dependency that will become increasingly strong, activated at first by the look; then, as his eyesight weakens, by the inner eye. The Levinasian situation of the face-to-face in its Kafkaesque version produces its own distinct description, which carries different implications. First, Kafka, like Levinas, does not describe an empirical condition, and emphatically not an anthropomorphic one. But in his fictive universe, the radical alterity expressed by the face is susceptible to metamorphoses: becoming-animal, or becoming-child. The rotting away that the man of the country observes attentively in the guardian, the fleas in his fur collar, and his own infantilization are accompanied by an attenuation, a softening. The real possibility of forming an ethical relationship is very far from the hyperbolic condition prescribed by Levinas. Here, friendship discovers, operates, and amplifies a human-animal repertoire that is indifferent from the ethical point of view and is rarely articulated. Kafka's story emphasizes the dimensions of fear, alienation, absurdity, negativity, fascination for the abject, and humiliation that are all implied in a meeting—a grotesque affective mixture exposed by two people who, apparently, are not at ease anywhere and who nevertheless achieve, with tiring patience, the construction of a little place for their own use. Derrida dedicated several essays to the theme of friendship, but only in *Given Time* does he confront its negative aspect. The book is about a story by Baudelaire, "Counterfeit Money," describing a scene of giving, of an offering, a generous gesture toward a pauper who embodies the law. In reflecting on that fictive situation, Derrida analyzes, via Baudelaire, the ambivalence articulated by the narrator-friend, who engages, during the entire time of their walking together, in judging his friend. Every act carried out by his friend implicates him immediately. Every act is ultimately addressed to himself, making him an accomplice. Derrida describes the animosity, the latent competition—is he generous, is he more generous than I am?—the resistance, the intolerance, the useless efforts at sweeping away, at ignoring, at overcoming, the need to forever affirm that rather strong and rather weak alliance—the incoherent emotional inventory situated at the basis of a relationship always already mediated by a third person, even an invented one, before the law. That negativity, which never appears as such in the discussions addressed to friends, living or dead, and which never appears in his writings on Paul de Man, in which it is expressed *a contrario*, by becoming self-incrimination and the taking up of an infinite responsibility—that negativity is presented here in this rigorous analysis of the internal monologue of the narrator, which accompanies what seems to be an innocent hour of grace, without contamination, but in fact divulges a neurotic and intense aggressiveness. The insistent deconstructive quest, which shows how our concepts, ideas, or conceptions implicate and contaminate what they reject, subjugate, or neutralize, cohabits in this way with a no less imperative requirement to be tactful and discreet, by ceaselessly seeking moderation. The tension between these two contradictory claims may also explain the polarity that constitutes the essay on Paul de Man's political journalism during the war, an essay that requires an independent discussion today, now that we are relatively far from the storm. But here, putting into practice his own sense of tact with respect to Baudelaire's text, Derrida responds in his own way to what can be read there. The respectable situation he describes, which appears to conform to the familiar model of a spiritual friendship, goes beyond Kafka's primal scene and bears a necessary tie to it. Derrida's sentences resound in Kafka as in the story of Genesis:

> The two friends are sentenced to pay, they are indebted and guilty as soon as it looks at them, as soon as the thing, the poor thing looks at them without talking to them. They are summoned to pay and to acquit themselves. They must restitute and enter again into the symbolic circle. They are on trial, they appear before the donee's court as before the law. With the result that in the final accounting, at the end of this trial, it will be a question of their own *gratitude* with regard to whoever accepts their damage payment and acquits them of their initial guilt, the guilt of their *situation*, by permitting them to acquit themselves of their debt. . . . since their *co-appearance* [comparution] before the law—in the sense in which they have to appear before the

eyes of the other that make a limitless demand as well as in the sense in which they appear *together*, they co-appear—places them in a situation of identificatory rivalry. . . . as friends, they are not only indebted with regard to the poor man; *they owe themselves each to the other*, they are indebted one with regard to the other. The comparison of their respective offerings is thus the very element of the story—as if they were giving themselves, were making (of) themselves an offering one *to* the other or one *for* the other, as if the poor man, the law, the third party were also but the mediation as well as the condition of their exchange.[23]

"I am going to close this door now," says the guardian at last. Couldn't you react otherwise? He raises his voice, committed, receptive, expressing his profound anguish but without judging: No. You, you couldn't react otherwise, we cannot, neither one of us, we who are subject to the law together, we who live the law, carry out the law, and besides, has anyone ever been luckier, can anyone, could anyone come in, and you, you smile like a child, you're not angry, not depressed, you are calm, after having worked so long, after having seen a more lucid light, the source of which is secret, and I am still here, your loyal witness, who glances at your revelation and who survives to tell your story, ours.

(Let us note in passing that the logic of this call—"You-my-friends-be-my-friends-and-although-you-are-not-yet-my-friends-you-are-already-since-that's-what-I-am-calling-you"—comes under the structure and the temporality of what we have been calling on several occasions a messianic teleiopoiesis.)[24]

The Story of a Friendship

What could one write to such a man, who had obviously run off the rails, a man one could be sorry for but could not help? Should one advise him to come home, to transplant himself and take up his old friendships again—there was nothing to hinder him—and in general to rely on the help of his friends? But that was as good as telling him, and the more kindly the more offensively, that all his efforts hitherto had miscarried, that he should finally give up, come back home, and be gaped at by everyone as a returned prodigal, that only his friends knew what was what and that he himself was just a big child who should do what his successful and home-keeping friends prescribed. And was it certain, besides, that all the pain one would have to inflict on him would achieve its object? Perhaps it would not even be possible to get him to come home at all—he said himself that he was now out of touch with commerce in his own country—and then he would still be left an alien in a foreign land embittered by his friends' advice and more than ever estranged from them. But if he did follow their advice and then didn't fit in at home—not out of malice, of course, but through force of circumstances—couldn't get on with his friends or without them, felt humiliated, couldn't be said to have either friends or a country of his own any longer, wouldn't it have been better for him to stay abroad just as he was? Taking all this into account, how could one be sure that he would make a success of life at home?[25]

It seems that one can tell the story of that friendship. It is about two friends who lived almost together, in geographical proximity, in intensive intellectual communication, first in Berlin, then in Muri near Bern during their studies, and when they parted, because of different existential choices, their relationship became epistolary. The passage could be described as a process of politicization in two senses: politicization in the sense developed by Derrida in *Politics of Friendship*, a movement that transforms absolute friendship into economic friendship, controlled, that is, transmitted by the sobriety of "O my friends, there is no friend," and politicization in a narrower sense, tied to events that took place during those years in Europe and Palestine. But both senses of the term are derived from the same source, from the same Kafkaesque tribunal, which interconnects the family scene, the (distant) friend, and the correspondence, which overshadows the friendship already during the eight years of its flourishing, years accompanied by bitter discussions on the economy of the two friends, on giving and taking, on the relations with money and the family home, and, consequently, on the morality and economy of friendship: "there lurked a deep-seated bitterness and disillusionment over the images of one another that we had fashioned for ourselves."[26]

As in Baudelaire's story, the latent and blatant conflict about money hinders friendship. The narrator-friend feels that the acts committed by his friend, which seem to be addressed to the other, especially those addressed to the family nexus, startle the bird of his soul, precisely because it is his friend; and he, the narrator, is implicated in his deliberations. Also, as in Baudelaire, we become familiar only with the position taken by the narrator-friend, who, in the case of Scholem-Benjamin, will survive his friend to tell their story, to explain causes and motivations, to reveal secrets, making hermeneutic and ethical decisions that raise the question: Did he truly pardon his friend? Is there not in the document he left us on friendship an expression of his refusal to pardon?

Indeed, the letters will no doubt aggravate elements that were always there: feelings of powerlessness, hindrances, the limited amount of help that could be given and was given, the limited amount that could be required, the limited availability, the feeling of risk caused by excessive proximity. The letters will amplify the hard silences, the giving—at once generous and avaricious—of time, the anguish of separation and the complex balance between reality and illusion. Even the way Scholem retrospectively describes the "crossroads" of their relationship is laden with ambivalence.

> Thus we were able to compare our prospects of *Habilitation* in the spring of 1922 and conclude that our situations were quite different. Both of us stood at a crossroads. Benjamin was still pursuing his aim of achieving an academic career via a *Privatdozentur*; this was his clear-cut ambition, and because he sought to obtain the resources for it from his parents, his relations with them were in constant turmoil. To me, however, the renunciation of ambition was a primary factor in my decision to go to Palestine, a plan that now approached the stage of realization. Anyone who went over there in those days could not think of a career, and that I would have one later could not be foreseen. The Hebrew University in Jerusalem was not yet in existence, and no one believed it would become a reality in the foreseeable future. To be sure, I had published a few German essays that had made some impression, as well as a book that no one was going to read. But I had to expect that in Judaic studies there would be far more thoroughly trained experts than I, one of the first in my generation who had taken up such studies quite independently and without any intention of becoming a rabbi. I believe it was the moral element in this decision that contributed to Benjamin's great trust in me, a trust that he continued to entertain for a long time to come.[27]

Clearly, politics in the narrow sense can intervene in a friendship, introducing an irreparable rift. That is what occurred between Benjamin and Wyneken, the hero of his adolescence, who was, moreover, much older than he. But the shadow that came over his relationship with Scholem is of another order, a fundamental one that predetermined their choices both in life and in respect to one another. In this perspective, did not Palestine make a difference? And was that difference a critical one? In what sense should we discuss the question of Palestine as posed by their friendship, beyond the factual givens — Zionism and judeity in Scholem versus the attitude of Benjamin, who never expressed his nostalgia for Palestine, which was not included in his concrete map or his imaginary one? At first glance, it would seem that Benjamin was much more exposed than Scholem, exposed by indirect means, means he found to communicate his feelings, by intimate notes here and there that he shared with Scholem after their separation ("In stirring as deeply as you have what in me is the most limited, the most painful"), as well as by the way he chose to confront his own childhood and to work in solitude, adopting a writing style that attempted to obliterate the boundaries between self-portrait and auto-fiction, between the personal and the social self. After his divorce, he wrote to Scholem (on June 14, 1930):

> For a very, very long time, I believed I would never have the strength to find my way out of my marriage; when this strength suddenly came to me in the midst of the deepest pain and profoundest loneliness, I of course clung to it. Just as the difficulties stemming from this step at present determine my outer existence — it is, after all, not easy to be without property and position, home and funds at the threshold of one's forties — this step itself is now at the basis of my inner existence, a foundation that feels hard but has no room for demons.[28]

When they lived in Muri, very close to one another, Benjamin was in the habit of sending letters to his friend by placing them in the doorway of his house. The spokesman of these shocking letters was Stephan, the son of Benjamin and Dora, who wrote in his mother's handwriting.[29] Thus, in a language at once strong, innocent, and crafty, the language used by children, the affective and anguished information of friendship was transmitted. Stephan addresses his "uncle Gerhard," who is older and wiser. When still an adolescent he had sold his collection of children's books to a Berlin antiquarian in order to be able to buy books of history, mathematics, and literature; at the end of his life, he will describe in his autobiography the most overwhelming family situations—like being barred from the house by his father—in a style that is anecdotal, ironic, but also factual and dry. In this case, however, Scholem cannot keep his nonchalant, avuncular pose. They both play at a family that becomes no less symbiotic and taxing than the one they left, even though they still avoid, in this phase of their relationship and development, working over materials from the past. At the heart of the amnesia that they both seek and into which they delve, perhaps it is not surprising to find these words written by Benjamin, the more Freudian of the two, addressing his friend (February 19, 1925): "I accidentally learned of your father's death when I saw the obituary in a newspaper. Will this cause a change in your situation?"[30] That icy phrase must be read together with the following testimony.

> One evening, when I was long asleep, there was a terrible row. First I thought it was another thunderstorm, but no, somebody was bawling and screaming so much that the walls shook. Do you have any idea what that was? I don't dare ask Mama, because she has been sad ever since. When I talk about you she usually gets snappish.
>
> Also, a book I prize very highly is missing from my library. I can't imagine who might have taken it. Now take care of yourself. I'm already quite anxious to go to the mountains. When, oh when will I finally get there?[31]

In his letters, Benjamin is divided between several instances that conflict with one another. A father, a friend, a wife, and a son; a father ambivalent toward his son, a friend ambivalent toward his friend, a son ambivalent toward his father, a husband ambivalent toward his wife, various voices produced to express a situation laden with jealousy, possessiveness, need, and loss. The details of the family tribunal that haunt each of the two friends, and naturally the friendship, are complex—two elder brothers, a sister, parents, figures that have been treated by Derrida in different contexts. And it is probably not merely coincidental that, in an exceptional note on the friendship between Scholem and Benjamin, Derrida should make a speculation—presented, moreover, as a fact—concerning the friendship between Benjamin and Werner, Scholem's brother; the one who, like Georg, Benjamin's brother, had committed himself to

Communist politics and who, like him, would go to his death under the Nazi regime. Here Derrida seems to exchange the phantasmatic experience that Scholem may have had, faced with the existential and intellectual choices of his friend, for objective reality. In a rather dense paragraph, Derrida juxtaposes the themes of place, friendship, ideology, and present-absent brothers, a configuration that he himself shares and that he identifies in *Memoirs of the Blind* as one of the negative, contaminated bases of intellectual choice.

> The American edition [of the *Moscow Diary*] opens with a preface by G. Scholem dated Jerusalem, where Benjamin wrote to him so frequently. I also emphasize these facts to usher in a certain *ellipse with two focal points*, Moscow and Jerusalem, which ... will not fail to cross another ellipse, if that is possible, the one that stretches between a para-Oedipal Greek mythology and a revelation of the Mosaic or messianic type: in 1926–27, Benjamin finds himself between Moscow and Jerusalem, between the German communist party that he hesitates to join and the Zionism to which he will never adhere, as between two brothers—the two Scholem brothers, Werner and Gershom—and two influences as well, his two friends the communist and the Zionist.[32]

At the conscious level, Scholem speaks of his connivance with his brother, despite the opposition, but at the same time he describes him as "a gifted demagogue" whose simplistic historical materialism lifted some eyebrows. These ridiculous exaggerations are not so different from the unworthy vocabulary with which he will react in the face of the transformation of his friend, which will be characterized as an inauthentic adventure, guided by bad faith and jeopardized by a spiritual suicide.

Their friendship hurts them, each in his own way. We learn through the book and the letters that Scholem was never unique in the life of Benjamin, and yet, like a benjamin (youngest child), he tries in vain to become unique in the world of his older brother. In the preface to the volume of Benjamin's correspondence that was edited and annotated by Adorno and himself, Scholem writes with bitterness and sobriety: "I am also convinced that he spoke to others about me with the same critical candor and ironic edge with which he expressed himself about others in his letters to me. We always knew where we stood with each other."[33]

Michal Ben Naftali ▪ *99*

These lines, and especially the correspondence about the question of Palestine, give well-hidden, yet exposed, expression to his weakness in that relationship. As already stated, the conflict about Palestine is a conflict about his place in the life and soul of his friend. During the twenties and thirties, Scholem changes his strategy with respect to his subjective situation. He is then and always has been, perfectly lucid. Already at the beginning, a third party haunted their friendship—whether it be masculine or feminine. Already, at the heart of their intimacy, another is implicated, who, imposing an emotive/erotic tension, disrupts their equilibrium. Scholem reports: "I have no doubt that the breakthrough and change in our relationship from acquaintance to friendship beginning in the summer of 1916 had much to do with Dora, to whom he had spoken about me."[34] Benjamin reads the letters he receives from Scholem to Dora, to ask her opinion. Dora, for her part, addresses a very exacting request to Scholem (Bern, November 12, 1917): "All the more urgent is the necessity to come to poor Walter's aid with suitable, i.e., male, eyes. Or, to put it quite plainly: Come as soon as possible."[35] As always, Stephan's words addressed to *dear uncle Gerhard* are even more stern and childish:

> You write that she never has time for you. I gave that a lot of thought once, and I believe I even wrote you about it. I believe she would have time if things were different; not having time is only a pretense, I think. I don't think it's like my mother not to have time because of external matters. After all, she always has time for Papa and me, and earlier, when she still wasn't feeling particularly well, people of your age, though not of your importance, would come and sit with her for as long as the Good Lord made the light shine, often even into the night. For all these she had time. But when I asked her in your name and we talked about it, suddenly many things became clear to us. It's hard for me to tell you, for I wouldn't want you to believe that your relationship with my Mama isn't all it should be. It is quite all right, but only on its own terms, as it were, for you would like it always to be something else. What you want from my mother she cannot give you, because you don't love her; she has known too many people who did to be mistaken about this. You could, however, get a great deal from her, but you don't realize this, because you want other, inadequate things.[36]

More than two years separate that letter from another, this time directly from Benjamin (February 14, 1921):

I continue to trust that the three of us will be able to work together as a team at some time in the future. I could not imagine Dora and me bound to any other third party in this way, but I am indebted to you for the direction my life and thought have taken and, as a consequence of this, Dora is indebted to you for the restoration of what was best in her upbringing.[37]

This triangle—which lasts while Scholem lives in Germany and leads him to believe later that, had he stayed, things might have taken a different direction between Dora and Benjamin—will change its members during their lives, and Scholem will describe the third member in a somber, sometimes even demonic way. That is how he describes Asja Lacis, for it was precisely she who, as Scholem perceives through amorous intuition, prevented the trip to Palestine, since her "place" was more important than his; so also Brecht, who (the same age as Scholem and six years younger than Benjamin) will occupy a dominant position in the intellectual life of Benjamin during the thirties and therefore be a dangerous rival. Scholem will allay his anger through overexcited, turbulent criticism of the "author as producer." Here we may perhaps again consider Derrida's suggestion. Choosing Brecht, and consequently choosing communism, signifies, to Scholem, following his brother's path—in other words, choosing his brother, preferring him. In the face of that fraternal economy, everything can, and in fact does, present a threat: Asja, Brecht, Werner, and obviously even Benjamin himself, who is incarnated in each of these figures to dispossess Scholem, his friend, his adopted brother, of what belongs to him. Perhaps we can divine here the profound frustration that his personality awakened in others. Since childhood Benjamin has been in the habit of sending a letter to a friend containing excerpts from his private diary, asking at the same time that the letter be shown to another friend. He shares with everyone his economic difficulties, the political atmosphere that weighs on him, the publication problems, his working conditions, the contours of his thought, the projects he has not yet begun, recommended readings, his travel impressions. In his diary he writes:

> I think of an afternoon in Paris to which I owe insights into my life that overcame me in a flash with the power of an illumination. It was precisely this afternoon that my biographical relationship to people, my friendships and comradeships, my passions and love affairs revealed themselves, in their liveliest, most hidden, interweavings. . . . I say to myself: it had to be

Paris where the walls and the quais, the asphalt, the collections and the debris, the railings and the squares, the arcades and the kiosks teach us such a strange language that our relationship to people in the loneliness that surrounds us, our sunkenness in that world of things, reach the depth of a sleep in which the dream-image awaits them.[38]

In this perspective, it seems that Benjamin is completely prepared, as if he had trained all his life, to create an economic friendship, by post. He has been waiting since forever, retiring, deconstructed, and when, because of objective conditions, he must correspond with his friends, this will be but an amplification of his profound conception of self and other, tied to the forgotten moment when he was transformed, became detached, passing like the work of art he describes elsewhere from an auratic position in relation to friendship to a mechanical one that obliterates the value of uniqueness of place and object. He is so invested in letters, so devoted. He nourishes and is nourished. He chooses the paper, the pens, the ink—like a priest directing a ritual. These letters are filled with emotion and participate actively in an incessant intellectual process—when, for example, he entrusts his archive and his memoirs to his addressees, while awaiting witnesses that he nonetheless ceaselessly rejects. At bottom, it is enough for him to know what his friends think of him, receptive as he is to their spectral presence, absorbing their anguish from afar and feeling at once protected by that anguish and protected from it. His development as a thinker is tied to the quasi-transcendental conditions of sending and operates in that modality in a persistent *praxis* that is irreducible to the specific character of any particular addressee. Already in 1913 (November 23) he writes to his friend Carla Seligson: "No one of us could proceed so happily and seriously if we were not aware that friends are watching."[39] And to Scholem from Paris (August 24, 1932):

> Unfortunately, it appears as though this European trip of yours is making you a witness to the most severe crisis that has ever befallen me. If at least you were an eyewitness! But I am sitting here without seeing any of my attempts to afford the most necessary things—at least to pay a bill— . . . and with the gloomiest thoughts. . . . Think over once more everything that concerns me. It is necessary.[40]

Deleuze and Guattari have examined the structural relationship between Kafka's correspondence and the system that activates his literary mechanism in general.⁴¹ There is considerable resemblance between Kafka and Benjamin in the concrete strategies they use to ensure the preservation of a distance in relation to their addressees — be they women in the case of Kafka, or friends in that of Benjamin. They transform themselves into prisoners of their objective condition, whatever the chains that hold them: their bodies, their families, their work, their finances, the political situation, or geographical distance. For their part, they did everything they could for things to work out: they planned, scheduled, hoped. And what eventually happened shows only their destiny, their powerlessness, their innocence. Writing therefore becomes the territory of friendship, or better yet, friendship has no place: "The essence of our relationship in the years from our separation to Benjamin's death is expressed in the detailed letters concerning Benjamin's work and many aspects of his life, and the most important of which are collected in *Briefe*. With few exceptions they are distinguished by complete frankness, a frankness based on trust."⁴²

Why are these letters almost exclusively about Benjamin's work? Why does Scholem insist on speaking of "total frankness," while the letters, but also other sources, show that they both avoided touching on certain dramatic events of their lives, as if they fled from precisely the essential, only to once again abruptly activate private dramas by their hesitating, calculating exchange of letters? What is the meaning of a delay? Why is that letter so short? Is it a response to something I myself wrote? Did I go too far? Should I be more tender, more sensitive, more guarded? Is a friend someone who dares and struggles against a given rule or space imposed upon him by his friend? Why is the word *confidence*, which Scholem uses rather often in his book — and Scholem has a very precise use of language — appropriate in this case? Is it adequate?

> Our physical separation in the long years until 1938 undoubtedly had a dual impact. In one sense it heightened the intensity of written communication that stayed alive over long periods of time. I was far away; what he told me stayed with me, and in his letters in which he often informed me about his inner and outer situations there vibrates a feeling of trust. But in a different sense the fact of his new development did intensify a feeling of remoteness. There were many things that Benjamin, being the way he was, could not express in letters — and this became increasingly true as the years advanced. This meant that we

sought no conflict but also that the things we avoided were magnified by silence.[43]

Not only did Benjamin not speak about women, he also hid his thoughts of suicide, and furthermore postponed on several occasions their projected meetings, even when Scholem went abroad. In 1932, he went to Rome to examine some Kabbalist manuscripts at the Vatican.

> We started discussions about possible prospects of a reunion. The eventual failure of all these plans made my heart heavy and gave me much food for thought that year. . . . Our reunion did not materialize, for from the beginning of August Benjamin stayed with Wilhelm Speyer in Poveromo for three months. From there he wrote me with unusual frequency, as though he wanted to make up for the breakdown of our plans for a meeting.[44]

Benjamin, for his part, after a few years complained in a similar fashion (March 29, 1936): "The manifold and disappointing fluctuations of the date of our reunion carry much weight in this regard. And they burden me still more when they cause me to wonder whether you are imbued with the importance, indeed the overdue nature, of our reunion as much as I am."[45]

The encounter does not take place and it sometimes seems that they recognize it—that they recognize that not only will it not take place, but that it cannot take place, as if it did not want to take place, and while it cannot / does not want to take place or the two friends cannot / do not want to, their discussion will exhaust their energy more and more. It will increase their despair, their frustration, and their malaise.

> When he sat down at his desk, it looked as if someone had been living in it. But it was he himself who was building his nest in the ruins. Whatever he did, he made a little house for himself out of it, as children do when they play. Similarly, just as children keep coming across things they have hidden away and then forgotten—in their pockets, in the sand, in a drawer—so it was with his mind, with his entire life.[46]

With the passing of time he becomes increasingly distressed by his solitude, and equally worried about losing it, as he gradually becomes estranged from his family, from his country, from the milieu of the

German immigrants in Paris, and from his friends. He moves rather frequently (thirteen different addresses in Paris) and seizes every opportunity to travel in Europe, because even without any place to look upon as his own, his spatial experience is exceptionally sensual and erotic. Places in Europe, which he delves into like an archaeologist, always in depth, are his means of historical and philosophical production, the substratum on which his critical imagination and aesthetic sensibility develop. To travel outside Europe, toward another absolute, without return, is not at all possible, despite his enormous suffering, despite his becoming increasingly excluded both politically and from the literary life in Berlin (which he leaves on March 18, 1933) and Paris. Obviously Scholem recognizes the depth of the refusal. Does he feel it as a refusal of himself, also of himself, that he projects onto him, onto his values? Palestine gives them a rare moment to reflect on their friendship and the paths to take to go toward one another without self-betrayal. The concatenation of events that led to the dream of Palestine and its failure is known, and so I will avoid presenting a detailed description of their continuous and troubled correspondence up until the avowal of concession. The explanations Scholem gives doubtless show that he always understood that affair, that he even reduced it to the terms of their relationship. In describing the conversation between Benjamin and Judah Leon Magnes, the rector of the Hebrew University of Jerusalem, in August 1927 in Paris, Scholem states clearly:

> He [Benjamin] said that his friendship with me had contributed to the increasing realization that his focal point would lie for him in an occupation with the Hebrew language and literature. . . . He said that he had a positive intellectual attitude toward the reconstruction work in Eretz Yisrael, though he had not concerned and identified himself particularly with the political aspects of Zionism. I myself was surprised by the firm, positive way in which Benjamin presented these thoughts. Of course, they had been expressed in one form or another often enough on previous occasions, and I had a certain share in them. . . . This encounter is more fantastic in retrospect than it seemed at the time. What appeared natural and possible to both of us at the time—a decision on the part of Benjamin to pursue a career and future within the Jewish fold—must seem all but incredible to present-day readers of Benjamin's later writings.[47]

And in a letter, while also expressing his anguish in the face of questions of place and of language, Scholem begs his friend:

I would like to have you not only come to terms with yourself
... but also explain your position to me with the same candor I
have shown you. I believe I have a right to expect more candor
from you with regard to this question than any other, so that
whatever happens we will not deceive each other with a personal apocalypse about the divergences of our autobiographies.
I am surely someone who will be able to accept with composure
and, perhaps, with some comprehension if you reveal that you
can no longer, and will no longer, in this life consider a true
confrontation with Judaism that lies outside the medium of our
friendship. I sometimes believe that, in speaking about these
matters, you do so with more consideration for me than for
yourself—as paradoxical as it may sound. I truly believe it to be
an accurate description of your attitude in some instances and I
would not feel the way I do about you if I did not suffer on
account of this situation.[48]

But it is the possibility of visiting Palestine, raised during the thirties (beginning in November 1934) and also condemned to repeated delays, that helps us better understand the problematic underlying both affairs. In his book, Scholem remarks almost exclusively on the obstacles that had been imposed yet again by Benjamin, reporting laconically the dramatic circumstances of his life at that time: his wife's illness, his divorce, his love for Fania, his student, who would become his wife. His letters of invitation set out the economic and logical considerations for and against the visit: the appropriate time and the length of the hospitality (during the summer, three or four weeks, then the spring, then the winter); the material conditions (it will be up to Benjamin to pay for the trip); and his doubts about Benjamin's adapting to the country, if he foresees such a possibility, given his psychological makeup. Even if he continues his literary work, Scholem insists, he and his wife Escha remain doubtful about the possibility of feeling at ease in that country without identifying with it and participating directly in its life. It is true that only experience will tell, but they think Paris is preferable for him, because there he will not be faced with the same moral and psychological challenges. Scholem begins to develop in this context an observation that will enable him to evaluate, among the German Jewish writers, certain remarkable individuals, such as Freud, Kafka, and Benjamin, who "never cut loose from that experience and the clear awareness of being aliens, even exiles." "I do not know," he concludes, "whether these men would have been at home in the land of Israel. I doubt it very much. They truly came from foreign parts and knew it."[49] Should we distinguish between these two aspects, the emotive vacillation expressed toward the friend and the grave and independent question concerning the adaptation of his friend, whom Scholem seems to treat with precaution, in attempting to internalize his friend's universe—his fears, his anxieties, his hesitations? In that reading, Scholem is saying to him: Even if it is cruel to hear, I don't see how you can have a place and an existence here. I don't think it is possible to live in Palestine keeping one's distance. Coming here will not be a superficial gesture of transferal. I don't think one can live by an act of solitary commitment. This place, therefore, cannot host you, cannot contain your difference, your European sensibility, and I speak to you this way—I who was a European, one among the thousands who have made their way to arrive here. This place requires of one who enters its doors to speak its language and transform himself, forget himself, fade away, in order to contain it, like a parent who must step back in the presence of his child. It asks you uncompromisingly to transform your intellectual choices. It calls out to you, mobilizes you, that you may adopt forthwith the same set of norms according to which it offers you its hospitality.

Is Scholem right? Does he have a lucid view of the relation between a life of writing and Palestine? Between the place and its inhabitants? Must its residents actively affirm it? Can one not live there as an outsider, as in the Diaspora? Is it typical of that place? Is there something in that place that intensifies the community spirit, that carries it to the an-economic, something that is like no place else? Is it true that Benjamin has no place in Palestine? Who makes that demand? Is it the place that demands it? Is a place a subject, with a will and requirements? Does it have its own representative? Does Palestine have its own representative? Is Scholem that representative? Has he ever been? Or is it rather the case of a friend making demands, putting himself in place of the place, representing that place he has chosen—a place to which he immigrated and in whose name he now speaks? A friend who in fact is competing for his place in Benjamin's heart and spiritual world? A friend who does not tolerate his friend's wavering (to live in ambiguity is destructive, he writes him in May 1931), who rejects Benjamin's ambivalence because it probably brings him face to face with his own, who cannot in the least bear the marginality of his friend, who causes him so much worry, guilt, and anger, who hardens him and weakens him alternatively, who haunts his existence in Palestine like a deconstruction for a man who has never really accepted the metaphysics of a place? Or perhaps he cannot stand his own ambivalence, his ambivalence toward his friend and toward his place, toward the choice he has made, toward his demanding experience of that place and the complex and painful reality he found there, an unpleasant feeling he discovers within himself, and therefore begs his friend—whose ambivalence is open and known—to have a 100 percent pure commitment both to him and to the place, as if he had wanted his friend to change, to become his alter ego and the ideal ego for himself and the place, because otherwise—absolutely not! It isn't possible! Never! Or perhaps he needs his friend in order to feel at home, because he lacks, after all, the sense of sharing he went quite far to find, despite his voluntaristic language, which seems not to echo these meditations expressed by Derrida via Levinas:

> we must be reminded of this implacable law of hospitality: the *hôte* who receives [the host], the one who welcomes the invited or received *hôte* [the guest], the welcoming *hôte* who considers himself the owner of the place, is in truth a *hôte* received in his own home. . . . The *hôte* as host is a guest. The dwelling opens itself to itself, to its "essence" without essence, as a "land of asylum or refuge." . . . this originary dispossession, this withdrawal by which the "owner" is expropriated from what is most his own . . . thus making of one's home a place or location one is simply passing through.[50]

Scholem, when he wrote the preface to their correspondence, which was published after *The Story of a Friendship*, had difficulty confronting what was revealed in that volume, his quite explicit priorities at that time, which totally ignored the tragic condition of his friend: "One other question will be raised by the reader of these letters: Why didn't I draw any direct conclusions from Benjamin's often catastrophic and distressing portrayal of his financial situation, which comes to light in this book? This question I could answer, but choose not to."[51] These lines are quite enigmatic. They imply that Scholem certainly recognizes the problem, that he can answer but chooses not to. In other words, he has supplementary factual or affective information underlying his decision. In retaining his right to silence as friend and editor—by a gesture that is contradictory with respect to his explicative *praxis*—he leaves the reader speechless. Did he avenge Benjamin with his disappointment? Did he pardon him?

Scholem brings us to consider the question of hospitality on the basis of two prisms that have not been articulated by the philosophical reflection, heterogeneous as it is, on friendship. What meaning is there in the welcoming of a friend? How are these two themes to be tied together: hospitality, the hyperbolic aspect of which seems to be manifested in the gesture of welcoming the stranger, and friendship? First, Scholem expresses a fear that is fundamental: the fear of welcoming the friend, the fear of having the friend at one's home, the audacity of welcoming the friend—a fear and an audacity that are not the equivalent of the psychic dynamics that have been played out in relation to the stranger. A friend who enters a house poses a distinct threat, perhaps an excessive one, because he has always existed in the host's heart, because he haunts his thoughts, and so his real entrance can intervene, transgressing invisible but existent, insistent, limits. The violent tension between love for the friend and fear of the friend is responsible for the sequence of letters in which the host-friend alternately invites and cancels his invitation. In the second prism, alluded to by Scholem, what is at stake is a different cruel rupture—that between intellectual friendship and intellectual work, which paradoxically seems to be ignored by the discourse that has intellectual intercourse as the nexus of its meditation. The spiritual substratum is certainly the condition of possibility of their meeting, but not only is it not appeasing and cooperative, it very often requires isolation, absence, and distance, which Benjamin termed a clerical closure (letter from Denmark, July 8, 1938), permitting neither noise nor intervention.

The confrontation between Scholem and Benjamin in relation to place was without remedy. Yet sometimes the most fragmented, the most damaged families find relief. In this case, the archive will suggest a compromise configuration. By means of the archive, Benjamin can be at once in Palestine and in Europe, and even not be and be—be in a place and out of it, move everywhere, transcend his center, the one he envisages in his testament in the National and University Library of Jerusalem, and therefore with his friend, his most loyal and stringent archivist. It is a cunning solution, for the archive is cunning. If, as Blanchot thought, the story of a friendship is necessarily the story of oblivion, because only oblivion can be translated into a story that contains its communicable meaning, there is neither friend nor archive that can annul the materiality of the archive, an ever-burning candle that preserves, in its persistent and implacable way, their friendship.

An innocent child, yes, that you were, truly, but still more truly have you been a devilish human being! — And therefore take note: I sentence you now to death by drowning![52]

Jacques Derrida and Kabbalistic Sources

MOSHE IDEL

> Rabbi Jeremiah in the name of R. Hiyya bar Abba said: it is written "They had deserted Me, and did not keep My Torah" [Jeremiah 16:11]. May they desert me but keep my Torah, because out of their studying Torah, the light within it will cause them to repent.
> —'Eikhah Rabbati, Petiheta II; Pesiqta de-Rabbi Kahanah, 16:5

The dialogue between Jacques Derrida's thought and that of some other Jewish thinkers is evident. We have only to mention the names of Sigmund Freud, Walter Benjamin, Franz Rosenzweig, Emmanuel Levinas, Edmond Jabès, Claude Lévi-Strauss, and, more recently, Yosef Hayim Yerushalmi to understand that Jewish thought constitutes a significant point of reference for this thinker, as important as the wide spectrum of European and American culture reflected in the principal line of his dialogues: Plato, Rousseau, Hegel, Mallarmé, Nietzsche, Husserl, Bataille, Heidegger, Austin, and Searle. I would like to mention another well-known name on the list of Derrida's Jewish references, that of Gershom Scholem, an author whose influence on Derrida has been but rarely noted, so far as I know. Scholem's colossal work had a substantial impact on contemporary thinkers whose concerns approached those of Derrida in one way or another. I am thinking, notably, of Harold Bloom and Umberto Eco. To my mind, a succinct review of the thought or texts of Scholem that may have marked Derrida could be fruitfully integrated into the theme of this colloquium.

The present study takes into account two important aspects of Derrida's approach, in light of the parallels between them and, I would go so far as to say, in light of their sources of inspiration. One of these aspects is found in kabbalistic texts. The first consists in the affirmation that there is nothing outside the text. The second concerns the juxtaposition of a mode of thinking grounded in the text and inherited from Jewish sources with a philosophical, even a logocentric approach that is Greek in origin. While these two aspects seem to me essential to understanding the genesis of Derrida's thought, I want to emphasize that my intention is neither to turn this thinker into a kabbalist nor to underestimate the importance of certain positive or negative developments intrinsic to European philosophy in the intellectual formation of Derrida. As the study of the likely Jewish sources of the concept of deconstruction is still in its incunabula, however, a great deal of work remains necessary before a balanced picture can come to light. I intend to suggest a few such paths at the end of the present essay.

God as Torah, or the Torah as God

It is well known that Jews, or a very small Jewish elite, were devoted to the study, the reading, the recitation, and the veneration of the sacred text. Here, there is not much to add to this stereotype, which does not lack a certain basis in truth. Nonetheless, it could be interesting to examine a relatively rare position, that of identifying the Torah with God. This approach is not without certain repercussions for a postmodern view of the status of the text. From the beginnings of the Kabbalah in Catalonia, we find a few assertions that point to the identification of the Torah with a body, no doubt a divine body.[1] According to a kabbalistic treatise drawn up in Girona by Rabbi Jacob in the middle of the thirteenth century, there is nothing in the world that is not contained in the letters of the Hebrew alphabet, which function as an instrument to incarnate the Platonic Ideas. Therein lies an interesting example of a subversion of Platonic ontology.[2] In another writing by the same kabbalist, it is the book of the Torah that is the site of the Ideas or forms, which, again, can be identified with the letters themselves.[3] We find an explicit identification of the Torah with God in the Zohar, the classic work of Kabbalah. This identification is expressed in the adage, "The Torah is none other than the Holy One, blessed be He." Let us now consider certain evocations of the Torah that are found in kabbalistic works from the end of the thirteenth century. The first one figures in a treatise that long remained forgotten, the "Book of (divine) Unity":

> God gave us the Torah entire and perfect from the [word] *Beres-hit* to the [words] *Le-einei kol Israel*.[4] Behold how all the letters of the Torah, in their diverse forms, whether assembled and separated, swaddled, curved or crooked, superfluous or elliptical, narrow or wide, inverted, with their diverse calligraphy, the pericopes open and closed, as well as the ordered pericopes—all of this constitutes the form of G-d, blessed be He. That resembles, *mutatis mutandis*, the act of painting, using [several] colors. In the same way, the Torah is, from the first to the last periscope, the form of God, great and awesome, blessed be He. For it is enough that one letter be missing or in excess in the Torah Scroll, or that a [closed] pericope be [written] as an open one, or an [open] pericope [written] as a closed one, for the Scroll of Torah to be invalidated, because this change in form caused it to lose the form of God, great and awesome, blessed be He. Does that not go without saying? And because every man in Israel must consider that the world was created for him,[5] God bound each one of them to write a Torah Scroll for himself. And the secret, implicit therein, is that each one of them has made God, blessed be He.[6]

According to this passage, the precise configuration of the canonical text of the Bible is identical to the form of God. Thus, the Bible constitutes, in its ideal form, an absolute book, containing the supreme revelation of God, as he is presented anthropomorphically and symbolically, member by member, in the midst of the various parts of the text. More important for understanding the status of the canonical text, however, is the identity postulated between the duty, incumbent on every Jew, to write or to have written for himself a Torah text and the concept of making or reproducing the image of God. No doubt the Scroll is conceived in iconic terms, as though it constituted a faithful representation of the form of God.

In the writings of the kabbalists that flourished in the thirteenth and the beginning of the fourteenth centuries, we read a phrase that asserts the total identity between the Torah, that is, the Pentateuch in the majority of cases, and God. The first such writing is the *Sefer ha-Yihud* ("Book of Unity"), a treatise composed in Castille at the end of the thirteenth century, a passage of which we have just examined. This book influenced Rabbi Menahem Recanati, an Italian kabbalist at the beginning of the fourteenth century.[7] This is what he writes in the Introduction to his *Commentary on the Meaning of the Precepts*: "All the sciences are evoked together in the Torah, since there is nothing outside of it. . . . Consequently, the Holy One, blessed be He, is nothing that is outside the Torah and the Torah is nothing that is outside of Him. This is why the sages of the Kabbalah have said that the Holy One, blessed be He, was the Torah."[8]

As extreme as it is, the concept expressed in this passage is echoed by another classic of Jewish thought and piety, that of Rabbi Isaïah Horowitz ha-Shelah, a kabbalist at the beginning of the seventeenth century. The identification of God with the Torah thus does not represent an extreme opinion, relegated to the margins of Judaism, but rather the particular stance taken up by two Jewish thinkers, from among the most conservative authors of the Middle Ages and the beginning of the modern period.

The identification of the author and the book allows us to reassert two values: the supremacy of the divine author and the sublimity of the sacred text. But it also contributes to changing these: the sacred book becomes equivalent to the realm of the divine, and the divine is conceived henceforth as the Torah. It seems to me that this is a logical evolution in a religion founded upon the centrality of a canonical book. Yet this development engendered extreme forms of mysticism. Although it has been preserved in numerous manuscripts, the *Sefer ha-Yiḥud* has not attracted the attention it deserves from Kabbalah scholars. Personally, I would not hesitate to see in this text one of the most important kabbalistic writings of the thirteenth century. However that may be, it had a remarkable impact on the works of Rabbi Menahem Recanati. Indeed, the book by Recanati that contains this identification of the Torah with God is preserved in a large number of manuscripts. It is one of the first kabbalistic texts to have been printed. Unlike other works of this kabbalist, however, which were translated into Latin and exerted a privileged influence on the Christian Kabbalah of Pico della Mirandola, this book was not translated into any European language, and that striking identification of the author with the book manifestly has left no trace on the development of modern hermeneutics. We can nonetheless find a non-negligible exception to this.

The passage from Recanati with which we were concerned above was highlighted in a brilliant study by Gershom Scholem on the concept of the Torah in the Kabbalah. Initially, this was a lecture given in German at the *Eranos* Colloquium, held in Ascona in 1954. As happens with some of these lectures, the study was published simultaneously in English and in French in the UNESCO journal of human sciences, *Diogenes*.

We will be interested here in the French translation, thanks to an eminent specialist of Jewish studies, Professor Georges Vajda. This translation was published in 1955–56.[9] To be sure that the French translation of Scholem's article was not just accessible in theory, but that it was in fact consulted by Derrida at least once in his career, I would like to point out that, without the slightest doubt, Derrida refers, in *Dissemination*, to another passage in the same article by Scholem. There, in question are the blank letters, hidden but destined to be revealed in the future. To my knowledge, this affirmation by Rabbi Levy Isaac of Berdichev has never been mentioned in any study written in a European language, except in the article by Scholem.[10] Here is how the passage on the identity of the Torah with God is formulated in Vajda's translation: "For the Torah is not outside of Him, no more than He is Himself outside the Torah."[11]

This is a faithful translation, even if it is not literal. Nevertheless, the original Hebrew contains nothing that corresponds to "He is not Himself outside the Torah." The term *Torah* that figures in this sentence is, in fact, the clarification of the anaphor inherent in the prepositional suffix *mimmenah*. To facilitate the understanding of the text, the translator gave the anaphor greater consistency, and he translated it as though the text contained *me-ha-Torah*. This is a difference in styles and not a difference in fundamentals. However that may be, it explains how the French formulation came about. The fact that this assertion of the identity of the Torah with God was accessible in the French translation from 1957 certainly plays some role in the emergence of one of the most postmodern propositions of literary criticism, "There is nothing outside the text." Derrida could well have read the translation of Scholem's article in French and adapted it to his own approach, as he had done with another important assertion found in a different kabbalist.[12] Derrida replaced Recanati's formula "There is nothing outside of it," that is to say, outside the Torah, with the assertion "There is nothing outside of the text" or, in yet another version, "There is no *hors-texte* [outside-text]."[13] In so doing, he replaced the term and the concept of "Torah" with that of the text. The first edition of Derrida's *Of Grammatology* dates from 1967, ten years after the appearance of Scholem's essay in French, in which a passage of Recanati's text can be found. Actually, Scholem had borrowed the formula "There is nothing outside of," understood in the theosophical sense, from Rabbi Azriel of Girona, who had a profound influence on the theosophy of Recanati.[14] However, whereas the Catalonian kabbalist was above all concerned to express his conception of the divine will, Recanati, while himself influenced by the Kabbalah of Castille, extended this pantheist conception to the divinity itself. In Recanati's thought, the concept of the divine will does not have the essential role that it has in the thought of Rabbi Azriel.

Curiously, one of Recanati's contemporaries, the Provençal philosopher Gersonides, whom Jewish sources know by the name of Rabbi Levy ben Gershom, expressed a quite similar conception of the Torah: "Behold, the book that God wrote is existence in its entirety, which is caused by Him. . . . Existence is compared to a book because, just as a book points toward the ideality from which it comes, so too the sensible world points toward the Law of the intelligible universe, which is [the ideality of] God, from whom the sensible world comes."[15]

In fact, the philosopher is referring to the whole book, insofar as it is a parable of divine creation. It is quite plausible that what is at stake here is not the dense textuality of the book, as is the case in many sources, but rather the fact that the ideal concept of divinity was materialized in creation, as when an author writes a book. Unlike Recanati and his kabbalistic sources, which evoke explicitly the identity of God with the Torah, it is created reality that here plays the role of the divine book. The book may well have been an analogue of the totality of the real: "it does not absorb" God, as it does in certain passages by Recanati, which I have analyzed elsewhere.[16] In other words, Gersonides' passage, which also recalls the ideas of Ben Sheshet as discussed above, is essentially logocentric. The text designates, here, a metaphysical or theosophical structure, defined by certain reverberations in the world of Ideas, according to a Platonic or Neoplatonic schema that was reinterpreted by medieval Neo-Aristotelianism. Concerning the qualities of the text qua text, that is, its particular texture, they are conspicuously absent.

I would like to compare for a moment the conception of the text as a totality in Recanati with its counterpart in Derrida. In the work of the Italian kabbalist, the book acquires an importance such that the author comes to assert, in the mode of hyperbole, that God himself is contained therein. On the book is conferred a fullness of meaning, since it is assimilated to the totalizing infinity characteristic of the divine nature and since it becomes the site of all knowledge. Besides, it is not too much to believe that despite the negative turn contained in the formula "There is nothing," the fact that it is a matter of divine presence allows us to confer a positive value on the text.

In Derrida, by contrast, we witness the obliteration of God and of all forms of metaphysical presence. His negative formulation "There is nothing" seems to be a tacit or oblique critique of the kabbalist who dared to insert God or metaphysics into the realm of the text.

Despite the efforts he exerts to take his distance from the kabbalistic formula and its metaphysical implications, in order to confer on the text its freedom and autonomy, Derrida does not seem to me to have completely set himself apart from the implications of the medieval source that he adopts and adapts. Ultimately—and this is an essential point for our subject—the book remains an important metaphor for reality. It even survives the attempt to rid it of God as such. If I use the word *attempt*, that is because my modest reading of Derrida has taught me that, for this thinker, the text is conceived as the carrier of an infinite number of meanings and that his system is in fact an alternative reading, slightly secularized, of the kabbalistic formula that identifies the canonical text with God. Indeed, this is not some transcendental entity that would confer meaning upon a text situated here on earth, it is, rather, an imminent divinity that assures the infinity of meanings in the midst of the human text. Rabbi Menahem Recanati, the conservative medieval kabbalist, and Jacques Derrida, the postmodern deconstructor, are in agreement on one essential point: the absolute centrality of the book for spiritual life. For Recanati, the book of the Torah was the transparent prism in which one could perceive the infinite God. For Derrida, the text is the prism that allows us to discover an infinity of meanings. What changes is the nature of the infinite, as considered by each of the two thinkers. Yet both assert, in an absolute fashion, the totalizing character of the text.

Derrida's formula suggests that, in a relationship between the author and the book, it is the author who is the great loser. He is completely excluded. In other words, the kabbalistic fusion of the author and the book prepared the ground for the resorption of the author into his text, the later stage called "deconstruction" by Derrida, even though in being absorbed into the text that author [God] gives it the most important of His attributes, that is, His infinity. I would like to explain the same suggestion from a different angle: the resorption of the author into the text has expanded the latitude or breadth of the reader to the extent that he can fashion at will the content of the text he has before him. The less the person of the reader is distinct, the more the meaning of the book is diffuse. With the identification of the text and the author, the infinity conferred on the text allows the full adoption of an attitude that I would call "the innovating Kabbalah."[17] According to this approach, it is the presence of the infinite author in the midst of the canonical text that guarantees the possibility of drawing an infinity of meanings from it. This hypothesis gives the reader a great deal of power. The idea of an infinite God attenuates the distinct character of His person and the clarity of his messages. This leaves to the reader the task of redefining the time as well as the content of the book he is reading. It is not the eclipse of the author that allowed the development of a creative hermeneutics in the Kabbalah. On the contrary, the assertion of the author's indelible omnipresence in the text creates a process of omni-semiosis. Modern hermeneutics, notably in its French version, sets forth as the essential characteristic of textuality the silence of the author upon the completion of the work. This is a decisive condition of the act of interpretation. For certain kabbalists, by contrast, it is the insistent but diffuse presence of the author that assures the proliferation of interpretations.

This hermeneutic observation can be formulated in terms more clearly centered on the sociology of knowledge. The absence of a directive author was necessary for the emergence of a secular theory of reading. This theory made possible the quality of omni-semiosis in the book. The less the author is directive, the greater is the authority of the reader or the listener. It is like being present at the democratization of the secular approach, which was, at its origin, an aristocratic or elitist attitude proper to the religious circles mentioned above. In describing this evolution, which preceded and to my mind inspired Derrida's postmodern theory concerning the priority of the text and the reader over the author, I have attempted to insert it within a more global framework, that of theories of the text in European culture. In so doing, I have relativized somewhat the novelty of Derrida's theses. Insofar as our observations have convinced the reader, it is apposite to consider the kabbalistic theories about the text as one of the sources of the Derridean concept of the text, together with the theories of Freud and Heidegger. This claim may be construed in Derridean terms, as part of a larger project according a greater role to forms of knowledge that, although formulated and transmitted in Europe during the Middle Ages and the Renaissance, have been neglected or repressed by the historiography of European culture. Is it reasonable to ignore precisely those forms of speculation about the text that are more consonant with the postmodern one? Is the linguistic turn in postmodern thought to be understood solely in terms immanent to the Enlightenment, to Christian visions of the text, or to modern secular developments alone? Is the postmodern speculation that we are examining here solely the culmination of processes that immediately preceded it, or should we not assume that a more "chaotic" history—which I propose calling a panoramic approach to European culture[18]—should give better consideration to ideas expressed by minorities like the kabbalists? Repressed by modernism, the kabbalists' theories found their way to the forefront once the more rationalistic mold of this thought began to break up. If this more comprehensive approach is adopted by modern historiography, the need for historical appropriations of Kabbalah, or at least for phenomenological comparisons, will become conspicuous. Postmodernism is not only the culmination of a process that immediately preceded it, discernible in modern time, but also a movement of recentering on some much older forms of intellectual concerns, characteristic of other periods in European history.

To put it in other terms: my reading of the history of the perception of the text as culminating in Derrida's deconstruction conceives that history as part of an ongoing, and thus still incomplete, process of secularization, one that has not yet attained its most extreme aspects, since it still believes not only in meaning but in a multiplicity, if not an infinity, of meanings. Henceforth, postmodern conceptions attribute the source not to the strong, monolithic author, possessed of an infinite mind, but to the infinity of readers making up a coherent community of individuals that succeed each other. The infinity of meanings of a text is now unfolding in history, as Gadamer put it explicitly, or as Derrida would allow in principle. Modern deconstruction has turned its attention to the nature of the text as dissociated from its author, but as strongly dependent on processes related to the reader. Following the cultural crises in the elites set in motion by the Nietzschean and Freudian revolutions, the instability of meaning has increasingly become a crucial issue, which betrays not only the fluid semantics of the texts interpreted, and the eclipse of the author, but also the flexible attitudes of readers. Once classical philology had been deprived of the power it assumed in the determination of the *intentio auctoris* or in that of the ideal meaning, we witness the emergence of discourses more subtle, more intricate, sometimes even excessively sophisticated, out of the possibilities implied in earlier discourses. This postmodern tendency, aiming to disclose the gap between the poverty of the author and the latent wealth of language, is a characteristic essential and inherent to a secular approach to literature, consisting in reading without the author being present. The unstructured elements of language, bound together by creative literary processes, are never totalized by the author. They transcend his original "intentions," causing a spectrum of meanings to appear that is vastly greater than that which could plausibly be attributed to him. However brilliant it may be, the mind—which cannot have a total mastery over its linguistic material—is necessarily incapable of dominating the variety of possibilities inherent in language and resulting from a long semantic evolution. This view of the secularized text supposes a crisis in a concept that until recently emphasized the identity and the thought of the author. This view proposes that we interest ourselves more in the contribution of the reader or, further still, in that of the sophisticated interpreter. Together, they complete the meaning, enriching the interpreted text with their own holdings. Let me conclude this paragraph by quoting a short passage from Edmond Jabès's "The Key": "The Jew lives in the intimacy of God, and God in that of the Jew, in the midst of the same words. A divine page; a human page. And both of them have, for their author, God; and both of them have, for their author, man."[19]

The Primacy of Language or the Primacy of the Logos

Abulafia's hermeneutic radicalism, which is expressed by the knowledge of God and even by access to mystical experiences, also had the comprehension of reality as its more scientific counterpart. Although these two results can be mentioned side by side, their coexistence is in no way a given. It is thus, for example, that in one of the last works of Abulafia we find an assertion that follows an enumeration of the books of Aristotle's *Organon*. The kabbalist declares that he has studied these treatises in depth; however, according to him, there exists a superior wisdom, "the path of the knowledge of the permutation of letters, which is more excellent than that [of Aristotle] and whose essence is explained in the commentaries of the *Sefer Yezirah*."[20]

The kabbalistic path, none other than Abulafia's own ecstatic Kabbalah, is placed above Aristotelian logic. In effect, the Kabbalah is the science of the "internal [and] higher logic," whereas Aristotle's logic corresponds to an "external and inferior aspect" by comparison.[21] To my knowledge, the expression "internal [and] higher logic"

(*Higayon penimi 'eliyon*) is without parallel in the Jewish literature. We nonetheless find an approximate equivalent in the *Ner Elohim*, an anonymous treatise coming out of Abulafia's school. The author of this book uses the term *Higayon ne 'elam* ("occult logic") to refer to a form of internal recitation that ostensibly corresponds to a middle term between the oral and the mental.[22]

The logic of the permutation of the letters, according to Abulafia, clearly resemblances the theories of the "higher etymology" about the combination of letters fashionable in Arabic literature starting in 1000.[23] This is not the place to treat this subject; nor will I pause to consider the affinities between the logic of Abulafia and the new logic invented by his contemporary Ramon Lull, whose profound interest in the techniques of letter combination is clearly attributable to the influence of a certain form of ecstatic Kabbalah.[24] In any case, Christian kabbalists like Pico della Mirandola were aware of this resemblance.

In his writings, Abulafia repeatedly evokes the sixth and seventh ways of interpreting the Torah by means of a host of eccentric techniques, certain of which are energetic techniques, as I have pointed out elsewhere.[25] All these techniques had been practiced by various kabbalists, even though they did not take on the form of systematic exegesis. I would point out that this passage had repercussions on a text written in the twentieth century by Rav David ha-Kohen, better known by the name of Rav ha-Nazir, a mystic who claimed to have prophetic experiences.[26]

Derrida, for his part, combines the combinatorial logic of Abulafia's Kabbalah with the definition of the role of poetry according to Stéphane Mallarmé. In *Dissemination*, we find a passage that refers explicitly to the Kabbalah: "The science of the combination of letters is the science of the internal higher logic; it works toward an orphic explanation of the Earth."[27] Derrida learned of this conception of Abulafia through the French translation of Scholem's *Major Trends in Jewish Mysticism*.[28] In that text, Scholem cites a brief extract of the text in which Abulafia discusses this subject.

We should also be aware of a question as fascinating as it is important: that of the influences kabbalistic theories may have had on the peculiar structure of Mallarmé's "Book." Though he was critical of the kabbalists, the poet seems to have come across certain kabbalistic conceptions.[29]

As Pico della Mirandola teaches, the *ars combinatoria* of the kabbalists has close affinities with the method practiced by Ramon Lull.[30]

Besides, Derrida's passage just cited is more easily understood when we acknowledge that in his theses Pico della Mirandola proceeds to a comparison and rapprochement of the orphic themes and discussions of the kabbalists, notably those of Abulafia's school.[31]

In conclusion, the concept of the infinity of meanings permitted the passage of the Torah from the status of a text motivated by its use in society to that of an instrument that mystics utilize for their personal perfection.

The Concept of *Setirah* Understood as a Deconstruction of the Text

As I pointed out above, Derrida knew that, for Abulafia, the combinations of letters represented a higher type of logic. It seems, moreover, that the affinities between Derrida and Abulafia cannot be confined to the brief extract from the medieval kabbalist to which the French philosopher refers. These affinities are also conveyed by the fact that both of them consider the text an entity whose signification is unstable. For Derrida, this instability is above all semantic in nature. In that respect, he comes close to theosophical Kabbalah, which held that the various pronunciations of the same consonant generated a variety of different meanings.[32]

By contrast, for Abulafia, new meanings of the text do not come only from novel associations or vocalizations that the reader projects onto the text, but rather from manipulations previously established for the consonants in a text, notably, in canonical texts. Here it is a question of the permutations noted above. They had been the object of a posteriori interpretations, which acquired the status of commentaries on the sacred text. The path of permutations, the sixth in Abulafia's sevenfold exegetical system, was intended for those who attempt the *imitatio intellecti agentes*. Those were solitary practitioners of the exercises in concentration which were supposed to confer "forms," that is, unforeseen and novel meanings, on the combinations of letters.[33] This attempt to imitate the Active Intellect should probably be interpreted as a process of expansion of the limits of consciousness.[34] Curiously, Abulafia describes his method of interpretation as concentric circles, whose largest ones represent the higher methods.[35] The expansion of the intellect thus amounts to the utilization of ever more complex hermeneutical methods, aiming at an increasingly encompassing comprehension of the Torah.[36]

Abulafia is attempting to transcend the natural interpretation of reality, which medieval philosophy connected closely with Aristotle's logic. Now, whereas Aristotelian logic is based on coherent sentences that generate conclusions about the natural world, the Kabbalah—here, the prophetic Kabbalah—has a specific logic that constitutes the only exegesis applicable to the text of the Bible. Intended to decipher the message of the Torah, the kabbalistic approach rests upon the "internal higher logic" discussed above. This logic operates not on concepts but on separated or combined letters. As we indicated, this method is deemed to be superior to Greek logic. In effect, it permits us to restore the canonical text to its original state, consisting in a continuum of letters, each one of them considered to be a name of God or a constitutive part of a divine name.[37] This implies the atomization of the interpreted text, the abolition of the meaning it carried, and the discovery or the invention of unforeseen meanings. Abulafia asserts explicitly that the method specific to his Kabbalah, "the path of the gematria, and all that belongs to this type, as well as the combinations of letters, the permutations in their place, as well as the permutations of their permutations, constitute a method more important and excellent than all the methods of logic."[38]

He cites, in this regard, an expression from the rabbinic literature that was controversial in the Middle Ages: "Keep your sons from *Higayon*."[39] In the rabbinic context, this saying is difficult to interpret. The word *Higayon*, above all, is enigmatic. In any event, it certainly does not refer to logic, much less to Greek logic. Yet this was the meaning that certain conservative authors attributed to it in the Middle Ages. According to them, the traditional Jew should abstain from studying, or at least from having his sons study, Greek logic and, by extension, Greek philosophy.[40] Abulafia makes the position of these authors his own, but he introduces his own particular interpretation of the term *Higayon*. According to him, the word encompasses two valid forms of logic: the one, inferior (that of the Greeks); the other, superior (the logic of the combination of letters). Unlike some other authors, Abulafia does not reject Greek logic; rather, he sees it as part of a more complex curriculum in which the in-depth study of Aristotle's *Organon* represents a relatively early stage. The role of logic—and, to my mind, of philosophy in general—consists in distinguishing what a revelation or an interpretation of the biblical text presents as significant or insignificant. Greek philosophy is clearly the principal instrument for this kind of triage of what is valid and what is not. In other words, philosophy provides a pale copy and yet, in a certain sense, the moment of resistance, or what could be called the reality principle, that restricts infinite semiosis. In Abulafia's thought, this restriction preserves a relatively wide margin, for he also has recourse to other languages in order to confer meaning on the various combinations of letters.[41] In a passage that precedes his discussion of Aristotle's logic and that immediately follows the warning to young students about Greek logic, Abulafia cites another rabbinic saying, which I would translate as follows: "The destruction done by elderly men is [tantamount to] a construction or building, the building of young people is [tantamount to] a destruction."[42] In the specific context of Abulafia's discussion, this means that the study of Greek logic, if begun at too early an age, risks being destructive. By contrast, Greek logic may prove to be constructive if it is undertaken at a more mature age, and if it is combined with the more advanced levels of the combinatory Kabbalah.

The Hebrew word that I translated as "destruction" is *SeTiRah*. In the Bible, the root *STR* is used in a context that refers to the hiding of the divine face.[43] Later on, the same root will contain increasingly complex semantic fields. In addition to the destruction of a building, it may designate the neutralization of an argument by way of a counter-argument,[44] at the end of a shift from the material sense to the intellectual one. Neither the material nor the intellectual form of destruction was applied to the realm of the text, however.

Abulafia was fascinated by the various significations of the root *STR*. In his commentary on the *Guide for the Perplexed*, he writes:

> The verse contains simultaneously two senses. When one places the first words together with the last words, the plain sense is more accessible than the hidden sense. But when the hidden and evidential sense of kabbalistic religion shall be understood by the perfect intellect, the articulations between the words in the plain sense will no longer have any importance. These articulations aim only to highlight the mystery[45] that flows from them and to remove what is hidden from the multitude of masters of the plain sense . . . what is hidden is the divine sense or topic and the plain sense is the human subject.[46]

The mystery, then, is not the deepening of some religious meaning that the ordinary text supports. It comes, to a certain degree, from dismantling the normal order of the words and the letters. Abulafia recognizes the coherence of the interpreted text, and he preserves its structure. But according to him, no hidden meaning could result from the fixed order of letters and words. Thus the emergence of the hidden meaning is closely tied to the deconstruction of the verbal structure. Since Abulafia attributes essential importance to the hidden meaning, we can understand the place of predilection that the process of deconstruction holds in his system. In fact, he asserts in another passage of the same book that the mystery hides itself in the midst of the plain sense, which constitutes, in some sense, a linguistic unity that one must then deconstruct to extract the hidden from the plain:

> The semantic content [namely, the consonants] of the *Sitrey Torah* ("secrets of the Torah") is pronounced in a certain way and can be interpreted in two ways that flow from the root *STR*: The first interpretation corresponds to the past tense of the verbal form *qal* of the complete roots; this form designates the destruction of something that is constructive, as for example a building and other things of the same sort. This refers also to the contradiction between words, as the sages expressed it in the formula: "Solomon! It is not enough that your words contradict those of your father, David. . . ."[47] To this is attached what the Rabbi [Maïmonides] said in the first part of the Introduction [to the *Guide for the Perplexed*] that precedes the chapters about *SeTiRah* or contradiction. It is a matter of the contradiction of an issue or subject. This meaning always flows from the *qal* form of the verb. We must verify if we should investigate whether this form can refer to another meaning, such as the dissimulation or the hiding of a subject. In any case, anything that can relate to the meaning of dissimulation flows from the *hif'il* of the verb. This is tied to the strong form of the verb, that consists in adding the letter *hi* at the beginning of the word, as in *histir*. On the one hand we have *soter*, "he contradicts," on the other, *histir*, "he dissimulates." This is why the word *STR* is a common term covering both senses whose authentic sense it expresses, that is, dissimulation and contradiction. And, in the eyes of the multitude, the hidden sense seems to contradict the plain sense. But this is not the case if we envision things from another perspective.[48]

Abulafia is not content with expatiating on the semantic field of a Hebrew root. According to him, the juxtaposition of two specific meanings implies a particular intent: even though these two meanings diverge at first glance, they are nonetheless held together by a certain coherence. To my mind, Abulafia is here referring implicitly to the profound difference separating the plain sense from the hidden sense in a given text. These two levels of meaning correspond respectively to the common and the elite ones. In many passages, Abulafia asserts not only that the two meanings coexist but, moreover, that they are not really contradictory.⁴⁹ According to another text, words are like covers, concealing secrets.

As if to add to the complication of this sketch, Abulafia is not content to pun on the two meanings of the root *STR*, insofar as it designates simultaneously hiding and contradiction. According to him, the secret also lies hidden in the numerical value of the word. Now, the gematria for the three consonants in the root *STR* is 660, the same as that of the expression *et qets* ("the time of the end"), which is found in the Book of Daniel. On a number of occasions in the *Gan Na'ul*, the word *seter* is used for its numerical value of 660, to which Abulafia attributes a messianic signification.⁵⁰ In other words, the quintessential secret is inherent in the very letters that express the idea of secrecy. The secret par excellence is none other than the eschatological secret.⁵¹

For Abulafia, the destruction of the old and the construction of the new was neither a mental game nor a mere exegetical device, still less an eccentric or contrived interpretation of some venerable passage out of the rabbinic literature concerning the construction or the deconstruction of synagogues or idolatrous temples. He himself took on the role of destroyer-constructor. This function, integrated into his method of self-perfection, aimed at transforming him into prophet and Messiah, and he applied it to his spiritual projects. In his prophetic work—written between 1285 and 1288, and one of the few apocalypses ever to be written by a kabbalist—Abulafia describes himself in these terms:

> Behold the time of deliverance and the day of redemption have arrived.
> But no one is paying attention to these and no one desires to know them.
> There is no redemption but by the name of *YHWH*.
> And His redemption is not for those who do not request it
> In virtue of His Name.
> This is why I, Zachariah [*Zekhariyahu*],
> Destroyer of the building⁵²
> And builder of destruction,⁵³
> Have written this little book,
> In the name of *Adonai* the small
> In order to disclose through it the secret of *YHWH* the great.⁵⁴

Zachariah (*Zekhariyahu*) is one of the theophoric names that Abulafia adopted.⁵⁵ It means "he who recites [or mentions] the Tetragrammaton." Its numerical value is 248, the same as that of Abraham, which is Abulafia's first or proper name. The dialectic is not very clear between the realms of the two divine names, *Adonai* and the Tetragrammaton. Nonetheless, we can deduce what its intention is from the context, as well as from a parallel text found in a book written by one of Abulafia's closest followers.⁵⁶ The situation of exile, which in Abulafia's thought designates something vaster than the social and political condition of the Jews, corresponds to the divine name *Adonai*, principal substitute for the Tetragrammaton, which was to be the predominant name at the time of redemption. Once again, redemption implies neither the political realization of Jewish hopes for a return to Zion nor the construction or reconstruction of a new or renewed order. It is, rather, a spiritual phenomenon. Thus, the two situations of exile exclude each other, even though the same person is concerned. One and the same person can be either in exile, when he places himself under the domination of the substitute for the divine Name, or redeemed, when he worships the Tetragrammaton. Thus, the ascent or the construction of one of the names implies the destruction of the other. According to the passage cited above, Abulafia is writing at a decisive moment in his life: he is still under the aegis of *Adonai*, but he is beginning to discover the Tetragrammaton. Therefore, the object of destruction and construction is linguistic. It is a matter of divine names and of the composition of a book, the *Sefer ha-Ot*. The process of construction consists in the revelation of a new name, which automatically provokes the concealment of the name dominant up until then. Out of this passage from the primacy of one name to that of the other name flows the technique of deconstruction of the biblical text by virtue of the exegetical technique that Abulafia calls internal logic and that consists in combining in a new fashion the letters of the sacred text.

Finally, the term *soter* ("destroy," "contradict"), when used in a context that has to do with redemption, is perhaps not without relation to the Greek word *kyrios* ("savior").⁵⁷

Toward an Alternative History of Western Thought: One Suggestion

In introducing an approach that we might call texto-centric, which goes against the grain of the dominant logocentrism, Derrida opened the way to an alternative description of the history of Western thought. This represented for him a means by which to criticize explicitly the history of Western thought proposed by Heidegger. His philosophical project may justly be interpreted as an effort to that end. One may write the history of philosophy in many ways. One of these, advocated by Harry A. Wolfson, claims that the history of European philosophy, from the end of antiquity through Spinoza, consists in a series of encounters between Greek philosophy and the Holy Scriptures, starting with Philo and passing through the various syntheses that succeeded each other over the course of the Middle Ages.[58] We can describe medieval Jewish thought according to still other types of confrontation between Greek philosophy and the Scriptures. It is a question of nuancing the concept of synthesis and of heightening—in light of Gadamer's and Derrida's thought—our awareness of the creative tension between the two terms.

Moreover, the crucial importance of letter combinations in Jewish mysticism—as well as among a small number of the bright lights of Western thought, such as Ramon Lull or Giordano Bruno, not to mention their impact on Leibniz and, more recently, on European thinkers like Stéphane Mallarmé—would require a study that examines in detail the cumulative impact of the infiltration of kabbalistic material on the development of the Western conception of the nature of language and of the text.[59]

The methodological supposition that structures many of the developments discussed above claims that, in the Europe of the Middle Ages and the Renaissance, works separated by significant differences interacted substantially with each other.[60] In the eleventh century, Europe witnessed the arrival of certain forms of Greek philosophy through the mediation of Syrian, Arabic, and Hebraic translations. This allowed for the creation of theoretical systems that sought to integrate diverse types of speculation, including Neo-Aristotelian, Neoplatonic, even Stoic or Pythagorean speculations into theological systems, which could rightly be called Helleno-Judaic or Judeo-Hellenistic. Thereupon, starting in the second half of the fifteenth century and following on the decisive impact of the translations of Marsilio Ficino and others, new corpuses supplanted the forms of medieval speculations. These new bodies of work acted upon the ancients, rapidly provoking the dissolution of some forms of medieval thought. One effect of this process was the disappearance of the elite intellectual culture that had once believed in the esoteric dimensions of religion and in the importance of mystery or secrecy. With postmodernism, esotericism has been completely abolished.

Yet mystery, or secrecy, is one of the principal problems that existing texts pose to deconstruction. Entire literary works avow the existence of secret messages in the canonical texts interpreted. More often than one might think, these works themselves create the secrets that they project onto the text in order to elucidate or, indeed, to hide it. The secrets invented by late commentators, which were set down on the texts they interpreted by means of what we could call a "process of arcanization," are not our concern here. They reflect a universe of imaginary representation superimposed on more ancient sources, even on archaic sources. This is the activity of elites seeking to legitimate their systems of thought or their idiosyncratic ideologies. While this projection was integrated into the dynamic process that was the rereading of these texts, the books that were thus reread may nonetheless have been founded upon codes supposing a coherence extrinsic to the text itself, whether this be the coherence of another text or indeed of an oral tradition.

The play of arcanization rarely unfolds in solitude. It is often part of a cultural struggle aiming to preserve, to reinforce, or to resurrect the vitality of the text; one either criticizes deliberately false interpretations to which the text was subjected (this, in the case of a *Kulturkampf*), or one stigmatizes the misunderstandings and scoffing to which it gave rise. In some cases, the new mystical reading takes on the form of a disjunctive approach that seeks to dismantle another interpretation—or even a competing esotericism. In others, the new reading is conjunctive or inclusive in attempting to harmonize, in one way or another, the ancient and the novel mystical interpretations.

To conclude, let us return for a moment to the kabbalistic sources studied above, which Derrida put to the uses noted earlier. The first of these sources reflects one of the principal postulates of the dominant current of theosophical Kabbalah, which gave rise to the richest kabbalistic literature. The second source, which consists in a passage from Abulafia, comes out of another kabbalistic school, secondary in a historical perspective, which has been called the "ecstatic Kabbalah." The first school promoted a conjunctive approach to exegesis, since it attempted to establish as close an affinity as possible between the secret and the plain senses of the canonical text. By contrast, the second school rarely perceived the relation between the two senses as something organic. The theosophical-theurgic approach is much closer to a logocentric vision of the world, at least in certain cases, whereas the ecstatic Kabbalah, which tends to be disjunctive, aims at a more flexible semiosis. The first school more readily allows for the possibility of presence, even though it functions on the basis of a dynamic theosophy. For this school, this supreme truth is reflected in the text, which serves to mirror transcendental processes and entities.[61] For Abulafia and his disciple Rabbi Nathan Harar, it is man who is supposed "to give" the forms, that is, to confer new meanings on the combinations of letters in the interpreted text.[62] More generally, religious literature advocates an almost "postal" conception, by virtue of which the message emanates from the sacred text. For Abulafia, the deconstruction of the text makes a reverse process possible. Since the succession of the letters in the sacred text is disorganized, the messages are transposed from the mind, or the imagination, of the interpreter to the interpreted text. The canonical text thus becomes the mailbox that receives a growing number of messages produced by the intense mental activity of the mystic. Once activated in this way, the human mind comes to resemble the Active Intellect, instilling its forms into the raw prime matter of the deconstructed canonical text.

Historicity and *Différance*

GIANNI VATTIMO

In the title I propose, I am well aware that the very term *historicity* may seem inappropriate, or may at least sound too "Italian" to be acceptable. But this language problem may also serve to signal an approach that is external, or rather "other," in the sense Derrida gives that word in his writings. This somewhat "discordant" title summarizes at least three questions.

1. Is there a history of Derrida?
2. Is there a history in Derrida, in his works?
3. Is there history—as a philosophically recognizable notion—in Derrida (again, in his writings and in the theory expressed therein)?

It seems to me that these three questions sum up, first, the historical meaning of Derrida's work—that is, what it means within the philosophical culture of our time, with all the problematic aspects that his critics invite us to discover in it (therefore, I repeat, a historicity in a sense that is more general, more generic, than the one to which our three questions refer)—and also its relation to Judaism, its "judeity," at least to the extent that I believe I recognize it (again, from a point of view that is external, foreign, etc.).

These three questions merely articulate one sole problem— one that is posed not in but by *Writing and Difference*, in which work we read that *différance* is not *in* history (which is a problem that since then has not, to my knowledge, been resolved in Derrida's subsequent works, and remains an open question—meaning that from that point of view nothing has changed . . .). What I have in mind are questions that might be considered, at first blush, foreign to Derrida's problematic. He has often refused, for example, to consider the question of the "evolution" of his thought:

> I learned . . . that my "thought" . . . was "in full evolution." . . . I would benefit greatly from such encouragement . . . if the value "evolution" had not always seemed suspect to me by all the presuppositions it harbors . . . , and if, above all, I had not always been wary of "thought." No, it is a question of textual displacements whose course, form, and necessity have nothing to do with the "evolution" of "thought" or the teleology of a discourse. . . . " *'thought' means nothing."*[1]

In these pages, which are from *Positions*, a 1971 colloquium, Derrida states that he is also wary of the concept of history.[2] And yet in these very pages there are elements with which we may reduce— even eliminate completely—the strangeness of the questions I have just raised. This is what, as an interpreter, I shall concern myself with doing: namely, with discussing, and eventually criticizing, a work *juxta propria principia*, according to its "formative form," as Luigi Pareyson would say (despite the Derridean refusal of an "organicity" of the text that would be the expression of an inner law or unifying intention). Just a few lines before the ones quoted above, Derrida says that deconstruction cannot neglect "the inscription ('historical,' if you will) of the text read *and* of the new text that deconstructionism itself writes."[3] And further down:

> the materialist insistence . . . within a very specific camp in our most contemporary situation . . . can function as a means of seeing to it that the necessary generalization of the concept of text, its extension with no simple exterior limit . . . does not wind up . . . as the definition of a new self-interiority, a new "idealism," if you will, of the text.[4]

The precautions that could be taken in that regard, it is true, are never sufficient.[5] The questions about historicity, in the many senses that I have just mentioned, are an attempt to proceed on the path of the precautions Derrida himself considered necessary in that same colloquium. It seems to me that the historicity of Derrida's work— albeit in its significance for today's culture, or in relation to judeity— becomes recognizable on the sole condition that there be a response to the questions I have just asked (and here I am alluding to a later aspect of the question, i.e., to my history as an interpreter of his texts).

I will dwell for a moment on that allusion to the history of my relationship with Derrida's texts, in order to deal at least with that aspect of the question. My choice of the title of these remarks is a fact of my biography, if I dare call it that. Underlying the three questions, there is the choice of a title, and that choice is a historical fact that depends upon *my* decision, which, however—this is the hermeneutic circle—is not unrelated to the historicity of the Derridean text, with its *Wirkungsgeschichte*, with the history of its *Wirkung*, its effects on *me*. If that were all there was to it, the organizers of this colloquium probably would not have accepted my title—although, since it is a meeting of Derrideans on Derrida, one might expect a certain tolerance . . . The history of the choice of the title is one aspect, and certainly not the only one, of the historicity of Derrida, of what his texts "mean" in today's culture. It is really not necessary to make that argument. We already know well enough (following a move so frequent in Derrida) why the question of historicity can be a question, or *the* question, of the meaning of Derrida's work in our culture. It seems that it can all be summed up in the phrase about the precautions that are never sufficient, taken in order to keep deconstruction from ending up being a kind of new idealism of the text. That is what the critics of deconstruction criticize Derrida for. According to these critics, the idealism of the text shows itself in the arbitrariness (apparent or real) of deconstruction, according to which, in several senses, there is no *hors-texte*. One may also not share that criticism in its grossest sense (consider, for example, the American "joke" . . .); but one cannot deny that it touches on a very specific aspect of Derrida's work, which has always concentrated on textuality, vindicating the importance of the text and of textual work. To put it more clearly: I think that, in this crass sense, the criticism of Derrida's textualism has little meaning; but the fact that it is possible, that it circulates in our cultural world (the very world in which deconstruction seems to come about as a movement that is not contingent on the arbitrary choices or genius of one sole thinker), appears to me to be strictly tied to the question of historicity and to other questions that it leaves open. What must be read in these questions is not the scandal of the absence of an *hors d'œuvre* [something outside the work], understood as a criterion for deconstructive work that would guarantee its validity on the basis of a concept of truth as "correspondence." On the other hand, in the choice of the title/theme of these remarks, the determining factor for me is the problem of the *project* of deconstruction. In the dissatisfaction with the real or supposed arbitrariness of the deconstructive practices of Derrida and so many of his imitators, I caught a glimpse, as authentic meaning, not reduced to a vulgar joke, of the question of the project that inspires deconstructive work. And here I claim proximity to, even agreement between, my approach and Derrida's own intentions. Without that, why take all the precautions he spoke of in the colloquium referred to above? The precautions are taken for the realization of a project, a project that—if I have understood correctly Derrida's refusal of the metaphysics of presence, which he shares with Heidegger (whom he even reproaches for not being sufficiently radical on this point)—cannot be only one of perceiving more clearly, more adequately than metaphysics did, the difference that ferments *within* all supposed *compactness* of being. In my personal history as a reader, friend, and student of Derrida, the question of historicity, or of the project, presents itself not as a question about the truth/validity of his method, of his theory, and so on, but as the problem of "What do we do now?" If I listen to Derrida, and not, say, to John Searle, Gadamer, or Habermas, what do I do in philosophy? In other words, is there a Derridean school? Or better yet: Does difference, or *différance*, make any difference?

Even in these somewhat peremptory and perhaps categorical terms, I do not think I am a stranger to Derrida's intentions. Again in the pages of the *Positions* colloquium with Jean-Louis Houdebine and Guy Scarpetta, where he talks about materialism (and about Lenin—a sign of the times), he denies that one can unambiguously characterize the concept of matter as metaphysical or nonmetaphysical. "That will depend on the work to which it gives rise."[6] True, it will depend on the work of textual deconstruction, but always on an effect, a result that is measured in relation to an end, that is, to a *project*.

Ultimately, then, why deconstruction? But should my title, then, not be "Historicity and Deconstruction" rather than "Historicity and *Différance*"? I might admit (another historico-biographical mark) that the title was chosen with the intention of borrowing the title of one of Derrida's best-known works. But not solely. For even if deconstruction is always an action, although its historicity—the fact of having a history, an unfolding, although with no certain goal—is obvious, what *has* no history, what is not *in* history, is *différance* itself:

"The differend, the *difference* between Dionysus and Apollo, between ardor and structure, cannot be erased in history, for it is not *in* history. It too, in an unexpected sense, is an original structure: the opening of history, historicity itself."[7]

If deconstruction is induced by *différance*—in two senses, as efficient cause and final cause, but perhaps also as formal cause (to deconstruct always comes down to bringing out differences, to dilating caesuras) and material cause, at least as an instrument with which, or a given upon which, one works—it is because it does not even have movement. The risk is, then, that deconstruction may assume the role of an *ipsum esse subsistens*.[8]

Does it suffice, in order to get out of metaphysics, or simply to sojourn in it with that duplicity of the look that Heidegger would call *Verwindung* and that Derrida himself considers to be the only way of "overcoming" it—does it suffice to work till one discovers at last a being or an origin no longer compact or intact, but fissured, worked over, split by the never-ending struggle between Dionysus and Apollo? What is metaphysics? Is it the thought of being as presence unfurled, as reconciled unity, or is it rather the presupposition that the task of thought, and emancipation itself, consists in the contemplation of true being, however it is conceived (even as a God not at peace with himself)?

As is quite clear, the three questions I asked at the beginning in order to clarify the meaning of the title have not yet been answered. But they have given rise to other questions (this is perhaps the work they produce?): the question about the historicity of the title itself, the questions about the possible transformation into *"other"* (no longer difference, but deconstruction), the question about the very meaning of the term "metaphysics" for Derrida and its relation to Heidegger. To return for at least a moment to the three initial questions, I will say that up to now, it seems to me that I have obtained, though elliptically, an answer, however provisional. Namely: Derrida's hesitation to speak of an evolution of his thought is, in the final analysis, bound up with his rejection of any kind of teleological vision of history, with a mistrust of its alleged linearity qua construction of meaning, which would contradict the antimetaphysical intent of working (toward)—or of grasping, dilating, corresponding with—the *différance* that "gives itself" in a certain way to us as a call, a fact in progress, and so on. A bit paradoxically, one might answer, then, that there is no one history of Derrida, no one evolution or development or "continuous," discursive, logical transformation of his thought, because for him there is no such thing as History, and that all of this depends on *facts* that are in turn historical, those my second question envisaged. It seems to me that it is in fact in historico-factual terms that Derrida explains the "why" of deconstruction, and primarily the "why" of grammatology. Let us recall here the almost *hapax legomenon* of the first part of *Of Grammatology*: "For some time now, as a matter of fact, here and there, by a gesture and for motives that are profoundly necessary, whose degradation is easier to denounce than it is to disclose their origin, 'language' has been used for action, movement, thought, reflection, consciousness, unconsciousness, experience, affectivity, etc. Now we tend to say 'writing' for all that and more."[9]

What we have here is obviously a sort of justification in "epochal" terms of the enterprise of deconstruction. In the later writings, however, beginning with the discussions I mentioned earlier, Derrida tends to drastically reduce, to the point of nullification, the meaning of these epochal references—which are apparently too close to the Heideggerian discourse on the "history of being" not to arouse in him the suspicion of a relapse into metaphysics.

Thus, in a more recent dialogue,[10] the absence of an explicit thematization of the deconstructive practices he carries out yet again in his texts—in which the "choice" of themes to be approached is made in an apparently arbitrary way—is justified in terms of "elliptic economy": the community of his readers already knows, shares with him the consciousness of the historical situation in which we live; it is, therefore, useless to give specific details. Nevertheless, in this dialogue, which I allow myself to consider as an introduction to my remarks today, Derrida also says other things, which appear to me more important and which make it possible to understand in what sense one can characterize the situation in which deconstruction acts as that which "goes without saying," to the point of not meriting a more intense theoretical attention. What takes place does not merit an attention comparable to that of Heidegger, because there is no history of being, nor any call that that history can address to us. *Of Grammatology* responds precisely to a situation of which one simply says that "something 'deconstructs.'"[11] But we respond to that situation not because it constitutes a true vocation—nor because one has understood by some sign that it is better to deconstruct than not to do so. "We are in the process of deconstructing and we must answer for it."[12] But why "we must"? If deconstruction does not arise from an initiative, a method, or a technique, but *is* what *happens*, why must we be answerable for an event that we simply observe?

"Here I have no answer," says Derrida. To go in the direction of deconstruction, however, does not mean simply to agree with what happens; on the contrary, deconstruction is the "anachrony of synchrony." "To attune to what happens" means to push it in the deconstructive direction that the event itself "reveals," contains, manifests. But, after all, "we must" do it in order for something to happen, "and it is better that something happen rather than not."[13] Here, to happen [*advenir*] in the sense of to occur and to happen in the sense of futurity, merge totally.[14]

One might inquire: Why in general a coming about [*advenir*] rather than immobility? It is abundantly clear that to happen—in the sense of to occur and in the sense of futurity—takes the place of the being of metaphysics. Does one truly get out of metaphysics? It seems to me that the reason why happening is preferable to its opposite—which may constitute, I believe, the last word in Derrida's theoretical itinerary to date—is the fact that "the future is the opening in which the other occurs [*arrive*]. . . . This is my way of interpreting the messianic. The other may come, or he may not. I don't want to programme him, but rather to leave a place for him to come if he comes. It is the ethics of hospitality."[14]

Even that attention to the other, which has never been absent from Derrida's text, but which has certainly increased in recent years, is perhaps an "external" historical mark that Derrida probably does not reject, but to which he gives no particular attention, in order to continue to avoid the risk of a "history of being." The event must truly be an event—and therefore also bear my signature, be witnessed by me—because the condition of salvation, of authenticity, of emancipation, in sum, of this "better" that from time to time turns up in Derrida's discourse, is that the other may always be able to come, because in him the messianic, if not the Messiah, is announced. (But can there be an announcing of these?)

At this point, we might again make the attempt, or give way to the temptation, to propose a point of arrival for Derrida's itinerary, or for our itinerary toward him: the epochal justification in *Of Grammatology*, and therefore the historico-factual enrootedness that appears to "found" it, is increasingly consumed in the development of Derrida's work. If there is a history of his thought, it may be the progressive obliteration of historicity, at least as the history of a meaning. Alongside this movement, the messianic orientation of his work, the idea that deconstruction is a way of responding to a certain ethical duty to give place to the other, asserts itself (or simply becomes more accentuated). Part of this same movement, in my view, is the institutional interest (in politics, the university) that, according to some of his interpreters, marks the second phase of his thought.[15] There has also been talk of an existentialist Derrida,[16] who would not be in contradiction to the image of a Derrida who is "committed" in politics and institutional critique. What I see in this, ultimately—and I know that it is a dangerous discourse to engage in from the point of view of French culture, but my status as a foreigner outside this history allows me to engage in it—is the Sartrean paradigm of historical commitment, which, at least up until the time of the *Critique of Dialectical Reason*, corresponds to no teleology and, in Sartre, is even the consequence of an absolute metaphysical pessimism. The messianism of Derrida's last period may even be much more faithful to an existentialist perspective than was Sartre's Marxist destination, despite the latter's statements in *Questions of Method* (Marxism/Theory and Existentialism/Ideology, etc.).

But if, with existentialism, Derrida too seems to place himself *on the level at which there is only man*—for which Heidegger criticized Sartre, upholding the history of being in opposition—are we not once again simply in metaphysics, at least in the sense of an existentialist metaphysics qua philosophy of finitude (of being)? What is in play here is a problem not devoid of foundation, if we think of the passage in *Writing and Difference* in which it is affirmed that *différance* "is not *in* history." Does messianism—the openness to the other who comes and thus ensures the advent, that is, being as event-advent—really remove the still-metaphysical character of this affirmation about *différance*? I ask this, bearing in mind a meaning of the word *metaphysical* with which I believe Derrida himself could agree, as I said earlier— namely, a conception of the task of thought as the uncovering of a structure, or archi-structure, before which we may stand (or which we may rediscover each time through the work of deconstruction). If *différance* has no history, the other who comes on the scene is always only the recollection and testimony of that archi-structure. Since there are no truly different moments in the relationship with that origin/nonorigin, even the alterity of the other will be nothing but an alterity that I would call purely *formal*. The other is messianic, because he is not me, because he is an event in relation to what was already there. I remember, though indistinctly, having heard Derrida say in the course of a discussion that "it is true that we are always in history." Precisely: we are always there; but what counts is precisely this "always," and not the determined moment of history in which we find ourselves. We always find ourselves in a determined moment, it is true; but it is for that very reason that one might say it is useless to seek its specific characteristics. And to get back to the other: if we know too much about him or her, if in a certain way we have expectations with respect to his or her physiognomy, even if they are negative, we will no longer be truly open to that alterity, that advent, which must always be *abrupt*.

Several things come to mind here (I beg you to forgive the elliptic character of this progression), especially from texts by Derrida, such as that page from *Of Grammatology* in which he says, *"In a certain sense, 'thought' means nothing."*[17] I have not been able to find a statement to this effect in the most recent writings of Derrida, but I assume he has not "retracted" it. Perhaps we should not take it literally, should not banalize it. Still, one wonders to what extent that statement may not confirm, if we read it as relating to the other, the presupposition that the alterity of the other is always accidental and that, to avoid falling back into metaphysics, we must think of it only in spatial, topographical terms.

That fundamental "hetero-logy" comes to us first and foremost from Derrida. It also comes to us from Levinas, for whom the look of the other calls to mind in a certain way the absolute Other, the divine Infinite. Thus the latter takes a decisive "leap" toward a way of thinking that replaces the hypocrisy of the Greco-Christian tradition with a return to the biblical heritage, to what the Christians call the Old Testament. Derrida does not make this "leap," and not because there is an abstract distinction between religious and philosophical discourse—which from his perspective should have no justification. But does the other, any other whatsoever, really always bear within him or herself the trace of the Infinite? Levinas has, after all, the Bible as a guide; for him, the messianic character of the other does not depend solely on his or her absolute diversity in relation to myself, which Derrida, by contrast, must emphasize, since he does not want to refer specifically to that revealed text. A Christian like Heidegger has the New Testament for his guide; thus, in the Introduction to the course *Phenomenology of Religion* (1920), conceived as a commentary on Saint Paul's two letters to the Thessalonians, the expectation of the *parousia*, of the promised return of the Messiah, is not a pure tension toward just any alterity, but an expectation "qualified" by what has already happened and the faithful already know.

In Levinas's case, the historicity of history, the specificity of events, is removed thanks to the choice of a vertical leap: the Last Judgment is at every moment; each alterity is in direct relation with God, but is also measured and judged in this very relation. In the case of Heidegger, despite the changes in his attitude with respect to the Christian tradition, which in my opinion do not affect his fundamental nature as a "Christian theologian," as he already writes in the thirties in a letter to Löwith, it is the directives that the faithful have already received by the teachings of Jesus that gauge the authenticity of the other. Directives that are, it is true, mainly negative ones: the Messiah will come "like a thief in the night"; do not allow yourselves to be fooled by the Antichrist, by the false messiahs we see round about us every day. That, then, is what you should do above all. Although Paul does not positively define the traits of the true Messiah, to the point where Heidegger is prompted to see in the attitude he recommends to the faithful a kind of translation of the phenomenological epoche, the example of the life and death of Jesus is nevertheless amply sufficient for the alterity of the coming Messiah not to be totally indefinite.

It is, basically, in that Christian ascendancy, often forgotten (in the course given in 1920, all the main elements of the analysis of the temporality of *Being and Time* and also of the antimetaphysical polemic of the *Kehre* are already present), that we can find the roots of the insistence with which Heidegger will always place the eventuality of being in a concept, indeed a problematic one, of the history of being.

The thesis I would like to advance here, by way of conclusion, could be formulated as follows. It is only on the condition that we accentuate and radicalize the notion of a historicity of being that we can remain faithful to the Heideggerian purpose—a purpose Heidegger himself has not always respected—namely, not to confuse being [*l'être*] with beings [*l'étant*], and therefore to seek a way of going beyond metaphysics. Similarly, for Derrida himself, desirous of furthering his antimetaphysical project, the point is to think the alterity of the other in concretely historical terms, beyond an "existentialist" perspective, which still runs the risk of an inadvertent relapse into metaphysics, because within that perspective being is conceptualized, no longer as a compact presence, but as (the presence of) a structure that is fissured, worked over, deferring. Either being (the archi-structure) truly falls into history, is consummated and differed (*si differisce*: the Italian may suggest here, with the verb *differire*, the verb *ferire* as well; hence "to be wounded," "to be thrown against") in history, or all the differences and deconstructions merely bring us back to contemplating, in a kind of paradoxical *amor dei intellectualis*, the archi-structure or originary being, merely place us back into its presence.

The other who is not concretely situated in a history endowed with "meaning"—even understood as progressive and indefinite consummation of presence and of its peremptory nature, which in my view is consistent with Heidegger even beyond the letter of what he says—cannot take on a messianic form and function otherwise than on the basis of a "subjective" attitude, that is, on the basis of my way of receiving him. The other's messianic character, devoid of any recognizable historical markings, is totally subjective: I can take as my starting point whatever term, concept, event, of whatever text, to get back to the originary difference, on the condition that I take up the "double look" that Derrida wishes. Even the predilection for the written text, as opposed to the phono-logo-centrism that would still be peculiar to Heidegger or to Heideggerians such as Gadamer, appears to be transformed into its opposite. The written text assures a definitive, monumental presence, but also turned over in each case to the deconstructing subject, who works on the text in the privacy of his study. What is important about the other is not his or her concrete historicity (which Plato identified with the ability of spoken discourse to defend itself) but the monument of the other, in which historicity is consumed in the constitutive finitude of existence, thus allowing the originary archi-structure to show through more clearly.

It seems to me that this risk of a metaphysical relapse—which is also that of Heidegger, and, here, of Derrida—comes, in the case of the latter, from his judeity. A messianism without a Messiah does not sidestep, in my view, the relapse into a structural conception of finitude, and therefore, into a negative theology, or a metaphysical existentialism. Levinas only succeeds in avoiding this risk by means of a deliberate "leap" into religious tradition. This "leap" Derrida does not take. Perhaps Dilthey was right when he said that the beginning of the end of metaphysics in the history of the Western world is the advent of Christianity, which is also, if I may say so, a *form* of judeity. In Derrida, we find at once these two souls, and the value of his texts consists perhaps in the fact that he allows us to discover these two souls in all their indispensable immediacy. But also in the fact of his bringing us face to face with a choice that he seems, for the moment, not to have made.

How to Answer the Ethical Question

JÜRGEN HABERMAS

I am grateful for the opportunity to participate in the exploration of the Jewish background of Derrida's thought, though my role will be marginal in several respects. Using a third language [English], I am painfully aware of an incapacity that excludes me from most of this philosophical exchange. An even greater obstacle is my distance from its major topics. Despite a long-standing relation to Gershom Scholem, I have not been working in fields specific to Judaism. And, in view of this distinguished circle, I am certainly the one with the poorest knowledge of Derrida's oeuvre. Derrida would be, of course, the first to explain why a marginal position is not necessarily a disadvantage. There were two reasons, anyway, for accepting the invitation: I want to express my respect for an exciting work, in which I recognize, across a certain distance, allied motives and shared intentions. And I cannot resist the opportunity to put "questions to Derrida." I have long been interested in the question: At what precise point do the philosophies of Heidegger and Derrida separate? This is not meant as a philological question; it is as much a philosophical as a political one.

In a lecture that he gave at the University of Frankfurt last summer [2000], Derrida talked about (what we in Germany are used to calling) the "Idea of the University."[1] He explained passionately the unconditional commitment of the academic community to freedom and truth. A university that does not betray its own idea has to provide the institutional space for the "profession" of such a faith. And it is the work of professors to express the performative meaning of that faith, in the sense of the "mise en oeuvre de la vérité [setting truth to work]." This phrase, the "ins Werk setzen der Wahrheit," reminds us of the world-disclosing function that Heidegger attributes to great books and works of art. Therefore, it did not come as a surprise that Derrida, with due irony, devoted the last part of his lecture to an act of evocation—calling for what he called the "arrival of an event [*l'arrivée d'un événement*]."

Speaking *intra muros*, this self-reflective gesture was intended to make the audience, gathered in a large amphitheater of the University of Frankfurt, aware of the very purpose that those walls are supposed to protect: "It is too often said that the performative produces the event of which it speaks.... One must also realize that, inversely, where there is the performative, an event worthy of the name cannot arrive. If what arrives belongs to the horizon of the possible ... of the 'I can' or the 'I may,' it does not arrive, it does not happen, in the full sense of the word.... only the impossible can arrive.... The force of the event is always stronger than the force of a performative."[2] In Derrida's words, there also resonates the voice we know from Heidegger's notes on "Of the Event."[3] In the years between 1936 and 1938, Heidegger first developed his conception of a devout overcoming of the totalitarian features of a subjectivism haunted by power. It was not until 1946 that Heidegger made this turn public. In his "Letter on Humanism," he explains his wholesale rejection of both the term and the meaning of the "humanist tradition" that feeds the normative self-understanding of modernity. By contrast, Derrida wants to save the substance of this "humanism," although, at the same time, he adopts Heidegger's attitude toward the "arrival of an event."

Human rights and the prosecution of crimes against humanity, a democracy that transcends national boundaries, a sovereignty freed from misleading connotations, a repeated reference to autonomy, and the encouragement of resistance, disobedience, or dissidence—everything that Derrida invokes in his interpretation of the purpose of our profession—is one more slap in the face of Heidegger's verdicts. My question is, therefore, simply this: How do Heidegger and Derrida differ in their precomprehension of the arrival of what each of them presents as an undetermined "event"? That divergence should explain the difference in attitude they adopt for and against "humanism." Again, we should not mistake the substantive question

I have in mind for a matter of terminology. It does not matter whether we use the term *humanism* in an affirmative or a pejorative sense. Either way, it is difficult to bring Derrida's purpose in line with the object of Heidegger's deepest contempt. I suspect that we face, here, a division between a neo-pagan betrayal of, and an ethical loyalty to, the monotheistic heritage.[4] Let us remember what Scholem said about such loyalty. "Authentic tradition remains hidden. Only when it goes to ruin is tradition turned into an object. Its decline, however, makes it manifest and allows us to perceive its greatness."[5]

Being aware of my own limits with regard to Derrida's work, I will proceed in a roundabout way, starting from a rather distant site. You must not expect an exegetical or deconstructive exercise, or a close reading of any kind. I will first explain the modern differentiation between moral and ethical theory, and then present Kierkegaard's postmetaphysical yet religious answer to the ethical question. The various attempts to appropriate Kierkegaard's ethical insights to philosophical or postreligious terminologies shall provide the arguments, finally, by which to specify the question I would like to put to Derrida.

Ethics was once the doctrine that could tell us how to lead "the right kind of life." Writing during and immediately after World War II, Adorno had, however, good reasons to present his *Minima Moralia* as a "melancholy science," barely apt to provide certain reflections from a "mutilated life." As long as conceptions of the whole of nature and history were still available or in force, philosophy could in good faith present a frame into which the life of individuals and communities might be expected to fit. The design of the cosmos and of human nature, the sequence of the stages of sacred or worldly history, all this was taken as value-laden facts that provided guidelines for "the right kind of life," guidelines permitting us to know "what to do with the time of our life," as Max Frisch would say. In this context, the expression "right" pointed to an exemplary way of life, worthy of being imitated at once by individuals and by communities. "Rightness" included both the value of the *good* life and that of the *just* one. But the faster an increasingly complex society changed, the shorter became the half-life that spelled the expiration dates of our ethical models—little matter whether the model of the ethical life came from the Greek *polis*, the social strata of the medieval *societas civilis*, or the state and society of the Prussian monarchy.

Political liberalism marks the end of this line. It reacts abstemiously to the facts of pluralism and individualization. John Rawls's "just society" cannot prescribe a specific mode of life anymore; it grants everybody equal freedom to develop and pursue an ethical self-understanding or a "conception of the good life" of her own. Modern philosophy by no means retreats from all normative questions, but it confines itself to the sharply defined issues of justice. We consider norms and actions from the moral point of view if we are concerned with what is in the equal interest of all, or with what is equally good for everyone thus affected.

The question "What is the right thing to do?" only appears to constitute the guiding question for both classical ethics and modern theories of justice. Yet the "should" of an ethical question must not be confused with the "ought" of a moral question. In the first case, we take care of our own well-being, whereas in the second case, equal concern is given to the well-being of everyone. A first-person reference is inscribed in the *selective* perspective of the question "What in the long run would be the best thing *for me* or *for us* to do?" By contrast, the moral point of view entails an *inclusive* we-perspective through which we acknowledge the rights and duties we accord each other, or those we expect *each from each*. Ethical questions, in the classical sense, change their meaning with the particular context from which they arise; they refer to an individual life history or a shared form of cultural life. They are intertwined with questions of identity—questions of who we are or would like to be, without blushing.

This logical differentiation has led to a split between moral and ethical theories. Since each individual is absolutely different from everyone else and has a right to remain an "other" to others, the search for what is equally good for everybody requires careful abstraction from exemplary images of a happy, good, or successful life, which are no longer shared by all. Our own existential self-understanding may still be nourished by the substance of religious narratives, metaphysical worldviews, or "strong traditions" (Alasdair MacIntyre) in general. But modern philosophy has lost the authority and competence to intervene in the struggle between comprehensive doctrines and to offer an impartial judgment of their competing claims. Philosophy has withdrawn to the meta-level of an inquiry into the formal properties of ethical discourse. It thereby abstains from taking a stand on precisely those issues that are most relevant to our personal and communal lives.

Moral and political theories have a high price to pay, however, for their division of labor with ethics proper. One consequence is the disconnection between moral judgment and moral action. Moral insights can effectively bind the will of an actor only insofar as these insights are embedded in an ethical self-understanding that places a person's individual concern for her own well-being in the service of an equal interest in justice and its motivations. While they may well explain the justification and application of norms, deontological theories lack moving arguments as to "why be moral" at all. Political theories of justice face a similar problem. When it comes to the question of why citizens should act, in relevant conflicts, according to constitutional principles rather than subjective preferences, these theories can do little more than hope for the emergence of the right patterns of political culture and socialization.

Philosophy not only pays a high price for its abstention; one might question the decision to abstain itself and ask why philosophy should leave the field to clinical theories like psychoanalysis, which claim competence, instead, in the treatment of disturbed or damaged lives. The conception of mental health by no means offers an unproblematic analogy to physical health. Compared with the body, the soul and mind lack the same sort of clearly observable parameters for states of "pathology." From the moment that pathologies are imperceptibly normalized on a grand scale and produce sufferings that do not so much as cross the threshold of consciousness for those enduring them, the only element at our disposition that could take the place of somatic indicators of health or illness (indicators that, as such, do not exist) is a normative interpretation of what might count as an undisturbed mode of human life. Why should philosophy abstain from a business that clinical psychology has to carry out in a conceptually more or less confused way? Why should philosophy not contribute to explaining the intuitions and glimpses of what we sometimes still dare to recognize, albeit hesitatingly, as "wrong" or "misspent" ways of life?

Kierkegaard was the first to give a postmetaphysical answer to the ethical question in terms of how "to be oneself." This level of abstraction corresponds appropriately to the challenge of pluralism. In *Either/Or*, Kierkegaard contrasts the ethical way of life with the hedonistic masquerade of life. He paints this kind of "aesthetic life" not without sympathy—in the attractive colors of early Romanticism—as a sensual mode of a leisurely but dispersed life, driven by the self-centered pleasures the ego derives from accidental and short-lived encounters. By contrast, the ethical self pulls itself together and achieves a consciousness of its own freedom and individuality. Ethical life gains continuity and transparency through self-reflection, since "he who lives ethically has himself as his task."[6] Only a person who has developed a deep concern for her own spiritual well-being, and has thereby become aware of the historicity of her existence, can thus acquire the strength to make responsible commitments to others.

Kierkegaard analyzes the structural, temporal, and modal features of an authentic mode of "being oneself." The extended choice-of-self is guided by an infinite interest in the imperiled success of one's own life project. Only through the self-critical appropriation of one's past life history—recollected and retrieved in light of future possibilities—can a person become a unique, irreplaceable individual and an autonomous subject at the same time. The ethical self can continuously give an account of her life and thus *become* the person she *is* only in the moral light of the sermon on the mount, which Kierkegaard always already tacitly presupposed. The individual develops an ethical self-understanding by repenting the problematic elements of his past—of which he is ashamed—and by affirming only those mental attitudes and actual habits with which he would be identified in the future. "Everything that is posited in his freedom belongs to him essentially, however accidental it may seem to be."

But Kierkegaard is far from Sartre's existentialism when he adds: "This distinction is not a product of his arbitrariness such that he might seem to have absolute power to make himself into what it pleased him to be. . . . The ethical individual dares to employ the expression that he is his own editor, but he is also fully aware that he is responsible—responsible for himself personally, responsible to the order of things in which he lives, responsible to God."[7] For Kierkegaard, an ethical life cannot be stabilized except in relation to God. His conception has no roots in a speculative interpretation of the entirety of beings, and in that sense it is *postmetaphysical*, but not *postreligious*. Faith must come to complement moral knowledge if the ethical question is to find a *compelling* answer.

Kierkegaard, that radical critic of contemporary culture, passionately denounces the ubiquity of a frivolous and cynical, and at best conformist and self-righteous, attitude toward the normalization of blatant injustice, humiliation, and suffering. It is this phenomenon, he argues, that cannot be explained by a *lack of knowledge*, but only by a *corruption of the will*. Those who *know* better are not *willing* to understand the disastrous state of mankind. Therefore, Kierkegaard speaks of "sin" rather than "guilt." As soon as we interpret guilt as sin, however, we come to realize that we must hope for an absolute power of forgiveness—a power that intervenes in and reverses the course of history for the purpose of resurrecting the integrity of its innocent victims. (In passing, that was what was at issue in the famous controversy between Walter Benjamin and Max Horkheimer during the thirties—even prior to the Holocaust.) For Kierkegaard, the promise of redemption is the motivating connection between the infinite concern for oneself and the moral commands of a post-conventional conscience. Faith in God, in the Savior, requires us "to go beyond" Socrates and Kant.

Climacus, the author of the *Philosophical Fragments*, is still satisfied to consider "the god in time" as a kind of "thought project." In the end, he remains undecided whether faith in the possibility of salvation is "more true" than the Socratic project of ethical knowledge.[8] Kierkegaard therefore introduces an Anti-Climacus, who presents us the striking phenomenology of a "sickness unto death," which leads to a final reversal of consciousness. He first describes the disquieting state of a person who becomes aware of the destination of "becoming a self," yet turns his back on this existential imperative, fleeing into equally despairing alternatives: either not to will to be oneself; or not to be a self; or again, to will to be someone else, to wish for a new self. When this person ends by discovering that the true source of his despair resides not in circumstances but in his own failed undertakings, he must then face the challenge of becoming oneself. In desperately willing to become oneself, he mobilizes all his resources toward an act of extreme self-assertion. To what does that lead?

The phenomena of an increasingly intense despair are so many manifestations of the ever more clearly recognized failure to reach a balance, one that alone would make possible an authentic mode of existence. The failure of the last *defiant* act of the ethical self resolutely to achieve this goal solely by its own powers marks the end of the therapeutic curriculum—the overturn of a secular self-understanding. It motivates the finite mind to transcend itself and to recognize its dependence on an Other, in whom its own freedom is rooted. Kierkegaard describes this condition of rebirth with a formula reminiscent of, but inverting, the initial paragraphs of Fichte's *Wissenschaftslehre*: "in relating itself to itself, and in willing to be itself, the self rests transparently in the power that established it."[9] Though the literal reference to a "power" in which the self is grounded ("gründet das Selbst in der Macht, die es setzte") does not signify more than the finitude of a human existence in history, Kierkegaard prefers a much stronger, a religious, reading. It is only through consciousness of sin that the self can reach, in the right way, an awareness of its own finitude, such that "this self takes on a new quality by being a self directly before God."[10]

Kierkegaard's ethical subject survives its hopeless despair only in the shape of a religious self that, in its relation to itself, receives its freedom by *devoting* itself to an "absolute Other," to whom "it owes everything." Obsessed over the course of his entire life by the Lutheran question of how to reach a merciful god, Kierkegaard is a radical Protestant. This orthodoxy must, of course, be an annoyance for his *philosophical* followers. He himself acknowledged that there is no way to form a consistent *conception* of God, neither by the *via eminentiae* nor by the *via negationis*. Every idealization remains parasitic on the basic predicates from which it starts; for the same reason, the attempt to encircle the absolute Other by way of negations fares no better. "Understanding cannot even think the absolutely different; for, unable to negate itself absolutely, it uses itself for this purpose and therefore thinks the difference [only] in itself."[11] The gap between knowledge and faith cannot be bridged by reason. This situation presents a dilemma to philosophers who wish to inherit Kierkegaard's postmetaphysical ethics but would deny any recourse to revealed truth. Let us consider rapidly the responses of Jaspers and Sartre, and then proceed to Heidegger and Adorno.

Jaspers maintained that philosophical knowledge must be conceived as another faith—faith in reason. Philosophy rejects revelation as a source of truth, yet it competes with religious doctrines for the right normative self-understanding of individuals, communities, and humanity in general. Socrates is set side by side with Jesus.[12] This strategy raises the difficult question of how to explain the paradoxical epistemic status of such a hybrid enterprise. Though it is still supposed to abide by normal standards of rational discourse, philosophy is said to share the domain of transcendent problems and the kind of dogmatic claims we know only from the great world religions.[13] This resemblance of postmetaphysical thought to faith is as implausible as the gap assumed between modern philosophy and science. A different, straightforwardly atheist strategy was adopted by Sartre. His conception of existential freedom ignored, however, the warning not to confuse self-conscious ethical life with defiant self-assertion. Yet that was the whole point of Kierkegaard's suggestive phenomenology of despair. Like Kierkegaard, Sartre wants to take into account both the fallibilism of human beliefs and the unconditionality of the moral claims he is confronted with. But he cannot elude the objection that, in these postmetaphysical conditions, the self cannot hope to satisfy its infinite ethical concern if it is not aware of its specific finitude—the dependence on an enabling power that escapes one's control.

A philosophy that would to be heir to Kierkegaard has to offer an interpretation of this enabling power. A naturalistic interpretation is ruled out, because the experience of a "transparent" dependency is bound to the dimension of an interpersonal relation. Defiant self-assertion is directed against an other, whom the self encounters as a second person. But it is far from obvious that this "other"—to whom the self must relate at the same time as it relates to itself—is identical with "the god in time." The linguistic turn offers, for its part, a deflationist interpretation. Interacting speakers are others to one another.

As historical and social beings, we find ourselves within a linguistically structured form of life. Caught in the restless concern not to waste our lives, we face in everyday communication a surpassing power on which we do indeed "rest transparently." As the medium of our communicative practices, language is no one's private property. No one individually holds an intersubjectively shared language at his disposal. No single participant is capable of controlling the course and dynamics of the interpenetrating processes of *mutual* understanding and *self*-understanding. How speakers and hearers make use of their respective communicative freedoms is not a matter of arbitrary choice. The logos embodied in ordinary language reaches through the individual freedoms of both speakers, who raise validity claims with their speech acts, and hearers, who meet them with their "yes" or "no." Both are free only by virtue of being subject to the *binding power* of the reasons they offer to, and receive from, each other.

This reading of dependence on an "Other" saves the fallibilist but antiskeptical meaning of "unconditionality" in a weak or proceduralist sense. We know how to learn what we owe to one another. And each of us—taken respectively as members of a community—can self-critically appropriate, in light of such moral obligations, our past histories with a view to articulating a proper ethical self-understanding. Yet the communication remains "ours," even though it is ruled by a logos that escapes our control. The unconditionality of truth and freedom is a necessary presupposition of our practices and lacks an ontological guarantee beyond the cultural constituents of our forms of life. The right ethical self-understanding is neither revealed nor "given" to us in any other way; it is achieved through a joint effort. From this perspective, the enabling power built into language is that of a trans-subjective rather than an absolute quality.

This modest interpretation does not fit Kierkegaard's idea that binding moral norms must be anchored in faith, that is to say, in some ethical self-understanding that unconditionally grants our life a "meaning." This is the sense in which we must understand Horkheimer's phrase that any attempt to salvage "an unconditional meaning" without God is in vain. For everyone who, like Horkheimer, is convinced that "together with God eternal truth is dying," philosophy faces an uneasy alternative.[14] It must either give in to a desperate skepticism or appropriate the theological substance of sin and salvation. Though I do not accept this alternative myself,[15] I would like to focus on an interesting consequence that has left its traces on the most important philosophical works of our century. If we accept this premise, then philosophy cannot overcome the nostalgic defeatism reflected in Horkheimer's remarks; it cannot do so unless it provides a reasonable translation for "the god in time"—and "reasonable" here means a translation of the God of Moses in terms of an impersonal conception of a temporalized absolute. Therein lies the key, I believe, to the works of Adorno and Derrida. Is it the key to Heidegger as well?

In respect to the question of loyalty to the monotheistic tradition, let me briefly compare Adorno with Heidegger. While the first draws on messianic sources of Western Marxism, the latter seems rather to follow Nietzsche in his attempt to reach back behind both the Jewish beginnings of monotheism and the Platonist beginnings of metaphysics.

Negative Dialectics can be understood as the elaboration of a Kierkegaardian thought, which Adorno first expressed in the final aphorism of his *Minima Moralia*: "The only philosophy which can be responsibly practiced in face of despair is the attempt to contemplate all things as they would present themselves from the standpoint of redemption. . . . Perspectives must be fashioned that displace and estrange the world, reveal it to be . . . as indigent and distorted as it will appear one day in the messianic light."[16] The counterfactual reference to such perspectives is justified with words that remind us of

Kierkegaard's famous remark about becoming aware of a finitude that does not debar the human mind from its relation to the infinite, the possible, and the transcendent. Adorno appears to interpret the self-transcending insight of the despairing self, which "is restlessly and tormentedly engaged in willing to be itself," when he adds: "The more passionately thought denies its conditionality for the sake of the unconditional, the more unconsciously, and so calamitously, it is delivered up to the world. Even its own impossibility it must at last comprehend for the sake of the possible."[17]

With this concluding sentence, Adorno withdraws the theological allusion and makes the reader aware of the innerworldly context from which he speaks: "Besides the demand thus placed on thought, the question of the reality or unreality of redemption itself hardly matters." What matters, however, is the strong moral implication of the revoked allusion to God, the Savior, and the Reconciler. Adorno lets us understand, indirectly, that his critical perspective remains loyal to the egalitarian universalism inscribed in the very conception of God, the *Deus absconditus*. On the Day of Judgment, when we step forward individually and see "Him" face to face, God will, through His comprehensive and charitable evaluation of the unique features of each single life, do justice to each of us equally. It is this normative substance of monotheism that Adorno wants to keep—and that gets lost with Heidegger.

Kierkegaard's existential analysis of what it would require to live a life beyond despair has certainly never found a more convincing philosophical explication than in *Being and Time*. It is, however, precisely the ontologizing translation of Kierkegaard's modalities of ethical life that deprives Heidegger's conception of authenticity of its normative core: "In the end, Heidegger and Kierkegaard move in opposite directions. Unlike Kierkegaard's ethical life, which constitutes a precondition to moral and social responsibility, Heidegger's methodological conception of authenticity is deeply anti-normative."[18] The empty appeal to a resoluteness that lacks any substance anticipates the emptiness of an implored arrival of Being. In his later writings, Heidegger retains the ontological perspective when he interprets the defiant self-assertion of the will to be oneself in terms of the subjectivism of the mentalist paradigm and when he goes on to substitute a history of Being for Kierkegaard's "god in history."

This historicized Being manifests itself in a contingent series of fateful, and in any case overwhelming, happenings—the shifts in world disclosure that are revealed through the mouth of distinguished poets and thinkers like Hölderlin or Heidegger himself. From the Socratic self-understanding of the ethical self to the awareness of one's dependence on the grace and judgment of the Savior, the conversion is replaced by the turn from the totalizing thought of metaphysics to a submission to something superior. The anonymity of a withdrawn and impersonal power demands from us the obedient attitude of someone listening to the uncertain arrival of an indeterminate message. The only content we know in advance is what we get from Heidegger's critical reading of the history of metaphysics. But in this regard, the "Letter on Humanism" only repeats what Heidegger had extracted from his earlier interpretation of Nietzsche, namely, that we have "to eliminate all conceptions of justice, which stem from Christian, humanist, Enlightenment, liberal and socialist morality."[19] The assimilation of ethics to ontology leads Heidegger in 1946 to answer the ethical question with a hint about the hollow ethos of *Schicklichkeit* ["rules of decorousness"]: he asks man to fit or respond to whatever might come from an indeterminate higher power—an absent power that, thus far, has had nothing to say.

The evacuation of all moral content from a temporalized Being results from the decisions on which Heidegger's conception of a history of Being rests. Heidegger first includes, under the rubric of onto-theology, the monotheistic tradition, which forms a part of the history of metaphysics. Judaism and Christianity thus fall under the critique of that history. The critique itself is driven, second, by a search for archaic origins that are "earlier," and supposedly more telling, than Socrates and Jesus—those two sources of Western thought and civilization that Kierkegaard appreciates and Nietzsche detests. As a result of this strange impetus, Heidegger is wont to talk about "gods," rather than God in the singular. You will remember the headline of his last interview in *Der Spiegel*: "Nur *ein* Gott kann uns retten." Adorno's critique of *Ursprungsdenken* ["thinking of the origin"] is the antithesis of Heidegger's *anfänglichen Denken* ["thinking of beginnings"].

Echoing Nietzsche's "last man," there is also a "last God." Heidegger declares that, with the death of this poor fellow, all types of "theism" have definitively reached their end. No surprise, then, that there is no moral trace left in Heidegger's Being and, in the awaiting of its arrival, no leftover from the egalitarian universalism that is inscribed in the monotheistic tradition. From this point of view, it is interesting to follow the dialogue that Derrida imagines at the end of his book on Heidegger, a dialogue between Heidegger and a few Christian theologians.[20]

The theologians ask Heidegger for a revision of his rejection of the monotheist tradition. He should better recognize that his own critique of onto-theology is the best possible interpretation of the experience of Christians, Jews, and Muslims in their encounter with the actuality of God in history. Derrida's Heidegger responds to this invitation in the way we would expect him to. He insists on the fundamentalist pretense of Heidegger's search for first origins, supposed to reach far back behind the beginnings of metaphysics and eschatology. Derrida, of course, fashions Heidegger's overbid in cautious terms, to avoid any suspicion about a regression toward paganism on the theologians' side. But Derrida does not leave the dialogue at that. The most remarkable aspect of the exchange is the fact that he gives the last word to Heidegger's unwavering opponents and allows them to restate their conciliatory interpretation. In the end, they embrace a reluctant Heidegger, who is presented as having unintentionally captured what faith can mean for Jews and Christians alike.

This surprising end seems to indicate that Derrida's own appropriation of Heidegger's later philosophy rests on a ground that is theological rather than pre-Socratic, and Jewish rather than Greek. His loyalty to Levinas, moreover, reveals the tendency to answer the ethical question from the perspective of the self's self-reflective relation to an Other, "who" speaks in each case through a second person. If I am not mistaken in this assumption, I can put my question as follows: Can Derrida leave the normative connotations of the uncertain "arrival" of an indefinite "event" as vague and indeterminate as Heidegger does? And moreover, what burden of justifications would follow from our accepting the demand to make those normative connotations more explicit, whatever they happen to be?

A Monster of Faithfulness

JOSEPH COHEN AND RAPHAEL ZAGURY-ORLY

What we will be saying together here, we'd like to think we also say it alone, each of us under the command of the *other* in each of us, and in the traces of an untranslatable silence. We write a text together, but it is as if we wrote it all alone. This writing will attempt to become the echo of two voices that did not know each other and that are irreducible to each other. Two voices that would never speak to each other. Would this be the *amorous encounter*—for we speak of nothing other—which would forbid any "lexical exchange," as Jabès would say, any communication in writing, any common language, any literature and any letter, letter of systems and/or antisystems, even any voice? Would these two voices be so foreign to one another that they could never meet, never give voice to one another, write one another? If *writing* alone were already in itself a betrayal and obliteration of the ineffable singularity of any amorous encounter—of what we tell ourselves about love—and thus recalls to presence what would withdraw from it, then to write as a twosome would imply a return of that treason, if not an intensification of writing, an even more intense return of presence and an irreversible loss of what one believed, of what one liked to believe, without words for us and between us.

It seems that the lexicon of the amorous encounter is irreducible to the motivation of the theoretico-practical; it does not allow itself to be treated by the ontological, metaphysical, or political synthesis.

The amorous encounter, if there is such a thing, comes to writing as an *event* beyond all conceptual or nonconceptual organization of meaning. There is no convergence, nothing but parallelism between us. As if our voices were superimposed upon one another with an only apparent coherence, so that they would never enter into dialogue with one another. It is as if the entry into our writing could only take place by turns, one by one.

But how can one continue to speak in two voices when these two singular voices only merge between us and through us, fuse, in spite of us, into the *essential* order of discourse? Is the safeguard of secret voices not bound in advance to fail in the friendly conversation—*so* interested, *so* disinterested—that we have kept up between each other for so long now on love and all the "objects" and "subjects" connected with it? Is it not additionally condemned to deteriorate in what will always be the public and universalizing translation that is part and parcel of the discursive process? Will not the perseverance of discourse—its *always-already-translating* process—ambush any singular voice, no matter how singular it may be? Will the logos not always in the end catch up with what attempts to break free from its presence? Furthermore, what language would be able to remain "faithful" to the untranslatable secret of the amorous encounter when the simple evocation or invocation of the word *faithfulness* would only affirm the grip of the theological or the religious, the inevitable economy of language and its immemorial *involvement* in the experience of the saintly, the saved, the safe and sound?

> Impossible to write today. Too unwell. You remember: everything had begun with the joyous decision not to write any more, the only affirmation, the only chance (no more letters, no more literature), the condition, what one has to give oneself so that something finally happens. Confess, let us confess: this was the failure, the triumph of communication, right (we should never have communicated anything in sum, not even together).[1]

Shall we, believing ourselves unique, do no more than rehearse the universality of the unique? In believing ourselves to be incomparable, do we not thereby already inscribe ourselves in judgment and comparison? That is perhaps what the two voices of this text will say to one another, each of them speaking of their love, but it is also what two lovers would say to each other in speaking of themselves and of the others.

Is the lover not the one who always says in the beloved's ear:

—*You are untranslatable, I would not have been able to love you in a language other than my own, we are untranslatable, we would not have been able to love one another in any other language but our own.*

He is, so to speak, the one who would always and everywhere say:

—*My love, one cannot, must never, speak of us. You and I, we will never use the language of the philosophers. We will love one another on the hither side of the separation and mediation of the concept.*

He would be the one to say "I am ashamed of emphasizing, of wanting to be intelligible and convincing (as if for others, really), I am ashamed of saying it in everyday language, of saying, therefore, of writing, of signifying anything at all in your direction."[2] To speak to one's love—that means always to (want to) speak to him or her in the singular, to echo the words of an enigmatic meeting, to speak to him or her *without* speaking to him or her.

—*You, you will never enter the trap of a language, a philosophy or literature. I would never thematize you, never lead you into the race of being.*

But might that not be the language of all lovers? Love's own language? Is there anything other than philosophy or literature, the "common language," the "language of knowledge," in which to speak of *us* and of love?

As long as we speak, we will trade in images and known words. As long as we write, we will express "our meetings," "our passions," and "our ecstasies," in the same words, and in one sole voice "our faithfulness," "our betrayals," "our tears"; everything we held jealously and eternally in secret. *Uttered*, the word snaps up; *written*, it grabs as in a fist. The moment it is said it takes on the grammatical categories, the proper name, the common noun. Does not "abject literature" lie in wait for the lovers' future? Hiding in wait, "crouching within language," despoiling them of everything, not even letting them enjoy the resumption of their voyage, leaving them stripped bare before one another, alive, separate, "out of reach."[3] And even if we were to submit language to a constant effort of reformulation, to an infinite attempt to *ex*-propriate the movement of universalizing translation, would we not be moving it still further in the direction of the most common element of language?

To claim without claiming an ineffable uniqueness for us lovers, to cry out without crying out for the urgent necessity of a different order of meaning for the *we*, to recommend without recommending a heterogeneous lovers' face-to-face for what is at the heart of the we, to cultivate without cultivating a taste for the absolute mystery of the we—this might be the even more extreme reinscription of the dreamed exceptionality of this *we* in what will always have already been there in the meeting. To announce in the intoxication of the possible that we must no longer write in order to be able to write, to write still better to one another, to try to give all its weight to the unconditional *we* relationship, to set up the conditions in order that the "totally other" may happen to the we, that it may happen in us and to us—to wish our end in order that everything may at last begin again: perhaps this boils down to suggesting that before us, below or above us, there is nothing but the fundamental universality of the *we*.

Would there ever be something like "a right distance" at the heart of the *we*? Something like "a right proximity," which would never be too much or not enough, a *proximity for proximity's sake*, to use Levinas's language?[4] What "to do" in order for the *we* to "find the best distance"?[5]

This is perhaps to intimate that the language of the universal betrays nothing, and that when it betrays it, that is because it is only by betrayal that love can be spoken of, only via a *common destination*, even a *communicatory destination*, and perhaps ultimately the betrayal does nothing but reveal love. There emerges here a certain *double bind*,[6] expressing the circumstance that simultaneously there is no betrayal in love, since it is in that very betrayal that love is expressed, that something like love is affirmed, and that as soon as one succeeds in expressing that love—something like its recognition, its manifestation or phenomenality—there remains nothing but its betrayal. It is a bit as if, in love, we were always and despite ourselves at the same time faithful and unfaithful, without our ever being able to assess the value of or the limits between faithfulness and unfaithfulness. Because faithfulness is not simply the opposite of unfaithfulness, and vice versa. Here we catch a first glimpse of the aporia that will continue to deepen in our discourse, which might be qualified, after Derrida, as a philosophical event, with neither intended recipient nor destination.

We will never be done unfolding the folds of this aporia. It is not so distant from another aporia that comes into play in the writing of this text. Between the secret, the intimate, the hidden within each of our individual voices *and* the universality, the publicity, the sharing of our two voices, writing seems to contain an aporia that precipitates its very possibility into an impossibility. Thus writing always solicits at once the massive presuppositions of subjectivity, will, identity of self with self, *and* the unshakable prejudices of universality, generality, and publicity. All writing of love seems to presuppose that the *we* of meeting is the most intimate secret, without any possible literary "experience," while presupposing that it is the most commonly shared "experience" in the world—the most common and the most general, the most empirical possible, the literary experience itself.

The restoration of the values faithfulness and unfaithfulness to their paradoxical nature, the manhandling of the purity of this relation, so metaphysically founded and charged, through all its registers, all its determinations, and according to each of its presuppositions, the problematizing of their clear distinction, the raising of all possible questions relating to the relationship between these two terms—such a deconstructive saga perhaps being a saga of love through and through—the pursuit of an immense, rebellious love, a madness of love. Such a deconstructive inquiry would be commanded tirelessly by a mad and undeconstructible idea of love, an idea infinitely sick with love.

So we must question the "compulsion" to set *faithfulness* and *unfaithfulness* in simple opposition and contradiction to each other, that is, to represent that contradiction simplistically. One should perhaps, while struggling with all the figures of stability, all the schemata of the proposition and conjunction "faithfulness-unfaithfulness," let their common "source," their "dependence" on one another, be felt, beyond that opposition and its determination—giving a sense of how they mutually nourish one another, signify through one another, and thus allow the reader to "divine" how the imperturbable and interminable movement of *faithfulness*, far from contradicting *unfaithfulness*, carries it within itself, presupposes and sustains it.

It will never be possible to establish by an act of judgment, be it determinative or reflective, whether faithfulness and unfaithfulness merely compensate for one another, indemnify one another in an oppositional, reciprocal back-and-forth movement, *or* whether they are commanded by an Idea of love that is *other*, an absolutely unconditional Idea of love. Similarly, it will never be demonstrated in a gesture of comprehension, be it speculative or hermeneutic, whether faithfulness and unfaithfulness live from their opposition, posit themselves in opposition to one another, co-determine one another in and through their contradiction, *or* if they are severally commanded by an Idea of love worthy of the name—a love that is infinite because always to come, heterogeneous with respect to determined forms of love, without any actual, concrete, real relationship with them, an

Idea radically devoid of adequation to all that has already come, to all that has already been qualified by the name of *love*.

Such is the risk of this interrogation, Derrida would say, the risk of this love. It is perhaps in this "place" of fuzzy, indecisive limits that the question of a certain *responsibility* of love in love plays itself out. Let us even say that it is only in this "place" without limits, this undecidable place, that something like an "experience" of love may perhaps come forth.

Now, the relationship between faithfulness and unfaithfulness would become complex on its own, in this place without place that is love. To free it from the metaphysically determined opposition faithfulness-unfaithfulness—that is our "task." We must try to rethink here the commonly accepted hierarchy, onto-theologically founded and too hastily associated with what may be called, not without a certain awkwardness, a "monotheism of the heart," and its opposite, a "polytheism of the heart."

Who is faithful? What does faithfulness mean? Is there any such thing as "of course I am faithful," and "I know my faithfulness"?

To be faithful, at first glance, might mean our *tautology*, something on the order of a tautology of love. A circularity in which the predicate would express nothing but the subject. There would always be a connecting thread, straight and taut, between speaker and addressee. It is always about a form that is certain and sure of itself, a form that is analytically true by virtue of its own syllogism: "I am faithful," as "I am the one who *is* faithful." That phrase is repeated ad infinitum and uninterruptedly, without contradiction or even hesitation. "I have an *experience* and a *knowledge* of faithfulness." "I am the witness par excellence to what faithfulness is—to its limits, its borders, its orientation, and its betrayal." "I bear testimony in advance to what *could occur* within it, through it, with or against it."

Each of these affirmations of faithfulness carries within it a powerful sovereignty for self and other, in the name of oneself and in the name of the other. They summon the other to a presence of self to self; they bespeak a total accompaniment. "I accompany the other everywhere; the other accompanies me everywhere." My presence to myself is always accompanied by that of the other. Similar . . . that we are, to the millimetric limits of absolute identity. Teleo-theo-geology of love. Espousal of an imperturbable face-to-face. Maximal illumination. Love without obstacles. Absolute memory of reciprocal recognition. Spatialized time, temporalized space. No time. No space. No illusions. Nothing but *us* between us. The inviolate map of meaning, sign, and reference. Seeing and hearing are *seeing* and *hearing*.

And what if the "willing of the will" of love in us were "that which wills and that which is willed in us"? Should we read in that analytic proposition our greatest fantasy of love? For it to be brought about that the *passage* between the word *faithfulness* and the thing faithfulness, between faithfulness [subject] and faithfulness [predicate] should remain forever unquestioned and unquestionable? The ordering of our syllogism in such a way that nothing would come along and destabilize it. With no intrusion into our "room," not even that of a different fantasy. Fantasy of the without-fantasy—would that not be our greatest fantasy? In our "room" there would be no one but *us* to love, without fear or trembling. To call faithfulness *faithfulness*, as one would call "an apple an *apple*," as one would love "to love to love." To write "so simply, so simply, so simply," *we are we*.

What is harbored within this amorous "willing of the will," this "willing to be" of an analytically unshakable faithfulness? What are we thinking when we say "we are we"? From what position can one *simply* assert "we are we," if not from a position that is objectively determined, always already overdetermined, a place closed in upon itself, unquestioned, without the slightest exteriority, unquestionable? Are we only "ourselves" when we see *ourselves* setting out from a *we* without questions? If it is true that not questioning ourselves is our most secret dream, it may also be the thing that pulls us inexorably toward our downfall. Ever "*self-justificatory*,"[7] the resemblance of faithfulness to itself may contain the seeds of its own undoing. The analogy is perfect, the reflection imperturbable, the mirror of the syllogism casts back the image of an immediate reciprocity. Between us the veil would be lifted, the mystery revealed; everything would be present in and by a syllogism that always already inscribes the relationship within the element of pure self-reference. At the very heart of the definitiveness of the enchainment of self to self, the other is always exposed, described, in reference to the present. Nothing cuts through the suffocating identity of the faithful we, the syllogistico-analytic *Diktat*. The other is other, but on the condition that he is no longer other. Here the other has no time, does not have his time. "I see only you, but I no longer see you." "I see only faithfulness, I think only of our faithfulness, but I no longer see you."

Is it not the case that lovers who love each other *definitively*, in and through the definitiveness of definitively, have forgotten each other? This is our first question with respect to the sort of faithfulness that is, so to speak, analytically constituted. Are the lovers faithful to one another in exchanging their vow of faithfulness mutually and immediately? One is tempted at this point to raise the question naively of whether they are *really* faithful to one another. Promising one's faithfulness, praising faithfulness in the presence of the other—is that the guarantee of faithfulness? The proposition faithfulness *is faithfulness* and its translation "I am faithful *as* you are faithful" bear within themselves an interminable question and solicit an infinite suspicion, which we will have to approach by way of another aspect of the same question. What is the *we* of this *we* that has too often been designated as faithfulness *is* faithfulness, and that has been understood as the mutual and reciprocal commitment to faithfulness?

Does not the *we faithful* always collide with its other? Does it not already feel its unfaithfulness? For if it did not go beyond its properly tautological formulation, if it did not advance beyond itself, it would never undergo the experience of its own meaning. That is to say, it would never undergo the experience of its own limits. It would never have an other; no temptation. And who can say that he or she remains faithful, truly, without having first touched, felt—in order to say one's faithfulness—the temptation and limit of unfaithfulness?

Who is unfaithful? What does being unfaithful mean? Is there such a thing as "of course I am unfaithful," or "I know my unfaithfulness"?

Let us attempt to elicit the emergence of something that would constitute a simple truth, something like, for unfaithfulness (if there is such a thing), a "first manifestation." When faithfulness so stated announces its own end, when its tautological affirmation involves its annihilation, a form of unfaithfulness that is just as tautological may arise. It would be an unfaithfulness voicing a lack of love, attesting to, almost confirming, a nonlove, that is, a certain unfaithfulness lodged in a virtual state within the petrified heart of faith, a (purely logical) unfaithful unfaithfulness, the counterpart, so to speak, of a faithful faithfulness. It would be derived from, a consequence of, the latter, with all its own self-justificatory terminology. Its own rights. What we have here is a certain faithfulness to one's unfaithfulness, a faithfulness to the other in the sense in which one might be faithful in confessing one's lack of love in a desire for sincerity, simplicity, and forthrightness. A faithfulness to nonlove, in the absence of love.

But unfaithfulness can also express itself in a declaration of love. As if it were necessary to "experience" it in order for the entire phenomenon of love to start over again, as if it were necessary to spoil everything in order endlessly to begin and begin yet again:

I have always known that we are lost and that from this very initial disaster an infinite distance has opened up

> this catastrophe, right near the beginning, this overturning that I still cannot succeed in thinking was the condition for everything, was it not, ours, our very condition, the condition for everything that was given us or that we destined, promised, gave, loaned—whatever—to each other.[8]

Unfaithfulness and betrayal would not be, in this view, the end of love, but the strongest commitment, the renewal of commitment ad infinitum. It is as if, in order to find the innermost essence of our *we*, it was necessary to destroy it, bring about its downfall, people it with images of our demise. As if the scandal of unfaithfulness were necessary to faithfulness, in the same way that betrayal would be necessary to loyalty, to affirmation, and as crisis would be the source of and need for philosophy. The we would then become present to itself in and by a negation emanating from within itself. The *we* always already present, always already including what it is not, could express itself in and by what shows itself as its negation.

Everything would begin here in the prejudice of a pure faithfulness, by the necessary presupposition of a faithfulness without fault that could stand the test of time, that could test time, that could venture forth to the limits of its unfaithfulness. A faithfulness that could be welcomed and undergone unto the ultimate test of its unfaithfulness, its betrayal, its "rending," to speak like Hegel.

Why this properly Hegelian insistence on this idea of *necessity*? Why the necessary *passage* from faithfulness to unfaithfulness as a sublime return of faithfulness? What we have here is a necessary reuniting of the we with we, of a we that always ends up ultimately affirming itself, in its beginning as in its end. The *we* becomes *other*, enters the stage as that which divides, or *unfaithfuls* itself, so to speak, the better to return to itself, outlive itself, become and come to itself. Unfaithfulness, in this perspective, is then the obligatory passage from faithfulness to a stronger faithfulness, self-assured, enlarged, filled with its faithfulness. One might almost see in this the *becoming* faithful of faithfulness, the coming to faithfulness in its becoming unfaithful, the occasion for the *we* to express itself in its faithful presence. In the same way faithfulness is pursued by the specter of unfaithfulness, the we is haunted by the specter of the non-we. But then how are we to understand an unfaithfulness at the service of faithfulness? How can one remain faithful even to the point of unfaithfulness?

Let us attempt to outline a few of the determinate forms of this "unfaithful faithfulness," or this "faithful unfaithfulness."

1. What if one wounds, tries to wound, the other, the loved one, the better to approach him or her? In the desire (conscious or unconscious) to inhabit that consciousness, to mark it with the imprint and name of the wound as if to say henceforth:

—You will think only of me, you will not forget me, you will not bury me away, henceforth we shall be inseparable, you will have only me, only we, on your mind. I will obsess you. My perfidious and unfaithful face will always be with you, everywhere you go, to elect domicile in your consciousness. It will accompany you permanently like the confession of an extreme and restless faithfulness. It will be your most faithful companion, always reminding you of our fragile and unshakable we. So that you may be forever preoccupied with our parting, that it be your only precious thing, your only memory of us, so that you may keep going over and over it till you break into a fever. The story of our we, I want to inflict it on you as one would inflict a torture.

2. What if one wounds, tries to wound, oneself, one's self that loves, loving in order to give oneself both the suffering of unfaithfulness and the memory of faithfulness? As if to say to oneself henceforth:

—I will carry with me, always and everywhere, the story of my own straying, as if to say to myself, I never should have replaced you, you are irreplaceable. In order already to be able, confronting me, to answer me, to give me the answer in advance, "I will always remember only us." As if the story of our we, I wanted to inflict it on myself, as one inflicts a torture on oneself.

3. What if we wounded, if we wounded our self, our amorous self, in order to accompany it always and everywhere with memories, with suffering, with the wound of a betrayal, our very own tragedy? There would seem to be something like a structurally shared unfaithfulness, something like a chronic unfaithfulness that would organize, give a rhythm to the we. The *we* would live and feed itself, then, from unfaithfulness. It would live and feed itself from a so intimately shared history of betrayal. This gives us the chance and the desire to live our *we* eternally beneath the sign of the catastrophe. It gives us

the chance and the desire for eternity, and to expose ourselves permanently to the apocalyptic danger of the *we*. Our fragility, our precariousness, would thus give us the strength to reactivate our amorous *we* perpetually. What if one destroys any scenario for confession between us, as if to say that between us there will be no home, no stability, no established place, no settling in, no declared love, no presence? What if we swear unfaithfulness to one another with the sole desire of preserving our *we* in memory, in order that the wound of the *we* remain forever open between *us*? As if to say to one another henceforth:

— *When will we be invisible to each other, illegible, incomprehensible, unfaithful, in order at last to be able to see each other, to see each other again and be absolutely faithful to each other?*

Or, in Derrida's words: "I recognize that I love—you—by this: that you leave in me a wound that I do not want to replace."[9]

Unfaithfulness, a certain vocabulary of disaster, may be the most hidden wish of the *we*, its most secret desire.

> I am not well this morning. There will never be any possible consolation, the disaster is ineffaceable. And yet, at this very moment when the ineffaceable appears to me as the self-evident itself, the opposite conviction is just as strong. The entire misfortune, the unlivable suffering that you know always will be capable of dissipating itself at this second, was in sum only due to a bad chance, a stroke of fate, an instant that we are no longer even sure had the slightest consistency, the slightest thickness of life. *Disaster—we have dreamed of it, no?* One day will suffice that . . .[10]

> "Disastrologies"—would be the title, do you like it? I think it suits us well.[11]

As if in order to survive the *we* needed to undergo the suffering of love or suffer the clutches of unfaithfulness, to paraphrase Jabès again. We could at last say everything, say it all to each other, everything about the *we*, catastrophe and luck, our catastrophe *is* our luck. It is in unfaithfulness that the *we* would finally find the privilege of its pain.

Ever undergone, thought, included, and "superseded,"[12] unfaithfulness reveals what is the most unfathomable between *us*, the most *abyssal*. The *we* would thus unveil itself to itself, would understand the absoluteness of its *all*, would find itself more loving than ever. It would be freed, individuated, constituted. A philosopher, in short. Holding in hand the *love phenomenon*, it would pinpoint the meaning and hence the authentic faithfulness of the *we*, the faithfulness that has survived unfaithfulness in appropriating it. Like the philosopher, this new *we* is the one who is not frightened of decrepitude, who explores the depths incessantly, who questions, makes use of what has happened; who acts as the master, the slave, who is the idealist, the realist, who stages the antinomy and its resolution, who proposes *the third way*, remembering everything, faithfulness and unfaithfulness, the ineffable letters, the hidden correspondences. It is in the memory of all these moments that it [i.e., the "we"] finds the remedy and meaning of the *we*. Life, love, the *we*. Faithfulness and unfaithfulness will always return to the all-encompassing *we*. Faithfulness does not have unfaithfulness outside itself, but within itself. It lives off it. Thus, one could almost imagine unfaithfulness as the salvation of the *we*, as one of the paths leading to its salvation.

When will we give ourselves the good fortune of being unfaithful?
To be unfaithful, to be unfaithful to one another; you would almost have *to thank each other* for unfaithfulness.

—Thank you *for having reawakened our* we, *our obsession with purity, our desire for loyalty and faithfulness. Everything that contradicts and confirms us at the same time, my love. Without unfaithfulness, without the "sacrifice" of our* we, *we would never have been able to recognize our faithfulness, never have been able to recognize our* we.

And what if no one has thought this through better than Hegel? The death of the *we*, its catastrophe, as he would have said, is indeed the placeholder of meaning, its *condition*, its very life:

> The life of Spirit is not the life that shrinks from death and keeps itself untouched by devastation, but rather the life that endures it and maintains itself in it. It wins its truth only when, in utter dismemberment, it finds itself. It is this power, not as something positive, which closes its eyes to the negative, as when we say of something that it is nothing or is false, and then, having done with it, turn away and pass on to something else; on the contrary, Spirit is this power only by looking the negative in the face, and tarrying with it. This tarrying with the negative is the magical power that converts it into being. This power is identical with what we earlier called the Subject, which by giving determinateness an existence in its own element supersedes abstract immediacy, i.e., the immediacy which

barely is, and thus is authentic substance: that being or immediacy whose mediation is not outside of it but which is this mediation itself.[13]

It is not til after having suffered the "absolute rending" of unfaithfulness, the supreme sacrifice, that the *we* reaches, according to Hegel, its authentic revelation. A revelation that expresses itself in and by its resurrection and conversion as infinite *love*. A love that faithfully/unfaithfully unifies the *we* in the spiritual unity of a faithfulness *of faithfulness and unfaithfulness*. Thus, lodged at the heart of infinitely faithful love are unfaithfulness and its sublation. The *we* is sublated at the very heart of the *unfaithful we* as the sublated totality of a faithful becoming. *We*, which Hegel also calls *love*. So it is that love contains in and for itself unfaithfulness: the infinite unfaithfulness of love as well as infinitely faithful love. Therefore there is for Hegel no betrayal, no catastrophe; there is only their faithful accomplishment, only the supersession of unfaithfulness in the most faithful love, that is, in the absolute presence of the infinite faithfulness of love.

Thus it is in its absolute faithfulness that the *we* finds the fullness of its infinite life. It finds within itself the co-adherence of all the elements of its *we* as the opening of its presence. Openness of its presence that is always already exposed as the movement of its *belonging* and its *nonbelonging*, its faithfulness and its unfaithfulness bearing the *we* beyond itself toward itself. The whole of the *we* is thus entirely anchored in its own openness, at the heart of its own authentic conjunction as absolute meaning of the *we*; a reciprocal conjunction between the horizon of its meaning and that of its rending, between its faithfulness and its unfaithfulness.

There is here, in sum, only *we*, only an absolute presence of the *we* that has integrated, converted, superseded its own "degradation," an absolute faithfulness of the *we* having entirely assimilated and reappropriated unfaithfulness. To Hegel, this faithful-unfaithful *we* is always already nothing but the reflection of the reappropriating power of Christianity. In what would be one of the possible segments of a *deconstruction of Christian memory* of the faithfulness-unfaithfulness relationship, or yet again, from the point of view of a "Christian deconstruction of Christianity," the *we* has found its originarity in an absolute faithfulness to self, an absolute faithfulness that would name no difference between its faithfulness and its unfaithfulness. The *we* has found the originary presence of its faithfulness, the presence of its own self to itself.

Here let us raise a few questions and leave them in suspense. Can one still pretend to pronounce on the word *faithfulness*, the truth of *faithfulness*, the *faithfulness* of the *we*, after knowledge has revealed the total presence of its meaning? To be more precise: What remains of *faithfulness* when it is thought speculatively and determined absolutely? What remains to be thought about the word *faithfulness* when its very *possibility* would seem to have been exhausted in and by the fullness of its meaning?

Should one then approach the *we* from another perspective? Might there be a *between-us* structured otherwise than the one that is absolutely present to itself, absolutely faithful to itself in and by its unfaithfulness? Another we than the *we* that is anchored in the speculative *movement* of its self-definition and self-reappropriation? In sum, the possibility of thinking a *we* that would live *otherwise than by the infinite dialectic of faithfulness and unfaithfulness*? Dialectic of faithfulness and unfaithfulness—the question of the *between-us* is perhaps not there. Is it not Levinas who taught us to ask these questions? And to conceive of a we (or a faithfulness) otherwise than in the framework of a speculatively determined love? Is it not Levinas who, in a certain way, allowed us to question and question yet again an entire philosophical discourse of Christian inspiration with respect to love? A certain Christic-philosophic-dialectico-speculative "self-evidence" of love? That is a possible reading, at least, of the Levinasian turn in the history of philosophy. To ask the question: Is love, along with each of these modalities (reciprocity, reconciliation, belonging, faithfulness, etc.), so devoid, so always already beyond and on the hither side of every strategy of sovereignty, of power, and of forgetting, so to speak?

To conceive of that other *we* is thus inseparable from the properly Levinasian exploit of "giving Judaism its philosophy" by carrying out a "Jewish deconstruction of Judaism," that is, a putting into question, always and everywhere, these two discourses on love as heterogeneous and as profoundly connected as are Hegelianism and Christianity.

In order to give all its potential to that other *we*, to a *between-us* without us, it would be necessary to overturn the semantics of presence as a reciprocal conjunction between the horizon of meaning and its rending, to "take leave" of the speculative law of the *we*, to "tear oneself free from" the *onto-theo-teleo-logical* order of absolute faithfulness. At which point a series of questions arises. How is one to think a faithfulness that would express itself in a language *other* than a *we* speculatively self-assured? How is one henceforth to proceed in seeking a mode of thought that would not be reducible to a "comprehending" of that which is thought in thinking? How can one pass from one "level" to the other, and how can one relocate the metaphysical "place" of the *we* by opening it up to another source of meaningfulness, one that cannot be thematized, a *between-us* modulated by the expression "one-*for*-the-other"?

In that attempt (to put it too hastily) at a certain form of *deconstruction of Jewish memory*, what would be necessary would be a descent from this level, at which a presence to self of the faithfulness of the *we* is deployed, toward *inspiration*, from which vantage point the *we* would be neither confirmed onto-theologically nor affirmed speculatively. The exploit of that deconstruction would consist in freeing up the passage from the *said* to the *Saying without a said*, from the *"we that is speculatively faithful to itself"* to the *between-us* of the "one-*for*-the-other." A *Saying* that would necessarily come to orient faithfulness otherwise, and that would always be formulated as "here I am," formulating the accusative of the subject and presupposing no nominative. *Saying*, prior to all, is a "vow of faithfulness," testifying to an unappeased faithfulness, to speak like Levinas. *Saying*, a prohibition against closing oneself in on oneself, against taking up a defensive position, would put the subject into question, interrupting it in its "routine of being," commanding it to faithfulness, that is, obliging it without limit, without respite, without any possibility of paying off the debt, toward others:

> Love without Eros. Transcendence is ethical, and the subjectivity that in the final analysis is not the "I think," or the unity of the "transcendental apperception," is, as responsibility for the other, subjection to the other. The I is a passivity more passive than any passivity, because from the outset in the accusative, oneself—which has never been in the nominative—under the accusation of another, although without sin. The hostage for another, the I obeys a commandment before having heard it; it is *faithful* to an engagement it never made, and to a past that was never present.[14]

Alterity thus elects the subject, awakens it to a responsibility that is unique, undeniable, and without any possible avoidance. Even before the subject has time to react, to take the time to exercise its will, to use free will, before all commitment freely assumed, it is already, always and already, *faithfully* committed to responsibility. That election of the self by and for the other is its awakening to an *extreme* and *dis-proportion-ate faithfulness*, that is, immemorially *obliged, indebted*. In other words, the "I" [*le moi*] does not have in itself the possibility of understanding that election to faithfulness. Faithful despite itself, it undergoes that election, being assigned to, placed in, the accusative. The responsibility for the other in which the I is already obsessed or besieged by the neighbor—signifies a faithfulness as infinite as it is anachronistic. Faithfulness would never have come to mind, would not have inspired it if it [faithfulness] had not been commanded to the subject before any command by the other person. The subject would, no doubt, be tempted to explain ontologically that faithfulness come from elsewhere, to submit the faithful *between-us* to the total unveiling of its meaning, but the other occurs first, before any temporal ordering, before any chronologically determined *before*, in announcing its exteriority to the *we*, to knowledge, to meaning. It invalidates this *we*, then opens it up to an otherwise and differently faithful *between-us*. It interrupts the "becoming we of the *we*" in opening up the possibility of a *between-us* in which the one-would-be-faithful-to-the-other through a commitment that it never itself made. For if the other does not announce a meaning, the other is *itself* the announcement. Now, what does it announce? The other announces: *you owe*, before all beginning, before all commandment, an infinite faithfulness to the other.

The I is complicit with faithfulness as it is with the *Good* in a pre-original *passivity*. Thus it is complicit with a faithfulness before having chosen it; it is always already indebted for it. Faithfulness is not rendered explicit in and by the reciprocity of the concept, but in the Abrahamic formulation "Here I am." This faithfulness, a dedication of oneself, is the opening up of the self that expresses an increasing requirement as the requirement of faithfulness is fulfilled.

The I does not unveil its faithfulness in the movement that consists in *testing oneself* in and by one's other, in and by one's mutual recognition with the other, but is awakened to faithfulness *without* an active taking up on its part and solely by the upsurge of the other. Here, the I is affected by the other, always already faithful to the other, more faithful than any faithfulness that it could bestow on itself, or in and by which it may always already have been recognized qua moment. Faithful to an immemorial past which is that of the preoriginal affection by the other.

Now, if we follow closely the path of the *otherwise than being* and its hyperbolic requirement that the I be awakened even *before* the call or command of the other, that is, immemorially faithful to faithfulness, we must believe that this I has no right to unfaithfulness. All we could conceive would be an infinitely devoted subjectivity, constantly loyal, always and everywhere overindebted to faithfulness. It would be as if the subjection of the I to faithfulness were prior to the very command of the other, and thus its hyperbolic faithfulness always already commanded.

That anteriority of faithfulness in relation to the very order of the other means, for Levinas, the goodness of the Good. There is an awakening of the subject to faithfulness beyond the speculatively conjoined couple of faithfulness and unfaithfulness. This would be the awakening of a faithfulness prior to the free-will faithfulness qua faculty possessed by man, prior to all self-possibilizing of faithfulness, prior to the faithfulness constituted in and by unfaithfulness.

Here alterity is never questioned in itself, never called to faithfulness. Alterity is there only to command, to awaken the subject to faithfulness. Thus, addressed by the other, there is no expectation of the other. Faithfulness is always already the lone subject's first and last *word*. It always answers before its own freedom but also already before the other with a *yes* that has been preoriginally determined by an unquestionable faithfulness. There is an eclipse of unfaithfulness in order to affirm solely the awakening of subjectivity in the modality of an *infinite faithfulness* to the other. In the "prehistory" of the I, the subject is hostage from head to toe, more anciently than *ego*. It is infinitely faithful. But this ethical subject—infinitely faithful—is it not also infinitely shut up in a stubborn *silence* with respect to the possibility of questioning, that is, to the possibility, the necessity even, of being unfaithful by way of the question addressed to its own faithfulness? And what if, for Levinas, the asking of a question (to the other or to oneself) were rooted in irresponsibility and at the same time a certain form of unfaithfulness?

Going a step further, in the hyperbolic acquiescence to ethics, in what Levinas calls *holiness*—in this commandment to be faithful before any reflective faithfulness, before any "should-be"—may there not be a more originary re-positioning of the subject even though conceived as a de-position? Might there not be, ultimately, something on the order of a "substantialization" or a "presentification" of faithfulness despite the attempt to snatch it away from these very terms? What strategy may lay hidden in that ordination to the other before any commitment, before any commandment, always already preceding even the possibility of the question? Is there a hidden strategy of the diachrony, the nonfoundation, the noninstitution, the "politics later" as a refusal of all political calculation and as supreme faithfulness? But also, and this is not without connection to those questions, it is even in a sense the raising again of the question that brings us all together here today—namely the question of *Judeities*: Does Judaism necessarily belong to that structure of subjection?

Let us ask a few questions here and leave them in suspense. Can one still pretend to pass judgment on the word *faithfulness*, when it has been "determined"—beyond our "faculty of knowledge" or our "power of understanding"—as a preoriginal acquiescence, immemorially established, when it will only allow to come to mind a faithfulness always already faithful, so to speak? From what place can we still pretend to pass judgment on faithfulness when the latter already commands, according to Levinas, when no question ever comes to trouble the ineffable place of its "determination," or to interrogate the sacrificial modality that orients it?

If, as we have suggested, in each of these two modes of deconstruction, one labeled of Christian memory, the other of Jewish memory, *faithfulness* is named, determined, and in that very process presentified, qua "faithfulness without unfaithfulness" (with definite nuances between those two sorts of discourse), the question we would like to ask, and to which we would like to remain faithful, could be framed as follows: In a manner of thought that envisages no other horizon than that of *faithfulness*—whether it be to pass through unfaithfulness and become strengthened as absolute faithfulness, or whether it be preoriginally indebted faithfulness—how can we still expect, hope for, believe in something like faithfulness? How can one still say his or her faithfulness; or faithfulness *tout court*? A faithfulness worthy of the name—should it not be subordinate, not to a Law that would consist in reaffirming it speculatively or hyperbolically, but to a Law "without" law, that is, empty and radically undetermined, and that a deconstruction faithful to itself would continually submit to the trial of its impossibility? This *place*, if there is such, would be undecidable and forever stretched *between* absolute faithfulness and preoriginally indebted faithfulness; it would forget everything about recognizable versions of faithfulness and unfaithfulness, phenomenalizable in continually recalling both faithfulness and unfaithfulness to their aporetic paradoxality. A faithfulness "not in on it," not in on anything, not in on the *signifyingness* of absolute faithfulness (the move of the perfect reciprocity between faithfulness and unfaithfulness) and outside the move of election to faithfulness (the move of ethics, of worry, of the unrepresentable, untouchable other), but just as much "in on it," in the move of absolute faithfulness and in the move of election to faithfulness. A faithfulness to the impossible decision between these two "moves." Moreover, who can still claim to be armed here with a power of decision? To possess a *logic* of decision? Is it possible to decide between being out of it and being in on it? These two paths are absolutely heterogeneous, as Jacques Derrida says: the one would exclude the other, be absolutely *without* the other. But what conjoins them is "this strange preposition *without*; this strange *without-with* or *with-without*."[15]

As if to say: "Through faithfulness to the secret demand you wanted to preserve, to preserve, me too, and here we are deprived of everything. I am still dreaming of a second holocaust that would not come too late. Know that I am always ready, this is my faithfulness. I am a monster of faithfulness, the most perverse infidel."[16] And to understand: "I" am faithful in the extreme, mad with faithfulness, the most religious and metaphysical of the faithful, the first and the last of the faithful, the most intolerant toward unfaithfulness, disproportionately, terribly faithful; but to give that faithfulness its chance, to give it the chance even of faithfulness, it is necessary "to me" to *upset* it constantly, to disturb it interminably, to turn it away from its goal, its *telos*, to keep on putting it into question, to subject it to the most perverse unfaithfulness . . . my own even.

We have spoken with one and with two voices of this strange relationship between faithfulness and unfaithfulness. Would it be to submit this report, already submitted on its own, to the law of undecidability? Might that undecidability be another word for Jacques Derrida's faithfulness to his *judeity*, to his *judeities*? His way of having his word stand or be maintained worthily? His way of calling judeity to its deepening, to its never being fixed or frozen into one determination, to invite it to an experience of indeterminacy? Would that be his *sending* [envoi] of a post card to . . . but to *whom* precisely? . . . to Israel, to God? His way of chanting . . .

As long as you want to stay, I am here, and even if you depart without turning back. I still do not know to whom, to what I am destining this faithfulness, to a morsel of myself perhaps, to the child I am carrying and whose features I try to make out.

You alone can help me to do so, but at the same time, since the child is to look like you more and more, you hide his features from me, you forbid me to see them, and for as long as I live with you I will understand nothing. The desire to free you from this "resemblance" at last, to see you appear, you, the other, and not only in the way a "negative" is developed. When I have seen you, we will leave each other. When we separate from each other, when I separate, I will see you. I will turn back toward you. But I have never known how to separate. I will learn, and then I will take you into me and there will no longer be any distance between us.[17]

The Shibboleth Effect:
On Reading Paul Celan

HENT DE VRIES

> In an art that is constantly obscuring and revoking itself, every determinate statement counterbalances the general proviso of indeterminateness.
> —Theodor W. Adorno, "Notes on Kafka"[1]

In his inquiries into the quasi-secret origin of the moral law and its relation to literature, that is, to a certain fictionality (an inquiry less of pure practical philosophy or formal pragmatics, in the footsteps of Kant and Habermas, than of "narrative pragmatics," a term that, in his pivotal essay on Kafka's "Before the Law," he borrows from Lyotard's *Just Gaming*),[2] Jacques Derrida addresses several theoretical issues commonly reserved for poetics or "poetology." In his readings of prose texts by Kafka, Joyce (*Ulysse gramophone*), Blanchot (*Parages*), Baudelaire (*Given Time*), and many others, he claims that narrative (the fable or *récit*) functions to encapsulate and reconfigure the singularity and unique temporal structure of both testimony and ethics. This would hold true a fortiori for poetry and especially for the lyric poem. Indeed, the structure of "the poematic," as Derrida will come to call it, comes to be the example par excellence of the literariness and quasi-fictionality of the moral law—of responsibility and ethico-political "acts"—and of the peculiar temporality it entails.

A powerful inquiry into the structure of the poetic singularities of language and the temporalities they receive or express, a structure without which all philosophical discourse and ethical experience would be meaningless, can be found in Derrida's reading of idiomatic language in the work of his onetime colleague at the École Normale Supérieure in Paris, Paul Celan.

Celan had translated Kafka's "Before the Law" into Romanian, and, in a letter of introduction that he carried on his flight from Romania across Hungary to Vienna, his mentor, Alfred Margul-Sperber, claimed that his poetry is "the only lyric counterpart to Kafka's work."[3] Does Derrida's analysis of the parallelism, even the intersection, between Kafka's parable and Kant's moral philosophy hold true for Celan as well?

Here, I will focus on how the singularity—the shibboleth, the date, and, what will turn out to be the same thing, the specter and the ashes—of philosophemes, theologemes, or ethico-political tropes is figured and disfigured in Celan's poetry and poetics in ways that reveal an important aspect of Derrida's own thinking. In what sense, then, does Derrida's reading of these poems, as well as of the poetics that accompanies them—a reading that in itself is the idiomatic recognition of a debt: a "Shibboleth," that is, "for Paul Celan"[4]— explore the elementary structure of obligation, resistance, and engagement as implied (but also obscured) by all philosophical, aesthetic, ethico-political, and religious categories? To what extent can Celan's poetry and poetics be said to exemplify or concretize what Derrida, in his early study on the work of Emmanuel Levinas, has called an "ethics of ethics"?

To begin with, it does so by analyzing the structure of a singular experience of temporality, an experience that, according to Celan, every poem inscribes in itself or, rather, within which every poem is inscribed. This aporetic structure reveals the inner logic of the philosophemes and theologemes in Celan's lyric and poetological work. This structure will also turn out to be the source of the peculiar form and force of these ethico-political figures. More importantly, the specific figuration, configuration, and refiguration of this temporality of poetic experience, which is also that of a radical diachrony, can almost be read as the paradigm of acts of utterance in general:

> What Kant said of time is no less valid for temporal language in Celan: it is the formal condition *a priori* of representation in general. In this way, Celan's poems speak—in a transcendental manner like only those of Hölderlin . . . —of the conditions of their own possibility. They do not name something determinate

but bring the very determining ground of speaking into language: its temporalizing character.[5]

Of course, many earlier texts of Derrida meticulously explore the question of the condition of possibility of absolutely singular meaning: notions of the *parergon*, the trace, the proper name, the address, to name only a few examples, all can be said to exemplify the preoccupation with this singular structure of differences, as well as the process of temporalization and spatialization, the *différance*, that brings them about. But nowhere does the supplementary but no less urgent problem, given this regime of an originary undecidability, of *how decisions are actually made* (in other words, how a difference is made) become clearer than in the inquiry into the shibboleths of Celan's poetry and poetics.

Does Derrida's study of the idiomatic aspects of Celan's poetic language, as well as the ethico-political implications they entail, signal a shift of attention away from a quasi-transcendental question that preoccupied the earlier work, barring a hasty transition from *différance* to singular difference? Does "Shibboleth" mark a *Kehre*, a turning away from the focus on the conditions of possibility (or the *ethicity*) of ethics in favor of an ethics understood in a more limited— and more strict—sense? Is it here that we should start looking to better understand the transition from his more formal grammatological investigations to the task of pragrammatology of which he speaks in *Limited Inc*?

Yet Derrida's reading of Celan also suspends this transition by constantly circling back to what seems to be the preliminary question of any such ethics of difference. That analysis is situated in a thought of the place and the gesture (rather than the act) of the gift, in whose light (or shadow) the contours of such shibboleths become possible. To a certain point, this fundamental problematic seems to supersede the analysis of these poetic singularities. Carefully reconstructing the stages of Derrida's text, I will try to unpack this paradox by confronting it with a powerful, if questionable, counterparadigm: Heidegger's interpretation of the relationship between the date, the *Datum*, and the gift in Hölderlin. I will conclude by briefly discussing the extent to which Heidegger's attempt to understand the date in light of the gift of Being leads to a secondarization of the singularity of the poetic date in Celan's work, thus countering the central moment that Derrida seeks to bring out. Is the poetic date in Heidegger's analysis, rather than being respected in the very ellipsis of its presentation, not in truth abandoned to a virtual eclipse? And if this is so, how does Derrida, while drawing on Heidegger in significant ways, avoid falling into the same pitfalls?

The Key to Poetics

It has become almost a commonplace that Paul Celan's poetry and poetics pose what might be the greatest challenge to the hermeneutic recuperation of meaning. Celan not only rejects the documentary and symbolic aspects of earlier poetry, by fracturing or dislodging syntax and semantics, his lyrics run the risk of exposing "nothing but" literature's unreadability. His texts seem to withdraw from narration and figuration to the point of giving themselves up in a gesture for which appropriate literary, aesthetic, rhetorical, or philosophical criteria are no longer available. Through the extensive use of personal data and conceptual reversals, his figures of speech seem no longer to exemplify any mimetic *mise-en-intrigue* of experience "in" language but rather, if anything, language's *mise-en-abîme*. Philosophemes, theologemes, and citations thus become tropes of a writing that overcomes the simple dichotomy between truth and nontruth, existence and nothingness, leaving us with nothing but a simple—emphatic, enigmatic, and idiomatic—saying. Yet the poetry never lapses into mere aestheticism, nor does it reduce poetic language to a haphazard but self-referential play of signifiers. Even the most extreme utterances in Celan's work make its readers aware of the degree to which a passivity—even a *passion*, to use Derrida's word—engraves itself in language, without condemning it to complete silence.

Accordingly, while Adorno considers Celan to be the most significant "hermetic" representative of contemporary postwar German lyric poetry,[6] he makes clear that in this work the experience of hermeticism (as defined in the epoch of *Kunstreligion* and *Jugendstil*) is turned inside out. This inversion, Adorno suggests, is no longer thinkable in terms of a further *Abdichtung* ("sealing off")[7] of the poem from the sociopolitical and historical world. On the contrary, the inversion is brought about by the contraction of the poetic word, haunted by the traces (the ashes) of a suffering that saps life of its vitality, exceeds the categories of possible experience, and ruins the tropes of its mimetic transfiguration or sublimation. Celan's poems, Adorno concludes:

want to speak of the most extreme horror through silence. Their truth content itself becomes negative. They imitate a language beneath the helpless language of human beings, indeed beneath all organic language: It is that of the dead speaking of stones and stars. The last rudiments of the organic are liquidated; what Benjamin noted in Baudelaire, that his poetry is without aura, comes into its own in Celan's work.[8]

Thus, as the poem "With a Variable Key" ("Mit wechselndem Schlüssel") describes,[9] there are no pre-established criteria or rules that might be of help in decoding this poetry. Both the conditions of the invention of the poetic word and the conditions of its possible interpretation are structurally unstable. This indeterminacy signals a wounding, an incision or circumcision,[10] of the word—and not just of the word but also of the flesh (in Celan's words: the eye, mouth, or ear)—that will always already have preceded any possible, deliberate, or calculated risk resulting from the purportedly conscious process of hermetically ciphering or coding a poem.

MIT WECHSELNDEM SCHLÜSSEL

Mit wechselndem Schlüssel
schliesst du das Haus auf, darin
der Schnee des Verschwiegenen treibt.
Je nach dem Blut, das dir quillt
aus Aug oder Mund oder Ohr,
wechselt dein Schlüssel.

Wechselt dein Schlüssel, wechselt das Wort,
das treiben darf mit den Flocken.
Je nach dem Wind, der dich fortstösst,
ballt um das Wort sich der Schnee.

WITH A VARIABLE KEY

With a variable key
you unlock the house in which
drifts the snow of that left unspoken.
Always what key you choose
depends on the blood that spurts
from your eye or your mouth or your ear.

You vary the key, you vary the word
that is free to drift with the flakes.
What snowball will form round the word
depends on the wind that rebuffs you.[11]

Poetic language, then, is neither the fluvial speech that Heidegger ascribes to Hölderlin—a saying that streams directly from the essence of language (the House, that is, of Being)—nor is it the hermetic absence of any saying or said. On the contrary, the "snow of that left unspoken" and the "flakes" in which the poetic word finds its element are characterized by a fractional crystallization of the sayable and the ineffable, of sense and nonsense. It is almost as if Celan inverts and displaces the poetological remarks with which Heidegger opens his *Elucidations of Hölderlin's Poetry*. Recalling and interpreting an image of the later Hölderlin, Heidegger writes: "Amid the noise of 'unpoetic languages' . . . , the poems are like a bell that hangs in the open air and is already becoming out of tune through a light snowfall that is covering it. . . . Perhaps every elucidation of these poems is like a snowfall on the bell."[12]

Celan's poem claims something different: in purity or absoluteness, far from the noise of inauthentic *Gerede* ("chatter"), the poem would have no meaning or signifyingness whatsoever. This does not mean that we could speak in general terms about the poem's meaningfulness. What we should be able to recognize (and pronounce) in a given situation is the poem's shibboleth, its *Schlüsselwort*, its *date*, a "cut or incision that the poem bears in its body like a memory, sometimes several memories in one, the mark of a provenance, of a place and of a time. To speak of an incision or cut is to say that the poem is first cut into there [*s'y entame*]: it begins in the wounding of its date [*commence par se blesser à sa date*]."[13]

Since the hermeneutic key must vary for the poem—the bell, to use Heidegger's image—to be able to resonate, any thematic reading that attempts to single out a particular imagery, metaphorics, or semantics, or any interpretation that seeks to address some general, existential, or ontological characteristics of this lyric poetry is bound to fail. This "information" precedes neither the poetic utterance nor its interpretation.[14] The poem does not conceal any determinable secret or, in Derrida's words, "a semantic content waiting behind the door for the one who holds a key."[15] What Adorno writes in his notes on Kafka, an author Celan revered, can be applied to Celan as well: "It is a parabolic system the key to which has been stolen; yet any effort to make this fact itself the key is bound to go astray."[16]

In the same vein, Derrida will note in his analysis of Celan's poem "Shibboleth" that no historicism, psychologism, sociologism, or empiricism can ever fully determine the place from which poetic singularities—which in and of themselves are insignificant, virtually nothing—are suddenly (and always provisionally) given a certain meaningfulness by an ambivalent stroke of luck and terror. In this poem, Celan commemorates the defeat of the Ephraimites by the army of Jephtah (the men of Gilead) as related in Judges and recalls the measure taken to prevent them from crossing the River Jordan and thus saving their lives: "When any Ephraimite who had escaped wished to cross, the men of Gilead would ask, 'Are you an Ephraimite?' and if he said 'No,' they would retort, 'Say "Shibboleth."' He would say 'Sibboleth,' and because he could not pronounce the word properly, they seized him and killed him."[17]

The commemoration of this biblical scene is not monumentalized or set aside in an archive. In Celan's poem, it *comes back to life* in the evocation of the Spanish Civil War, where the slogan of the republican guards, *no pasarán*, served as a similar sign of alliance and exclusion, thereby repeating the diacritical function of the shibboleth. The repetition demonstrates that this word is more than a figure whose origin and meaning could be determined historically, geographically, or even politically:

> A *shibboleth*, the word *shibboleth*, if it is one, names, in the broadest extension of its generality or its usage, every insignificant, arbitrary mark, for example, the phonemic difference between *shi* and *si* when that difference becomes discriminative, decisive, and divisive [or cutting, *coupante*]. The difference has no meaning in and of itself, but it becomes what one must know how to recognize and above all to mark if one is to make the *step* [*faire le pas*], to step across the border of a place or the threshold of a poem, to see oneself granted the right of asylum or the legitimate habitation of a language. So as no longer to be outside the law.[18]

The recognition (and pronunciation) of the shibboleth not only gives or refuses access to a linguistically defined community, it also always already presupposes such participation. This ability (or inability) to utter the vital key word has nothing to do with pre-established, that is, biological or ontological, properties or categories. On the contrary, it is the capacity to make a difference, which is less a deconstructable *vouloir dire* (wanting to say) than a *pouvoir dire* (being able, free, or empowered to say) that, in a sense, suspends or interrupts the ultimate undecidability of linguistic meaning and distinguishes "the strange from the strange." As Derrida explains: "The meaning of the word [*shibboleth*] was less important than the way in which it was pronounced. The relation to the meaning or to the thing was suspended, neutralized, bracketed: the opposite, one might say, of a phenomenological *epokhē*, which preserves, above all, the meaning [*le sens*]."[19]

This gesture, this attempt to find the right tone, so to speak, resonates within a given cultural frame without being completely reducible to the coordinates, that is, the topography and topology, of that space. This essential discrepancy makes it impossible to identify the gesture with a performative speech act as it is commonly defined, namely, as an utterance that is thinkable (or successful) only in terms of certain conventions and does not as such mark or inaugurate our adherence (or opposition) to them. In sum, the singularity of the shibboleth (or the date) opens up (*donne lieu à*) the space of calculability without itself being calculable in any possible economy: "This is the gift of the poem, and of the date, their condition made up of distress and hope, the chance and the turn, the tone and the *Wechsel der Töne*."[20]

Taken in isolation, the shibboleth, although a terrifying discriminative sign that separates friend and foe, life and death, is insignificant, nothing more than an ever-present potential for confusion in language. But as it operates within war and partisanship, this linguistic differentiality, in itself meaningless, can be seen as the beginning of all meaningfulness, "insignificant difference as the condition of meaning [*sens*]."[21] This explains why in a given situation the diacritical value of a shibboleth may turn upside down; why, in its circulation, it can be distorted as a sign of discriminatory exclusion instead of functioning as the sign of solidarity and an emancipatory alliance; why, finally, it can become devalued or trivial. There is always an element of tragedy in this derailment of the tone, to the extent that the shift exceeds the intentions, the decisions, and even the political skills of the individuals and the collectives involved. In all the events to which Celan refers, the shibboleth, the *no pasarán*, is pronounced or exclaimed in vain. Small wonder that the fourth stanza of the poem "Shibboleth" honors a less triumphant flag and orders:

Setz deine Fahne auf Halbmast,
Erinnrung.
Auf Halbmast
für heute und immer.

Set your flag at half-mast,
memory.

> At half-mast
> today and forever.²²

It is in this tragic ambiguity, then, that the shibboleth "exemplifies" a "general structure" (terms that are to be used with great caution) discernible in every idiom that incises itself in (or cuts through) language. Insofar as this aspect of poetic writing forms the paradigm of performative utterance in general, it characterizes the nature of every possible philosopheme, theologeme, or ethico-political imperative. Like the poem, like any shibboleth, these examples signal the ineradicable duplicity of any possible opening or closure.

It is no accident, then, that in his "Letter to Hans Bender" Celan identifies the singularity of the poem with "nothing but" a gesture, more precisely, with a handshake. Moreover, the performative rather than constative language of poetry, that is, its communication of communication as such rather than any information contained by this communication, is likened to a gift to those who are attentive. The speech on the occasion of receiving the Georg Büchner Prize in 1960, entitled "The Meridian," further develops this moment by emphasizing that a certain *Aufmerksamkeit*, an attentiveness and concentration, a vigilance and wakefulness (and not a thematic content) defines the formal characteristics of the commemoration, mourning, or blessing performed by the poetic "subject." Celan writes: "This language, notwithstanding its inalienable complexity of expression, is concerned with precision. It does not transfigure or render 'poetical'; it names, it posits, it tries to measure the area of the given and the possible."²³

This almost geometric precision of a "prosaic" (rather than aesthetic or purely indeterminate) meaning is never "simply given." "What" it gives, if anything, it gives only to those who are attentive enough to perceive.²⁴ Celan continues: "True, this is never the working of language itself, language as such, but always of an 'I' who speaks from the particular angle of reflection which is his existence and who is concerned with outlines and orientation."²⁵

But if the poetic gesture of writing, speaking, reading, hearing, or perceiving is an absolutely singular gesture, how could we ever hope to isolate and determine the relative weight of the philosophemes, theologemes, and ethico-political figures in Celan's lyric poetry? How could we ever succeed in *measuring* the precise displacement that their purported original meaning has undergone? And what, finally, would it mean when Celan writes in the speech on the occasion of receiving the literature prize of the city of Bremen: "the poem is not timeless. Certainly, it lays a claim to infinity, it seeks, through time, to reach through all the time, through time all the time, not above and beyond it."²⁶

At this point we must take up the paradoxical or, rather, aporetic structure of the date, its *Uhrzeigersinn*: the intricate relationship of its uniqueness *and* iterability. While the date is haunted—and haunts itself in its very repetition as other, as the other of itself that it itself "is"—it is also *in anticipation of* and *projected toward* the future to come as if it were a "dress rehearsal" (*répétition générale*).²⁷ Indeed, Derrida writes, the date has the structure of a "future anterior,"²⁸ one whose futurity parts ways with the ontological primacy of the future and the coming about, the *Zukunft* and *Ankunft*, in Heidegger, and whose modality, if we can still use this term, also eludes the Bergsonian distinction between the *quantitative* mode of succession of separate spatiotemporal moments that characterizes homogeneous time, or *temps*, and the *qualitative* succession that singles out the multiple unity, the *unité multiple*, or the concrete real duration, *durée réelle*.²⁹ The spectral ideality toward which the date is already stretched out, by which it is uncannily divided in and against itself as if by its own double, should not be misunderstood as an ontological possibility, that is to say, as a potentiality, as Heidegger claims. It signals itself, if at all, otherwise than being and otherwise than this otherwise than being, to use a terminology that he borrows from the later Levinas. And if its repetition or *revenance* is above all experienced as a living on of a certain pastness, then this *survivance*, to cite another Bergsonian concept, escapes the opposition between physicalism and psychologism (or reflected intuitionism) on which it hinges in Bergson.

Diachrony, *Contretemps*, Unzeit

In large measure, Derrida's "Shibboleth" can be read as an inquiry into the politics no less than the poetics (or, for that matter, the rhetoric) of temporality. This analysis should be sharply distinguished from the phenomenology of originary temporality (in contradistinction to vulgar time) that Heidegger proposes in the second division of *Being and Time*, and that Derrida had been attempting to problematize since "*Ousia* and *Grammē*."³⁰ Whereas that text seeks to deconstruct Heidegger's destruction of the metaphysical concept of time by holding up a mirror, "Shibboleth" politicizes this previous exchange. This rearticulation is also a renegotiation of the borderlines between the ontological and the theological, which Heidegger had vainly claimed to protect. Consider the following formulation of the aporia that governs Derrida's analysis: "How can one date what does not repeat if dating [*la datation*] also calls for some form of return, if it recalls in the readability of a repetition? But how can one date anything other than that which never repeats itself?"[31] All modalities of the date (the clock, the calendar, and even the toponomy) obey the same paradoxical structure. They all hint at a temporality that is neither an indivisible presence or now, nor a moment of retrospective retention or anticipatory protention, nor their total annihilation. Every date "presents," that is, it marks a time that circumvents or cuts across these apparent extremes of appropriation, projection, and oblivion.

The date—but we could also speak here of the signature of the poet or the poem (as well as of the reader and the reading, for that matter) in short, of any mark—would be nothing if it were not an absolutely singular "event." At the same time, the date, in its very particularity, has a far-ranging general (and, perhaps, universal) implication, intent, or purport. It is something "ab-solute," in the etymological sense of the word: loosened from every determinable context. Celan evokes this paradox in "The Meridian" by exclaiming: "But the poem speaks! It is mindful of its dates, but it speaks. True, it speaks only on its own, its very own behalf. But . . . the poem has always hoped, for this very reason, to speak also . . . *on behalf of the other*, who knows, perhaps of an *altogether other*."[32] The poem speaks, although, strictly speaking, it does not have a referent. It addresses a vacancy, an otherness, an empty transcendence, as it were, that still has to be set free and that is nevertheless always already turned toward, perhaps in expectation of, the poem.

In the very errancy of its destination, even while it appeals to nobody (who exists) or to nothing (determinate)—that is, to *Niemand* and *Nichts*,[33] designations that recall the tradition of mysticism and negative theology from the Kabbalah through Meister Eckehart and, perhaps, even Heidegger[34]—the address still somehow, somewhere, sometimes *takes place*. This gesture "is" not nothing, it "is" not an effect of an abstract negation or denegation, nor does it signal a purely nihilistic act. As Martine Broda comments: "One should not confuse this provocative gesture, which concerns 'no one' [*niemand*] . . . with an absence of address [*Nicht-Anrede*]. 'No one' introduces a dissymmetry into the dialogical relationship, through which it is problematized but not annulled." Yet this transcendence pushes the dialogism to—perhaps beyond—its limits: "It represents the condition for what

Celan names 'encounter' [*Begegnung*]. But is an encounter that presupposes such an absolute dissymmetry of positions still a dialogue?"[35]

In fact, the poem *cannot not speak*, cannot *avoid* speaking. The "destinerrance" or "clandestination" of poetic meaning described above is the very condition of the possibility of its signification, of its (poetic) "signifyingness." Derrida's analysis in "Shibboleth" thus echoes the theme of prayer discussed in more detail in his Jerusalem address on negative theology, "How to Avoid Speaking": "To address no one is not exactly not to address any one. To speak to no one, *risking*, each time, singularly, that there might be no one to bless, no one who can bless — is this not the only chance for blessing? for an act of faith? What would a blessing be that was sure of itself? A judgment, a certitude, a dogma."[36]

To return to my original question, how does the structure of a date — or, provided such a thing is possible, of dates in general — reveal the modality of the ethico-philosophical aspects of Celan's poetry, of the literary criticism devoted to his work, and of the political engagement it might inspire, provoke, or problematize? The answer can be found in the way in which singular inscription and universal import *take place* together or presuppose one other. The date is not an indivisible *hic et nunc*, an atomic point in time and space. From its very inception, the date will always already have broken the silence of a pure singularity. How can this occur?

The paradox of this mutual implication of singularity and universality cannot, Derrida maintains, be mastered by a dialectics that would reconstruct — like Hegel's *Phenomenology of Spirit*, with its analysis of sense certainty, the "this," and meaning — the movement in which the punctual and deictic sensation (or, in the text under consideration, the syntactic, semantic material of tropes) is negated and sublated in a knowable, conceptual (or readable) generality or experience.[37]

If we follow this analysis, it becomes difficult if not impossible to insist on answering or even asking the question "What is a date?" — not only because no univocal response seems possible but also because any such questioning presupposes what is in question. In its very generality, the formal structure of this inquiry is (has) in itself (become) *dated*: "the question 'What is . . . ?' has a history, a provenance; it is signed, engaged, commanded by a place, a time, a language or a network of languages, in other words, by a date in relation to whose essence this question has only a limited power, a finite claim, its very pertinence contestable."³⁸ If we still acknowledge its persistent legitimacy (as we must, for philosophy and the history of thought would be nothing without it), this insufficiency should teach us something about the confines of philosophical discourse as such. And it is this insight that forces Derrida to place the "performative modality" of poetic singularity rather than its possible denotative "content" at the center of his argument. This performative modality of the dates of the poem—itself a singular constellation of singularities—is described as (and in) a gesture, as (and in) an address and, again, a *gift* (and, as *Given Time* reminds us, "*There were there is gift, there is time*"³⁹): "The gift or the *envoi* will carry us beyond the question given in the form 'What is?' A date is not, since it withdraws in order to appear . . . perhaps there is (*es gibt*) something of the date—even if the date does not exist."⁴⁰

Thus, Derrida does not propose a fundamental or even quasi-ontological exposition of this gift of the poem. Nor does he reduce the date to an aesthetic (or, for that matter, meta-, that is to say, pre- or beyond ethical) aspect of poetry. "Shibboleth," like its subject, Celan's poetry and poetic writing, cuts across these disciplinary distinctions. The very premises of its analysis forever complicate our attempts to *single out* the distinct systematic, that is, philosophical or ethico-political implications of this or any text, whether lyric or narrative. Seen in this light, the (literary) text does not simply illustrate or exemplify a preexisting systematic thought constituted prior to and without the help of rhetorical tropes and figures. Nor, inversely, can the systematic content of a text be reduced to the disseminative effects of these poetic aspects of thought, which, in turn, do not exist *as such*. The absolute poem, in all its purity, is impossible. With its figures, images, dates, and address, the poem has always already transgressed a limit. From the very moment of its inception, poetic singularity cuts through the opposition of what is commonly considered to be either essential or empirical, either necessary or contingent, sacred or profane. As a result, the distinction between philosophy (ethics, aesthetics, even theology or mysticism) and poetics is blurred, but not completely erased. The experience of this originary complication, productive of boundaries, limits, and delimitations, is, contrary to what most "separatists" claim, the experience of philosophy itself. Just as we cannot hope to dissociate Celan's theoretical, systematic, and poetological remarks concerning the theme of the date from his poetic practice of implementing dates, we cannot separate philosophy from its singular spatiotemporal inscription.

Drawing attention to an "old poem from the Scandinavian Edda" that serves as an epigraph at the opening of Marcel Mauss's *The Gift*, Derrida writes, in *Given Time*: "Why must one begin with a poem when one speaks of the gift? And why does the gift always appear to be the *gift of the poem*, the *don du poème*, as Mallarmé says?"[41] The co-implication of the gift and the poem, of the one as the other, is no accident, but is based on a structural necessity according to which the gift "will be linked to the—internal—necessity of a certain narrative [*récit*] or of a certain poetics of narrative.... The thing as given thing, the given of the gift arrives, if it arrives, only in narrative. And in a poematic simulacrum of narrative."[42] This is why *Given Time* takes its point of departure in the reading of a narration—Baudelaire's "Counterfeit Money"—in order to render the structure of the gift, of the giving of time, visible, intelligible, operative. The gift, Derrida insists, "is" always the gift of a writing, whether a poem or a narrative. This is to suggest not that these texts are auxiliary to the gift or its "external archive" but rather that they are "'something' that is tied to the very act of the gift, *act* in the sense both of the archive and the performative operation [*la mise en oeuvre performative*]."[43]

In a reply to a questionnaire whose subject was "The Problem of the Bilingual," Celan remarks: "Poetry is by necessity a unique instance of language [*Dichtung—das ist das schicksalhaft Einmalige der Sprache*]."[44] But the poem has always already transgressed the confines of its own idiomatic language. Insofar as it hinges on an iterable meaning—and a date, we found, is not only singular but also repeatable in its reappearance, that is, not *sensu stricto* but as (its own) specter—the poem itself can always be recognized as a philosopheme, theologeme, or ethico-political topos. Its universal "intent," its status as a commemoration of a singular event that is addressed, open, and vulnerable to everybody and everything, allows us to speak of this philosophical (as well as theologico- and ethico-political) relevance or supplementary effect. Moreover, it is in this paradoxical universality of what gives itself as something unique, as something ab-solute, that the work of hermeneutics—of reading poetry and the poematic—can begin to take hold.

Insofar as we read the poem as, for example, a philosopheme, we do not simply abstract or infer from concrete "prephilosophical" experiences. On the contrary, the trace of the poetic word (the *Wortspur*)—which in spite of, or thanks to, the incision or circumcision of language can be a "letter in a bottle" (*Flaschenpost*) and is "en route" (*unterwegs*)—is a wound to be read (*Wundgelesenes*) and "wounded by reality" (*wirklichkeitswund*).⁴⁵ Only in this wound, scar, petrified tear, or crypt—in the words of the poem "À la pointe acérée," in "Unwritten things, hardened / into language [*Ungeschriebenes, zu / Sprache verhärtet*]"⁴⁶—does the originary passivity or passion of all poetic utterance betray itself, opening up an image of the other—an Otherness and a wholly Other that "lay bare / a sky [*legt / einen Himmel frei*]" or, as "The Meridian" puts it, an abyss (*Abgrund*).⁴⁷ Only the incision or circumcision of the word (compare the injunction "circumscribe the word [*beschneide das Wort*]")⁴⁸ could provoke the *Atemwende*, the "turning of breath," announced in "The Meridian."

Insofar as the singularity of the literary oeuvre is defined by its status as an untranslatable idiom, that is, by the fact that it is something more and other than a parasitical instance of rigorous argumentation, there can be no such thing as a systematic, general—that is, philosophical or ethico-political—implication, relevance, or effect of literature. The absolute poem is never given as such, in its purity. Moreover, it would not be able to give (anything). The idiosyncratic, hermetic poem, "the hundred- / tongued pseudo- / poem [*das hundert- / züngige Mein- / gedicht*]," if it were possible at all, would be nothing other than "the noem [*das Genicht*]": a virtual nothingness, nothing in the order of what exists, nothing that *is*.⁴⁹

Only after being made transparent through the language of the other, only after being transformed into a petrified gesture, a "crystal of breath" (*Atemkristall*), would the poem be able to reflect, or to give, an unmistakable, "irreversible witness" (*unumstössliches Zeugnis*), or testimony.⁵⁰ This testimony, Derrida reminds us, is at once inexhaustible, structurally incomplete, and nontotalizable. Perhaps this is because there seems to be no "absolute witness" outside or beyond the poematic address who could provide us with the key, all the keys, to its interpretation.⁵¹ Which is not to deny that if Celan writes: "No one / bears witness for the / witness [*Niemand / zeugt für den / Zeugen*],"⁵² this no one (*Niemand, Nul*) does not stand for the absence of just anybody (as nobody), but evokes a witness that is absolute in the strict sense of the word. In this infinite distance and retreat from an infinity misunderstood in terms of presence, omnipresence, omniscience, omnipotence, and simplicity, Celan locates the unconditioned condition of testimony no less than its impossibility. In all the ambiguity of this formulation: no one (*Niemand*, that is) makes this testimony possible. That's all there is to say: "The poem speaks, even if none of its references is intelligible, none apart from the Other, the one to whom the poem addresses itself and to whom it speaks in saying that it speaks to it. Even if it does not reach [or touch, *atteint*] the Other, at least it calls to it. Address takes place."[53] It is this taking place that encrypts, although not one particular secret, nor a symbolism describable in terms of a given rhetorical tradition, "be it of a religious kind" *alone*.[54]

What thus appears to make any philosophical interpretation of a literary text possible—the paradoxical structure of its poetic, idiomatic, meaning, which in its very idiosyncrasy addresses nothing, nobody, *and* everything, anybody—also forms a barrier to any attempt to formalize the poetic "performance." There is no method—no path we could follow—that might bring us closer to this enigma of poetic meaning: like so much else, poetry burns all bridges behind us; "La poésie, elle aussi, brûle nos étapes."[55]

This circumstance does not necessarily render the formal analyses of a philosophical hermeneutics and poetics obsolete. Instead, it makes the interpreter aware of the forgotten common "ground," "origin," or condition of possibility of these different disciplines, which both stand and fall with the attempt to thematize an idiomatic language of dates, places, situations, and proper names they cannot master, control, or reconstruct meta-linguistically, meta-historically, transcendentally. In that sense philosophy, hermeneutics, and poetics begin with the unknown, or, more precisely, with the unknowable. What they contribute to our knowledge and experience begins with a forgetfulness, although not, as Heidegger would have it, a forgetfulness of a neutral dimension or horizon of Being obfuscated by a reified thought preoccupied with beings. What is forgotten is a "concrete" idiom that in and of itself is always already sinking into oblivion. The conceptual violence of forgetting that initiates philosophy and all other systematization (which is never unrelated to violence in an empirical sense) is not simply, or brutally, imposed on a remembrance that would characterize the language or silence of poetry. Like philosophy and formal poetics, literature is affected *from within* by a forgetting that is not merely accidental. This forgetting belongs to the structure of what it forgets and thus can be said to be constitutive of the very memory of dates. In becoming a readable, commemorable—as it were, remarkable—mark, the date cannot but emancipate itself from the stigma of the singularity that it seeks to commemorate. *It outlasts what it recalls only by becoming a certain ideality.* And this fidelity through betrayal is not something that takes place *a posteriori* (as if it could also not have taken place): "Annulment is at work everywhere a date inscribes its *here* and *now* within iterability.... Of a date *itself* nothing remains, nothing of what it dates, nothing of what is dated by it. No one remains—*a priori*. This 'nothing' or 'no one' does not befall the date after the fact, like a loss—of something or someone—nor is it an abstract negativity."[56]

The annulment in question is evoked, by Celan no less than by Derrida, in violent figures: "destruction by fire," "cremation," "incineration," "consummation," leaving nothing but "ashes," "without being"—and thus "almost nothing"—in other words, the "remnance" or *restance* of the "tub of Being, the *Seinstrog*."[57] More or less nothing, more and less than nothing, the ashes would be the point of departure from the poem of which the date speaks. Whence the relation of the "burning up" of the date to the topic of the all-burning, the *brûle-tout*. While it casts its shadow throughout "Shibboleth," Derrida only briefly indicates it explicitly: "there is certainly today the date of that holocaust we know, the hell of our memory; but there is a holocaust for every date, and somewhere in the world at every hour. Every hour counts its holocaust.'"[58] Given with every date is already the "threat of an absolute crypt," of "amnesia without remainder," and so on.[59] Indeed, these annihilations are nothing but ontological possibilities of the date, since they continue to haunt it in its very genesis and structure. In fact, Derrida seems to suggest that there is no iteration of the date without a certain memory of hell or, in this century, without the "hell of memory." While unique, while "being" a "cipher of singularity," the date would be nothing without the risk of the worst and without the "holocaustic generality of return and . . . the readability of the concept."[60] Like the absolute poem, the absolute date is impossible. Everything here hinges on what Derrida calls a "*writing of Nothing*," the performance, if one can still say so, of an "operation on Nothing."[61] A parenthetical remark, indeed, mention of the "necessity of an immense parenthesis," indicates that this *passage by way of Nothing* conjures up an inevitable confrontation with Heidegger, with "the question of Nothing and the meaning of being in Celan, of a truth of being that *passes* through the *experience* of Nothing, for the question . . . left unanswered at the time or date of Todtnauberg."[62]

Not only the origin of the date, then, but also its future commemoration will always be divided and threatened. After all, a single date may do more than recall several separate events (the more elusive the date, the more numerous the events it commemorates). In the absence of a witness with which it will inevitably be confronted, the date will also signal a deserted place or no man's land: that is, become a no one's and nothing's date, a "Nevermansday,"⁶³ a *jour de personne* or *Datum des Nimmermenschtages*, as the poem "Huhediblu" has it.

In consequence, the date can only come to life time and again as the ghostly reappearance of what it once "was." If this possibility were not constitutive of every date, its commemoration would hardly be an "act" (or "passion") of remembrance but, on the contrary, the programmed, mechanical repetition of coded information that is somehow, somewhere, stored in a *database*. In assigning an ab-solute singularity, dates must—at the same time and with the same gesture—annul this very singularity. Every date entails an idiom that summons thought as well as commemoration and blessing. In so doing, the date points beyond itself and effaces itself. The date relates to an event or a sequence of events that can be distinguished from the particular moment of its inscription and subscription. In this partition, which, as before, is not merely external or accidental, the poetic date reveals from its very inception a metonymic structure. Yet this referral (to avoid the word *reference*) has little in common with any "thetic relation to meaning or referent,"⁶⁴ or with any symbolic representation or metaphoric substitution, forms that are always in danger of postulating a past (or future) identity of signifier and signified and hence suggest an illusory sameness of language and its other. On the contrary, the referral marks a movement in which the poetic date loses itself, touches upon *allegory*, that is, upon a decentered, centrifugal, narrative sequence ("Count and recount, the clock / even that, runs down [*Zähl und erzähl, die Uhr, / auch diese, läuft ab*]"⁶⁵). Insofar as this particular movement of poetic figures of speech is exemplary of the displacement of philosophical and aesthetic figures in general, it can be said that "Philosophy finds itself, *finds itself again* in the vicinity [*dans les parages*] of poetics, indeed, of literature. It finds itself again there, for the indecision of this limit is perhaps what is most thought provoking."⁶⁶

What has been argued with respect to philosophemes also applies to theologemes or all ethico-religious tropes. They are not figures of thought borrowed from a pre-existing constellation of meaning, but spectral images of a fictional or fabulous origin. As they are invented by the poem and directed against the canon, they reinvent tradition in an antinomical turn or return that is neither rejection nor simple repetition. To define Derrida's contemplations on the date as something like a contemporary "midrash" on Celan's text (as has been suggested by the editors of an earlier, English version of "Shibboleth"[67]) is therefore trivial, so long as one does not analyze this peculiar modality of belonging and denial, interpretive history (or "effective history," *Wirkungsgeschichte*) and partition, in short: the *partage* of tradition. Like the poetic date, all the philosophemes, theologemes, and ethico-political tropes that are addressed to us do not simply lose themselves in the very process of affirmation and negation or recontextualization and reinscription to which we subject them. More importantly, they were always already lost, marked, incised. There is no confession but circumfession.[68] And it "is" the circumcision of the word, while dated or itself a date, that does not take place *in* or *as* history. On the contrary (if there is contradiction), this circumcision "opens history" and everything that comes with it.[69]

Immediately before entering into the discussion of circumcision in part 7 of "Shibboleth," Derrida raises the issue of mourning:

> Spectral errancy of words. This revenance does not befall words by accident, following a death that would come to some or spare others. *All* words, from their very first emergence, partake of revenance. They will always have been phantoms. . . . One cannot say that we know this *because* we experience death and mourning. That experience comes to us from our relation to this revenance of the mark, then of language, then of the word, then of the name. What is called poetry or literature, art itself . . . in other words, a certain experience of language, of the mark, or of the trait *as such*—is perhaps only an intense familiarity with the ineluctable originarity of the specter. One can, naturally, translate it into the ineluctable loss of the origin.[70]

The spectrality of dates of which the poem—and not only the poem—speaks thus signals the experience of mourning, the impossibility of a single attribution of the origin, of loss, as well as the impossibility of a return. This, Derrida suggests, can be read from the very structure of the date, its different modalities, its systems of notation, its spatiotemporal plottings, and its toponomy, in Celan's poems and elsewhere:

> These coded marks all share a common resource, but also a dramatic, fatal, and fatally equivocal power. Assigning or consigning absolute singularity, they must mark themselves off simultaneously, *at the same time*, and from themselves, by the

possibility of commemoration. Indeed, they mark only insofar as their readability announces the possibility of a return. Not the absolute return of precisely what cannot come again: a birth or a circumcision takes place but once, nothing could be more self-evident. But rather the spectral revenance of that which, as a unique event in the world, will never come again. A date is a specter. But this revenance of impossible return is marked *in* the date.[71]

"Jewish is not Jewish": The Parallel Structure of Dates and Judeities

In reading Celan's prose piece "Conversation in the Mountains," Derrida underscores the resonances of the phrase "and July is not July."[72] This dialogue on the nature of being Jewish, on the relation between nature and the Jew (whose proper name is, as it is said, "unpronounceable") argues that what is proper to a Jew is to have no proper property or essence: "Jewish is not Jewish."[73] The affirmation of Judaism in Celan's (and Derrida's) texts thus seems to obey at least the formal scheme that can be discovered in the date.[74] It reveals an engagement that is neither the awareness nor acceptance of a fact of life, nor a matter of fact, nor, conversely, an arbitrary decision, but rather a singular responsibility for a singular—"unchosen"[75]—destination that has always already preceded the "I" who says and reiterates "yes" (or "yes, yes"). As in "Circumfession," where Derrida introduces the figure of the last and the least of the Jews, the last and the least of the eschatologists, "Shibboleth" touches upon a similar logic of identity, singularity, and universality: "I am Jewish in saying: the Jew is the other who has no essence, who has nothing of his own or whose own essence is to have none. Whence, *at the same time*, both the alleged universality of the Jewish witness ('All poets are Jews,' says Marina Tsvetaeva, cited in the epigraph to 'Und mit dem Buch aus Tarussa') *and* the incommunicable secret of the Judaic idiom."[76]

And yet, the intricate relationship between the date, testimony, and tradition (here, Judaism) is more complex still, for it is in this context that a paradox similar to the one to be witnessed in the structure of confession (in Augustine and others) reappears. The aporia of the date, its being at once unique, singular, or idiosyncratic, *and* repeatable or iterable, leaves its trace in the very structure of interpretation and citation, affirmation and attestation that the poem—as the example par excellence of any singular marker—calls forth. Again, this seems nowhere clearer than in Celan's poetry, as has been aptly demonstrated by the uncertainties with which it confronted its readers from the outset (I am thinking in particular of Peter Szondi's discussion of "Eden" in his *Celan Studies*).[77] Derrida alludes to this difficulty in a passage that, I think, sheds light on the question of traditionality, of the simultaneous persistence and obsolescence of figures of thought, speech, and modes of experience:

> concerning the circumstances in which the poem was written or, better, concerning those which it names, ciphers, disguises, or dates in its own body, concerning whose secrets it partakes, witnessing is *at once* indispensable, *essential* to the reading of the poem, to the partaking that it becomes in its turn, and, finally, *supplementary, nonessential*, merely the guarantee of an excess of intelligibilty, which the poem can also forgo. *At once* essential and inessential.[78]

Similarly, the structure of all prayer, supplication, and blessing (or of any other gesture of faith) reveals itself only in the very elusiveness of the poetic utterance, in the invocation of rest "without being" that calls for music, incantation, and that remains to be sung (in Celan's words: a "singable remainder," *singbarer Rest*). Moreover, in echoing Celan's association of "When, whenwhen, / manywhens, yes mania — [*Wann, wannwann, / Wahnwann, ja Wahn*]" (in the poem "Huhediblu"), Derrida notes:

> A date is mad, that is the truth.
> And we are mad for dates.
> For the ashes that dates are. Celan knew one may praise or bless ashes. Religion is not necessary for that. Perhaps because a religion begins there, before religion, in the blessing of dates, of names, and of ashes.[79]

The question is therefore not Can the tropes of the tradition called the "religious" be recuperated in philosophy or be more easily expressed by texts called "literary"? The very dichotomy with which this question operates must be drastically reformulated. To assume that the trace of the Other can only be addressed in an aporetic thought, one that is neither strictly hermeneutical, nor purely narrative, nor poetical, let alone aesthetic, is to doubt the very pertinence of the common lines of demarcation that are drawn between philosophy, literature, and theology, without thereby effacing them completely. It is thus false to see poetic singularity as the paradigm of performative utterance in general. It is still unclear to what extent philosophical and theological thought can distance themselves—in form, style, and content—from their supposed referents, contexts of origination, and horizons of expectation.

The fact that one encounters insurmountable problems when one ascribes these philosophemes or theologemes to a certain well-defined thought or religious faith that would precede their inscription, illuminate their original meaning, and put their purported displacement into perspective becomes even clearer when one focuses on the relationship between Celan's work and that of thinkers who seem to be both extremely close to him and tending in almost opposite directions. In the following section, I shall focus on a significant parallel and contrast between Celan and Heidegger that plays a crucial but largely implicit role in the reading that I have taken as my guide, Derrida's "Shibboleth."

Dates and *Datum*: The Gift of the Poem and the Gift of Being

In relating the date to a more general consideration of the gift, Derrida follows a path different from Heidegger's. His reading of Celan's poetry and poetics implies a radical shift away from Heidegger's analysis of the relationship between thought (*Denken*) and poetry or poetics (*Dichtung*), the shift to a more general consideration of the gift, traversed by Celan's insistence on a poematic singularity that allows the poem to speak. Of course, Celan notes in the letter to Hans Bender: "Poems are also gifts—gifts to the attentive. Gifts bearing destinies."[80] But these words are hardly a confirmation of Heidegger's thought. How, then, do Celan's and Derrida's notions of the gift illuminate or affect the paradoxical structure of the date as we have reconstructed it? Where does the difference between Celan, Derrida, and Heidegger become most visible?

In his illuminating remarks on the singular temporal structure of the poem in Celan, Jean Greisch recalls that Heidegger runs the risk of virtually obliterating the resistance of the poetic word to every hermeneutic horizon by merging the notion of the gift or donation with that of *Datum* as it occurs in Hölderlin's hymns. Of the first line of "The Ister"—"Now come, fire! [*Jetzt komme, Feuer!*]"—Heidegger writes: "No calendrical date can be given for the 'Now' of his poetry. Nor is any date needed here at all. For this 'Now' that is called and is itself calling is, in a more originary sense, itself a date, that is to say, something given, a gift; namely, given via the calling of this vocation."[81] And yet, Greisch indicates, Celan's poetry—in which Hölderlin's *"Pallaksch, Pallaksch,"* like the caesura or "counter-rhythmic rupture" (*gegenrythmische Unterbrechung*),[82] takes different forms and resounds more and more intensely—obliges us to read this intricate relationship between the date and the gift also or even primarily in an opposite sense. Instead of (re)affirming the primacy of the call (*Berufung*), as Heidegger suggests, "the originary temporality that gives ought to be referred, in turn, to unforgettable 'historical' dates."[83] The summoning (the *dictare*) that Heidegger thinks accompanies poetry can thus no longer be defined in terms of a response to a call of Being that somehow precedes writing. On the contrary, the poem "is" at least contemporaneous with this call and perhaps even comes first.[84] Moreover, if that is so, this primacy would be more fundamental, more "originary," than any supposed ontic priority. Is it an accident, then, that Celan speaks of "the hour's message of comfort" (*Zuspruch der Stunde*)? Derrida identifies this as an "exhortation, perhaps a consolation, but above all a word addressed," which confirms the privileging of the "institution of the calendar" and the "clock," that is to say, of years, months, days, hours, minutes, and seconds—in short, of the codes of time that Heidegger deems secondary, derived, and grounded in a more originary datability.[85] In Derrida's account, Celan's poematic "words of comfort" (*Zuspruch*) seem to mark the Heideggerian "promise" (*Zusage*) at least as much as they are opened by it.

Yet it is important that Greisch puts the decisive adjective "historical" in quotation marks. What is at stake in this reference of the *Datum* to the date is a momentary time (as well as this time's very momentum) that can neither be reduced to the coordinates of any physical or cosmic time nor objectivized in the sociohistorical construction of a calendrical time. Invoking one of the multiple associations—indeed, commemorations—that one of Celan's most significant dates, cited in"Shibboleth," might solicit, Derrida writes: "And what if there were more than one thirteenth of February? Not only because the thirteenth of February recurs, becoming each year its revenant, but above all because a multiplicity of events, in dispersed places—for example, on a political map of Europe, at different epochs, in foreign idioms—may have come together at the heart of the same anniversary."[86] *Jänner, Februar* (and *Feber*) revive different events at once. They recall not only Büchner's Lenz walking through the mountains but also the Wannsee conference, not only the worker strike in Vienna but also, Derrida surmises, the Parisian demonstrations protesting the atrocities that accompanied the Algerian war. As the imperative of the third stanza of the poem "Shibboleth" describes, the date is at least doubled, accompanied by its double or "twin" (*Zwilling*):

Flöte,
Doppelflöte der Nacht:
denke der dunklen
Zwillingsröte
in Wien und Madrid.

Flute,
double flute of night:
remember the dark
twin redness
of Vienna and Madrid.[87]

But beyond the polyinterpretability of these calendrical indices of whose (to whose or from whose) diachrony the poem speaks is a "gap in the calendar" (*Kalenderlücke*), a counter-time (a *contre-temps* or, in Celan's own words, an *Unzeit*).[88] If such a notion of time can still be said to "exist" or make itself felt, it cannot but disrupt the traditional concept of the *nunc stans*, every thinkable modification of an abiding present or eternal time, as well as their conceptual and figural representation or narration.[89]

Thus, the poem "The Trumpet Part," in the cycle of Jerusalem poems in *Timehalo*, describes the metonymy of an at once sacred and profane revelation in terms of a suspension of temporality, as well as of narration. The place of the trumpet "is" that of a virtual nonplace: its sound echoes—takes place—"deep in the . . . empty-text [*tief im . . . Leertext*]," "in the time hole [*im Zeitloch*]."[90]

In our context, such a counter-time "is" of an order entirely different from the originary temporality revealed by the Heideggerian appropriative event of Being, or *Ereignis*. It precedes, exceeds, and perhaps even secondarizes the event of appropriation that, according to Heidegger, would make all derived and vulgar modifications of time possible and would be signaled in Hölderlin's "now." This is what is at stake in Heidegger's reading of "The Ister": "The 'Now' names an event [*Ereignis*]."[91] Greisch sketches the effects of the other order, of the time of the other in Celan's poetry and poetics in unmistakably Levinasian terms, suggesting a closer proximity between this thinker and the poet for whose *Dichtung* Heidegger fails to provide appropriate terms: "the time of the other forbids passing over in silence the link between certain 'dates' and the 'destination.' 'Originary' temporality, if it exists, cannot be indifferent to such dates."[92]

Of course, we should ask whether Heidegger himself allows for such a reading in other contexts:

> Hölderlin puts into poetry the very essence of poetry—but not in the sense of a timelessly valid concept. This essence of poetry belongs to a definite time. But not in such a way that it merely conforms to that time as some time already existing. Rather, by providing anew the essence of poetry, Hölderlin first determines a new time. It is the time of the gods who have fled and the god who is coming. It is the *time of need* because it stands in a double lack and a double not: in the no-longer of the gods who have fled and in the not-yet of the god who is coming.
>
> The essence of poetry which is founded by Hölderlin is historical in the highest degree, because it anticipates a historical time.[93]

Whatever answer we give to his question—"And what if there were more than one thirteenth of February?"—we touch upon the point at which it becomes clear how far Derrida distances himself from the most problematic and troubling aspects of Heidegger's rethinking of the relationship between datability, originary temporality, and the gift in light of a massive reinterpretation of the epochal history of onto-theology, metaphysics, and technology. The silent "axiomatic," "axiological," and "axio-poetological" presuppositions of Heidegger's *Destruktion* of this history had already been explicitly problematized in "*Ousia* and *Grammē*," "*Khōra*," the essays on *Geschlecht*, and *Of Spirit*, to name the most important texts.[94] Presumably, the strands of argument that Derrida unfolds in these readings are not without relevance for the question, so central to the argument of "Shibboleth," of the singularity and the singular universality of the date, singularities that are, as we have seen, "virtual," "virtualities," and even "virtual virtualities."[95]

To be sure, Heidegger's insight, as formulated in *Being and Time*—"Temporality 'is' not an *entity* at all. It is not, but *temporalizes* itself."[96]—has revealed that time "is" the transcendental horizon of any genuine, if not necessarily generous, repetition of the question of the meaning (*Sinn*) of the Being of beings. Heidegger demonstrates that time cannot be interpreted in terms of the movement or succession of things in physical nature (that is, as an atomic *Jetztfolge* or

Jetzt-Zeit,⁹⁷ as, Heidegger claims, Aristotle would have it). Nor can time be reduced to an empty form of the inner sense of perception of the (transcendental) subject (thereby understood, as in Kant and Husserl, as the formal condition of internal and external phenomenality as such⁹⁸). Nor, finally, can time be seen as the open dimension in which the Hegelian Spirit unfolds dynamically. At the same time, even though Heidegger had shown convincingly that the problem of time cannot be relegated to that of nature or the soul, objectivity or subjectivity, these classical-modern coordinates of "outside" and "inside," as well as the premises on which they were based, are displaced, at least in *Being and Time*, only minimally.⁹⁹

The reason for this is clear. The very distinction between an originary conception of temporality and a derivative conception of intratemporality, a distinction that should have made the destruction of these traditional and "vulgar" conceptions possible, presupposes what it seeks to dismantle. Up to a certain extent, Derrida writes, Heidegger would (have to) acknowledge that, for this continuity is inscribed in the quest for *meaning* (or *Sinn*) as such.¹⁰⁰

The very idea of a *lapsus* (a *Fallen* and *Verfallen*) from a proper into an inauthentic temporality is inconceivable without privileging the linear notion of duration that it tries to overcome, that is, the interpretation of time as an open, homogeneous space (*ein Vorhandenes*) *in which* things or events occur or *in which* things and events are mastered, calculated, or encountered.¹⁰¹ In Derrida's words, the very analytical and figural opposition between the primordial or originary and the derivative, that is to say, between the proper and the improper, is "still metaphysical":

> Is not the quest for an *arche* [archie] in general, no matter with what precautions one surrounds the concept, still the "essential" operation of metaphysics? Supposing, despite powerful presumptions, that one may eliminate it from any other provenance, is there not at least some Platonism in the *Verfallen*? Why determine as *fall* the passage from one temporality to another? And why qualify temporality as authentic—or *proper* (*eigentlich*)—and as inauthentic—or improper—when every ethical preoccupation has been suspended? One could multiply such questions around the concept of finitude, around the point of departure in the existential analytic of *Dasein*, justified by the enigmatic proximity to itself or by the identity with itself of the questioning . . . , etc.¹⁰²

In other words, the very assumption of a fall or decline—of the Spirit *into* time no less than of factical existence *from* originary temporality—is irrevocably tied to an onto-theological predetermination that Heidegger pretends to circumvent. This topos of the fall, in all its ambiguity of falling and the decline, is, writes Derrida, a concept that "no precaution—and Hegel took no fewer precautions than Heidegger—can lift from its ethicotheological orb [*orbe*]. Unless, in the void, the term of the orb in question is itself redirected toward a *point of falling* still further off."[103]

But Heidegger does not push the fallen, the *Verfallen*, to the edge, let alone over the edge, to the point of a *mise en abîme* that would force it beyond a falling and fallenness of *Dasein*, of being-there and, ultimately, of Being itself, of the one Being, which articulates itself in multiple ways (*pollagoos legetai*). Both Aristotle's and Hegel's texts would *already* and *still* perform—or allow us to read—what Heidegger, in *Being and Time* and in more detail in *Kant and the Problem of Metaphysics*, seems to reserve for the Kantian transcendental aesthetic alone:[104] to mark and remark the "play of submission and subtraction" that prepares the Heideggerian "breakthrough" [*la percée*] and that makes this "sole thinking excess of metaphysics"[105] nothing but its (not always generous) *repetition*. This acknowledgment, Derrida concludes, cannot take the form of an external critique. In a sense, it is already anticipated and accounted for in Heidegger's own text, just as that text is anticipated and accounted for in the text of another that preceded (and followed) him. If we sum up by saying that there is "perhaps" no such thing as a vulgar concept of time, then this "perhaps" trembles in Heidegger's text no less than in the texts that *Being and Time* makes tremble in turn. Derrida explains:

> The concept of time, in all its aspects, belongs to metaphysics, and it names the domination of presence. Therefore we can only conclude that the entire system of metaphysical concepts, throughout its history, develops the so-called "vulgarity" of the concept of time (which Heidegger, doubtless, would not contest), but also that an *other* concept of time cannot be opposed to it, since time in general belongs to metaphysical conceptuality. In attempting to produce this *other* concept, one rapidly would come to see that it is constructed out of other metaphysical or ontotheological predicates.
>
> Was this not Heidegger's experience in *Being and Time*? The extraordinary trembling to which classical ontology is thus subjected here still remains within the grammar and lexicon of

metaphysics. And all the conceptual pairs of opposites which serve the destruction of ontology are ordered around one fundamental axis: that which separates the authentic from the inauthentic and, in the very last analysis, originary from fallen temporality.[106]

Heidegger, in reiterating this metaphysical topos or commonplace—and, thereby, in relapsing into a metaphysics of presence—can only fall short in determining the singular nature of the (poetic) date.[107] Unlike the diachronical temporality manifested by so many of Celan's poems, the originary time that Heidegger retraces in *Being and Time* is irreversible.[108] Nowhere in his work could one find the inversion that haunts the following lines, from the second stanza of "Welldigger in the Wind":

Dies Jahr
rauscht nicht hinüber,
es stürzt den Dezember zurück, den November,
es gräbt seine Wunden um,

This year
does not roar across,
it hurls back December, November,
it turns the soil of its wounds,[109]

words that suggest a reversibility of time, a falling, but this time backward, a regressive restoration of its pastness, as it were.

For Heidegger, time, as it escapes the dilemma of being reified in its objectification or of vanishing in its subjectification, could never become such a specter (or *Phantom*, to use his own word[110]). When time does not belong to that which is ready at hand, that is, when Heidegger writes of time that it is "*'earlier'* than any subjectivity or Objectivity, because it presents the condition for the very possibility of this 'earlier,'" this primacy is subsumed under what remains (at this point in his overall oeuvre) an ontological hypothesis. Time, in a sense, "has 'more being' [i.e., "is," "*seiender*"] than any possible entity [*Seiende*]."[111] The hermeneutic articulation of the "now" entails another discourse, one that no longer speaks in terms of astronomical time or calendar dates but pushes the exploration of these derived and secondary modes of datability in the direction of time proper (to be distinguished from "the most primordial way of *assigning a time* [die ursprünglichste Zeitangabe])."[112]

The other temporality (the time of the other), which in Celan's postwar lyric poetry engraves itself in language, leaving nothing but a trace of mourning and ashes—a fate or *Schicksal*, rather than a generous gift (notions that in the later Heidegger seem to merge)—is no longer conceivable against this background of an effluorescent and fluvial giving in which authentic temporality would be placed.

To be sure, like the temporality disclosed in the "originary" gift of time (*Zeitangabe*), in the *Vorlaufen* into the utmost possibility that is death, and in the "moment" (*Augenblick*), the circumcision of the poetic word is not datable or localizable *in* time, *in* space, or *in* history. In a sense, the poem *has no* date (or age) of its own but "opens the place of and for the date."[113] In so doing, the poetic date opens up any history of being and its consecutive epochal interpretations (in philosophy, in religion, in onto-theology). However, the status of this gift (the *Geschenk*) of the poem is hardly that of the Heideggerian gift of Being (*es gibt*)[114] or destiny (*Geschick*). The "madness" of the date, its "monstrosity" rather than generosity,[115] its being always already other than it "is," destined to (be) virtually nothing, "is not an effect of being, of some meaning of being."[116] Celan's words "everything is less, than / it is, / everything is more [*alles ist weniger als / es ist, / alles ist mehr*]" make clear this "otherwise"—less *and* more—than being.[117]

Derrida comments that the effect—the shibboleth effect—of these lines hinges on the singular mention and use made of the *als*, which cannot be retrieved via the Heideggerian interpretation of the apophatic *als* in *Being and Time*: "The ambiguous *als*, emphasized by its position at the end of the line, after the pause of a comma, disengages the *als est ist* (as it is, insofar as it is, as such, such as it is) from the apparent syntax of comparison with which it nonetheless plays."[118] The remembrance of dates in Celan does not inaugurate or celebrate a "thinking-of" (*Andenken*) Being. Celan's steps are far from "moor-wandering" (*heidegängerisch*).[119] On the contrary, the poem, the *place* (*Ort*) in which all tropes are pushed beyond themselves to the point of absurdity, no longer allows its addressees the hope of "dwelling poetically on earth." And while poems, Celan claims, address the utopian ("they are headed toward. Toward what? Toward something open, inhabitable, an approachable you, perhaps, an approachable reality"[120]), this notion must also be thought of in terms other than those of a regulative idea, a messianic telos, or any other authentic experience of temporality. Such interpretations presuppose a temporal space that would remain to be (ful)filled or appropriated, progressively or abruptly.

In the last chapter of *La parole heureuse*, Greisch draws the line between the thinker and the poet even more sharply: "That the 'dates' in question are for Celan equally givens goes without saying, but contrary to Heidegger the date is not forgotten in favor of the gift and the pure giving of the *Ereignis*. On the contrary, it is the 'date' that defines the giving."[121] Whether or not we accept these formulations and the primacy of the date over the gift they imply is not important at this point, although I will return to this question. What should be emphasized is Greisch's hint that the notion of the date is not *unilaterally* or *asymmetrically* opened up by the thought of the gift, nor does it simply follow in its wake. The caesura of the date cuts through this alternative. The date "is" that which makes the gift possible, elicits or summons its occurrence, and thereby precedes and discloses its coming into presence no less than its futurity and pastness. The consequences of such an interpretation could be far-reaching. Again, I cite Greisch: "One might surely ask oneself whether this dialectic or tension between datability and giving does not engage, in turn, another thought of *Différence*, one that is simply the harmony between *Ereignis* and *Différence*."[122] One must thus ask oneself whether in the gesture of thinking, of preparing oneself to think, this gift is not a gesture with a date of its own, always already dated. In consequence, the apparent comprehensiveness (unity or simplicity) of the gift—the contention that it manifests a single destiny or sending forth of Being (*Geschick des Seins*) beyond all conceptual (read: metaphysical) or figural (read: aesthetic) grasp—is an inevitable (transcendental) illusion. It is "nothing but" the haunting idea that we might talk about or even hint at a dimension (the gift, the *Ereignis*) that is presupposed by the perpetual linguistic displacement of the forms and contents of our experience, without *ipso facto* betraying the absolutely singular performativity of this address. Although Heidegger states explicitly that the existential analysis remains forever ontically rooted, the basic tenet of his argument seems to lie in forgetting this singular embeddedness in favor of pursuing the question of the *Sinn* of Being as such (*als solches*), of Being *überhaupt*. Doing so, however, amounts to obliterating its time, which is not its *Datum*, but the singularity and spectrality—again, the shibboleth—of its given date, a date that is neither proper nor vulgar, or, if one wishes, both at once.[123]

Now and then it would appear that, despite the de-transcendentalizing and singularizing gesture of his text—of his "Shibboleth," that is, "for Paul Celan"—Derrida claims that the diacritical function of such an address, as well as any other shibboleth, takes shape only in light of (or in contrast to) an element or situation that gives this saying (pronunciation) of a said its *place*. This place or situation, while being itself no part of (or irreducible to) any discernable linguistic or sociohistorical constellation, would be the opening in (or through?) which all pragmatic conventions receive and suspend a certain provisional *and* decisive signification.

> Babel within *a single* language. *Shibboleth* marks the multiplicity within language, insignificant difference as the condition of meaning. But by the same token, the insignificance of language, of the properly linguistic body: it can take on meaning only in relation to a *place*. By place, I mean just as much the relation to a border, country, house, or threshold as any site, any *situation* in general from within which, practically, pragmatically, alliances are formed, contracts, codes, and conventions established that give meaning to the insignificant, institute passwords, bend language to what exceeds it, make of it a moment of gesture and of step, secondarize or "reject" it in order to find it again.[124]

It would almost seem, then, that in this context Derrida inadvertently follows Heidegger by ascribing a certain privilege to a *quasi*-transcendental—open and nonsubjective—horizon in whose light or shadow alone all singularity becomes possible (thinkable, sayable, or performable).[125] Should we conclude that Derrida himself secondarizes the date in favor of a more comprehensive notion of the *place*, of any situation in general, and thus recoils from pronouncing their shibboleth?

Singularity, Ideality, Universality

A less ambiguous statement will modify, however, a Heideggerian misreading of this passage and demonstrate that, for Derrida, the singular date and the general situation and place that give it its distinction are at most equi-primordial, the one conditioning the other at least as much as the other way around, thus exemplifying a paradox—an aporia, rather—of temporality as well as of the invocation of Being "as such." Indeed, Derrida also says of the poem (in a remarkable claim that applies to any shibboleth, philosopheme, theologeme, and ethico-political topos or trope):

> the date, by its mere occurrence, by the inscription of a sign "as a memorandum," will have broken the silence of pure singularity. But to speak of it one must also efface it, make it readable,

audible, intelligible *beyond the pure singularity* of which it speaks. Now the beyond of absolute singularity, the chance for the poem's exclamation, is not the simple effacement of the date in a generality, but *its effacement in front of* another date, the one *to which* it speaks, the date of an other, masculine or feminine, which is strangely allied in the secret of an *encounter*.[126]

The attempt to formalize the experience of such singular meaning is inevitable. A minimal degree of abstraction marks the inception and the transcendental illusion of all thought, at least as much as the experience of an originary undecidability. This apparent transcendentalism could easily make us forget that any discourse on the shibboleth—of, for instance, religion, indeed, judeities—also entails a supplementary reconsideration of the transcendental "schematism," of "imagination,"[127] and, ultimately, of the law of genre of that which resists all genre. If anything, the completion of this task, of this translation, transition, or transferral, is the Ethics of ethics that is sought, the singular (i.e., remarkable and sole) condition of its possibility. Indeed, as Derek Attridge formulates it: "Neither the language of communality and historical laws nor the language of individuality and pragmatic freedom matches deconstruction's insistence on the structural interconnectedness of the absolutely singular and the absolutely general, necessitating a new understanding of both 'absolutes.'"[128] Whenever, wherever, however the date or shibboleth is seen in the shadow of the gift or from the perspective of a place or situation, we always have to ask: *What* is traced, inscribed, incised, exorcized, and effaced *in this very opening*? If the question "What is?" is, as is likely, found wanting, overdetermined as it is by a metaphysics of presence, the same could not so easily be maintained with respect to the other formulation that gestures to the address by the other (or, rather, at our always already being addressed by the other), that is, the question "Who?"[129] Derrida seems to make this clear by giving his reading of Celan, again, an almost Levinasian turn: "The *shibboleth* is given or promised by *me (mein Wort)* to the singular other."[130]

It would certainly not suffice to insist on the apparently dialogical or even personalist overtones in Celan's poetological writings, which indeed speak of *Dasein*, although always in terms of a specific angle or "angle of reflection" (*Neigungswinkel*),[131] which cannot be reduced to the notions of "mineness" (*Jemeinigkeit*), "care" (*Sorge*), "being with" (*Mitsein*), let alone "being toward death" (*Sein zum Tode*). In

Celan's poems, "thou" (*Du*) becomes a spectral "thou," an *Aber-Du*, as elusive as a "superstition" (*Aberglaube*), that is, as the faith in "no one and No One" (*niemand und Niemand*).[132] The un-Heideggerian motifs of individuation and "creatureliness" (*Kreatürlichkeit*) do not suggest that there is still an identifiable self left to which these designations might apply, nor that such a self pre-exists the poetic utterance, nor even that it is constituted in this speech. Even though Derrida reminds us that the poem "constitutes" a "sign" in the form of "one person's language become shape [*gestaltgewordene Sprache eines Einzelnen*],"[133] this singular structure is also one of "solitude." These notions come together in the simple gesture of the handshake, a gesture that Levinas rightly recognizes as a "saying without a said," a prelogical and presyntactical gesticulation that reveals a "modality of the *otherwise than being*" and as such precedes and opens up every possible manifestation of Being.[134]

In *Poetry as Experience* (in the part significantly entitled "Remembering Dates"), Lacoue-Labarthe writes of the "event of poetry (and as such, poetry *is* event . . .)." He says further "there is no poetry, poetry does not occur or take place . . . except as the event of a singularity."[135] Moreover, he maintains that the notion of "the human" in "The Meridian" does not intend an ethical response to what can only insufficiently be called Heidegger's "ontology."[136] But this loses sight of a conceptual and figural displacement that is crucial for Celan, Levinas, and Derrida. It is not simply that the almost invisible step beyond art that Lacoue-Labarthe ascribes to Celan's poetics—in reference to a key motif in Derrida's reading of Blanchot, *le pas-d'art* or *le pas-de l'art*[137]—marks a decisive interruption or suspension of the thought (and the truth) of Being. More importantly, Levinas's descriptions of the *ethicity* of Celan's poetic gesture go hand in hand with more radical figures and disfigurations, which seem to approach the alterity of the other and of the self as other no longer dialogically, but differently and more closely. When Levinas opens the central chapter of *Otherwise than Being* with an epigraph from Celan's poem "Praise of Distance"—"I am you, when I am I [*Ich bin du, wenn ich ich bin*]"[138]—these words should not be read as the ellipsis of the dialogical or phenomenological, let alone as a dialectical constitution of the "I" by the "other." The substitution of the "other" for the "I" suggested by the other is an intrigue in which these two poles neither merge nor remain what they "are." The de-centering of the subject makes it into another other, and the other that (or, rather, *who*) unsettles the subject is more elusive than can be anticipated, to the point of being confused with the absurd sonority of the *il y a* (a complex notion for which no single parallel in contemporary thought, e.g., the Heideggerian *es gibt*, can be found).

Following Derrida's reading of Celan, the poetic passage to a distinct, for example, ethical tonality is not an immanent linguistic confusion of referentiality as such: a confusion definable in terms of, say, a "rhetoric of temporality."[139] Nor can we identify it as the echo of some unequivocal (e.g., Kantian) transcendental and, in a certain sense, transcendent imperative. On the contrary, the moment, as well as the momentum, of ethical judgment always signals a "history," a date inexhaustible by philosophical or hermeneutical categories alone. It is here, then, that the poetics and the politics of temporality intersect.[140]

The "experience of writing," in Celan as well as in reading Celan, is also "'subject' to an imperative: to give space for singular events; to invent something new in the form of acts of writing, something which is no longer theoretical knowledge but takes the form of constative statements; to give oneself to a poetico-literary performativity analogous to that of promises, orders, or acts of constitution and legislation which do not merely change language, or which, in changing language, change more than language."[141]

Instead of furnishing us with a theory of the acquisition of practical wisdom, instead of appealing to a (reinterpreted) faculty of reflective judgment, Derrida's "Shibboleth" gives us another, possibly closer look at the "structure" (or should we perhaps say the "stricture"[142]) of a singular sensitivity to singular cases and apparently random dates that summon us to pronounce the right word, to do the right thing. It is in this sense that inquiry into the contingency of making a decision (or of making differences), of suitable judgment, of ethics and politics, is at the center (the heart or the "heart's mouth [*Herzmund*]"[143]) of Derrida's thought, in "Shibboleth" and throughout.

In Celan, the most succinct example of an obligation devoid of any determinable, reconstructible, or in any other way justifiable norm can be found in the elliptical theory of justice formulated in one of the aphorisms Celan published in 1949 under the title "Backlight." It reads: "Our talk of justice is empty until the largest battleship has foundered on the forehead of a drowned man."[144] The paradox of the inversion of universality and singularity that characterizes this phrase, let alone its "foundation," "implication," or "application," cannot easily, if ever, be conceptualized. To ask what could count as its realization or implementation would be to miss the point. This "type" of poetic utterance, of which many other "examples" can be found in "Backlight" and elsewhere in Celan's works, seems to be twisted by a permanent paradox, a persistent resistance, a coherent incoherence. What such phrases seek to express, grasp, or stammer, rather than describe or state, is nothing less than the shibboleth of experience, of ethics, of politics, and of other realms as well. Such phrases hint at its aporia, which etymologically, Derrida notes, points to a barred passage, a *no pasarán* that keeps one from making sense of and from entering into the Law.

It is only to the extent that a shibboleth belongs to the order of the impenetrable (or unreadable) that it prescribes and operates as a "pre-script" (*Vor-Schrift*), to use a word from the poem "Do not work ahead."[145] Precisely insofar as it prescribes, it remains, in a way, something unwritten (*Ungeschriebenes*). "Before the Law" we cannot but make a "step of (not) writing" (*pas d'écriture*).

Derrida, of course, speaks of the "without writing," "un-writing," "unwritten" (*sans écrit, anécrit, non-écrit*).[146] Going even further, every step, every remembrance, every word written, unwritten, or pronounced, can be said, in a sense, to burn up. In *The Post Card*, Derrida cites the opening stanza of the poem "With Letter and Clock": "Wax / to seal the unwritten / that guessed / your name, / that enciphers / your name. [*Wachs, / Ungeschriebenes zu siegeln, / das deinen Namen / erriet, / das deinen Namen / verschlüsselt*]."[147] As the wax seals what—in the letter, at a given hour—remains unwritten, it betrays as much as it obscures the name. In this, the structural ambiguity of any marking of the wax evokes the wax with which one seals a letter or the wax of a candle that one beseeches to deliver its radiance at this hour—the poem asks "Swimming light, will you come now? [*Kommst du nun, schwimmendes Licht?*]." The wax also recalls the seal and the decomposition, the disclosure and concealment, of the metaphysical category par excellence, substance as it figures in Descartes' thought experiment in the *Meditations*. In addition, it evokes the fragility of the gift of memory, the mother of the Muses, according to a traditional genealogy reflecting oral poetry (cf. Hesiod's *Theogony*) and invoked by Plato. At the beginning of his *Memoires for Paul de Man*, Derrida cites the passage from the *Theaetetus* where part of the mind is compared to a wax block into which impressions are imprinted.[148] As the second stanza of Celan's poem relates, this traditional topos is subjected to a painful melting away of the fingers—and thus of the hands—which are pushed through rings and burn up in cycles of time and alliances.

If the shibboleth is a *pas d'écriture*, we can only hope to circumscribe or visualize the shibboleth of all ethico-political utterance by resorting to the figure or, rather, the image of the *ellipsis*. The ellipsis has, in literary studies, most often been interpreted as a rhetorical figure, that is, as a descriptive term for the suppression or omission of at least one of the linguistic elements necessary for a complete syntactic or narrative construction. Clearly, this rhetorical use of the term is applicable in the context of Celan's work. A poetry that no longer imposes itself but exposes itself,[149] in a hyperbolic positioning of language that reveals its sudden inversion into the simple gestural "saying without a said," always runs the risk of being stripped of all determinable meaning. This defection from a certain order of meaningfulness is a risk, one more serious than that of an economy of expression or a deliberate ambiguity or obscurity, a risk that the elliptic poem *must* run. The poem must risk being meaningless to the point of bringing about its own virtual eclipse.

> Commemorating what can always be forgotten in the absence of any witness, the date is exposed in its destination or in its very essence. It is offered up to annihilation, but in truth it *offers* itself up. The threat is not external; it does not stem from an accident that would suddenly come along and destroy the archive's material support. The date lets itself be threatened in its coming due [*son échéance*], in its conservation and its readability, by them, insofar as it remains, and gives itself to be read. Risking the annulment of what it saves from forgetting, it may always become no one's and nothing's date, the essence without essence of ash, about which one no longer even knows what was one day, only once, under some proper name, consumed there. . . . This does not happen *empirically*, like a fact, which might come about once under certain conditions and which could be avoided at other times, for example, by multiplying precautions—or by chance.[150]

In "The Meridian" Celan does not primarily ascribe the progressive muteness of his later lyric poetry to the abyssal character of language. The silence that affects speech and discourse (in particular, poetic utterance) from within cannot, he notes, be explained with the help of the rhetorical interpretation of the ellipsis alone. It is also the manifestation of the singular historicity and temporality revealed in (or revealed by) the date: "the poem, the poem today, shows—and this has only indirectly to do with the difficulties of vocabulary, the faster flow of syntax or a more awakened sense of ellipsis . . . —the poem clearly shows a strong tendency toward silence. The poem holds its ground . . . on its own margin."[151] In consequence, poetic language neither immediately flows from the essence of language as such, nor is it its (however distanced) (re)appropriation. Nor, Celan notes, is it a correspondence, an *Entsprechung* (a qualification that presumably refers to Heidegger's essay on Trakl, "Language in Poetry").[152] On the contrary, poetic utterance must be redefined as "language actualized" (*aktualisierte Sprache*) in the sense of provoking an instance of concentrated memory, a provocation that is nothing else than "individuation."[153] Only in this way is the poetic word unpredictable, only thus does it fail to obey the *dictare*, the *vor-sagen*, that Heidegger hears in the word *Dichten*. Only in this way does the poetic word fail to double or mimic what exists, inventing instead a new constellation.

Naturally, the attentive retracing of such poetic constellations (but also that of other dates and shibboleths, in whose wake all rhetorics, philosophy, theology, ethics, politics, and, last but not least, all thinkings of the gift *take place*) is a task whose structurally undelimitable character can hardly be overestimated. This remembrance, after all, cannot but perform the singular gesture that it seeks to describe. It therefore has to obey—to repeat—the paradox that governs every poetic date. But if the date is indeed a specter, then this gesture of circling back can never really come to closure. A date is elliptical when it does not come back and when, far from being a *hic et nunc*, it is from its very inception divided, doubled, tripled, or even further multiplied within itself. It draws a line or traces a loop, one that no longer encircles one fixed focus, the purported origin and center of its movement. The short text entitled "Ellipsis," which concludes and reiterates the trajectory that marks *Writing and Difference*, describes this iteration: "Repeated, the same line is no longer exactly the same, the ring no longer has exactly the same center, *the origin has played*. Something is missing that would make the circle perfect."[154] Any reading that, like this short text itself, succeeds in retracing this kind of repetition is elliptical, that is, the doubling of a singular, virtual point (or *point de vue*). How should we understand the *ellipticity* of such a—poetic and more than simply lyrical—figure? In what terms can we describe its divergence from, say, a hermeneutic circle?

"From a circular sense [*sens*] to an elliptical sense: How is one to think, how is one to live that?"[155]

One might be tempted to stress that reference to ellipsis also invokes another, nonrhetorical figure that falls short of completing a certain movement or of filling up a certain middle. I mean the mathematical, geometric *ellipse*, an oval figure, a structurally incomplete circle whose center has been omitted, evacuated, or split and doubled into two foci, which orient every point on the periphery. It is perhaps no accident that the last lines of "The Meridian" speak of such a connective, through which poetic utterance, an "encounter," becomes possible, that is, becomes "something as immaterial as language, yet earthly, terrestrial, in the shape of a circle which, via both poles, rejoins itself and on the way serenely crosses even the tropics: . . . *meridian*."[156] In a letter from 1961, Celan relates this figure, which crosses (out) all figures by leading them *ad absurdum*, to a motif found in Keppler, the astronomer who discovered that the heavenly bodies do not move in circles but in ellipses. The citation follows an implicit critique of a (or, rather, *the*) Heideggerian topos, namely, by reading "the 'to be placed' as the 'place' that is both 'nowhere' and everywhere [or always] actual [*das 'zu Ortende' als der 'nirgends' und jeweils aktuelle 'Ort'*]." The reference to Keppler situates this dis-placement, an echo of the earlier determination of language as an actualized individuation, in a quasi-theological perspective: "God is symbolized as a sphere [*Kugel*]. A cut through a sphere constitutes a circle; this designates the human [*den Menschen*]. . . . Perhaps poems are planes of projection of this hyper-Uranian place, 'without meaning' [*deutungslos*]—but sensible [*sinvoll*] through the pneumatic contour that can be allotted to them when they keep themselves open to what is above, what below."[157]

In this passage, Celan seems to envisage an absolute of almost cosmic dimensions that nevertheless falls short—again, elliptically—of coinciding with itself. The figure describes a u-topy that as such finds nowhere a place, never takes place, and is for that very reason always out of place, always already dis-placed.

Do these ellipses in Celan's poetry and poetics help us intuit the irreducible polarity and mutual implication of singularity and universality, shibboleths and partisanship, ashes and remembrance, distancing and *Ereignis* of the date and the gift? Is the blindness of one of these poles not the insight of the other—and vice versa? Can both of these constitutive moments not be said to oscillate in what could be called a permanent, open dialectic?

In another context,[158] Derrida treats a model that describes thought without cutting it short in a vicious circle of pure repetition and without paralyzing it before the abyss of an exclusively idiosyncratic or hermetic language. Between the horns of this dilemma, he writes, a strategy of alternation could take place in which the archaeological and anarchic extremes of our discourse keep each other in (or, rather, off) balance. Could a similar elliptical construction guide our attempt to understand the relationship between a date and the gift as it figures in "Shibboleth"? Neither the date nor the gift, the two foci of every utterance, could ever fully determine or synchronize poetic experience and synthesize it around *one* center. Not unlike the ellipse, which decenters the circle, the apparent repetition or recurrence of dates draws a ring only in a peculiar, inflected, or even contorted way. No date could ever be recuperated by an archaeology or stored in an archive, a database, of sorts.

Similarly, to speak of an-archy—with a privative intent—with respect to an affirmative gift (the gift of affirmation) would be equally awkward. Yet could not the very formal structure of the ellipse as the interplay of two foci that are mutually exclusive and yet always already point to each other help us *visualize, figure, and, indeed, think* the paradoxical structure of both of these polar constellations (of archaeology and anarchy, that is, as well as of the date and the gift)? Between the poles of archaeology and an-archy, adds Derrida, only the difference, the suspension and inversion of a breath, the enactment of thought, its pause and turning of breath (*Atempause* and *Atemwende*), can decide. Subsequent emphasis on one of the poles would be almost nothing, "nothing but" the pronunciation of a shibboleth or, more precisely, its declaring itself a shibboleth. With this *nonformalizable* gesture, the date—the gift of the date or the date of the gift—once again, time and again, would thereby, after all is said and done, reaffirm its priority, a primacy without precedent.

The Judeo-Christian

JEAN-LUC NANCY

By way of epigraph, at the end of this colloquium, and to return to Gérard Bensussan's initial presentation: might the "last of the Jews" not be the first of the Christians? This is a question that we can rightly call "historial."[1] It is, in any case, the one I will pose today to Jacques Derrida.

"Judeo-Christian" is a fragile designation. The word appears in the *Littré* dictionary with a historical definition that restricts it to the religion of the first Christian Jews, of those who considered that non-Jewish Christians should first "be associated with, or incorporated into, the nation of Israel." This signification sets aside the partisans of the measures of the order taken in Jerusalem under James's authority and reported in Acts 15. It is no longer the same meaning as in Harnack at the end of the century, which indicates only a preferential place for the Jewish people as the distinctive trait of the Judeo-Christians. Harnack thus distinguishes them from those whom he will call the "pagan-Christians" (who will also be called "Helleno-Christians" or "Hellenic-Christians"). Today, the use of the term *Judeo-Christian* is still less restrictive, as a function of complexities that historians have brought to light. At the same time, certain among them have expressed doubts about the validity of the category, if only because of the diversity of movements or stances that it is able to cover.

In the meantime, usage of the term has authorized a still broader and nonhistorical role when one speaks, for example, of

Judeo-Christian culture or tradition to designate a certain interweaving, at the base of European civilization, of the two enemy sisters or, indeed, of the mother and the daughter, the Synagogue and the Church. In truth, this composite term so far has been taken to designate an imbrication or conjuncture essential to our identity or our thought, even "the most impenetrable abyss that Western thought conceals," as Lyotard wrote of the *trait d'union* [hyphen]² that holds this composition together or de-composes it at its core—which makes of its center a disunion.

The enigma of this noncomposable composition should interest us in more than one respect; in fact, it should interest us in five respects.

1. Insofar as the name *Judeo-Christian* can go so far as to posit a—or even *the*—salient characteristic, that is, the incisive and decisive, if not essential, characteristic of a civilization that will call itself "Western," its stake is then nothing other then the composition and/or the decomposition, in and for itself, of this "civilization."

2. Insofar as its name de-composes what we have agreed to call, in our culture, "religions," it implies, within the determination of Western thought (and in its self-determination), a hyphen drawn between "religion" and "thought," precisely where thought—in the name of "philosophy," itself albeit otherwise self-composed—was determined as non-religious, even anti-religious, thereby drawing its line *over* religion, to destroy it or de-compose it. This name thus implies an irritation or a vexation of the West in itself and for itself.

3. Insofar as it implicates philosophy—if only in the guise of an offense or contradiction—this name communicates in some sense with that other composite: the Greek-Jew and/or Jew-Greek. This composite names nothing other (before becoming a name forged in Joyce's language of de-composition) than the *vis-à-vis* of Judeo-Christianity, understood as pagan-Christianity or Christian Hellenism (and from the latter began properly the missionary expansion of Christianity, which may also be the fact of Jews speaking or thinking in Greek, and designating their new religion, moreover, as one more philosophy). For this motif, there is no Judeo-Christianity, under the circumstances, that is not also Judeo-Greco-Christianity, and philosophy cannot hold itself apart or stand free from this double mark of dis-union.

4. Insofar as this mark multiplies at least once by itself, its reduction [*sa démultiplication*] will not cease thereafter: it draws or traces from itself a general de-composition. This de-composition first dis-unites the three religions called "of the Book," and thus composes

with Islam another assemblage and another discontinuity relative to the West, another dis-orientation and re-orientation (after all, as we know, the aftermath of historical Judeo-Christianity exerted very specific influences upon the birth of Islam, just as it had, a few centuries earlier, on the formation of Manichaeism). This reduction once again de-composes Judaism*s*, Christianism*s*, and Islamism*s* among themselves, setting in play each time a new form of contrariety with, or attraction to, philosophy. For its part, philosophy itself only presumes to be one insofar as (and at the least among other motives) across its extreme synchronic and diachronic disparity; it posits itself as distinct from religion (or again, within religion itself, as essentially distinguished from faith).

5. Insofar as the Judeo-Christian composition thus conceals or stimulates what we could call the general dis-position of the West (or indeed, what we should spell, in Greco-Latin, its dys-position), it so happens that this composition espouses formally a schema whose recurrence and extent/amplitude are not insignificant in our entire tradition of thought: this is the schema of *coincidentia oppositorum*, whose declensions include, among others, the oxymoron, the *Witz*, the Hegelian dialectic, or mystical ecstasies. From which of these four species the Judeo-Christian composition comes is perhaps not the question to ask, for it may arise from all of them or compose them all. But it is a constant that the most general law of this schema (like the structure of the Kantian schematism, which forms a species of the same genre) is to contain at its center a gap [*un écart*] around which it is organized. The hyphen passes over a void that it does not fill. Upon what could this void open? That is the question that a consideration attentive to the Judeo-Christian composition cannot avoid posing. Such a consideration is perhaps virtually a reflection on the composition in general of our tradition and within our tradition; that is, ultimately, on the possibility of the *cum* ["with"] considered in itself. How could the *cum*, how could the *communion*—taken as a generic term (that term of Cicero, taken up later on in Christianity to absorb and sublate the *koinōnia*, the *societas*, and the *communicatio*)—include constitutively the voiding of its center or its heart? How, consequently, can this voiding call to the deconstruction of this composition: that is, the penetration in the midst of the possibility, which is a possibility of composition that is both contracted and combated?

(A parenthesis for two axioms. 1. A deconstruction is always a penetration; it is neither a destruction, nor a return to the archaic, nor, again, a suspension of adherence: a deconstruction is an intentionality of the to-come [*l'à-venir*], enclosed in the space through which the con-struction is articulated part by part. 2. Deconstruction thus belongs to a construction as its law or its proper schema: it does not come to it from elsewhere.)

Here, deconstruction is therefore none other than the logic, altogether historical and theoretical, of the construction of what one might readily call in the language of painting "short-stroke composition" ["*la composition au trait d'union*"].[3] To be sure, composition, or the composed or composite characteristic, is not an exclusive trait of Christianity or the West. Nonetheless, Christianity never ceases designating, by itself and as itself, a communication or placing-in-common, a *koinōnia* that appears according to circumstances as its essence or as its *acme*, and it is indeed Christianity that has marked the West, or even as what is Western itself, with the intentional drive toward a "pleroma of peoples [*plērōma tōn ethnōn, plenitudo gentium*; cf. Romans 11:25]" whose restored community with Israel must be the touchstone, according to this text of Paul. Likewise, the pre- or para-Christian Judaism of the *Qumran* is a strain that considered the community to be the true Temple. From the religion of the Temple to communitarian or "communal" faith, from the religion of the sons to the religion of the brothers—all the way to republican fraternity and to the comparison Engels developed between the first communists and the first Christians or, more precisely, those Jews he called "still unconscious Christians" (referring, above all, to the John of Revelation)—from this passage, then, which also brings to its end a generalized abandonment of the Temples of antiquity and leads toward the constitution of a "church," which means, above all, an "assembly" (just like a "synagogue"), up to the question of what the *koinōnia* of our globalization or becoming-global and its being-in-common in every sense of the term could mean, there is an insistent continuity of a com-position that would carry in itself, in its *cum* itself, the law of a deconstruction: What is there beneath the hyphen and in the hollow of the assemblage?

Over what and from what is the hyphen drawn? And how is this hyphen drawn from the one to the other—from the one to the other edge and from the one to the other "self"? How is it drawn such that it might withdraw while at the same time remaining intact: not untouchable but intact, remaining intact throughout the entire Greco-Judeo-Christo-Islamo-Euro-planetary history, an intact spacing that has perhaps never yet come to light, having perhaps never yet taken form or substance, but remaining always residual, the uncomposable and undecomposable non-thought of our history?

I am drawing no conclusions, for the moment, from this enumeration of headings for the uncomposable composition that requires our attention. I propose today to examine only one of the most remarkable tendencies of Judeo-Christianity: that which was incorporated, ultimately, in the Christian canon of the "New Testament," even at the price of remarkable doubts and resistances, which have persisted, in some cases, up to our day. I mean, here, the epistle attributed to James.

That letter is the first of those a very ancient tradition designates "catholic." This name does not designate, at its origin, some particular orientation of these texts toward the Roman Church, but rather, as in the initial expression *katholikē ekklēsia*, their general or, if you will, universal destination. In this sense, rather than being addressed to a community, to a synagogue, or to a determinate church (like the Pauline epistles), they are addressed to a larger whole, which each time arises from the *diaspora*. That catholicity and diaspora might initially have to do with one another is something worth reflecting upon: do the "whole" and the "dispersion" produce a whole out of dispersion, a dispersion of the whole, or, indeed, a whole in dispersion? In a sense, the entire question lies there: I mean that the entire question of the West as totality and/or as dissemination resides therein.

Today, then, for us, the Judeo-Christian will be James. And it will be, in a manner that remains to be discerned, a secret thread or a hyphen that could tie the historic James to that other James [*Jacques*] around whom, or on whose pretext, we have come together here; and who is another Judeo-Christian, or indeed another Judeo-Helleno-Christian. This secret tie has nothing contrived or arbitrary about it; nor am I proposing it as an ad hoc rationalization. At the very least we should venture the risk, here, of its relevance. That relevance would be tied simply to this: if it is possible, at the end of the twentieth century, that a philosopher, and thus in principle a Greek, experience the necessity of re-interrogating a category of faith or of a faith act, or, again, that he or she speak of the real as resurrection— and if it is possible that this philosopher do so in a reference that might be at the same time Jewish (i.e., holiness, borrowed from Levinas) and Christian (i.e., a "miracle of witnessing"), then in what relationship can this take shape within historical Judeo-Christianity and what could this allow us to discern, and deconstruct, in our own origin or provenance?

(Parenthesis: before reading the Epistle of James, I would like to make it clear that I am going to proceed without furnishing any erudite sources, for that could only be excessive here. Recent studies on the many Judeo-Christianities and on the messianisms of James's time are multiplying. This is no doubt also a sign. But I neither want nor am able to do the work of a historian, no more than I intend a commentary on Derrida: I intend to work precisely between the two.)

The James to whom we attribute the letter in question has been distinguished as "the minor," from James the major, whom all of Europe went to venerate at *Compostello*. The tradition also names him "the brother of Jesus," and we believe we have finally identified him as the head of the Church of Jerusalem or of the "Holy Church of the Hebrews," who brings down the decision, reported in Acts 15, in favor of the non-Jews by declaring that "God chose for himself a people in his name . . . so that other men would seek the Lord, all those nations over which his name was invoked." With these words, James confers his authority (and that of a citation from Amos) on the words that Peter had pronounced when he said: "God has borne witness to the nations in giving them the holy spirit just as he did for us." God is a witness, that is, a *martyr*, for all men: the witness of their holiness or of their call to holiness (which is to say, to his proper holiness). Such was the message that the assembly sent Paul and Barnabas, along with a few others, to deliver to Antioch, where tempers had to be calmed in regard to what was due to the Jews, and what to the others. God bears witness for all men insofar as he is the one who "knows human hearts [*ho kardiognostēs*]." Israel is thus the singular site chosen for this witness about hearts: the visible or visibly marked (by circumcision) site starting from which the Holy One attests to the invisible and uncircumcised holiness of all humanity, or of the pleroma of his peoples.

It is from this angle that I will approach the Epistle of James. In it one reads, at 1:18, that God sought "to engender us from a word of truth such that we might be the first-born of his creatures." "We," here is first "the brothers" of the "twelve tribes of the dispersion," to whom the letter is addressed. It is thus the Jews who must be the "first-born of the creatures." The first-born represent the part reserved for the gods of a harvest or a herd. The relation of the Jewish churches to the rest of humanity stands, here, in this single verse.

The Jews who have faith in Jesus consecrate to God his own creation. Now, the letter reminds us further on that "men are made in the image of God" (3:9). (No doubt, the "we" of this verse can just as well tend to designate all men as the first-born of creation in its entirety: we shall come back to that.)

The resemblance of men to God, and with this a thematic and problematic of the image that are infinitely complex, belongs to the essential core of biblical monotheism. This resemblance occupies an important place in the thought of Paul, for whom Jesus is "the image of the invisible God" (Colossians 1:15). But the Epistle of James stops at this mention of the well-known verse of Genesis and ventures nothing in particular about the relationship between man-as-image and Jesus. The mediation of this relation remains at a certain distance. As we shall see, it is not the economy of a Christo-centric salvation that organizes James's thought: it is, as it were, directly, a certain relation of man to holiness that becomes an image in him.

Before proceeding we must make a remark about methodology. An absence of Christology, and even of theology in general, characterizes this text—which we could call more parenetic or spiritual than doctrinal—to the point that this has aroused suspicion about its authenticity, or about whether to consider it simply a Jewish text. In passing, it is remarkable that Harnack does not even mention James in his *History of Dogma*: in fact, one can grant him that this epistle does not provide us much, by contrast to those of Paul, for the development of a discourse about the contents of faith (I would readily put it as the contents of a knowledge of faith, but that would be to anticipate too much). The epistle is wholly given over—as we shall show—to the act of faith.

I am not claiming to reconstitute (others have done so much better than I could) the backgrounds or the implicit thematic (Essene, in particular) of this text. I am taking it in the form in which it is given. Now it is given at once as a text rather thin in theological speculation (as Luther said, "an epistle of straw") and as a text whose intention is not to oppose Paul but to correct a tendentious interpretation of Paul that tended to cut faith off from all action. James's theological reserve seems therefore intentional. But that means we must look here not for theological thinness but for a retreat of theology, or for a theology in retreat, that is, a withdrawal of any representation of contents in favor of an active information by faith—which is also to say that we must look for that alone which activates the contents. It is not another theological position, even less an opposed thesis: it is the position that stands precisely between two theological elaborations, and thus perhaps also between two religions, the Jewish and the Christian, like their hyphen and their separation [*trait d'union et d'écartement*], but also of their com-possibility, whatever the status of this "com-" might be: like their construction and their deconstruction taken together. That is to say that this position is like one of those points, one of those situations, in which the construction in question, like any construction, according to the general law of constructions, exposes itself, constitutively and in itself, to its deconstruction.

Let us return, then, to the internal logic of this letter. If humans were engendered according to the image (*gegonotes kath'omoiōsin theou*), then what is this *homoiōsis*? To what or to whom are humans similar or *homogeneous*? The God of the letter is described rather briefly. He is unique, to be sure, but therein does not lie what is essential to the faith, which concerns more the works of man than the nature of God (James 2:19: "you believe that there is but one God, and you do well. The demons also believe this and they tremble," which is to say, this is not enough to qualify your faith). This God is not the God of Israel in his jealous exclusivity, but neither is it properly speaking the God either of the Trinity or of love (nonetheless, the love of others plays a primordial role in the letter).

God is "Lord and Father" (James 3:9), and this is uttered in the same verse that mentions *homoiōsis*, just as in 1:17–18, where it is said that he "engendered us as the first-born of his creatures." The father is father of and in his resemblance (we could even say that paternity and resemblance share a reciprocity here), just as in Genesis, in the second story of creation, the resemblance of Adam to God passes into the resemblance between Adam and his son Seth: in this way opens the genealogy that will lead through Noah to Shem, Ham, and Japheth. This resemblance distinguishes man in creation; it makes of him the first-born of creation, which is to say that it is (and that through it man also is) the mark or the homogeneous trace that dedicates the world to its creator. This resemblance therefore does not depend on generation (as we are accustomed to thinking); it is rather generation that consists in the transmission of the trace. The created world is less a produced world than a marked world, a world traced, simultaneously imprinted and traversed by a vestige (as Augustine will say later on), that is to say, traced by that which remains withdrawn and by the withdrawal of an origin.

From what, then, is this *homoiōsis* made, this trace of the creator as such? The letter names him "Father of lights" (1:17) — he who opens the world in the division of light from what it illuminates (according to a very ancient cosmogonic schema). Immediately thereafter, it is said that from him comes "every beautiful gift, every perfect donation [*pasa dosis agathē kai pan dōrema teleion*]": that is, every action of giving and all things given, the first being literally called "good," and the second "fulfilled," "completed." God is first the giver. And it is as such that he is the "Father of lights, with whom there is neither change nor a shadow of variation." He gives as light and what he gives is first, essentially, his light (the Latin allows us to specify: *lux*, illuminating light, not *lumen*, the glimmer of the illumined thing). He gives not so much some thing as the possibility of the clarity in which alone there can be things. If the logic of the gift is indeed, as the other James [*Jacques*] enjoys thinking, that the giver abandons him- or herself in his or her gift, then that is what is taking place here. In giving, in fulfilling the gift, God gives himself just as much as he remains in himself without shadows, since it is this dissipation of the shadow, this clearing of light that he gives, and since he "gives to all, simply" (James 1:5). To give and to withhold, to give oneself and to withhold oneself, these are not contradictories here and, correlatively, to be and to appear would be identical: a phenomenology that is theological, but not theophanic.

The logic of the gift and the logic of the *homoiōsis* are superimposed: the *homoios* is of the same *genos* as that which engendered it (this theme, which displaces the pre-Greek and pre-Jewish relation of man to the divine, runs from Pythagoras via Plato up to Cleanthes, from whom Paul will borrow in addressing himself to the Athenians), and that which engenders or which engenders itself, gives itself, gives precisely its *genos*.

Further on, the letter names the thing given. In James 4:6 we read: "He gives a grace better than covetousness," and again, "he gives this grace to the humble" (a citation from Proverbs 3:34). Grace is favor, that is, at once the election that favors and the pleasure or the joy that is thereby given. Grace is a gratuity (Émile Benveniste shows that *gratia*, which translates *kharis*, gave us both *gratis* and *gratuitas*).[4] It is the gratuity of a pleasure given for itself. In verse 4:6, the *kharis* is opposed to the desire that is *pros phthonon*, the desire of envy or jealousy. The latter is associated with voluptuous pleasures (*hēdonai*). But the logic of the text cannot be reduced to the condemnation of the *philia tou kosmou* ("the love of this world"). Or again, perhaps this condemnation should be understood according to the ampler and more complex logic in which it is inserted. James says, in effect, that the desire of envy proceeds from lack: "you covet and you have not, so you kill" (4:2). *Phthonos* is the envious desire for the good or for the happiness of the other (as we know, the *phthonos* of the Greek gods takes aim at the man whose success or happiness irritates them). Now, James continues: "but you have not because you ask not." And then: "you ask and you receive not, because you ask wrongly, in order to spend for your sensuous pleasures." There is thus a logic of lack and of jealous appropriation here, as well as a logic of asking in order to receive that which cannot be received other than by the gift or as the gift, that is, the favor of grace. This *kharis* is the opposite neither of desire nor of pleasure: it is desire and pleasure qua receptivity of and to this gift. This receptivity must equal the donation in gratuity.

This gift gives nothing that might be of the order of an appropriable good. (We must also remember, so as to come back to it again shortly, that this epistle is the most vehemently opposed to the rich in the entirety of the New Testament.) This gift gives itself, it gives its own gift's favor, which is to say, a withdrawal into the grace of the giver and of the present itself. The *homoiōsis* is a *homodōsis*. To be in the image of God is therefore to be asking for grace, to give oneself in turn to the gift. Far from coming out of an askesis, one may justifiably say that this logic of grace arises out of enjoyment, and this enjoyment itself comes out of an abandon. That supposes, no doubt, according to the letter of the text, "unhappiness" and "bereavement," "weeping" and "humiliation," but these are not a sacrifice: they are the disposition of abandon, in which joy is possible. To be sure, something is abandoned, and it is lack, along with the desire for appropriation. But that is not sacrificed: it is not offered and consecrated to God. James is not preaching renunciation here: he is laying bare a logic separated as much from envy as from renunciation. And this logic is that of what he calls faith.

As we know, the letter of James—while it may not be as opposed as one might think to the thought of Paul—is clearly distinguished from the latter, at least by its great insistence on the works of faith. (That was, moreover, the first reason for Luther's severity toward this text.) But it is important to understand clearly that the works of faith in question here are not opposed to faith: they are, on the contrary, faith itself.

The relationship of faith to its works is set forth in chapter 2, whose most famous verse is the eighteenth: "show me your faith without works, and I will show you my faith by my works." The injunction or the challenge does not concern the necessity of proving one's faith. Besides, the preceding verse has just stated: "without works faith by itself is dead [*kath'heauten*, by itself, in itself, as to itself]." These works do not stand in the order of external manifestation, or in that of a demonstration through the phenomenon. And faith does not subsist in itself. This is why what is in question here is to show faith *ek tōn ergōn*, on the basis of works, and coming out of them. Instead of works proceeding from faith, and instead of works expressing it, faith here exists only in the works: in works that are its own and whose existence makes up the whole essence of faith, if we may put it that way. Verse 20 states that faith without works is *argē*, that is, vain, inefficient, and ineffective (curiously, the Vulgate translates this term by *mortua*, like the *nekra* of verse 17). *Argos* is a contraction of *aergos*, which is to say without *ergon*. James is thus stating a quasi-tautology. But it means: the *ergon* is existence here. That also means, then, that the *ergon* is understood in a general sense, as effectivity much more than as production; it is understood as being-in-act much more than as the *operari* of an *opus*.

This logic is so precise and so restrictive that it obliges us to set aside a certain comprehension of the *ergon* to which we are more habituated, and even our Platonic and Aristotelian understanding of *poiēsis*—a word that appears in 1:25, tied to *ergon*, and which everything makes us think, following several translators, in the sense of "practice" (thus, of "*praxis*"), that is, if *praxis* is indeed action in the sense of *by* or *of* an agent and not the *praxis* exerted *upon* an object.

One might say: *pistis* is the *praxis* that takes place in and as the *poiēsis* of the *erga*. If I wanted to write this in a Blanchotian idiom, I would say that faith is the inactivity or inoperativity [*désœuvrement*] that takes place in and as the work [*dans et comme l'œuvre*]. And if I wanted to pass from one James to the other [to Jacques Derrida], I would say that faith, as the *praxis* of *poiēsis*, opens in *poiēsis* the inadequation to self that alone can constitute "doing" ["*faire*"] and/or "acting" [l'"*agir*"] (both concepts implying the difference within or unto self of every concept or the irreducible difference between a *lexis* and the *praxis* that would seek to effectuate it). Extrapolating from there, I would say that *praxis* is that which could not be the production of a work adequate to its concept (and thus, production of an object), but that *praxis* is in every work and it is *ek tou ergou*, that which exceeds the concept of it. This is not, as we commonly think, that which is lacking in the concept, but rather that which, in exceeding it, thrusts the concept out of itself and gives it more to conceive, or more to grasp and to think, more to touch and to indicate, than that which it itself conceives. Faith would thus be here the *praxical* excess of and in the action or in the operation, and it would be this excess, insofar as it aligns itself with nothing other than itself, that is to say, also with the possibility for a "subject" (for an agent or for an actor) to be more, to be infinitely more and excessively more than what it is in itself and for itself.

In that sense, this faith can no more be a property of the subject than it can be the subject's "work": this faith must be asked for and received—which does not prevent it from being asked for with faith, quite the contrary. (In James 1:6, one must "ask with faith without turns or sidestepping": there is at the heart of faith a decision of faith that precedes itself and exceeds itself.) In this sense, faith cannot be an adherence to some contents of belief. If belief must be understood as a weak form or an analogy of knowledge, then faith is not of the order of belief. It comes neither from a knowledge nor from a wisdom, not even by analogy. And it is also not in this sense that we should understand Paul's opposition of Christian "madness" to the "wisdom" of the world: this "madness" is neither a super-wisdom nor something symmetrical to wisdom or to knowledge. What James, for his part, would have us understand is that faith is its own work. It *is* in works, it *makes* them, and the works *make* it. Taking a step further, even a short step, we could extrapolate from James a declaration like the following: "It is false to the point of absurdity to see in a 'belief,' for example, in the belief in redemption by the Christ, that which characterizes the Christian; only Christian *practice* is Christian, a life like that *lived* by him who died on the cross"—a declaration that we could read in Nietzsche.

Spinoza, for his part, asserts that "God demands, by the Prophets, of men no other knowledge of himself than that of his divine Justice and his Charity, that is to say those attributes which are such that men might imitate them by following a certain rule of life," by which he is referring implicitly to the citation from James's epistle, which he mentioned earlier in the same text.

That faith might consist in its practice is the certainty that commands James' interpretation of Abraham's act or of that of Rahab (Genesis 2:21–25). Contrary to Paul (Romans 4), James maintains that Abraham is justified by his work, designated as the offering of Isaac. For his part, Paul does not mention this episode, but rather that of Sarah's sterility (in Hebrews 11:1 ff., the sacrifice is evoked, but the fundamental argument remains the same). According to Paul, what is important is that Abraham *believed* that God could give him a son, against all natural evidence. His act thus depended on a knowledge postulate (or it consisted in one; in the text of the letter to the Hebrews, we find the word *logisamenos*: Abraham judged that God could). For James, on the contrary, Abraham did. He offered up Isaac. It is not said there that he judged, considered, or believed. (Likewise, Rahab the prostitute saved the emissaries, and James says nothing, by contrast with Paul, about her belief in the promise the emissaries had made her, whereas the Letter to the Hebrews reminds us that Rahab expected that her life would be saved.)

In a certain sense, James's Abraham believes nothing, does not even hope (Paul says that he "hoped without hope": even this dialectic is absent in James). James's Abraham is not in the economy of assurances or substitutes for assurance. Abraham is neither persuaded nor convinced: his assent is not in the *logismos*. It is only in the *ergon*. If the notion of "faith" must be situated in the "logical" or "logistical" order (as the origin of *pistis* in *peithō* would invite us to think: "to persuade," "to convince"), then this faith resides in the inadequation of one's own "*logos*" to itself. The reasons that this faith has "to believe" are not reasons. Thus it has nothing, in sum, with which to convince itself. This faith is but the "conviction" that gives itself over in act—not even to something "incomprehensible" (according to a logic of the "I cannot understand but I must or I may still believe," and still less according to a logic of the *credo quia absurdum*), but to that which is another act: a commandment. Faith is not argumentative; it is the performative of the commandment—or it is homogeneous with it. Faith resides in inadequation to itself as a content of meaning. And it is in this precisely that it is truth qua truth of faith or faith as truth and verification. This is not sacri-fication but veri-fication. That is, also, the contrary of a truth *believed*. This faith, above all, does not *believe*. It is neither credulous nor even believing in the current sense of the term. It is a faith not believed. *It is a non-belief whose faith guarantees it as non-believable.*

The concept of "trusting oneself to" ["*se fier à*"] or "confiding in" ["*se confier à*"] opens on two sides: on the one hand, it is a matter of a kind of assurance, of a postulated certainty, something wagered, by a confidence poised upon some anticipation risked toward an end (analogous to the Kantian postulates, which are precisely those of a rational or reasonable belief into which Christian faith metamorphosed or by which it was eclipsed). But faith, according to James, is effected entirely in the inadequation of its enactment to any concept of that act even if it be a concept formed by analogy, by symbols, or by an "as if." The work of Abraham is the acting or the doing of this inadequation: a *praxis* whose *poiēsis* is the incommensurability of an action (to offer Isaac up) and of its representation or its meaning (to immolate his son).

Faith as work could very well be knowledge—or nescience—of the incommensurability of acting with itself, that is, of the incommensurability of the agent, of the actor, or of the acting entity insofar as it exceeds itself and *makes* itself in the act, or *makes itself* exceed itself, or be exceeded by itself therein: thus, radically, absolutely, and necessarily, it proves to be the being-unto-the-other of its being-unto-self. In this, faith would be the very act of a *homoiōsis* with the gift itself, understood in the sense of its act. *Homoiōsis* as *heteroiōsis*, the identity of the concept (of "knowledge" or of "thought") qua the incommensurability of the conceiving *in actu*. This incommensurability would be tied to the following: this faith ("persuasion," "wager of confidence," or "assurance of faithfulness") must come from the other, this faith must come from outside, it is the outside opening in itself a passage toward the inside.

This faith would be—or, again, the Judeo-Christian and Islamic faith would be—the act of a non-knowledge as non-knowledge of the necessity of the other in every act and in every knowledge of the act that could stand at the level of what James here calls (5:21, 24–25) "justification": that which makes just, that which creates a just one (which could never be, could above all not be in the adequation of the knowledge of its own justice). This act would be tied first to faith in the other—which the other James, or Jacques [Derrida], calls "the relation to the other as the secret of testimonial experience," if by "testimony" we mean, as he does, the attestation of truth that all words postulate in the other or from the other, and in me qua other to myself (just as, Platonically, I "dialogue with myself"). The just one or the justified one would be he who lets himself be attested, borne witness to, in the other.

This truth and this justice open most precisely where it is no longer a sacred presence that assures and guarantees, but the fact itself—the act and the work—of not being assured by any presence that might not be of the other, and other than itself, other than the presence of sacred gods: in a sense, or if one wishes, the sacred itself or the holy (to fuse them for an instant), but as not given, not posited, not presented in an order of divine presence—on the contrary, "God" "himself" as unlike any god, as gift and as the gift of the faith that is given to the other and that believes in nothing. With this, then, the Judeo-Christianism of James as deconstruction of religion and, consequently, also as self-deconstruction: leaving nothing subsisting, if this is indeed subsistence at all, but the hyphen and its spacing.

This is why the work of faith, the *poiēsis-praxis* of *pistis*, presents itself in the letter under three aspects: the love of the neighbor, the discrediting of wealth, and the truthful and decided word. In these three forms, in question each time is an exposition to what cannot be appropriated, to what has outside itself, and infinitely outside itself, the justice and truth of itself.

In question is what the letter calls "the perfect law of freedom" (James 1:25 and 2:12). Unlike Paul, James does not sublate the law (supposedly ancient) into freedom and/or into a law (reputedly new). The "law of freedom"—of which no precept is really foreign to Judaism—is the arrangement or framework that would have it that acting should expose itself to the other and be nothing other than this very exposition: it is the *acting* of relationship or proximity rather than the *doing* of desire or appropriation; the *acting* of the word and the truth, rather than the "logistical" *doing* of representation and meaning. This formula—"law of freedom" (*nomos tēs eleutherias*), which is perhaps a *hapax* in the Scriptures—could be understood with a Stoic resonance, and we would have, in that case, one of the marks of the implication of philosophy in this Christianity *in statu nascendi*. If something like this could be attested, then that should refer us to the deepest level of Stoicism's understanding: not the submissive acceptance of an order that escapes me, but the sharing (*nomos*) of the event as the opportunity of a becoming-self. In this we can hear Jacques Derrida's text on Abraham resonate with Deleuze's lines on Stoicism: "to become worthy of what befalls us, thus to want it and to set it forth in its event, to become the son of one's own events . . . and not of one's works. For the work is itself produced only by the son of the event." The *nomos* is thus the following: that we are only liberated by the truth that does not belong to us, that does not devolve to us, and that makes us act according to the inadequation and the inappropriation of its coming.

It would be outside the scope of this conference to analyze the triple determination of the "law of freedom" according to love, the word, and poverty. I will therefore not attempt to do so today and I will conclude simply with that which can no longer be deferred: namely, Jesus Christ.

In a certain sense, the only indubitable attestation of the Judeo-*Christian* composition of James's letter is his mention of Jesus. This mention is made from the first verse, in the formula, also used by Paul, "James, servant of God and of the lord Jesus Christ." Then, in the first verse of chapter 2: "my brothers, you who have faith in our Lord Jesus the Christ of glory." On the one hand, as I have already noted, this mention of the Christ stands withdrawn from any Christology. On the other hand, and at the same time, this mention alone determines faith, no longer according to its (praxical or operative) nature, but according to its reference, its scaffolding, its support, or its guarantee. Mere faith in the uniqueness of God, as we have seen, is not, by itself alone, truly faith. Faith, in order to be, that is, in order to act, draws its consistency from somewhere else: from a proper name. Being the carrier of no specific theology, the proper name does not turn into a concept. This proper name is no introduction to a logic of the mysteries of incarnation and redemption. At the most, we may suppose, beneath the name *Jesus*, an implicit reference to the teaching transmitted by the gospels, especially that of the Sermon on the Mount. For everything else, this name serves only to identify Christ, that is, the messiah. If the messiah is named, it is because he is come, because he is present in one way or another. He has presented himself. The name states this presence come to pass. A reader unaware of this would have no reason to think that this Jesus is no longer of this world. This presence is not that of a witness who would give reasons to believe, or some example of faith. The presence named here refers only to the messianic quality.

The expression "messiah of glory" could be, itself, a *hapax*. The messiah is the anointed one. Anointing is, in Israel—which inherited it from other cultures—the gesture that confers and signs the royal, sacerdotal, or prophetic function (a later Christology will attribute these three functions to Jesus). To be sure, whoever says "messiah," in Israel, understands this triple function, and foremost, the first one, that of the reign—which verse 2:5 names here, speaking of the "reign that God promised to those who love him" (four verses after the "Christ of glory"). A reflection on messianism cannot forgo consideration of this royalty or kingship. (Without wanting to go into details here, I would say that the somewhat biased reduction of the meaning of *messiah* to the idea of a "savior" overlooks the functions implied by anointment and the fact that this "salvation" requires these functions—which also implies, eventually, a dehiscence of or a disparity between these functions, like that between priesthood and prophecy.) A messiah "of glory," whether he be anointed with glory or glory be the splendor of his unction, is an absolutely royal messiah: resplendent with the magnificence that the Scripture never ceases to attribute to God, and which the oil, luminous and perfumed, reflects as it flows over the hair and onto the beard of the anointed one. Royalty according to glory is not firstly of the order of power. Or again, it is not of that order without being identically in and of the order of light and dispensation, the order of the "beautiful gift and perfect donation."

(Glory, *éclat*, or splendor is a very ancient attribute, divine and/or royal, in Assyrian and Babylonian representations, in whose context one also finds it allied with seduction and pleasure, especially on the part of feminine deities: this is the splendor associated with favor. In this regard, a great Hellenist once wrote: "It is with the Greek notion of *kharis* that the *rapprochement* is unavoidable between charm, external grace, power of seduction, but also the luminous sparkling of jewels and materials, bodily beauty, physical wholeness, sensual delight, the gift that woman makes of herself to man.")

Ultimately, there would no longer be messianism here, but charisma, an inappropriable gift.

Glory purely and simply gives itself, and precisely as that which is not appropriable—not even by the one from whom it emanates—it is only admirable, and perhaps admirable to the point of not being able to be contemplated. Faith in glory or faith of glory (*pistis tou Kuriou Iēsou Christou tēs doxas*) is faith in the inappropriable: and once again, as the inadequation of the work or the inadequation at work. This faith receives itself from inappropriable glory, it is in glory in the sense that it comes from glory, where that glory provides faith its assurance, which is not a belief. The *doxa* of Jesus is his appearing: the fact that he is come, that the glory of his reign has appeared, already given as faith. *Jesus* is thus the name of this appearing—and he is this *doxa* qua name: the proper name of the inappropriable (that is, as we know, the very property of the name or, if you prefer, its divinity). And it is thus a name for any name, for all names, for the name of every other. The whole verse says: "take no account of persons in your faith in the Lord Jesus the Christ of glory," in order to introduce considerations about the poor. In a certain sense, we can only attempt to understand, likewise, that it is a matter of not taking account of the person of Jesus (either his face, his *prosōpon*, or his *persona*).

Thus a deconstruction comes to pass even before construction, or during construction and at its very heart. The deconstruction does not annul the construction, and I have no intention to reject, in James's name, the subsequent study of Christian construction—I do not want to take up again the gesture of "returning to the sources" and of "puri-fication" of the origin, so obsessive in Christianity, monotheism, and the West. But this deconstruction—which will not be a retrocessive gesture, aimed at some sort of morning light—henceforth belongs to the principle and plan of construction. Deconstruction lies in its cement: it is in the hyphen, indeed it is *of* that hyphen.

For the present, here, of the hyphen in "Jesus-Christ" there remains but the dash that ties a name to glory. There remains this dash or hyphen, like a schema, in the sense of the conjunction of a concept and an intuition, but above all, in the more precise sense according to which, in this conjunction, each of the edges, exceeding the other, remains incommensurable with it. And so there remains the schema like a name, which is always the name of an other, the way the name *James* is the name of more than one James (as the other one would say), always the name of an other, even if it were my own—and the *doxa* of what shows itself, the fame of the name so far as it puts faith to work, and a faith that creates a work, as at first blush, the deconstruction of religion as of the onto-theology that awaits it in its history—that awaits it to deconstruct itself therein.

But now, glory is only what it is insofar as it does not shine like gold or silver (unlike the jewels and the clothes of the rich man in verse 2:2). Glory is monstration, the exhibition of faith in the act (the *deixon* of the "show me your faith" carries the same semantic root as *doxa*), and yet for all that, glory is the exhibition of inadequation or incommensurability. It is in that way that glory is the anointing of the messiah: that is, the messiah exhibits the withdrawal of that with which he is anointed. This withdrawal is not a sacred separation: it is, quite precisely, the withdrawal of the sacred and the exhibition of the world to the world. To be sure, anointment is a consecration. But it is the non-sacrificial consecration that does not seal within the offering a transgression of the sacred separation, but which pours upon the world, in the world and as the world—as the work of creation—the very withdrawal of the divine.

James's letter says, toward the end (5:8), that "the coming of the Lord is near [literally: has approached, has become near]." The *parousia* is nigh: this is to say that *parousia* is and is not in proximity. Proximity is what never ceases closing and opening itself, opening itself in closing (it is not promiscuity, which would be a mixture). *Parousia* is—to be set apart from the very thing that approaches, to be a gap with and in itself [*l'écart de soi*]. *Parousia*—or presence close to—differs and is deferred: in this way it is there, imminent, like death in life.

What is changing, in the instituting configuration of the West, is that man is no longer the mortal who stands before the immortal. He is becoming the dying one in a dying that doubles or lines the whole time of his life. The divine withdraws from its dwelling sites—whether these be the peaks of Mount Olympus or of Sinai—and from every type of temple. It becomes, in so withdrawing, the perpetual imminence of dying. Death, as the natural end of a mode of existence, is itself finite: dying becomes the theme of existence according to the always suspended imminence of *parousia*.

The conclusion of James's letter recommends anointing the sick with the "prayer of faith" and the mutual confession of sins. The Catholic Church will found what it calls the sacrament of extreme unction on precisely this text, albeit much later. We must understand that the unction supposed to "heal," as the text says, heals the soul and not the body ("the prayer of faith will save the ailing one, the Lord will pick him up, and the sins he committed will be forgiven him," 5:15). This is to say that unction signs not what will later be called a life eternal beyond death but the entry into death as into a finite *parousia* that is infinitely differed or deferred. This is the entry into incommensurable inadequation. In this sense, every dying one is a messiah, and every messiah a dying one. The dying one is no longer a mortal as distinct from the immortals. The dying one is the living one in the act of a presence that is incommensurable. All unction is thus extreme, and the extreme is always what is nigh: one never ceases drawing close to it, almost touching it. Death is tied to sin: that is, tied to the deficiency of a life that does not *practice* faith—that cannot practice it without failing or fainting—at the incommensurable height of dying. Yet despite this, faith gives; it gives dying precisely in its incommensurability ("to give death," "the gift of death," he says):⁵ a gift that it is not a matter of receiving in order to keep, any more than is love, or poverty, or even veridicity (which are, ultimately, the same thing as dying).

Not sacrifice, or tragedy, or resurrection—or, to be more precise, no one of these three schemas, insofar as it would give to death (one way or another) a proper density or consistency, whereas death is absolute in-consistency, if it *is* at all. (Hegel writes: "Death, if we would give a name to this non-effectivity.") Each of these schemas gives consistency to death: sacrifice seals in blood the reconciliation of a sacred order; tragedy soaks in death the bloodied iron of destiny (the utter rending of the irreconcilable); resurrection heals and glorifies death within death itself. Whether in one mode or another, each of these schemas gives a figure to the defunct and substance to death itself.

No doubt, each of these schemas can be understood differently— each one, or all three together, in some composition that remains to be set forth and that could well be, precisely, Christianity in its most elaborate form.

But we can draw from these still another thread or splinter; that is, an inconsistency of death that would be such that the mortal does not "sink" into it, and still less escapes into it or from it,⁶ but rather, remains safe from it at the precise point where he disappears qua mortal (and thus disappears "in death," if you will: but in death there is nothing, no inside, no domain). At this point where he dies, the mortal touches, making the only possible contact, upon the sole immortality possible, which is precisely that of death: it is inconsistent, inappropriable. It is the proximity of presence. The only consistency is that of the finite so far as it finishes and finishes itself.⁷ For this reason, death can do nothing to the existent—except that, in its irreconcilable, inadequate way, it makes that existent exist, after a birth expelled it into death. Death thus puts the existent in the presence of existing itself.

In the Epistle of James, everything unfolds as though faith, far from being a belief in another life, that is, some belief in an infinite adequation between life and itself, were the setting in act [*la mise en œuvre*] of the inadequation in which and as which existence exists. How did faith, one day, with the West, start composing a decomposition of religion? That is what still places that curious day before us, ever before us, ahead of us, like a day that would be neither Jewish, nor Christian, nor Muslim—but rather like a trace or hyphen drawn to set space between every union, to untie every religion from itself.

Jean-Luc Nancy ■ 233

Contributors

Gil Anidjar is Associate Professor of Near Eastern Languages and Comparative Literature at Columbia University. He is the author of *The Jew, the Arab: A History of the Enemy* (2003) and *"Our place in al-Andalus": Kabbalah, Philosophy, Literature in Arab Jewish Letters* (2002).

Michal Ben Naftali is currently Fellow at the Van Leer Jerusalem Institute. She has taught in the Departments of Comparative Literature at the Hebrew University, Jerusalem, and the University of Bar Ilan. The author of an Oxford thesis entitled "Effects of the Holocaust on Three Post-Modernist Thinkers: Levinas, Lyotard and Derrida," she has published *The Visitation of Hannah Arendt* (2005, in Hebrew).

Gérard Bensussan is Professor of Philosophy at the University Marc Bloch, Strasbourg. He is also Permanent Visiting Professor at the École Normale Supérieure, Paris. He has recently published *Le temps messianique: Temps historique et temps vécu* (2001) and *Franz Rosenzweig: Existence et philosophie* (2000). He is the co-editor of many books, among them *Levinas et la politique* (2002–2003) and *Franz Rosenzweig, confluences: Politique, histoire, judaïsme* (2003).

Bettina Bergo is Associate Professor of Philosophy at the University of Montreal. Author of *Levinas Between Ethics and Politics* (1999), she has translated works by Emmanuel Levinas—including *On Escape / De l'évasion* (2003), *God, Death, and Time* (2000), and *Of God Who Comes to Mind* (1998)—and by other authors.

Hélène Cixous is Professor Emeritus of English Literature at the University of Paris and founder of the Centre d'Études Féminines. Among her recent works are *Hyperrêve* (2006), *Portrait of Jacques Derrida as a Young Jewish Saint* (2004), and *Veils*, with Jacques Derrida (2001).

Joseph Cohen is Visiting Professor of Philosophy at the Hochschule für Gestaltung in Karlsruhe, Germany, and Program Director at the Collège International de Philosophie. He has published *Le sacrifice de Hegel* (2006) and *Le spectre juif de Hegel* (2005). Author of many articles, he recently edited *Heidegger—le danger et la promesse* (2006), a critical collection on Heidegger and the end of history.

Jacques Derrida (1930–2004) was Director of Studies at the École des Hautes Études en Sciences Sociales, Paris, and Professor of Humanities at the University of California, Irvine. Among his most recently published works are *Geneses, Genealogies, Genres and Genius: The Secrets of the Archive* (2006), *Sovereignties in Question: The Poetics of Paul Celan* (2005), and *Philosophy in a Time of Terror: Dialogues with Jürgen Habermas and Jacques Derrida* (2003).

Jürgen Habermas is Professor of Philosophy Emeritus at the Johann Wolfgang Goethe University in Frankfurt am Main and former director of its Institute for Social Research. He is also Permanent Visiting Professor at Northwestern University. The most recent of his many books in English translation are *Truth and Justification* (2003) and *Religion and Rationality: Essays on Reason, God, and Modernity* (2002).

Moshe Idel is Max Cooper Professor of Jewish Thought at the Hebrew University, Jerusalem. Winner of the Gershom Scholem Prize for Research in Kabbalah, he is the author of many works, including *Kabbalah and Eros* (2005), *Absorbing Perfections: Kabbalah and Interpretation* (2002), *Messianic Mystics* (1998), and *Kabbalah: New Perspectives* (1988).

Gabriel Malenfant is Administrative Coordinator for Environmental Affairs at SNC-Lavalin, Québec. He has published on Jewish philosophy, environmental philosophy, and the questions of exile. He has a master's degree in philosophy from the University of Montreal.

Jean-Luc Nancy is Distinguished Professor of Philosophy at the University Marc Bloch, Strasbourg. The most recent of his many books to be published in English are *Listening* (2007) and *The Ground of the Image* (2005).

Michael B. Smith is Professor Emeritus of French and Philosophy at Berry College. He is the author of *Toward the Outside: Concepts and Themes in Emmanuel Levinas* (2005). He has translated many works, especially by Emmanuel Levinas, notably *Alterity and Transcendence* (1999), *Entre-nous: On Thinking-of-the-Other* (1998, co-translated with Barbara Harshav), *Proper Names* (1996), and *Outside the Subject* (1994).

Gianni Vattimo is Professor of Philosophy at the University of Turin. Among his many works are *Dialogue with Nietzsche* (2006), *Nihilism and Emancipation: Ethics, Politics and Law* (2004), and *After Christianity* (2002).

Hent de Vries is Professor of Humanities and Philosophy at The Johns Hopkins University and Professor of Philosophy at the University of Amsterdam. He is the author of *Minimal Theologies: Critiques of Secular Reason in Adorno and Levinas* (2005), *Religion and Violence: Philosophical Perspectives from Kant to Derrida* (2002), and *Philosophy and the Turn to Religion* (1999). Among the volumes he has co-edited are, with Lawrence E. Sullivan, *Political Theologies: Public Religions in a Post-Secular World* (2006) and, with Samuel Weber, *Religion and Media* (2001) and *Violence, Identity, and Self-Determination* (1998).

Raphael Zagury-Orly is Professor of Philosophy at the Bezalel Academy of Fine Arts in Jerusalem and Researcher in Philosophy at the University of Tel Aviv. He has translated Gilles Deleuze and Jacques Derrida into Hebrew and is the author of many articles.

Notes

Abraham, the Other, Jacques Derrida

1. Franz Kafka, "Abraham," trans. Clement Greenberg, in *Kafka: Paradoxes and Parables* (New York: Schocken Books, 1958), 40–45.

2. Since Derrida has offered the phrase *plus d'une langue* provisionally to define deconstruction, the difficulty of translating its form and derivatives has been noted by commentators and translators. *Plus d'un*—a recurring phrase in Derrida—reinscribes this difficulty as well. More than one, no more than one, no longer one, and one no more, the One no more, no one no more are some of the possibilities that will have to be kept in mind here.—Trans.

3. Jacques Derrida, *The Gift of Death*, trans. David Wills (Chicago: University of Chicago Press, 1995); *Donner la mort* (Paris: Galilée, 1999).—Trans.

4. Respectively, President and Director of the Jewish Community Center of Paris, where the Judéités conference took place.—Trans.

5. These two words are in English in the original.—Trans.

6. Y. H. Yerushalmi, *Freud's Moses: Judaism Terminable and Interminable* (New Haven: Yale University Press, 1991).

7. As Derrida makes clear in the way he deploys the phrase, *garder du judaïsme* can be read as "keeping, conserving, or protecting Judaism," as well as "keeping or protecting (someone, something) *from* Judaism." The reflexive form—*se garder*—functions in a similar way. Hence, *je me garde du Judaïsme* would perhaps first be read as "I keep Judaism at bay," but can just as well be read as "I keep some Judaism for myself." *L'un se garde de l'autre* is another instance of such rhetorical complexity.—Trans.

8. *Argumentaire* is not simply an argument, but arguments advanced in order to sell something—Trans.

9. Jacques Derrida, "Circumfession," trans. Geoffrey Bennington in Geoffrey Bennington and Jacques Derrida, *Jacques Derrida* (Chicago: University of Chicago Press, 1993), 154, trans. modified.

10. Jean-Paul Sartre, *Anti-Semite and Jew*, trans. George J. Becker (New York: Schocken Books, 1948), 69; *Réflexions sur la question juive* (Paris: Gallimard, 1954), 83–84. The translation has been slightly altered here because my edition includes a strange and significant typo: one reads, "une homme: le Juif est une homme [the Jew is a—female article—man]." All further references to this work will be given in the text, with English page number followed by the French pagination.

11. Trans. slightly modified.—Trans.

12. The English translation here has "ugly and upsetting" (75).—Trans.

13. This last phrase, "et le respect qu'ils lui portent est empoisonné" was omitted from the English translation—Trans.

14. Respectively, in December 1945 in *Les temps modernes*, and in 1946 with editor Paul Morihien.

15. Alain Finkielkraut, *The Imaginary Jew*, trans. Kevin O'Neill and David Suchoff (Lincoln: University of Nebraska Press, 1994).

16. Freud, "Preface to the Hebrew Translation," in *Totem and Taboo*, quoted in Yerushalmi, *Freud's Moses*, 14.

17. See Jacques Derrida, *Archive Fever: A Freudian Impression*, trans. Eric Prenowitz (Chicago: University of Chicago Press, 1995), 75 ff.

"The Last, the Remnant . . . (Derrida and Rosenzweig), Gérard Bensussan

1. Jacques Derrida, "A Testimony Given . . .," in *Questioning Judaism: Interviews with Elisabeth Weber*, trans. Rachel Bowlby (Stanford: Stanford University Press, 2004), 43; "Un témoignage donné," in *Questions au Judaïsme: Entretiens avec Élisabeth Weber* (Paris: Desclée de Brouwer, 1996), 79. In following citations of this and all other works, page numbers of the English translation will precede those of the French original.

2. Jacques Derrida, "Shibboleth: For Paul Celan," trans. Joshua Wilner, in Jacques Derrida, *Sovereignties in Question: The Poetics of Paul Celan*, ed. Thomas Dutoit and Outi Pasanen (New York: Fordham University Press, 2005), 1–64; *Schibboleth: Pour Paul Celan*. (Paris: Galilée, 1986). Jacques Derrida, "Circumfession," trans. Geoffrey Bennington, in Jacques Derrida and Geoffrey Benningtion, *Jacques Derrida* (Chicago: University of Chicago Press, 1993); "Circonfession," in Geoffrey Bennington and Jacques Derrida, *Jacques Derrida* (Paris: Seuil, 1991). Jacques Derrida, *Monolingualism of the Other; or, The Prosthesis of Origin*, trans. Patrick Mensah (Stanford: Stanford University Press, 1998); *Le monolinguisme de l'autre: ou la prothèse d'origine* (Paris: Galilée, 1996).

3. Derrida, "A Testimony Given," in *Questioning Judaism*, ed. Weber, 42/78. See also "Circumfession," 154/178.

4. In his "White Mythology: Metaphor in the Text of Philosophy," Derrida speaks of metaphysics as the *"relève de la métaphore."* The translator, Alan Bass, points out that the term *relève* is "untranslatable." He adds, "if *relève* is taken as a noun, the subtitle would read: 'Metaphysics—the *relève*, the *Aufhebung* of Metaphor.' If relève is taken as a verb . . . it can be understood in its usual sense, i.e., not as a translation of *Aufhebung*," but rather as relief or change. Change in the sense of the change of the guard. Derrida was the first to propose the *relève* for the Hegelian *Aufhebung*. See "White Mythology," in *Margins of Philosophy*, trans. Alan Bass (Chicago: University of Chicago Press, 1982), 258.—Trans.

5. G. W. F. Hegel, *Phenomenology of Spirit*, trans. A. V. Miller (Oxford: Oxford University Press, 1977), §156, p. 95.

6. "I have long struggled with myself in what looks like a logical paradox . . . over this figure of exemplarity"; see Derrida, "A Testimony Given," in *Questioning Judaism*, 41/76 (trans. modified).

7. "An inversion of the limiting concept into precondition, of defect into source, of abyss into condition, of discourse into locus" (Emmanuel Levinas, *Proper Names*, trans. Michael B. Smith [Stanford: Stanford University Press, 1996], 56; *Noms propres* [Montpellier: Fata Morgana, 1976], 66).

8. Jacques Derrida, *Writing and Difference*, trans. Alan Bass (Chicago: University of Chicago Press, 1980), 77–96; *L'écriture et la différence* (Paris: Seuil, 1967).

9. Ibid., 92/112.

10. Cf. Giorgio Agamben, *Remnants of Auschwitz: The Witness and the Archive*, trans. Daniel Heller-Roazen (New York: Zone Books, 1999), 163–64; *Ce qui reste après Auschwitz* (Paris: Rivages, 1999), 214–15.

11. The Just One refers either to the messiah or to the last of the Tsadiks, the proverbial thirty-six perfectly just men who, for each generation, bore the weight of the wrongs of the entire community.—Trans.

12. "The son of David will not come before the moment at which one shall have despaired of his coming." Cf. *Treatise Sanhedrin*, 97a.

13. Franz Rosenzweig, *The Star of Redemption*, trans. W. W. Hallo (New York: Holt, Rinehart and Winston, 1970), 404. [In *The Star of Redemption*, Rosenzweig writes: "In Judaism, man is always somehow a remnant. He is always somehow a survivor, an inner something, whose exterior was seized by the current of the world and carried off while he himself, what is left of him, remains standing on the shore. Something within him is waiting. And he has something within himself," 405.—Trans.]

14. "The Jewish people . . . preserves itself by subtraction, through a process of contraction, by the incessant formation of new remnants" (ibid., trans. modified.)

15. "The goal [*das Ziel*] is there where it has no need to go further beyond itself, there where it finds itself, and where the concept corresponds to the

object and the object to the concept" (Hegel, *Phenomenology of Spirit*, §80, p. 51).

16. Derrida, *Writing and Difference*, 92/112.
17. Derrida, "A Testimony Given," in *Questioning Judaism*, 41/76.
18. Rosenzweig, *The Star of Redemption*, 254.
19. Ibid., 256–57.
20. Ibid., 259.
21. Jacques Derrida, *Of Grammatology*, trans. Gayatri Chakravorty Spivak, corrected edition (Baltimore: The Johns Hopkins University Press, 1997), 65; *De la grammatologie* (Paris: Minuit, 1967), 96.
22. The French term *ajointement* is not in everyday use but combines the Latin *ad* ("toward") and *junctus* ("to join"). — Trans.
23. Rosenzweig, *The Star of Redemption*, 259.
24. Ibid., 256–57.
25. For *relève*, see n. 4, above. In addition, the word means a host of things from "concrete inscription," to "taking the place of," to "preserving in transmission." — Trans.
26. Franz Rosenzweig, "Cedars of Lebanon XVI: On Being a Jewish Person," in *Commentary* 1, no. 1 (November 1945); "Der jüdische Mensch," in *Gesammelte Schriften* (The Hague: Martinus Nijhoff, 1984), 3:561.
27. Derrida, "Circumfession," 75/74.
28. *Megillah*, 9b.
29. *Midrash Rabba*, Noah 36:8.
30. Jean-Luc Nancy, "Of Divine Places," trans. Michael Holland, in Jean-Luc Nancy, *The Inoperative Community*, ed. Peter Connor (Minneapolis: University of Minnesota Press, 1991), 128; *Des lieux divins* (Mauvezin: Trans-Europe-Repress, 1987), 22.
31. Rosenzweig, *The Star of Redemption*, 198, trans. modified.
32. Ibid.
33. Jacques Derrida, *Of Spirit: Heidegger and the Question*, trans. Geoffrey Bennington and Rachel Bowlby (Chicago: University of Chicago Press, 1989), 125–27; *De l'esprit* (Paris: Galilée, 1987), 115 ff.
34. "The real word that 'calls' [*heisst*] the object by its name ... the origin-word has pro-mised [*ver-heissen*]" (Rosenzweig, *The Star of Redemption*, 90). Rosenzweig overloads his play on *sprechen* and *versprechen*, "to speak" and "to promise," with another play on *heissen* and *verheissen*, "to call or be called" and "to promise and be promised"; that is, he loads the play on the Name and the Promise (the Promised Land is called in German "*das Land der Verheissung*"). See Martin Heidegger, *What Is Called Thinking?* trans. J. Glenn Gray (New York: Harper and Row, 1968), 114–19.
35. Rosenzweig, *The Star of Redemption*, 102.
36. Ibid., 119.
37. Derrida, *Monolingualism of the Other*, 68/127.
38. Rosenzweig, *Gesammelte Schriften*, 1.2:754.

39. Hannah Arendt, "Only the Mother Tongue Remains," *Esprit* 6 (Paris: Gallimard, 1985), 19–38. ["Was bleibt? Es bleibt die Muttersprache, "Interview with Günter Gaus, German television, 1964; translated into French in *La tradition cache, le Juif paria*, trans. Sylvie Courtine-Denamy (Paris: Bourgois, 1987). A complete English translation of the interview appears never to have been published.—Trans.]

40. We might consider here the famous stylistic economy of Kafka and the service-German [*Beamtendeutsch*] he uses as the writing of this very dispossession, or at least this dis-appropriation that the orality of language reveals.

41. Rosenzweig, *The Star of Redemption*, 90.

42. Ibid. To evince "speaking" as the site of a "revelation," of a passage from the "mute" to the "sonorous," from the "secret" to the "patent," from the "closed" to the "open," Rosenzweig plays, on this page (whose translation is very difficult), on the meanings of *Wort* ("word") and *ant-worten* ("answer" or "respond"), the meanings of *Anfang* ("beginning") and *auf-fangen* ("receive" or "welcome"). See Gérard Bensussan, *Franz Rosenzweig: Existence et philosophie* (Paris: Presses Universitaires de France, 2000), 59 ff.

43. We might counter that Rosenzweig "attenuates" the depropriation by attributing it to the "Jewish people" according to "three ways" (relative to German, to the Jewish languages, and the Hebrew), something Derrida has highlighted in a remarkable note in *Monolingualism of the Other*, 79–84. We may, in any case, attempt to indicate that the modalities of depropriation's radicalization, if they can be discussed, do not sweep away the true reappropriations.

44. Rosenzweig, *The Star of Redemption*, 252–53.

45. Ibid., 253.

46. Ibid.

47. Obviously Rosenzweig did not take into account the question of the revitalization of Hebrew into modern Israeli, which would then fall under the common status of the languages of "everyday life."

48. Translated as "The Eyes of Language: The Abyss and the Volcano," trans. Gil Anidjar, in Jacques Derrida, *Acts of Religion*, ed. Gil Anidjar (New York: Routledge, 2001), 189–227.—Trans.

49. French translation by Stéphane Mosès in *Archives de sciences sociales des religions*, nos. 60–61 (Paris, 1985), 83–84. Reprinted in S. Mosès, *L'ange de l'histoire* (Paris: Seuil, 1992), 239–41. (The letter is absent from the principal collection of Scholem's correspondence in English translation, Gershom Scholem, *A Life in Letters, 1914–1982*, ed. Anthony David Skinner [Cambridge: Harvard University Press, 2002].)

This Stranjew Body, Hélène Cixous

1. This extremely imagistic sentence combines the tension of Marrano-dissimulation (*Marrano* designated a Jew or Muslim who converted to

Christianity out of compulsion, and hence was not above suspicion of preserving the old religion) with the animal metaphor (*ébrouer*) of shaking off sweat or saliva and with what escapes all images: those names that no longer have a face. — Trans.

2. See Franz Kafka, "The Wish to Be a Red Indian," in *Franz Kafka: The Complete Stories*, ed. Nahum N. Glatzer (New York: Schocken Books, 1971), 390. — Trans.

3. In French, *Menti-né* combines two past participles: lied-to (*menti*) and born (*né*). But it immediately calls to mind *matinée*, as in the *matinée de sa vie* or the early morning of his life, an expression used to denote childhood. — Trans.

4. Marcel Proust, *In Search of Lost Time*, vol. 5, *The Captive and the Fugitive*, trans. C. K. Scott Moncrieff and Terrence Kilmartin (New York: Modern Library, 1999). In the original text, the section is entitled "La Fugitive: Albertine disparue." — Trans.

5. The Latin term *liquor* comes from the Greek *leípō*. It signifies, essentially, "to leave," or "to leave behind." This leaving comes from the fact of liquidity itself, comprising everything that flows away; thus the cognates: *liquidate, delinquent, delicto, relic*, even *derelict* and *deliquescent*. In Romance languages, the Indo-European root *leikw* has come to signify "to find oneself deficient, to be lacking or missing from that place where one should be." See Émile Benveniste, *Le vocabulaire des institutions indo-européennes*, vol.1, *Économie, parenté et société* (Paris: Minuit, 1969), 194; translated into English as *Indo-European Language and Society*, trans. Elizabeth Palmer (London: Faber, 1973). — Trans.

6. *Antonommé* — an impossible past participle that combines "to antonym," or give the opposite name to something, and "antonomasia" (both with *an* = counter, non, or *ana* = repeatedly, and *onoma*, or name, in Greek), a trope that characterizes a person by a common noun or a phrase. — Trans.

7. *Le sens apaisant du sang* means the meaning, the feeling, but also the *direction* (of the blood), as the French language speaks of one-way streets, *rue à sens unique*. — Trans.

8. In English in the text. — Trans.

9. *Tachet* is not a noun. It is a misspelling that suggests an epithet. Derived from the verb *tacheter*, "to speckle or fleck with brown or black spots or markings, as on an animal pelt," it suggests at the same time "stain" and "brown spot," or, by extension, one who is marked or sullied. — Trans.

10. The *Contre-allée* carries a strong connotation of a side path or service road. I have translated it as "frontage road" to preserve that sense, as well as Cixous' reference to the graffiti facing incoming travelers from the sea. The English translation is Catherine Malabou and Jacques Derrida, *Counterpath: Traveling with Jacques Derrida*, trans. David Wills (Stanford: Stanford University Press, 2004). — Trans.

11. Émile Benveniste reminds us that *hostis* comes into Latin as *hostis* and *hosti-pet* (where *-pet* is one of the suffixes from *pte* and *pse*, which gave us the words *despotes*, "despot," and *ipse*, "himself"). In both cases, *host-* designates the foreigner and a certain equality established by exchange or compensation. The foreigner (like the Greek *xenos*) who compensates the gift of the host by offering a return gift is the positive foreigner, or guest, apt to receive the hospitality of the host. The foreigner who does not participate in such an economy of gifting becomes the *hostis*, who is thus "hostile," the enemy. The host (which in French denotes simultaneously host and guest) is tied to the master by virtue of the form *hosti-pes*, as the master is the one who is most eminently "himself" or *ipse*, or again: the *despotes*. All these related terms are in Derrida's reflection. See Benveniste, *Le vocabulaire des institutions indo-européennes*, 1:87–93; and Jacques Derrida, "Hostipitality," in Jacques Derrida, *Acts of Religion*, ed. and introd. Gil Anidjar (New York: Routledge, 2002), 356–420. — Trans.

12. For his discussion of *Le parjure*, see Jacques Derrida, *Without Alibi*, ed. and trans. Peggy Kamuf (Stanford: Stanford University Press, 2002), 161– 201. The concept *parjure* is larger than the English term *perjury*: it includes false sermons, faithlessness, and betrayal; it is both adjective and noun. — Trans.

13. *La bête et le bête*. Benveniste shows that the French *bête*, by its ties to *bestia* or *bétail*, and to ancient Indo-Iranian (*paso-vira*, or "men-cattle," is related to the Greek *probaton* and the Latin *pecus*, etc.), refers to movable, domestic living things. By extension, in contexts where cattle or domestic beasts are the referent, all domestic persons, house slaves, are covered by this same term. See Benveniste, *Le vocabulaire des institutions indo-européennes*, 1:48/292. — Trans.

14. See Jacques Derrida, "Composing 'Circumfession,'" in *Augustine and Postmodernism: Confessions and Circumfession*, ed. John D. Caputo and Michael J. Scanlon (Bloomington: Indiana University Press, 2005), and also Hélène Cixous, *Portrait of Jacques Derrida as a Young Jewish Saint*, trans. Beverley Bie Brahic (New York: Columbia University Press, 2004). — Trans.

15. This is a play on *déjà j'arrive* or *déjà arrivé*, plus *ance*, which makes the term into a processual noun: "already happened-ing," "already I arriveness." *Al Djezaïr* is the Arabic name for Algiers. — Trans.

16. Hélène Cixous is weaving into her text the beginnings of her novella *Un vrai jardin* (Paris: L'Herne, 1971). This is the story of a Jewish student in a grammar school who, being completely ignored by the faculty and hounded by his fellow students, develops an obsession with the earth and the sand. — Trans.

17. Cixous is playing on the homonymy of *essai* or *des essais*, this time writing *des c*. She means the combined process of discovering the children's garden called *kindergarden* and discovering the abc's. Clearly, the children were beginning to write, if not essays, at least something like assays. With

this comes the whole psychoanalytic theory, developed by Lacan, of the signifier and the letter that traces limits and boundaries on the raw excess of experience. — Trans.

18. The French homonymy continues from *d'essai* to *des lettres c*, to *des c'est*, ultimately to *Décès*, where death culminates essays and trials like a new thorny outcropping or a strange tree. — Trans.

19. Cixous appears to mean the lush garden that frames the beginnings of Genesis, which the Jewish Bible calls *Bereshit*, or beginning. — Trans.

20. In French, to unscrew is *dévisser*. To stare someone down is *dévisager*, playing on the face of the house and the face of her father, the screw, *la vis*, and the face, *vis* or *visage*. Cixous creates a symbolic murder whose beginnings are exclusion and, for the time being, result in the removal of the professional sign or shingle. — Trans.

21. It is not habitual to speak of rising in iron, *monter en fer*," the *en fer* immediately calls to mind *enfer*, or hell. That is, the bars rose, in iron (and as hell) up to the blue sky; as if hell (*enfer*) rose up to a pure, blue heaven. — Trans.

22. *Renvoir* is untranslatable, because it is not a French word. It combines the verbs *renvoyer*, *revoir*, and, indirectly, *voir ailleurs*. *Renvoyer* denotes the dismissal or suspension of an employee or student. In a more general sense, it means to send back or to return. In a literary sense, it means to refer an image or idea to another one. *Revoir* denotes seeing again. It can mean to witness again, as in the case of terrible events, and it can mean to revise or to go over a text again. With the repetitions in these words comes a distinct affective intensification. *Voir ailleurs* has been added here because the verb-neologism *renvoir* lends itself to an imperative: "Get out of here, go somewhere else." — Trans.

23. In *fuite sèche*, Cixous combines *fuite*, "flight," and *séchai l'école*, "to cut class or play hookey." What she creates is a new meaning: *fuite sèche*, which for the French ear is like *panne sèche*, when a car stops dead, because it is out of gas. The words that follow, *secret sec*, combine a dry, simple secret with a secret that stops you from advancing. — Trans.

24. The French reads "les yeux fuient tant de pleurs et de larmes, les siens, les siennes et celles et ceux": the pronouns refer, respectively, to the masculine *pleurs* and the feminine *larmes*, but the pronouns are much broader in scope and refer to his eyes but also to the weeping and tears of men and women, saints and secular ones, victims of the necessity of fleeing. — Trans.

25. Playing on the popular Latin *persus* and on the classical Latin *persicus*, Cixous is following Derrida in relation to Catherine of Siena, whose eyes were *pers*, of a changeable color, and whose eyes, including his own, pierced through the obscurity of the times, of the world, of philosophy, to see the light. — Trans.

26. On the eighth day, by Jewish law, the male child is circumcised. — Trans.

27. The reference is to Proust and his autobiographical Albertine. Not until 1987 were the fragments entitled "Albertine disparue" recognized as intended for inclusion in *À la recherche du temps perdu*. Inclusion of the Albertine saga, which remains fragmentary and describes a flight, was rendered difficult by the incomplete character of that work. Thus, "Albertine disparue" amounts to a *texte de renvoi*, a fragment that belongs to the text but refers us continually beyond the version that we have come to know. It functions like a kind of *différance*.—Trans.

28. *Imaginez-le* means simultaneously "imagine him" and "imagine it."—Trans.

29. Recall Lacan's analysis of the letters on the body and his *pas-de-trace*. I see a step (*pas*) in the sand; it is up to me to choose whether this is an indeterminate trace, a hollow, or the sign that a human foot was there. In so doing, an utterance escapes my lips. I say "step [*pas*]." But already, in saying *pas*, I have introduced the trace into a complex network of homonyms and antonyms, spoken signifiers; I am, therefore, already fleeing the indeterminacy of which I chose, half-consciously, to "make sense." The disjunction between the real and the letter, or trace, can be assimilated to a letter that draws boundaries and imposes form on the formless. Such letters are also inscribed on human bodies, like the *Tachet* mark that Cixous described earlier. See Philippe Julien, *Pour lire Jacques Lacan* (Paris: Seuil, 1995).—Trans.

30. Here, *prises de vie* echoes *prises de vue*, or photo shots, and *prises de sang*, blood samples.—Trans.

31. Cixous writes *l'abyme*, evoking the old French spelling of a word now written *l'abîme*.—Trans.

32. The ambiguity here is due to the fact that the subject is *imminence*, but every noun that follows is also feminine. Thus, when Cixous writes, "elle signe en meme temps le verdict," the feminine pronoun, *elle*, refers likewise to death and to the epoch.—Trans.

33. Elpinor was one of Odysseus's men. Having gotten drunk on Circe's island, he fell from a roof, broke his neck, and died. On Odysseus's visit to Hades, Elpinor implored him to return to the island and bury his body, so that his soul could leave Hades.—Trans.

34. *Gradiva* was Wilhelm Jensen's "Pompeian" fantasy piece, which Freud analyzed.—Trans.

35. Cf. the theme of the cave in Hélène Cixous, *Tombe* (Paris: Seuil, 1973), and in her discussion of Derrida's "Circumfession" in "Ce qui a l'air de quoi," *Modern Language Notes* 121 (2006): 828–49. The latter condenses Cixous's presentation in *L'événement comme écriture: Lire Cixous et Derrida se lisant*, ed. Marta Segarra Montaner (Paris: Campagne première, 2007).

36. Through Cixous, Derrida is playing on two meanings of "donner au chat sa langue": literally, it is giving your tongue or your language to a cat, which has none. The more frequent meaning is simply "I don't know."

Under the circumstances, Derrida is transgressing, miming the cat. Derrida does not know what he is doing—but knows precisely that much.—Trans.

37. At least four homophonies are here: *ver*; or "worm"; *vers*, or "verse"; *vers* as the preposition denoting movement in time or space; and *ver* as the beginning of *ver-ité*.—Trans.

38. Cf. Cixous, *Portrait of Jacques Derrida as a Young Jewish Saint*—Trans.

39. Derrida first plays on the first person indicative of "to be [*suis*]," and of "to follow [*suis*]." But he says "Je le suis à la trace": I *follow* it meticulously; I *am* this foreign body through the trace.—Trans.

40. Cixous writes, "je qui est ce corps." The proper French would be "je qui suis ce corps;" here, the *est* makes the *je*, or I, into an object. In addition, *est* plays on *hait* from the verb *haïr*, or "to hate."—Trans.

41. In French, a *bête rayée* is any animal with stripes. But another emphasis is present as well: the animal crossed out, eliminated in its integrity or its definability. Hence the mixture of half-god and half-animal..—Trans.

The Story of a Friendship: The Archive and the Question of Palestine, Michal Ben Naftali

1. Gershom Scholem, *Walter Benjamin: The Story of a Friendship* (Philadelphia: The Jewish Publication Society of America, 1981), 21.

2. Jacques Derrida, *Memoires for Paul de Man,* Revised edition, trans. Cecile Lindsay et al. (New York: Columbia University Press, 1986).

3. Jacques Derrida, "Like the Sound of the Sea Deep Within a Shell: Paul de Man's War," trans. Peggy Kamuf, first published in *Critical Inquiry* 14, no. 3 (Spring 1988). This essay was later republished in the revised edition of *Memoires for Paul de Man*, 157–263, incorporating changes made by Derrida for its publication in *Responses: On Paul de Man's Wartime Journalism*, ed. Werner Hamacher, Neil Hertz, and Thomas Keenan (Lincoln: University of Nebraska Press, 1989), 127–64.

4. Jacques Derrida, *Acts of Literature,* ed. Derek Attridge (New York: Routledge, 1992), 313. [Trans. modified.—Trans.]

5. Jacques Derrida, *Politics of Friendship*, trans. George Collins (London: Verso, 1997), 294.

6. Jacques Derrida, "Fors: The Anglish Words of Nicolas Abraham and Maria Torok," trans. Barbara Johnson, in Nicolas Abraham and Maria Torok, *The Wolfman's Magic Word: A Cryptonomy*, trans. Nicholas Rand (Minneapolis: University of Minnesota Press, 1986), xi–xlviii.—Trans.

7. Jacques Derrida, *Archive Fever: A Freudian Impression,* trans. Eric Prenowitz (Chicago: University of Chicago Press, 1996), 62–63.

8. Gershom Scholem, *Fidélité et utopie: Essais sur le judaïsme contemporain*, trans. M. Delmotte and B. Dupuy (Paris: Calmann-Lévy, 1978).

9. Franz Kafka, "Before the Law," in *The Complete Stories*, ed. Nahum N. Glatzer (New York: Schocken Books, 1946), 3–4. [Trans. modified.—Trans.]

10. Derrida, *Politics of Friendship*, 297–98.

11. Walter Benjamin, "Franz Kafka," trans. Harry Zohn, in Benjamin, *Selected Writings*, vol. 2, *1927–1934*, ed. Michael W. Jennings, Howard Eiland, and Gary Smith (Cambridge: Harvard University Press, 1999), 809–10.

12. Franz Kafka, *Letter to His Father* (New York: Schocken Books, 1966), 73. [Trans. modified.—Trans.]

13. Walter Benjamin, *Illuminations*, ed. Hannah Arendt, trans. Harry Zohn (New York: Schocken Books, 1969), 124.

14. "[T]he attitude taken by the biographer [Brod] is one of supreme bonhomie. Its lack of detachment is its most salient feature. . . . On account of the author's striking lack of tact, of a feeling for thresholds and distances, feuilletonistic clichés have seeped into a text that should have been obliged to exhibit a certain dignity. . . . It oversteps moderation both in the way in which he pays homage to Kafka and in the familiarity with which he treats him" (Letter of June 12, 1938, in *The Correspondence of Walter Benjamin, 1910–1940*, ed. Gershom Scholem and Theodor W. Adorno [Chicago: University of Chicago Press, 1994], 560–62).

15. Kafka, *Letter to His Father*, 17.

16. Derrida, *Politics of Friendship*, 282.

17. Genesis 4:7.

18. Walter Benjamin, "On the Image of Proust," trans. Rodney Livingstone, in Benjamin, *Selected Writings*, vol. 2, 244–45.

19. Kafka, *Letter to His Father*, 7. [Trans. modified—Trans.]

20. Derrida, "Devant la Loi," in *Kafka and the Contemporary Critical Performance*, ed. A. Udoff (Bloomington: Indiana University Press, 1987), 141. [Trans. modified, and "friend" substituted for "law" in Derrida's text.—Trans.]

21. Kafka, *The Complete Stories*, 392–93.

22. Derrida, "Devant la Loi," 128.

23. Jacques Derrida, *Given Time: I. Counterfeit Money*, trans. Peggy Kamuf (Chicago: University of Chicago Press, 1992), 144–45.

24. Derrida, *Politics of Friendship*, 235.

25. Kafka, "The Judgment," *The Complete Stories*, 77–78.

26. Scholem, *Walter Benjamin: The Story of a Friendship*, 68.

27. Ibid., 113–14.

28. Ibid., 162–63.

29. These fictive "letters from Stephan" (Stephan was only months old at the time) were written by Dora, but with Walter's knowledge and perhaps even with his participation. See Scholem, *Walter Benjamin: The Story of a Friendship*, 68.—Trans.

30. *The Correspondence of Walter Benjamin, 1910–1940*, 262.

31. Scholem, *Walter Benjamin: The Story of a Friendship*, 73–74.

32. Jacques Derrida, "Back from Moscow, in the USSR," trans. M. Quaintaire, in *Politics, Theory, and Contemporary Culture*, ed. Mark Poster

(New York: Columbia University Press: 1993), 200–21. In his *Memoirs of the Blind*, Derrida speaks of the family or fraternal economy at the basis of the intellectual choice, which is thus contaminated by guilt or negativity: "wounded jealousy before an older brother whom I admired, as did everyone around him, for his talent as a draftsman. . . . And the fratricidal watchword: *economizing on drawing*" (Jacques Derrida, *Memoirs of the Blind: The Self-Portrait and Other Ruins*, trans. Pascale-Anne Brault and Michael Naas [Chicago: University of Chicago Press, 1993], 37; my emphasis).

33. *The Correspondence of Walter Benjamin, 1910–1940*, xiii.
34. Scholem, *Walter Benjamin: The Story of a Friendship*, 33.
35. Ibid, 47.
36. Ibid., 74–75.
37. *The Correspondence of Walter Benjamin, 1910–1940*, 175.
38. Walter Benjamin, "A Berlin Chronicle," trans. Edmund Jephcott, in *Selected Writings*, vol. 2, 614.
39. *The Correspondence of Walter Benjamin, 1910–1940*, 58.
40. Scholem, *Walter Benjamin: The Story of a Friendship*, 189.
41. "Letters to this or that woman, letters to friends, letter to the father; nonetheless, there is always a woman behind these letters who is the real addressee [*destinataire*]—the woman that the father is supposed to have made him lose, the one that his friends hope he will break from, and so on. To substitute for love the letter of love? To deterritorialize love. To substitute for the feared *conjugal contract* a *pact with the devil*. The letters are inseparable from such a pact; they are this pact itself" (Gilles Deleuze and Félix Guattari, *Kafka: Toward a Minor Literature*, trans. Dana Polan [Minneapolis: University of Minnesota Press, 1986], 29; my emphasis).
42. Scholem, *Walter Benjamin: The Story of a Friendship*, 120.
43. Ibid., 193.
44. Ibid., 182, 189.
45. Ibid., 199.
46. Walter Benjamin, *Ibizan Sequence*, trans. Rodney Livingstone, in *Selected Writings*, vol. 2, 591.
47. Scholem, *Walter Benjamin: The Story of a Friendship*, 137–39.
48. Letter of February 20, 1930, in *The Correspondence of Walter Benjamin, 1910–1940*, 363.
49. Gershom Scholem, "Walter Benjamin," trans. Lux Furtmüller, *Yearbook of the Leo Baeck Institute* 10 (1965), 131.
50. Jacques Derrida, *Adieu to Emmanuel Levinas*, trans. Pascale-Anne Brault and Michael Naas (Stanford: Stanford University Press, 1997), 41–42.
51. Scholem's preface to *The Correspondence of Walter Benjamin and Gershom Scholem, 1932–40* (Cambridge: Harvard University Press, 1992), 7.
52. Kafka, "The Judgment," *The Complete Stories*, 87.

Jacques Derrida and Kabbalistic Sources, Moshe Idel

1. See: Gershom Scholem, *On the Kabbalah and Its Symbolism*, trans. R. Manheim (New York: Schocken Books, 1969), 44–47; Moshe Idel, "The Concept of the Torah in Heikhalot Literature and Its Metamorphoses in Kabbalah," *Jerusalem Studies in Jewish Thought* 1 (1981): 49–52 (in Hebrew); Elliot R. Wolfson, *Through a Speculum That Shines: Vision and Imagination in Medieval Jewish Mysticism* (Princeton: Princeton University Press, 1994), 247–51, 376.

2. R. Jacob of Girona, *Sefer Meshiv Devarim Nekhohim*, ed. Georges Vajda (Jerusalem: G. Vajda, 1969), 154–155. On this kabbalist, see Georges Vajda, *Recherches sur la philosophie et la Kabbale dans la pensée juive du Moyen Age* (Paris: Mouton, 1962), 33–113.

3. See R. Jacob of Girona, *Sefer ha-'Emunah ve-ha-Bitahon*, in *Kitvei ha-Ramban*, ed. H. Chavel (Jerusalem: Rav Kook Institute, 1964), vol. 2, chap. 18, p. 409. Also, Moshe Idel, "Sefirot above Sefirot," in *Tarbiz* 51 (1982): 265–267 (in Hebrew). For R. Isaac ibn Latif's interpretation of this Platonic position as formulated by Maimonides, see S. O. Heller Wilensky, "Isaac ibn Latif: Philosopher or Kabbalist?" in *Jewish Medieval and Renaissance Studies*, ed. Alexander Altmann (Cambridge: Harvard University Press, 1967), 188–89, esp. n. 26.

4. I assume that the idea of perfection is related also to the fact that the first and last letters are conceived of as next to each other. This idea is found, to a certain extent, in Nahmanides' introduction to his *Commentary on the Torah*, from which also comes the description of the visual aspect of the Torah in the following lines.

5. See *Tanna de-Bei 'Eliyahu*, chap. 25.

6. *Sefer ha-Yihud*, MS. Milano-Ambrosiana 62, 113b ff., printed and discussed in Idel, "Concept of the Torah," 62–64. See also Idel, *R. Menahem Recanati, the Kabbalist* (Jerusalem: Schocken, 1998), vol. 2, chap. 16 (in Hebrew). Also: Scholem, *On the Kabbalah*, 43–44; Charles Mopsik, *Les grands textes de la Kabbale* (Paris: Verdier, 1993), 278–87, 560–65; Michael Fishbane, *The Garments of the Torah: Essays in Biblical Hermeneutics* (Bloomington: Indiana University Press, 1989), 43; and Barbara A. Holdrege, *Veda and Torah: Transcending the Textuality of Scripture* (Albany: State University of New York Press, 1996), 361.

7. See Moshe Idel, "R. Joseph of Hamadan's Commentary on Ten Sefirot and Fragments of His Writings," in *'Alei Sefer*, vols. 6–7 (Jerusalem, 1979), 81–84 (in Hebrew).

8. See R. Menahem Recanati, *Commentary on the Rationales for the Commandments*, ed. H. Liebermann (London: H. Liebermann, 1962), 2a-b ff.; checked with the version found in Ms. Paris, Bibliothèque nationale 825, 1b–2a ff. On this quote, see: Scholem, *On the Kabbalah*, 44, 124; Isaiah Tishby, *The Wisdom of the Zohar: An Anthology of Texts*, trans. D. Goldstein (London: The Littman Library, 1991), 1:284.

9. See *Diogenes*, vol. 14 (Paris: Gallimard/UNESCO, 1955): 1–16; vol. 15 (1956): 2–40. For an easily available reprint of the French translation, see Gershom Scholem, *Le nom et les symboles de Dieu dans la mystique juive*, trans. M. R. Hayoun and G. Vajda (Paris: Le Cerf, 1983), 111.

10. Jacques Derrida, *Dissemination*, trans. Barbara Johnson (Chicago: University of Chicago Press, 1981), 345. For further discussion of this issue, see Moshe Idel, *Absorbing Perfections: Kabbalah and Interpretation* (New Haven: Yale University Press, 2002), chap. 2, pp. 69–74.

11. For further reference to this quote, see Mopsik, *Les grands textes*, 279. See also: Idel, "The Concept of the Torah," 58–62; Moshe Idel, *Kabbalah: New Perspectives* (New Haven: Yale University Press, 1988), 244–47; Holdrege, *Veda and Torah*, 200–201, 334, 492.

12. See Idel, *Absorbing Perfections*, 45–110.

13. Jacques Derrida, *Of Grammatology*, trans. Gayatri Chakravorty Spivak (Baltimore: The Johns Hopkins University Press, 1976), 163, 158, respectively. For other similarities between Derrida and Jewish mystical thought, though without claiming a historical nexus, see Elliot R. Wolfson, *Circle in the Square: Studies in the Use of Gender in Kabbalistic Symbolism* (Albany: State University of New York Press, 1995), 166n41. Compare also Umberto Eco's remarks in *Foucault's Pendulum*, trans. W. Weaver (New York: Harcourt Brace Jovanovich, 1989), chap. 110, p. 565.

14. See Gershom Scholem, "New Remnants from the Writings of R. Azriel of Gerona," in *The Gulak and Klein Memorial Volume* (Jerusalem, 1942), 207, *'Ein davar hutz mimmenu*. This phrase is characteristic of R. Azriel's terminology, though it was rarely related to God but more often to the Divine Will. I assume that Derrida did not have access to the pertinent passage in the original Hebrew, but could nevertheless have read either the German version in Scholem's fuller description of the beginnings of Kabbalah, *Ursprung und Anfänge der Kabbala* (Berlin: De Gruyter, 1962), or in the French translation, *Les origines de la Kabbale*, trans. Jean Loewenson (Paris: Aubier Montaigne, 1966), 447. The French reads: "rien n'existe hormis Lui." See also the English version, *Origins of the Kabbalah*, ed., R. Z. J. Werblowsky, trans. A. Arkush (Philadelphia: Jewish Publication Society, 1987), 423–24, 434: "Nothing exists outside of Him." Scholem pointed out the plausible source of R. Azriel in a formulation of Duns Scotus. See *Origins*, 438n.170. See also Chaim Wirszubski, *Pico della Mirandola's Encounter with Jewish Mysticism* (Cambridge: Harvard University Press, 1988), 103, for the Latin translation of R. Azriel of Girona, prepared for Pico della Mirandola.

15. See R. Levy Ben Gershom, *Commentary on the Torah* (Venice, 1547), 113b-c ff. Compare also with the translation of Jose Faur, *Golden Doves with Silver Dots* (Bloomington: Indiana University Press, 1986), xxii.

16. See Idel, *Absorbing Perfections*, 122–24.

17. Idel, *Kabbalah*, 212–13.

18. On the need to resort to a panoramic approach to Jewish culture in Hasidism, see Moshe Idel, *Hasidism: Between Ecstasy and Magic* (Albany: State University of New York Press, 1995), 9–15.

19. See Edmond Jabès, "La clé," in *Le Parcours* (Paris: Gallimard, 1985), 88.

20. Abraham Abulafia, *Sheva' Netivot ha-Torah [Philosophie und Kabbalah]*, ed. Adolf Jellinek (Leipzig, 1854), 1:14. On the twelve commentaries on *Sefer Yetzirah* studied by Abulafia, see Moshe Idel, *R. Menahem Recanati: The Kabbalist* (Jerusalem: Schocken Books, 1999), 1:33–35 (in Hebrew).

21. *Sheva' Netivot ha-Torah*, 14–15; *L'épître des sept voies*, trans. Jean-Christophe Attiah (Paris: Éclat, 1992), 72. See also: Scholem, "The Name of God and the Linguistics of the Kabbalah," *Diogenes* 80 (1972): 190; Moshe Idel, *Language, Torah, and Hermeneutics in Abraham Abulafia* (Albany: State University of New York Press, 1989), xvi; and Idel, *Absorbing Perfections*, 91, 267.

22. Cf. Ms. München Bayerische Staatsbibliothek Heb. 10, 136b ff.

23. See Henri Corbin, *Histoire de la philosophie islamique* (Paris: Gallimard, 1964), 206–7.

24. See: M. Idel, "Ramon Lull and Ecstatic Kabbalah," in *Journal of the Warburg and Courtauld Institutes* 51 (1988): 170–74; Umberto Eco, *The Search for the Perfect Language*, trans. James Fentress (Oxford: Blackwell, 1995), 53–69; Andreas Kilcher, *Die Sprachtheorie der Kabbala als Ästhetisches Paradigma* (Stuttgart: J. M. Metzler, 1998), 152–75; Harvey J. Haimes, *The Art of Conversion, Christianity and Kabbalah in the Thirteenth Century* (Leiden: Brill, 2000), 217–22. For further on ecstatic Kabbalah, see Wirszubski, *Pico della Mirandola*, 63, 73–74, 81.

25. Idel, *Language, Torah, and Hermeneutics*, 97–101.

26. Dov Schwartz, *Religious Zionism Between Logic and Messianism* (Tel Aviv: 'Am 'Oved, 1999), 305–6 (in Hebrew).

27. Derrida, *Dissemination*, 344.

28. Gershom Scholem, *Major Trends in Jewish Mysticism* (New York: Schocken Books, 1995); translated as *Les grands courants de la mystique juive*, trans. M. M. Davy (Paris: Payot, 1950). See p. 390n50 of the French translation for the same translation occurring verbatim in Derrida. See also George Steiner, *After Babel* (London: Oxford University Press, 1976), 60–61. On orphic language, see the important remarks of Susan A. Handelman, *Fragments of Redemption: Jewish Thought and Literary Theory in Benjamin, Scholem, and Levinas* (Bloomington: Indiana University Press, 1991), 33–35. Umberto Eco also refers to Lullian techniques of letter combination in describing Mallarmé's method of combining pages. See Umberto Eco, *The Open Work*, trans. Anna Cancogni (Cambridge: Harvard University Press, 1989), 1–23. See also Idel, *Absorbing Perfections*, 90–91.

29. Thomas A. Williams, *Mallarmé and the Language of Mysticism* (Athens: University of Georgia Press, 1970), 55–56. See also Idel, *Absorbing Perfections*, 76–77 and notes.

30. Pico della Mirandola, *Apologia*, in *Opera Omnia* (Basel, 1557), 180. On this text, see Idel, "Ramon Lull and Ecstatic Kabbalah."

31. Wirszubski, *Pico della Mirandola*, 196–99.

32. Moshe Idel, "Infinities of Torah in Kabbalah," in *Midrash and Literature*, ed. Geoffrey H. Hartman and Sanford Budick (New Haven: Yale University Press, 1986), 146–47.

33. Cf. Idel, *Absorbing Perfections*, 90–91, 361–67.

34. See Abulafia's recurrent motif of unknotting the knots of the soul as part of mystical progress; Moshe Idel, *The Mystical Experience in Abraham Abulafia*, trans. Jonathan Chipman (Albany: State University of New York Press, 1988), 134–37.

35. Abulafia uses the term *Galgal* ("circle or sphere") in order to refer to *nativ* ("path," i.e., way of interpretation). He starts with the smallest sphere and progresses toward the largest one. Compare Gregory the Great's interpretation of Ezekiel's *'Ofan* as referring to an exegetical method, hinted at in Henri de Lubac, *L'écriture dans la tradition* (Paris: Aubier Montaigne, 1966), 276. On the concept of *Galgal* in Abulafia, see also Idel, *Absorbing Perfections*, 39–40.

36. This is an interesting parallel to Origen's view: "extenditur anima nostra, quae prius fuerat contracta, ut possit capax esse sapientia Dei [We enlarge our soul, which was previously contracted, in order to be capable of receiving the Wisdom of God]." See *Patrologia Latina*, vol. 25, 627c ff. See also: de Lubac, *L'écriture dans la tradition*, 285; Umberto Eco, *Semiotics and the Philosophy of Language* (Bloomington: Indiana University Press, 1984), 150.

37. Moshe Idel, "On the History of the Interdiction Against the Study of Kabbalah Before the Age of Forty," *A.J.S. Review* 5 (1980): 17–18 (in Hebrew); and Idel, *Absorbing Perfections*, 267–68, 324–32.

38. Abulafia, *Sheva Netivot ha-Torah*, 13–14.

39. *Berakhot*, 28b ff.

40. Mordechai Breuer, "Mine'u Bneichem min ha-Higayon" ["Keep your children from Higayyon"], in *Memory Book for Rabbi David Ochs* (Ramat Gan: Bar Ilan, 1978), 242–61 (in Hebrew); Frank Talmage, "Keep Your Sons from Scripture: The Bible in Medieval Jewish Scholarship and Spirituality," in *Understanding Scripture: Explorations of Jewish and Christian Traditions of Interpretation*, ed. Clemens Thoma and Michael Wyschogrod (New York: Paulist Press, 1987), 90–91; Idel, "On the History," 15–20.

41. Cf. Idel, *Language, Torah, and Hermeneutics*, 20–22. See also R. Nathan ben Sa'adyah Harar, *Sha'arei Tzedeq*, ed. Elijah Porush (Jerusalem, 1989), 41.

42. *Meggilah*, 31b ff.; *Nedarim*, 40a ff.; Yalqut Shime'oni on Kings, para. 196.

43. Samuel Balentine, *The Hidden God: The Hiding of the Face of God in the Old Testament* (Oxford: Oxford University Press, 1984).

44. Robert Gordis, "Studies in the Relationship of Biblical and Rabbinic Hebrew," in *The Word and the Book: Studies in Biblical Language and Literature* (New York: Ktav Publishing House, 1976), 158–84. See also *Louis Ginzberg Jubilee Volume* (New York: American Academy for Jewish Research, 1946), 173–200.

45. *Lehaflig ha-hester*: this can also mean "the hiding" or "accentuating the destruction."

46. *Hayyei ha-Nefesh*, Ms. Munich, Bayerische Staatsbibliothek, 408, 9b ff. (in Hebrew).

47. *Sabbath*, 30a ff.

48. *Sefer Hayyei ha-Nefesh*, Ms. Munich, Bayerische Staatsbibliotek 408, 71b–72a ff. See also: Alexander Altmann, "Maimonides' Attitude Toward Jewish Mysticism," in *Studies in Jewish Thought: An Anthology of German Jewish Scholarship*, ed. Alfred Jospe (Detroit: Wayne State University Press, 1981), 200–19; Aviezer Ravitzky, *History and Faith: Studies in Jewish Philosophy*, Amsterdam Studies in Jewish Thought (Amsterdam: Gieben Publishers, 1996), 2:250–51, for the earlier view of R. Shmuel ibn Tibbon, see pp. 262–63; Idel, *Language, Torah, and Hermeneutics*, 74.

49. *Sefer Sitrey Torah*, Ms. Paris, Bibliothèque nationale 774, 151a ff.

50. See, e.g., Ms. Munich, Bayerische Staatsbibliothek, Heb. 58, 328b ff.

51. On Abulafia's calculations of the end, using the noun *seter*, see Moshe Idel, "'The Time of the End': Apocalypticism and Its Spiritualization in Abraham Abulafia's Eschatology," in *Apocalyptic Time*, ed. Albert Baumgarten (Leiden: Brill, 2000), 180.

52. *Hores ha-binyan*.

53. *Boneh ha-horbban*.

54. A. Jellinek, ed., "'Sefer ha-Ot': Apokalypse des Pseudo-Propheten und Pseudo-Messias Abraham Abulafia," in *Jubelschrift zum siebzigsten Geburtstage des Prof. Dr. H. Graetz* (Breslau, 1887), 79.

55. Ibid., 75, 77, 78.

56. R. Nathan ben Sa'adyah Harar, *Sha'arei Tzedeq*, 17.

57. Moshe Idel, *Messianic Mystics* (New Haven: Yale University Press, 1998), 302.

58. See, e.g., Harry A. Wolfson, *Philo: Foundations of Religious Philosophy* (Cambridge: Harvard University Press, 1982). See also Moshe Idel, "On Binary 'Beginnings' in Kabbalah-Scholarship," in *Aporemata: Kritische Studien zur Philologiegeschichte* (Göttingen: Vandenhoeck and Ruprecht, 2001), 5:313–37.

59. For Lull, see above, n. 24. For Bruno, see Eco, *The Search*, 132–39. On Leibniz and Kabbalah, see: Allison Coudert, *Leibniz and the Kabbalah* (Dordrecht: Kluwer, 1995); Susanne Edel, *Die individuelle Substanz bei Boehme und Leibniz* (Stuttgart: Steiner, 1995), 163–205. For more recent thinkers, see Paolo Rossi, *'Clavis Universalis': Arti mnemoniche e logica combinatoria da Lullo a Leibniz* (Bologna: Il Mulino, 1983); and Eco, *The Search*.

60. The relatively significant divergences between the main concepts that inform the different works mentioned above should not minimize the fact that earlier contacts between them, in Europe or in the East, preceded the medieval episodes, and even facilitated them, by "allowing" some later figures like Pico della Mirandola and Johann Reuchlin to claim that there were basic concordances between these works. See Idel, *Absorbing Perfections*, 250–54 and 482–92.

61. Idel, *Kabbalah*, 247–49.

62. Idel, *Language, Torah, and Hermeneutics*, 101, 103; *Sha'arei Tzedeq*, 39.

Historicity and *Différance*, Gianni Vattimo

1. Jacques Derrida, *Positions*, trans. Alan Bass (Chicago: University of Chicago Press, 1981), 48–49. [Derrida is quoting himself from *Of Grammatology*, trans. Gayatri Chakravorty Spivak, corrected edition (Baltimore: The Johns Hopkins University Press, 1998), 93. — Trans.]

2. Derrida, *Positions*, 59–60.

3. Ibid, 47.

4. Ibid., 66, trans. modified.

5. Ibid.

6. Ibid., 65, trans. modified.

7. Jacques Derrida, *Writing and Difference*, trans. Alan Bass (Chicago: University of Chicago Press, 1978), 28.

8. A self-subsistent being. — Trans.

9. Derrida, *Of Grammatology*, 9, trans. modified.

10. Jacques Derrida and Maurizio Ferraris, *A Taste for the Secret*, ed. Giacomo Donis and David Webb, trans. Giacomo Donis (Cambridge: Polity Press, 2001).

11. Ibid., 80.

12. Here I have chosen to remain as close as possible to Vattimo's French, since his wording, which appears to stress a personal responsibility, is crucial to the logic of his question for Derrida. — Trans.

13. Derrida and Ferraris, *A Taste for the Secret*, 83, trans. modified.

14. Ibid.

15. See Maurizio Ferraris, *Nuova Corriente* (Rome: Laterza, 1991).

16. See Maurizio Ferraris, Introduction to the Italian translation of Jacques Derrida, "La main de Heidegger," *La mano di Heidegger*, trans. G. Scibilia and G. Chiurazzi (Rome: Laterza, 1991).

17. Derrida, *Of Grammatology*, 93. Quoted in *Positions*, 49.

How to Answer the Ethical Question, Jürgen Habermas

1. Jacques Derrida, "The University Without Condition," in *Without Alibi*, ed., trans., and introd. Peggy Kamuf (Stanford: Stanford University Press, 2002), 202–37. Also published in English as "The Future of the Profession or the University Without Condition (Thanks to the "Humanities,"

What *Could Take Place* Tomorrow)," in *Jacques Derrida and the Humanities: A Critical Reader*, ed. Tom Cohen (Cambridge: Cambridge University Press, 2001), 24–57.

2. Derrida, "The Future of the Profession," 54.

3. Martin Heidegger, *Contributions to Philosophy (From Enowning)*, trans. Parvis Emad and Kenneth Maly (Bloomington: Indiana University Press, 1999); *Beiträge zur Philosophie: Vom Ereignis* (Frankfurt a. M.: Vittorio Klostermann, 1994).

4. Jürgen Habermas, *The Philosophical Discourse of Modernity: Twelve Lectures*, trans. Frederick G. Lawrence (Cambridge: MIT Press, 1991), 357 ff.; *Der philosophische Diskurs der Moderne* (Frankfurt a. M.: Surhkamp 1985), 414 ff.

5. Gershom Scholem, "Zehn unhistorische Sätze über Kabbala," in Scholem, *Judaica III* (Frankfurt a. M.: Suhrkamp 1973), 264 [Habermas's translation; slightly modified—Ed.].

6. Søren Kierkegaard, *Either/Or*, pt. 2, in Howard V. Hong and Edna H. Hong, eds., *Kierkegaard's Writings*, vol. 4 (Princeton: Princeton University Press, 1987), 256.

7. Ibid., 260.

8. Søren Kierkegaard, *Philosophical Fragments*, in Howard V. Hong and Edna H. Hong, eds., *Kierkegaard's Writings*, vol. 7 (Princeton: Princeton University Press, 1985), 111.

9. Søren Kierkegaard, *The Sickness unto Death*, in Howard V. Hong and Edna H. Hong, eds., *Kierkegaard's Writings*, vol. 19 (Princeton: Princeton University Press, 1980), 14 and 131.

10. Ibid., 79.

11. Kierkegaard, *Philosophical Fragments*, 45.

12. Karl Jaspers, *Socrates, Buddha, Confucius, Jesus: From the Great Philosophers*, vol. 1, ed. Hannah Arendt, trans. Ralph Mannheim (Harvest, 1966); *Die Grossen Philosophen*, vol. 1, (Munich: Piper Verlag, 1957).

13. Karl Jaspers, *Philosophical Faith and Revelation*, trans. Ernst Basch Austin (New York: Harper and Row, 1967), 54; *Der philosophische Glaube angesichts der Offenbarung* (Munich: Piper, 1962), 100 ff.: "There the confrontation is not between knowledge and faith, but between faith and faith. Yet this philosophical opposition, while refusing to bow and obey, does not negate. Only a dogmatic theology and a dogmatic philosophy, both fatally insistent on the absoluteness of their supposedly known faiths, exclude each other. The two faiths as such, in revelation and in reason, are poles which affect each other, cannot wholly understand each other, but do not stop trying. The individual can acknowledge in another, as the other's faith, what he rejects in and for himself."

14. Max Horkheimer, "Theismus-Atheismus," *Critique of Instrumental Reason: Lectures and Essays since the End of World War II*, trans. Matthew J. O'Connell et al. (New York: Seabury Press, 1974), 48; *Gesammelte Schriften* (Frankfurt a. M.: S. Fischer, 1996), 7:184, trans. modified.

15. Cf. my response in Jürgen Habermas, "To Seek to Salvage an Unconditional Meaning Without God Is a Futile Undertaking: Reflections on a Remark of Max Horkheimer," trans. Ciaran P. Cronin, in *Religion and Rationality: Essays on Reason, God, and Modernity*, ed. Eduardo Mendieta (Cambridge: Polity Press, 2002), 95–108; "Zu Horkheimers Satz Einen unbedingten Sinn zu retten ohne Gott, ist eitel," in Habermas, *Texte und Kontexte* (Frankfurt am Main: Suhrkamp, 1991), 110–126.

16. Theodor W. Adorno, *Minima Moralia*, trans. Edmund Jephcott (London: Verso, 1984), 247.

17. Ibid.

18. P. J. Huntington, "Heidegger's Reading of Kierkegaard Revisited," in *Kierkegaard in Post/Modernity*, ed. Martin J. Matustik and Merold Westphal (Bloomington: Indiana University Press, 1995), 43–65.

19. Martin Heidegger, *Nietzsche* vols. 3 and 4, trans. David Farrell Krell (San Francisco: HarperSanFrancisco, 1991), 243–44; *Nietzsche*, vol. 2, (Pfullingen: Neske, 1961), 325: "Of course, in order to think the essence of justice in accord with this metaphysics, we must exclude all notions of justice that derive from Christian, humanistic, Enlightenment, bourgeois, and socialist moralities."

20. Jacques Derrida, *Of Spirit: Heidegger and the Question*, trans. Geoffrey Bennington and Rachel Bowlby (Chicago: University of Chicago Press, 1991), 110 ff.

A Monster of Faithfulness, Joseph Cohen and Raphael Zagury-Orly

1. Jacques Derrida, *The Post Card: From Socrates to Freud and Beyond*, trans. Alan Bass (Chicago: University of Chicago Press, 1987), 30.

2. Ibid., 7–8. [Trans. modified—Trans.]

3. Ibid., 29.

4. Emmanuel Levinas, *Proper Names*, trans. Michael B. Smith (Stanford: Stanford University Press, 1996), 41.

5. Derrida, *The Post Card*, 78.

6. In English in the original.—Trans.

7. In English in the original.—Trans.

8. Derrida, *The Post Card*, 19. [Trans. modified.—Trans.]

9. Ibid., 25.

10. Ibid., 77; my emphasis.

11. Ibid., 115.

12. *Relevée*, i.e., *aufgehoben*, in the Hegelian sense.—Trans.

13. Hegel, *Phenomenology of Spirit*, trans. A. V. Miller (Oxford: Oxford University Press, 1977), 19.

14. Emmanuel Levinas, *Of God Who Comes to Mind*, trans. Bettina Bergo (Stanford: Stanford University Press, 1998), 68. [Trans. modified.—Trans.]

15. Jacques Derrida, "Sauf le nom (Post-Scriptum)," in *On the Name*, ed. Thomas Dutoit, trans. David Wood et al. (Stanford: Stanford University Press, 1995), 76. [Trans. modified.—Trans.]

16. Derrida, *The Post Card*, 24.
17. Ibid., 42–43. [Trans. modified.—Trans.]

The Shibboleth Effect: On Reading Paul Celan, Hent de Vries

NOTE: An earlier, much shorter version of this essay appeared as "Le schibboleth de l'éthique: Derrida avec Celan," in *L'éthique du don: Jacques Derrida et la pensée du don*, ed. Jean-Michel Rabaté and Michael Wetzel (Paris: Métailié-transition, 1992), 212–38, and as "Das Schibboleth der Ethik: Derrida und Celan," in *Ethik der Gabe: Denken nach Jacques Derrida*, ed. Michael Wetzel and Jean-Michel Rabaté (Berlin: Akademie, 1993), 57–80.

1. Theodor W. Adorno, "Notes on Kafka," in *Prisms*, trans. Samuel and Shierry Weber (Cambridge: MIT Press, 1981), 247; Adorno, "Aufzeichnungen zu Kafka," in *Gesammelte Schriften* (Frankfurt a. M.: Suhrkamp, 1977), 10.1:257.

2. Jacques Derrida, "Before the Law," trans. Avital Ronell, in Jacques Derrida, *Acts of Literature*, ed. Derek Attridge (New York: Routledge, 1992), 181–220.

3. Cited in John Felstiner, *Paul Celan: Poet, Survivor, Jew* (New Haven: Yale University Press, 1995), 51, cf. 46.

4. Jacques Derrida, "Shibboleth: For Paul Celan," trans. Joshua Wilner and Thomas Dutoit, in Derrida, *Sovereignties in Question: The Poetics of Paul Celan*, ed. Thomas Dutoit and Outi Pasanen (New York: Fordham University Press, 2005), 1–64; *Schibboleth pour Paul Celan* (Paris: Galilée, 1986). See also P. Forget, "Neuere Daten über Paul Celan: Zu Jacques Derrida, 'Schibboleth pour Paul Celan,'" *Celan-Jahrbuch*, ed. H. M. Speier (Heidelberg, 1987), 1:217–22.

5. Werner Hamacher, "The Second of Inversion: Movements of a Figure Through Celan's Poetry," in Hamacher, *Premises: Essays on Philosophy and Literature from Kant to Celan*, trans. Peter Fenves (Cambridge: Harvard University Press, 1996), 352; "Die Sekunde der Inversion: Bewegungen einer Figur durch Celans Gedichte," in *Paul Celan*, ed. Werner Hamacher and Winfried Menninghaus (Frankfurt a. M.: Suhrkamp, 1988), 94.

6. Theodor W. Adorno, *Aesthetic Theory*, trans. Robert Hullot-Kentor (Minneapolis: University of Minnesota Press, 1997), 321–22; Adorno, *Ästhetische Theorie, Gesammelte Schriften* (Frankfurt a. M.: Suhrkamp, 1970), 7:477. See also Thomas Sparr, *Celans Poetik des hermetischen Gedichts* (Heidelberg: C. Winter, 1989).

7. Adorno, *Aesthetic Theory*, 321/475.
8. Ibid., 322/477.
9. "Mit wechselndem Schlüssel" is also the title of one of the epicycles of *Von Schwelle zu Schwelle*, the book in which the poem "Schibboleth" can be found.

10. The use of this term in "Shibboleth" should, of course, be read in light of Derrida's "Circumfession," trans. Geoffrey Bennington, in Geoffrey Bennington and Jacques Derrida, *Jacques Derrida* (Chicago: University of Chicago Press, 1993), 3–315; "Circonfession," in Bennington and Derrida, *Jacques Derrida* (Paris: Seuil, 1991), 7–291. See, on this text, my "Instances: Temporal Modes from Augustine to Derrida and Lyotard," in *Augustine and Postmodernism: Confessions and Circumfession*, ed. John D. Caputo and Michael J. Scanlon (Bloomington: Indiana University Press, 2005), 68–88.

11. Paul Celan, "With a Variable Key," trans. Michael Hamburger, in *Poems of Paul Celan* (New York: Persea Books, 1988), 89; "Mit wechselndem Schlüssel," in *Gesammelte Werke*, ed. B. Allemann and S. Reichert (Frankfurt a. M.: Suhrkamp, 1986), 1:112.

12. Martin Heidegger, *Elucidations of Hölderlin's Poetry*, trans. Keith Hoeller (Amherst, N.Y.: Prometheus Books, 2000), 21–22; *Erläuterungen zu Hölderlins Dichtung* (Frankfurt a. M.: Klostermann, 1971), 7–8.

13. Derrida, "Shibboleth," 18/36.

14. Cf. Jean Greisch, "*Zeitgehöft* et *Anwesen*: La diachronie du poème," in *Contre-jour: Études sur Paul Celan*, ed. Martine Broda (Paris: Cerf 1986), 176.

15. Derrida, "Shibboleth," 33/61.

16. Adorno, "Notes on Kafka," 246/255.

17. Judges 12:5–6 (The Revised English Bible).

18. Derrida, "Shibboleth," 26/50.

19. Ibid., 22/44. The phrase "the strange from the strange" is from Paul Celan, "The Meridian," trans. Rosmarie Waldrop, in Paul Celan, *Collected Prose* (Riverdale-on-Hudson, N.Y.: Sheep Meadow Press, 1986), 47; "Der Meridian," *Gesammelte Werke*, 3:196. See also Paul Celan, *Der Meridian: Endfassung, Entwürfe, Materialien*, ed. Bernhard Böschenstein and Heino Schmull (Frankfurt a. M.: Suhrkamp, 1999).

20. Derrida, "Shibboleth," 40/72. Derrida refers here to the Hölderlinian motif of the *Wechsel der Töne*, a motif that also plays an important role in his *The Post Card: From Freud to Socrates and Beyond*, trans. Alan Bass (Chicago: University of Chicago Press, 1987); *La carte postale; De Socrate à Freud et au-delà* (Paris: Flammarion, 1980); and "On a Newly Arisen Apocalyptic Tone in Philosophy," trans. John P. Leavey, Jr., in *Raising the Tone of Philosophy: Late Essays by Immanuel Kant, Transformative Critique by Jacques Derrida*, ed. Peter Fenves (Baltimore: The Johns Hopkins University Press, 1993), 117–71; "D'un ton apocalyptique adopté naguère en philosophie," in *Les Fins de l'homme: À partir du travail de Jacques Derrida*, ed. Philippe Lacoue-Labarthe and Jean-Luc Nancy (Paris: Galilée, 1981), 445–79.

21. Derrida, "Shibboleth," 28–29/54.

22. Paul Celan, "Shibboleth," trans. Hamburger, *Poems of Paul Celan*, 97; "Schibboleth," *Gesammelte Werke*, 1:131.

23. Paul Celan, "[Reply to a Questionnaire from the Flinker Bookstore, Paris, 1958]," trans. Waldrop, in *Collected Prose*, 16; "[Antwort auf eine Umfrage der Librairie Flinker, Paris (1958)]," *Gesammelte Werke*, 3:167.

24. Celan cites Benjamin's essay on Kafka, in which Malebranche is quoted: "Attentiveness is the natural prayer of the soul." See Walter Benjamin, "Franz Kafka," trans. Harry Zohn, in Benjamin, *Selected Writings*, vol. 2, *1927–1934*, ed. Michael W. Jennings, Howard Eiland, and Gary Smith (Cambridge: Harvard University Press, 1999), 812 (trans. modified); *Gesammelte Schriften*, ed. R. Tiedemann and H. Schweppenhäuser (Frankfurt a. M.: Suhrkamp, 1972 ff.), 2.2:432. In this essay, Benjamin describes Kafka's whole oeuvre as a "code of gestures" (801/418).

25. Celan, "[Reply to a Questionnaire from the Flinker Bookstore]," 16/3:167–68.

26. Paul Celan, "Speech on the Occasion of Receiving the Literature Prize of the Free Hanseatic City of Bremen," trans. Walter Billeter, in Celan, *Prose Writings and Selected Poems* (Carlton, Vic.: Paper Castle, 1977), 21, trans. modified; cited in Derrida, "Shibboleth," 46; Celan, "Ansprache anlässlich der Entgegennahme des Literaturpreises der freien Hansestadt Bremen," *Gesammelte Werke*, 3:186.

27. Derrida, "Shibboleth," 23/45.

28. Ibid., 23/48.

29. Cf. the second chapter of Henri Bergson's dissertation, first published in 1889 and titled *Essai sur les données immédiates de la conscience* (Paris: Félix Alcan, 1921); translated as *Time and Free Will: An Essay on the Immediate Data of Consciousness*, trans. F. L. Pogson (Mineola, N.Y.: Dover, 2001); as well as Martin Heidegger, *Being and Time*, trans. Jon Macquarrie and Edward Robinson (New York: Harper and Row, 1962), 500–501nxxx; *Sein und Zeit* (Tübingen: Max Niemeyer, 1993), 433n1; and Jacques Derrida *Margins of Philosophy*, trans. Alan Bass (Chicago: University of Chicago Press, 1982), 57, 57–58n34, 59–60, and 62n36; *Marges de la philosophie* (Paris: Minuit, 1972), 66, 66n22, 68–69, and 72n24.

30. Jacques Derrida, "*Ousia* and *Grammē*: Note on a Note from *Being and Time*," *Margins of Philosophy*, 29–67; "Ousia et grammè," in *Marges de la philosophie* (Paris: Minuit, 1972), 31–78.

31. Derrida, "Shibboleth," 2/13.

32. Celan, "The Meridian," 48/196.

33. See Jacques Derrida, *Glas*, trans. John P. Leavy, Jr., and Richard Rand (Lincoln: University of Nebraska Press, 1986), 79, right column, "The *glas* is for (no) one. (No) one"; *Glas* (Paris: Galilée, 1974), 92, right column, "Le glas n'est de personne." Needless to say, this *personne* cannot be associated, let alone identified, with an alienated individual or collective subject, as is suggested by Marlies Janz, *Vom Engagement absoluter Poesie: Zur Lyrik und Ästhetik Paul Celans* (Frankfurt a. M.: Syndikat, 1976), 130, in her reading of "Psalm": "To the no one [*Niemand*], the god who is no longer present to hand, not merely unnamed god, corresponds the 'nothing' [*Nichts*], the absence of a life worthy of humanity." On the range of possible meanings of *Niemand*, see Martine Broda, "'An Niemand gerichtet': Paul

Celan als Leser von Mandelstamm's 'Gegenüber," in *Paul Celan*, ed. Hamacher and Menninghaus, 209.

34. Does not Heidegger describe the "call of care" (*Ruf der Sorge*) in terms that at first seem similar? The "caller," the voice of "conscience" (i.e., *Dasein* itself) is "'nobody,' when seen after the manner of the world" (*Being and Time*, 323/278). Of course, we should not forget that Heidegger's introduction and use of the term *Dasein* in *Being and Time* not only forbids the deeply rooted desire to narrate histories (*muthon tina diegeisthai*; *Being and Time*, 26/6, with reference to Plato's *Sophistes* 242 c), but is also at odds with Celan's attempt to sing songs "beyond the human" (*jenseits des Menschen*).

35. See Broda, "'An Niemand gerichtet,'" in *Paul Celan*, ed. Hamacher and Menninghaus, 214–15.

36. Derrida, "Shibboleth," 42/76. Jacques Derrida, "How to Avoid Speaking: Denials," trans. Ken Frieden, in *Languages of the Unsayable: The Play of Negativity in Literature and Literary Theory*, ed. Sanford Budick and Wolfgang Iser (New York: Columbia University Press, 1987), 3–70; "Comment ne pas parler: Dénégations," in Derrida, *Psyché: Inventions de l'autre* (Paris: Galilée, 1987), 535–93.

37. This Hegelian analysis is not unrelated to a dialectical determination of time, notably in the second part of the *Enzyklopädie der philosophischen Wissenschaften* (par. 254 ff.). There, as Heidegger is quick to point out, the thinking of the *Jetzt-hier*, and thereby of vulgar temporality, takes place within the context of an elucidation of the philosophy of nature, mechanics, and space, just as in another context it is subsumed under the heading of the "system of the sun" and premised on such Aristotelian notions as the "boundary" (*horos, Grenze*), the "point" (*stigmē, Punkt*), the "absolute this" (*tode ti, absolute Dieses*), and the "circular course" of time (*sphaira, Kreislauf*). (See *Being and Time*, 481 ff. and 500–501nxxx / 429 ff. and 432n1.) The relationship of "filiation" (*Filiation*) between Aristotle and Hegel notwithstanding, Heidegger writes that for the latter defining time involves not establishing the ontological order (*Fundierungszusammenhang*, ibid., 500–501nxxx/432n1) that founds the relation between these traditional notions (as Aristotle sets out to do) but stating that time is the truth of space, more precisely, of its punctuality (*Punktualität; Enzyklopädie*, par. 254; *Being and Time*, 481/429). The possibilization of the latter is the "now": "time is primarily understood in terms of the 'now,' and indeed in the very manner in which one comes across such a 'now' in pure intuition" (*Being and Time*, 483/431). If for Hegel time is "simply abstract, ideal," then this means, Heidegger claims, that it is intuited not as real but as "ready-at-hand only 'ideally'" (ibid., trans. modified). This does not exclude this ready-at-handness being simultaneously determined as an "intuited becoming" (*angeschaute Werden*) or, more radically, as an "abstraction of consuming" (*Abstraktion des Verzehrens*). These expressions do nothing, according to Heidegger, to remove the primacy of the most extreme formalization and leveling off of time in terms

of a series of negated "nows," the *Jetztfolge*, which ultimately reduces the dialectical concept of time to a merely formal or abstract negation of negation (cf. ibid., 483–84/432). In fact, Heidegger concludes, in the final chapter of the *Phenomenology* Hegel formulates time as the fate and necessity of Spirit, which has not yet come full circle or to its inner completion ("time appears as the very fate and necessity which spirit has when it is not in itself complete," cited in ibid., 486/435).

The basic thrust of Derrida's argument in "*Ousia* and *Grammē*" is that Heidegger's "originary temporality" takes the form, if not of a real or ideal, then at least of a virtual ready-at-handness. Put otherwise, temporality properly speaking does not escape or circumvent the determination of improper, vulgar temporality. Proper temporality is proper. And since there is no improper temporality without there being proper temporality, it — "proper" temporality — is not "improper" either. Nor, I will maintain, is it *time*. And if, finally, it is called the condition of possibility or the possibilization (*Ermöglichung*) of chronometrics, of chronology, of the determination of days, months, years, seconds, minutes, and hours — in short, of *dates* in the most general sense of the word — then these determinations can in turn be said to condition and possibilize this singular time.

38. Derrida, "Shibboleth," 14/31. Cf. Derrida, *Glas*, 167/188: "What does *there is* [il y a] mean (to say), as soon as what there is is removed out of reach of the *it is*, the *this is*, the *c'est*, the *ceci est*, out of reach of the exposition [*ostension*] of all presence? Apropos the propriation process (*Ereignis*), Heidegger sets free the *es gibt*, in *es gibt Sein*, of Being's all-powerful precession. The value of the *gift* (*Gabe*), a value foreign to the *there is*, the *il y a*, we wager that that value will have preoccupied all."

39. Jacques Derrida, *Given Time: 1. Counterfeit Money*, trans. Peggy Kamuf (Chicago: University of Chicago Press, 1992), 41; Derrida, *Donner le temps* (Paris: Galilée, 1991), 60.

40. Derrida, "Shibboleth," 15/33, trans. modified.

41. Derrida, *Given Time*, 40/59. The reference to Mallarmé is to S. Mallarmé, *Oeuvres complètes* (Paris: Gallimard, 1945), 40.

42. Derrida, *Given Time*, 41/60.

43. Ibid., 44/63.

44. Paul Celan, "[Reply to a Questionnaire from the Flinker Bookstore, Paris, 1961]," 23/3:175.

45. *Wortspur* and *Wundegelesenes* are from Paul Celan, "Dein vom Wachen stößiger Traum," *Gesammelte Werke*, 2:24; the other phrases are from the closing paragraphs of the Bremen address, trans. Waldrop, in Celan, *Collected Prose*, 35, trans. modified; *Gesammelte Werke*, 3:186.

46. Paul Celan, "À la pointe acérée," trans. Hamburger, in *Poems of Paul Celan*, 193; *Gesammelte Werke*, 1:251.

47. Ibid.; Celan, "The Meridian," 52/3:200.

48. Celan, "To one who stood before the door," trans. John Felstiner, in *Selected Poems and Prose of Paul Celan* (New York: Norton, 2001), 171, trans.

modified; Celan, "Einem, der vor der Tür stand," *Gesammelte Werke*, 1:242–43.

49. Paul Celan, "Etched away from," trans. Hamburger, in *Poems of Paul Celan*, 231; "Weggebeizt," *Gesammelte Werke*, 2:31. Both referring to his earlier discussions of translatability in "Des Tours de Babel" (trans. Joseph F. Graham, in Derrida, *Acts of Religion*, ed. Gil Anidjar [New York: Routledge, 2002], 104–34; in *Psyché*, 203–36) and *The Ear of the Other: Otobiography, Transference, Translation* (trans. Peggy Kamuf, ed. Christie McDonald [Lincoln: University of Nebraska Press, 1988]; *L'oreille de l'autre* [Montreal: Vlb, 1982]) and anticipating his analysis in "*Sauf le nom*" of Angelus Silesius's exclamation "The most impossible is possible" (trans. John P. Leavey, Jr., in *On the Name*, ed Thomas Dutoit [Stanford: Stanford University Press, 1995], 44; *Sauf le Nom* [Paris: Galilée, 1993], 33), Derrida remarks: "One should specify that untranslatability does not stem only from the difficult passage (*no pasarán*), from the aporia or impasse that isolates one poetic language from another. Babel is also this *impossible impasse*, this *impossible pass* [*ce pas impossible*; meaning at once "this impossible step" and "this not impossible"; see translator's note to the translation by Joshua Wilner in *Word Traces*, ed. Aris Fioretos {Baltimore: The Johns Hopkins University Press, 1994, 71n16] — and without transaction to come — stemming from the multiplicity of languages within the uniqueness of the poetic inscription." ("Shibboleth," 29/54). It should be noted, however, that the formulation *pas impossible* does not necessarily imply that a possibility of this *pas* would be mere privation.

50. Paul Celan, "Etched away from," 231/2:31.

51. Derrida, "Shibboleth," 32/60.

52. Paul Celan, "Ash-glory," trans. Joachim Neugroschel, in Celan, *Speech-Grille and Selected Poems* (New York: Dutton, 1971), 241; "Aschenglorie," *Gesammelte Werke*, 2:72.

53. Derrida, "Shibboleth," 33/61.

54. Ibid.

55. Celan, "The Meridian," 45/194.

56. Derrida, "Shibboleth," 40–41/72–73.

57. Ibid., 43/77; cf. Paul Celan, "Mit der Aschenkelle geschöpft," *Gesammelte Werke*, 2:236.

58. Derrida, "Shibboleth," 46/83. On the motif of the Shoah, see Amir Eshel, *Zeit der Zäsur: Jüdische Dichter im Angesicht der Shoah* (Heidelberg: C. Winter, 1999), and Ulrich Baer, *Remnants of Song: Trauma and the Experience of Modernity in Charles Baudelaire and Paul Celan* (Stanford: Stanford University Press, 2000).

59. Derrida, "Shibboleth," 46/83.

60. Ibid., 48/87.

61. Ibid., 61/109.

62. Ibid., 62/110; cf. Paul Celan, "Todtnauberg," trans. Hamburger, in *Poems of Paul Celan*, 293; *Gesammelte Werke*, 2:255. See Hadrien France-Lanord, *Paul Celan et Martin Heidegger: Les sens d'un dialogue* (Paris: Fayard, 2004).

63. Derrida, "Shibboleth," 36/66.

64. Jacques Derrida, "'This Strange Institution Called Literature': Interview with Jacques Derrida," in *Acts of Literature*, ed. Derek Attridge (New York: Routledge, 1992), 45.

65. Celan, "Voiceless, above," trans. Hamburger, in *Poems of Paul Celan*, 109; "Oben, geräuschlos," *Gesammelte Werke*, 1:188.

66. Derrida, "Shibboleth," 44/80. On Celan's extensive reading of the philosophical tradition, as well as contemporary authors, see Paul Celan, *La bibliothèque philosophique / Die philosophische Bibliothek: Catalogue raisonné des annotations*, ed. Alexandra Richer, Patrik Alac, and Bertrand Badiou, Preface by Jean-Pierre Lefebvre (Paris: Rue d'Ulm, 2004).

67. Geoffrey Hartman and Sanford Budick, Introduction to *Midrash and Literature* (New Haven: Yale University Press, 1986).

68. See my "Instances."

69. Derrida, "Shibboleth," 64/112.

70. Ibid., 53/96.

71. Ibid., 18/37. The word *revenance* is used in Emmanuel Levinas, *Otherwise than Being, or Beyond Essence*, trans. Alphonso Lingis (The Hague: Martinus Nijhoff, 1981); *Autrement qu'être ou au-delà de l'essence* (The Hague: Martinus Nijhoff, 1974), to indicate the modality of the manifestation of the Other, as well as the insistent recurrence of the performative contradiction of a discourse that, like skepticism, signals (or says and writes) what cannot be said or written. See Hent de Vries, *Minimal Theologies: Critiques of Secular Reason in Adorno and Levinas* (Baltimore: The Johns Hopkins University Press, 2005), 494–97. On the parallels between Levinas's and Stanley Cavell's interpretations of "skepticism," see my "From Ghost in the Machine to Spiritual Automaton: Philosophical Meditation in Wittgenstein, Cavell, and Levinas," *International Journal for the Philosophy of Religion* 60, nos. 1–3 (December 2006): 77–97.

It can be argued that the date's spectrality—its shibboleth—comes to occupy a place similar to that of the *hama* in Aristotle's *Physics*. The motif of the *hama*, Derrida reminds us in *"Ousia* and *Grammē,"* is that of the *clavis*, the "small key that both opens and closes the history of metaphysics" from Aristotle through Kant and Hegel all the way up to Heidegger. Like the *hama*, the date marks the instant of a "together," an "at the same time," the "duplicity of the *simul*," of a simultaneity that "does not yet reassemble, within itself, either points or nows, places or phases," but rather evokes the "complicity, the common origin of time and space, appearing together [*comparaître*] as the condition for all appearing of Being. In a certain way it [the *hama* but also, we might add, the *date*] says the dyad as the minimum" (*Margins of Philosophy*, 56/64). Aristotle (like Celan) does not say this in these terms or *as such*, nor, for that matter, does Derrida. The key to this key is not given, or not given *as such*. In consequence, the discourse on the date—and thereby the dating of this date—must take place in what can only be described as a "generous repetition" of Aristotle's text and all of its historical rearticulations. Not unlike *différance*, the *simul* is "not a determination of Being, but the very production of Being" (ibid., 56/64).

72. Paul Celan, "Conversation in the Mountains," trans. Waldrop, in *Collected Prose*, 19; *Gesammelte Werke*, 3:170.

73. Derrida, "Shibboleth," 35/64.

74. Ibid., 49/90.

75. Ibid.

76. Ibid., 50/91.

77. Peter Szondi, *Celan Studies*, trans. Susan Bernofsky with Harvey Mendelsohn (Stanford: Stanford University Press, 2003), 83–92.

78. Derrida, "Shibboleth," 17/35 .

79. Ibid., 37/68. *Glas* cites Sartre's *Saint Genet*: "The structure of the poetic sentence very accurately reflects the ontological structure of saintliness" (14).

80. Paul Celan, "[Letter to Hans Bender]," trans. Waldrop, in *Collected Prose*, 26; *Gesammelte Werke*, 3:177–78. Heidegger, in *Elucidations of Hölderlin's Poetry*, also speaks of the poem—Hölderlin's *Dichtung*—as a "gift" (*Geschenk*; 63/39).

81. Martin Heidegger, *Hölderlin's Hymn "The Ister,"* trans. William McNeill and Julia Davis (Bloomington: Indiana University Press, 1996), 9; Heidegger, *Hölderlins Hymne "Der Ister,"* *Gesamtausgabe* (Frankfurt a. M.: Klostermann, 1984), 53:8; cited in Derrida, "Shibboleth," 194, note to p. 15 / 121, note to p. 33. The citation is preceded by a concise answer to the question concerning the essence and temporality of the poem ("Yet what is that—poetizing? How can poetizing determine a time, lend distinction to a now?"). I quote the entire passage, which deserves a more extensive commentary that I can undertake here:"'To poetize,' *dichten*—in Latin, *dictare*—means to write down, to fore-tell something to be written down. To tell something that, prior to this, has not been told. A properly unique beginning thus lies in whatever is said poetically. Something like a time stemming from and determining the poetry—a poetic time—would then be given. Its "points in time" cannot be established in accordance with the calendar; they cannot be 'dated.' Sometimes, in terms of the numbers by which we calculate time, we can indeed give the year and the day, even the hour when a poem was 'composed' or completed. Yet such temporal ordering of the activity of poetizing is not straightforwardly identical, nor even the same, as the timespace of that which is poetized. Moreover, poetic time is also different in each case, in accordance with the essential nature of the poetry and

of the poets. For all essential poetry also poetizes 'anew' the essence of poetizing itself. This is true of Hölderlin's poetry in a special and singular sense. No calendrical date can be given for the 'Now' of his poetry" (8–9/8).

Greisch and Derrida also recall in this context that Heidegger's *The Basic Problems of Phenomenology* insists on a similar discrepancy between datability and the calendrical date: "The date itself does not need to be calendrical in the narrower sense. The calendar date is only one particular mode of everyday dating. . . . The dating can be calendrically indeterminate, but it is nevertheless determined by a particular historical happening or some other event" (Martin Heidegger, *The Basic Problems of Phenomenology*, trans. and introd. Albert Hofstadter [Bloomington: Indiana University Press, 1982], 262; Heidegger, *Die Grundprobleme der Phänomenologie, Gesamtausgabe*, 24:371).

82. Friedrich Hölderlin, "Remarks on 'Oedipus,'" trans. Thomas Pfau, in Hölderlin, *Essays and Letters on Theory* (Albany: State University of New York Press, 1988), 102; Hölderlin, "Anmerkung zum 'Ödipus,'" Hölderlin, *Sämtliche Werke* (Stuttgart: Kohlhammer, 1944–85), 5:196. See Philippe Lacoue-Labarthe, "Catastrophe," in his *Poetry as Experience*, trans. Andrea Tarnowski (Stanford: Stanford University Press, 1999), 41–70, where this phrase is quoted on p. 49; *La poésie comme expérience* (Paris: Bourgois, 1986), 61–103, 74.

83. Greisch, *"Zeitgehöft* und *Anwesen,"* 180, cf. 183.

84. The structure of the *dictare* is highly problematic, not only in the philosophical heritage (from Socrates to Plato) but also in the purportedly more originary *Geschick* of *Denken* und *Dichten* with which Heidegger hoped to overcome this metaphysical tradition. This is made clear by Derrida's analyses of Plato's apparent "dictation" (*dictée*) to Socrates in *The Post Card*, 19 and passim / 25 and passim.

85. Paul Celan, "Night," trans. Hamburger, *Poems of Paul Celan*, 123; "Nacht," Celan, *Gesammelte Werke*, 1:170; Derrida, "Shibboleth," 44–45/81.

86. Derrida, "Shibboleth," 21/42.

87. Celan, "Shibboleth," 97/1:131. This original, or even originary, duplicity is not overcome in the (Christian) symbol for the *coincidentia oppositorum*, as the word "unicorn" (*Einhorn*) might suggest:

Einhorn:
du weisst um die Steine,
du weisst um die Wasser,
komm,
ich führ dich hinweg
zu den Stimmen
von Estremadura.

Unicorn:
you know about the stones,
you know about the water,

come,
I shall lead you away
to the voices
of Estremadura. (97/1:131–32)'

The first line of this concluding stanza should also be read as a proper name, addressing Erich Einhorn, the friend with whom Celan shared his revolutionary sympathies. See I. Chalfen, *Paul Celan: Eine Biographie seiner Jugend* (Frankfurt a. M.: Suhrkamp, 1983), 114.

88. *Kalenderlücke* appears in Paul Celan, "Merkblätter-Schmerz," *Gesammelte Werke*, 2:321. For *contre-temps*, see Greisch, "*Zeitgehöft* et *Anwesen*," 182. For *Unzeit*, see Paul Celan, "Und mit dem Buch aus Tarussa," in *Die Niemandsrose*, and "Nacht," in *Sprachgitter*. Werner Hamacher has explored the intricate resonances of the counter-concept of the *Unzeit* in "Des contrées des temps," in *Zeit-Zeichen: Aufschübe und Interferenzen zwischen Endzeit und Echtzeit*, ed. G. Tholen and M. Scholl (Weinheim: Acta Humaniora, 1990), 29–36. Greisch's analysis points in a different direction, one that echoes a fundamental essay by Levinas (mentioned neither by Greisch nor by Hamacher), "Reality and Its Shadow," trans. Alphonso Lingis, in Levinas, *Collected Philosophical Papers* (Dordrecht: Martinus Nijhoff, 1987), 1–13; "La réalité et son ombre," *Les temps modernes* 38 (1948): 771–89. In this early study, the aesthetic experience—which at this point in Levinas's oeuvre is not clearly distinguished from what he will later call poetic "saying" (*Dire*)—is seen as the irruption of an "entre-temps." See also my *Minimal Theologies*, chap. 8, "Levinas on Art and Truth," 409–42.

89. For Heidegger, the "gaps" (*Löcher*) in time signal above all the living along of *Dasein*'s everydayness, the privileging of the *Jetzt-Zeit*, and the covering up of the originary temporality of its most proper possibility of being-toward-death, as well as the *Augenblick* (cf. *Being and Time*, 461–62/409). Only against this backdrop can we understand how Heidegger can characterize his own exposition of originary temporality qua *Geschichtlichkeit* as incomplete, or *lückenhaft*, so long or insofar as it has not yet demonstrated that to this *Zeitlichkeit* belongs "something like world-time" (*so etwas wie Weltzeit*, ibid., 457/405). ("World-time" is based upon an "existential-temporal conception of the world"; ibid.)

Moreover, while Heidegger cites the *nunc stans* as the epitome of the hypostasis of the one modality of presence, he leaves room for another possible interpretation, a temporality neither that of Dasein's finiteness nor that of a full presence but a notion of "eternity" that leads us back to the question of negative theology: "The fact that the traditional conception of 'eternity' as signifying the 'standing "now"' (*nunc stans*) has been drawn from the ordinary way of understanding time and has been defined with an orientation toward the idea of 'constant' presence-at-hand does not need to be discussed in detail. If God's eternity can be 'construed' philosophically, then it may be understood only as a more primordial temporality which is 'infinite.' Whether the way afforded by the *via negativa et eminentiae* is a possible one remains to be seen" (ibid., 499nxiii/427n1). On the intemporal in the sense of the *Unzeitliche* and the *Überzeitliche*, which are in themselves to be considered temporal or *zeitlich*, see ibid., 39–40/18–19 and Martin Heidegger, *Kant and the Problem of Metaphysics*, trans. Richard Taft (Bloomington: Indiana University Press, 1997), 168; *Kant und das Problem der Metaphysik* (Frankfurt a. M.: Vittorio Klostermann, 1991), par. 44, p. 240.

90. Celan, "The Trumpet Part," trans. Hamburger, in *Poems of Paul Celan*, 343, trans. modified; "Die Posanenstelle," *Gesammelte Werke*, 3:104. See Stéphane Mosès, "Patterns of Negativity in Paul Celan's 'The Trumpet Place,'" in *Languages of the Unsayable: The Play of Negativity in Literature and Literary Theory*, ed. Budick and Iser, 209–24.

91. Heidegger, *Hölderlin's Hymn "The Ister,"* 9/9, trans. modified.

92. Greisch, *"Zeitgehöft et Anwesen,"* 180.

93. Heidegger, *Elucidations of Hölderlin's Poetry*, 64–65/47.

94. Derrida, *"Ousia* and *Grammē,"* in *Margins*, 29–67; "Khōra," trans. Ian McLeod, in *On the Name*, ed. Dutoit, 89–127; *Khōra*, (Paris: Galilée, 1993); "*Geschlecht*: Différence sexuelle, différence ontologique" and "La main de Heidegger (*Geschlecht II*)," in *Psyché*, 395–454; *Of Spirit: Heidegger and the Question*, trans. Geoffrey Bennington and Rachel Bowlby (Chicago: University of Chicago Press, 1989); *De l'esprit: Heidegger et la question* (Paris: Galilée, 1987). The three terms cited are used by Derrida, with certain reservations, in *Of Spirit*, 14/32; see also 8/23.

95. From Aristotle through Heidegger—at least according to the common interpretation of their work, Derrida reminds us—the "now" (*nunc, Jetzt*) "*is* (in the present indicative) the impossibility of coexistence *with itself*: with itself, that is, with an other self, an other now, an other same, a double [*un double*]." (*Margins*, 55/63). The date, by contrast, as conceived by Celan and read by Derrida, is precisely such a double. In Aristotle's and Heidegger's terms, then, the very structure of the date—as double—is aporetic.

96. Heidegger, *Being and Time*, 377/328.

97. Ibid., 473–76/421–23.

98. Establishing a continuity between book 4 of Aristotle's *Physics*—which, as *"Ousia* and *Grammē"* reminds us, "unites time and movement in *aisthèsis*" without, however, relegating the latter to some "sensory exterior content" or, for that matter, "objective movement" (*Margins*, 49/56)—and Kant's first *Critique*, Derrida cites the "Transcendental Exposition of the Concept of Time": "Time is not something which exists of itself, or which inheres in things as an objective determination, and it does not, therefore, remain when abstraction is made of all subjective conditions of its intuition." (cited in *Margins*, 48/55).

99. See Derrida, *Of Spirit*, 25 ff, esp. 28–29 / 46 ff., esp. 50–51.

100. Cf. Derrida, *"Ousia* and *Grammē," Margins*, 51–52/58–59: "one seeks in vain to extract the question of meaning (the meaning of time, or of anything else) as such from metaphysics, or from the system of so called 'vulgar' concepts. Such also would be the case, therefore, for a *question of Being* determined, as it is as the beginning of *Being and Time*, as a question of the *meaning of Being*, whatever the force, necessity, and value . . . of such a question. Heidegger doubtless would acknowledge that as a question of meaning, the question of Being is already linked, at its point of departure, to the (lexical and grammatical) discourse of the metaphysics whose destruction it has undertaken. In a sense, as Bataille gives us to think, the question of meaning, the project of *preserving* meaning, is 'vulgar.' This is his word too."

101. To be sure, Heidegger intends to demonstrate that factical existence "'falls' as falling *from* primordial, authentic temporality" (*Being and Time*, 486/436). But the opposite is also the case. The last paragraph of *Being and Time* recapitulates this first part's trajectory by saying: "that which our *preparatory* existential analytic of Dasein contributed *before* temporality was laid bare, has now been *taken back* into temporality as the primordial structure of Dasein's totality of Being. In terms of the possible ways in which primordial time can temporalize itself, we have provided the 'grounds' for those structures which were just 'pointed out' in our earlier treatment" (486–87/436). Yet the reverse holds true as well. Temporality is equally illuminated by the structures of Dasein that the first division of *Being and Time* articulates in astonishing detail. The description of time, whether originary or derived, proper or improper, does not drop from heaven, but arises, in a sense, from the very falling and fallenness that the analytic of Dasein depicts. One might well wonder, then, whether this analytic is just one way among others ("nur *ein Weg*"; ibid., 487/437). In a marginal note, Heidegger adds: "not 'the' only one [*nicht "den" einzigen*]" (ibid., 445) — or, worse still, whether it is a *way* alone. Is the fundamental ontology that takes its point of departure in Dasein, in the being that we are, a mere provisional or preparatory analysis? The importance of that analysis is doubly relativized by the facts that: (1) though coming first, it is secondary and only a vehicle with respect to its purported *telos* (*Ziel*), to wit, the "elaboration of the question of Being *überhaupt*"; and (2) while being for us the best available access for illuminating the understanding of Being, it must at the same time *in advance* be guided in its very "thematic" and "formally indicating" analyses by the searchlight of the "idea" of Being as such ("The *thematic* analytic of existence, however, first needs the light of the idea of Being in general, which must be clarified beforehand"; ibid., 487/437). In the attempt to interpret time or, rather, originary temporality as the horizon for "any understanding whatsoever of Being" — which is, according to the first page of *Being and Time*, Heidegger's "provisional aim" (*vorläufiges Ziel*) — the very idea or "idea" of Being itself

or as such has the first and the last word. Heidegger leaves no doubt that the understanding of Being and the idea/"idea" by which it is assisted *rises up from* and *collapses back into* the being that we are. If we stretch the point, we could say that, paradoxically, Dasein remains the alpha and omega of the first and last word that is reserved for Being alone, provided one does not take this to be a reluctant endorsement of *Existenzphilosophie* (cf. ibid., 445). Is this what Heidegger allows us to read when he reiterates his formulation from the introduction? He writes: "philosophy 'is universal phenomenological ontology, and takes its departure from the hermeneutic of Dasein, which, as an analytic of *existence*, has made fast the guiding-line for all philosophical inquiry at the point where it *arises* and to which it *returns*'" (ibid., 487 cf. 62 / 436, cf. 38). True, Heidegger continues, this assertion should not be taken dogmatically (*als Dogma*) but as the index of a problem that "still remains 'veiled' [*noch "eingbüllten"*]." He then reformulates that problem as a question to which the final answer is, here at the end, left open: "can one provide *ontological* grounds for ontology, or does it also require an *ontical* foundation? and *which* entity must take over the function of providing this foundation?" (ibid., 487/436). It would almost seem as if Heidegger is reluctant to acclaim *de jure* what he deems true *in fact*, namely, Dasein's primacy over the idea/"idea" of Being as such. The latter, Heidegger knows, can never (*nie*) be elucidated with the help of a "formal-logical 'abstraction'" (ibid., 487/437). For it to come into view at all, one must embark upon a way, if one does not want to acquiesce in being without way or without way out. This "Being without passage [*Ohne-Weg-Sein*]" or "not getting through [*Nicht-durchkommen*]" (Heidegger, *Basic Problems of Phenomenology*, 233/330) is the very definition of *aporia*. To be on the way or underway (*unterwegs*) is the precondition for being able to judge whether the road taken was the right one. More precisely, the struggle (*Streit*) over the interpretation of Being—one is reminded here of the *gigantomachia peri tes ousias* of which Heidegger speaks on the first page of the Introduction (*Being and Time*, 21/2)—can only be decided after it has been "enkindled" or *ignited* (*entfacht* or, as *Kant and the Problem of Metaphysics*, 168/239, has it, *entbrannt*, which is poorly rendered by "broken out"), if only by one's choice of a method and after one has followed this path to its end, "after one has gone along it" (*nach dem Gang*). The way that triggers the conflict over interpretations no less than one's awareness of it is at the same time a necessary, perhaps the best, preparation for that struggle. More paradoxically still, the setting alight or igniting of the struggle is itself already in need of preparation, that is to say, of the preparation for this very struggle: "the conflict . . . cannot get enkindled unless preparations are made for it" (ibid., 487–88/437).

102. Derrida, "*Ousia* and *Grammē*," *Margins*, 63–64/73–74, trans. modified.
103. Ibid., 50/45.
104. Cf. Ibid., 48–50/53–57.

105. Ibid., 62/72, trans. modified.

106. Ibid., 63/73, trans. modified. According to Derrida, the central question raised in "*Ousia* and *grammē*" thus remains, in a sense, "interior to Heidegger's thought" (ibid., 64/74, trans. modified). This thought, however, already points beyond itself, disrupting *and* reestablishing its continuity with itself: "It is not in closing but in interrupting *Being and Time* that Heidegger wonders whether 'originary temporality' leads to the meaning of Being. And this is not a programmatic articulation but a question and a suspension. The displacement, a certain lateralization, if not a simple erasure of the theme of time and of everything that goes along with it in *Being and Time*, leads one to think that Heidegger, without putting back into question the necessity of a certain point of departure in metaphysics, and even less the efficacy of the 'destruction' operated by the analytic of *Dasein*, for essential reasons had to go at it otherwise [*s'y prendre autrement*] and, it may be said literally, to *change horizons*. // Henceforth, along with the theme of time, all the themes that are dependent upon it (and, par excellence, those of *Dasein*, of finitude, of historicity) will no longer constitute the transcendental horizon of the question of Being, but in transition will be reconstituted on the basis of the epochality of Being" (ibid., 64/74).

107. Heidegger, *Being and Time*, 459/407, raises the question whether "this dating is factically done with respect to a 'date' on the calendar," and continues: "Even without 'dates' of this sort, the 'now,' the 'then,' and the 'on that former occasion' have been dated more or less definitively."

108. The possibility of reversibility, Heidegger suggests, would be consistent with the leveling off and covering up of originary temporality. To the extent that the ordinary interpretation misunderstands its own implications and has it that time is irreversible, it points beyond itself or, rather, is haunted (cf. *Being and Time*, 477/425) by the temporality in which it remains grounded. Thus, Heidegger says, "even in this pure sequence of 'nows' which passes away in itself, primordial time still manifests itself throughout all this leveling off and covering up. In the ordinary interpretation, the stream of time is defined as an *irreversible* succession. Why cannot time be reversed? Especially if one looks exclusively at the stream of 'nows,' it is incomprehensible in itself why this sequence should not present itself in the reverse direction. The impossibility of this reversal has its basis in the way public time originates in temporality, the temporalizing of which is primarily futural and 'goes' to its end ecstatically in such a way that it 'is' already towards its end" (ibid., 478/426). The thesis of the irreversibility of time, then, is for Heidegger irreversible. But this irreversibility is founded not in time as we know it most of the time but in the structure and the *Augenblick* of originary temporality. The vulgar characteristic of time has a certain—natural yet limited—right of its own (Heidegger does speak, literally and in italics, of a "*natural justification*"; ibid.). It belongs to the mode of Dasein in its everydayness and fallenness. It only loses this right when it oversteps

its limit and presents itself as the "true" and only possible horizon of time. Conversely, only the analysis of the concept and the structure of original temporality enable us to "follow," "see," "estimate," and "judge" its derivation and "vulgarizations": "*why and how world-time belongs to Dasein's temporality* is intelligible only in terms of that temporality and its temporalizing. From temporality the full structure of world-time has been drawn; and only the Interpretation of this structure gives us the clue for 'seeing' at all that in the ordinary conception of time something has been covered up, and for estimating how much the ecstatico-horizonal constitution of temporality has been leveled off. This orientation by Dasein's temporality indeed makes it possible to exhibit the origin and the factical necessity of its leveling off and covering up and at the same time to test the arguments for the ordinary theses about time" (478–79/426). Heidegger hastens to add: "On the other hand, within the horizon of the way time is ordinarily understood, *temporality is inaccessible in the reverse direction*" (479/426). This is why Heidegger thinks one can speak of the derivation of the *Jetzt-Zeit* from temporality proper and identify the latter in terms of an original, originary time (*die ursprüngliche Zeit*, ibid.). This time temporalizes itself above all in terms of the future, whereas the ordinary interpretation of time is based on a restricted, indeed *circumcised*, "now" called the "present": "In the way time is ordinarily understood . . . the basic phenomenon of time is seen in the '*now*,' and indeed in that pure 'now' which has been shorn [*beschnittenen*] in its full structure — that which they call the 'Present'" (479/426–27, cf. also 474/422). Macquarrie and Robinson lose Heidegger's (unintentional) allusion to circumcision in the verb *beschneiden*. For Heidegger, then, the contrast between originary and ordinary time is one between fullness and circumcision. The use of equipment for measuring time, Heidegger writes somewhat earlier in the text, is "cut out from the determination of time [*auf die Zeitbestimmung zugeschnitten*]" (*Sein und Zeit*, 404), which Macquarrie and Robinson translate simply as "determined" (*Being and Time*, 456).

109. Paul Celan, "Well-digger in the Wind," trans. Hamburger, in *Poems of Paul Celan*, 319; "Brunnengräber im Wind," *Gesammelte Werke*, 2:336.

110. In another context (pertaining to the notion of spirit in Heidegger's reading of Trakl in *On the Way to Language*), Derrida notes: "'*Revenant*' is not a word of Heidegger's, and no doubt he would not like having it imposed on him because of the negative connotations, metaphysical or parapsychic, that he would be at pains to denounce in it" (*Of Spirit*, 91/142–43).

111. Heidegger, *Being and Time*, 472/419. But the relation between originary time and time as ordinarily conceived is complex, indeed, aporetic. Whereas the former grounds or conditions and fundamentally structures the latter, the subsequent analysis of the latter also in a sense justifies the (analysis of) temporality properly speaking. Simple determination in terms of ontological primacy and derivation — "The ordinary conception of time owes its origin to a way in which primordial time has been leveled off" — is

folded back on itself in that the conditioned becomes a condition of possibility of the conditioning instance, in turn: "By demonstrating that this is the source of the ordinary conception, we shall justify our earlier Interpretation of temporality as *primordial time*" (ibid., 457/405, cf. 478–79/426).

112. Ibid., 460–61/408, trans. modified.

113. Derrida, "Shibboleth," 64/112.

114. In *Being and Time* the *es gibt* functions differently from the way it does in, say, 'Time and Being" ("Zeit und Sein"). In the former text, it is an index of the improper, of everydayness, of temporality as ordinarily conceived, etc. (cf. *Being and Time*, 272–73, 463–64 / 230, 411).

115. Derrida, "Shibboleth," 37, 57 / 68, 102–3. Note that in *Basic Problems in Phenomenology* (240/340) Heidegger uses the formulation "prodigy" (*das Ungeheur*) to indicate the nonlocalizable character of time: "But really, then, where is this prodigy at home?"

116. Derrida, "Shibboleth," 38/68.

117. Paul Celan, "Cello Entry," trans. Hamburger, *Poems of Paul Celan*, 253, trans. modified; "Cello-Einsatz," *Gesammelte Werke*, 2:76.

118. Derrida, "Shibboleth," 38/69.

119. Paul Celan, "Largo," trans. Hamburger, *Poems of Paul Celan*, 327; *Gesammelte Werke*, 2:356.

120. Celan, Bremen address, trans. Waldrop, in Celan, *Collected Prose*, 35; *Gesammelte Werke*, 3:186.

121. Jean Greisch, *La parole heureuse: Martin Heidegger entre les choses et les mots* (Paris: Beauchesne, 1987), 354. See also Lacoue-Labarthe, *Poetry as Experience*, 66/97: "Celan is not saying time itself, but rather, speaking of the other who is, in every instance, a particular other, *his* time. The poetic act (the poem) is a singular experience, the dialogue is a singular dialogue. And this is of course what distinguishes poetry from thought proper."

122. Greisch, *La parole heureuse*, 360.

123. Already in the Introduction to *Being and Time* it is clear that the second "Abschnitt" is less concerned with an interpretation of "time" "itself" than with an interpretation of time as the meaning (*Sinn*) of Being. This, I would claim, results in an ontologization of time as temporality (and later epochality), whose fundamental—and fundamentally metaphysical—presuppositions Heidegger will from then on never revoke. Heidegger writes: "We shall point to *temporality* as the meaning of the Being of that entity which we call 'Dasein.' If this is to be demonstrated, those structures of Dasein which we shall provisionally exhibit must be Interpreted over again as modes [*modi*] of temporality" (38/17). But in this "interpreting Dasein as temporality" (ibid.), temporality is not only—or not primarily—described as the horizon, dimension or, indeed, *Sinn* of the being of the being called Dasein that we are. The structures of temporality seem, in turn, to be reduced to those of Dasein, as if they were *modi* or modes of Dasein rather than the other way around. Heidegger himself seems to allow for this

interpretation when he writes not only "that whenever Dasein tacitly understands and interprets something like Being, it does so with *time* as its standpoint" and "Time must be brought to light—and genuinely conceived—as the horizon for all understanding of Being and for any way of interpreting it" but also "In order for us to discern this, *time* needs to be *explicated primordially as the horizon for the understanding of Being, and in terms of temporality as the Being of Dasein, which understands Being*" (39/17).

Dasein is thus the transcendental horizon, the *Sinn*, and the truth of temporality *at least as much* as the inverse relation, on which Heidegger puts so much emphasis. But this logic of presupposition is already relativized by the fact that, in spite of repeated declarations, the existential analysis no less than the temporal interpretation it receives in the second division is both preliminary and secondary to an ulterior articulation of the meaning of Being "in general" (*überhaupt*) or "as such" (*als solches*), which, it should be noted, remains indefinitely postponed, well beyond the closing of *Being and Time*. Fundamental ontology, then, remains the alpha and omega of *Being and Time*, and perhaps not of this first part alone. One might well wonder, then, whether time, or rather, temporality—as distinguished from time in its everydayness or ordinary understanding—is ever discussed in its own right or as such at all. Certainly, Heidegger writes: "If Being is to be conceived in terms of time, and if, indeed, its various modes and derivatives are to become intelligible in their respective modifications and derivations by taking time into consideration, then Being itself (and not merely entities, let us say, as entities 'in time') is thus made visible in its 'temporal' character. But in that case, 'temporal' can no longer mean simply 'being in time.' Even the 'non-temporal' and the 'supra-temporal' are 'temporal' with regard to their Being, and not just privatively by contrast with something 'temporal' as an entity 'in time,' but in a *positive* sense" (40/18–19). This *"positive"* meaning of the temporal, however, is nothing but a subtle echo or doubling of the modifications and derivations of Being "itself" or "as such." The temporal interpretation of the second division of *Being and Time* is in this sense a repetition, or *Wiederholung*, which does not add anything new but explicates time as that which is and as how it is. The temporal determination of Being—its being "determined primordially in terms of time," the articulation of the "*Temporality of Being*" (40/19)—is at the same time the leveling off, so to speak, of time (or at least of originary time) into the ultra-modality of being as being-possible. Faithful to the phenomenological method, which he seeks to mobilize as an ally in a work of destruction that he keeps in reserve for phenomenology as well, Heidegger is not willing or able to consider any time that is not ultimately or originarily Dasein's own, that is to say, its ownmost horizon and *Sinn*, its utmost possibility, and thereby the time of its life and of its being toward death. In other words, temporality does not make possible Dasein's "understanding of Being" (*Seinsverständnis*) and "address ... to entities" (*Ansprechen von Seiendem*; 458/406); rather than having some "being" of its own, its temporalization (*Zeitigung*) is just another word for the fundamental modality of this understanding of Being. In conclusion, when Heidegger ends *Being and Time* with two rhetorical questions—"Is there a way which leads from primordial *time* to the meaning of *Being*? Does *time* itself manifest itself as the horizon of *Being*?" (488/437)—the reverse of these formulations might just as well be true. This is the ground of our suspicion. In other words: Is there a way that leads from *Being* (as Being-possible) to the meaning of primordial *time*? Does *Being* manifest itself as the horizon (as the meaning) of *time*?

124. Derrida, "Shibboleth," 28–29/54.

125. See, for the notions *Situation* and *Ort*, Heidegger, *Being and Time*, 345–48/299–300.

126. Derrida, "Shibboleth," 9/22–23.

127. Ibid., 11/26.

128. Attridge, "Introduction," *Acts of Literature*, 26.

129. The question "Who?" must, however, be approached with the greatest caution. See Jacques Derrida, "'Eating Well,' or the Calculation of the Subject: An Interview with Jacques Derrida," trans. Peter Connor and Avital Ronell, in *Who Comes after the Subject?* ed. Eduardo Cadava, Peter Connor, and Jean-Luc Nancy (New York: Routledge, 1991), 96–119; Derrida, "'Il faut bien manger': Entretien (avec J.-L. Nancy)," *Confrontations* 20 (1989): 91–114.

130. Derrida, "Shibboleth," 61/108.

131. Celan, "The Meridian," 49/3:197.

132. See Broda, "'An Niemand gerichtet,'" in *Paul Celan*, ed. Hamacher and Menninghaus, 215 and 221n15.

133. Celan, "The Meridian," 49/3:197–98; quoted in Derrida, "Shibboleth," 5/18.

134. Emmanuel Levinas, "Paul Celan: From Being to the Other," in *Proper Names*, trans. Michael B. Smith (Stanford: Stanford University Press, 1996), 40, 46; Levinas, *Noms propres* (Montpellier: Fata Morgana, 1976), 59, 66. Greisch writes of Levinas: "If the hand possesses a metaphysical significance and if this significance rediscovers itself in the poem, turning the entire poem into the expression of an outstretched hand, then the significance of this gesture can be thought only on the basis of the primary character of the-one-for-the-other. Now, in the eyes of Heidegger, the gesture of the outstretched hand already supposes the gesture of being and the gestation of the world" (*La parole heureuse*, 387).

135. Lacoue-Labarthe, *Poetry as Experience*, 44, 43 / 65, 64.

136. Ibid.: "The human is in no way an 'ethical' category, and moreover, no category of this kind can resist the question of Being" (132n13/73n7). See also Martin Jörg Schäfer, *Schmerz zum Mitsein: Zur Relektüre Celans und Heideggers durch Philippe Lacoue-Labarthe und Jean-Luc Nancy* (Würzburg: Königshausen & Neumann, 2003).

137. See Jacques Derrida, "Pas," in *Parages* (Paris: Galilée, 1986), 20–116.

138. Paul Celan, "Praise of Distance," trans. Felstiner, *Selected Poems and Prose of Paul Celan*, 25; "Lob der Ferne," *Gesammelte Werke*, 1:33.

139. Cf. Paul de Man, *Allegories of Reading: Figural Language in Rousseau, Nietzsche, Rilke, and Proust* (New Haven: Yale University Press, 1979), 206.

140. In a note, Derrida refers to the third volume of Paul Ricoeur's *Time and Narrative*, subtitled *Narrated Time*, which had come to his attention while reading the proofs of "Shibboleth." This book, Derrida writes, "includes, in particular, a rich analysis of calendar time and the institution of the calendar. This 'institution constitutes the invention of a third form of time,' between 'lived time' and 'cosmic time.' The 'transcendental' analysis proposed (120 ff. / 153 ff.), above and beyond the genetic and sociological approaches, is developed specifically by means of a critique of the Heideggerian concept of 'ordinary time' and the elaboration of a philosophy of the trace, which is both close to and different from that of Levinas." This analysis, he adds, would merit a longer and more careful discussion than is possible in a note, at the moment of proofreading, though he hoped to return to the issue elsewhere ("Shibboleth," 195, n. to p. 15 / 121–22 n. to p. 33; quoting Paul Ricoeur, *Time and Narrative*, vol. 3, trans. Kathleen Blamey and David Pellauer [Chicago: University of Chicago Press, 1988]; *Temps et récit: Le temps raconté* [Paris: Seuil, 1985]).

141. Jacques Derrida, "'This Strange Institution Called Literature': An Interview with Jacques Derrida, in *Acts of Literature*, ed. Attridge, 55.

142. Cf. Derrida, *The Post Card*, 262/278, and *Glas*, 244 / 271, 272, left column.

143. Celan, "Shibboleth," 206/1:270.

144. Celan, "Backlight," trans. Waldrop, *Collected Prose*, 11; "Gegenlicht," *Gesammelte Werke*, 3:163.

145. Celan, "Do not work ahead," trans. Hamburger, *Poems of Paul Celan*, 315; "Wirk nicht voraus," *Gesammelte Werke*, 2:328.

146. Derrida, "Shibboleth," 2/13.

147. Celan, "With Letter and Clock," trans. Hamburger, *Poems of Paul Celan*, 107; "Mit Brief und Uhr," *Gesammelte Werke*, 1:154. See Derrida, *The Post Card*, 198/213. See also Derrida, "Shibboleth," 19/38–39.

148. *Theaetetus*, 192 c and d, cited in Jacques Derrida, *Memoires for Paul de Man*, trans. Cecile Lindsay, Jonathan Culler, and Eduardo Cadava (New York: Columbia University Press, 1986), 3; *Mémoires pour Paul de Man* (Paris: Galilée, 1988), 27.

149. "La poésie ne s'impose plus, elle s'expose" (Celan, *Gesammelte Werke*, 3:181).

150. Derrida, "Shibboleth," 36/65–66. For the need to risk meaninglessness, see Jacques Derrida, "Edmond Jabès and the Question of the Book," trans. Alan Bass, in Derrida, *Writing and Difference* (Chicago: University of

Chicago Press, 1978), 74; Derrida, *L'écriture et la différence* (Paris: Seuil, 1967), 111.

151. Celan, "The Meridian," 48–49/3:197.

152. See Martin Heidegger, "Die Sprache im Gedicht: Eine Erörterung von Georg Trakls Gedicht," in Heidegger, *Unterwegs zur Sprache, Gesamtausgabe* (Frankfurt a. M.: Klostermann, 1985), 12:75.

153. Celan, "The Meridian," 49/197.

154. Derrida, "Ellipsis," in *Writing and Difference*, 296/431. On the circle, see also *Margins*, 52–53n32, 60 / 60–61n20, 69.

155. Jean-Luc Nancy, "Sens elliptique," in *Revue philosophique* 2 (1990): 336. See also Werner Hamacher, "Hermeneutische Ellipsen: Schrift und Zirkel bei Schleiermacher," in *Texthermeneutik: Aktualität, Geschichte, Kritik*, ed. U. Nassen, (Paderborn: Schöningh, 1979), 113–48; and Jean Greisch, "Le cercle et l'ellipse: Le statut de l'herméneutique de Platon à Schleiermacher," in *Revue des sciences philosophiques et théologiques* 73 (1989): 161–84.

156. Celan, "The Meridian," 55/202.

157. Quoted in Otto Pöggeler, *Spur des Worts: Zur Lyrik Paul Celans* (Freiburg: Alber, 1986), 162.

158. See Jacques Derrida, "The Principle of Reason: The University in the Eyes of Its Pupils," trans. Catherine Porter and Edward P. Morris, in Derrida, *Eyes of the University: Right to Philosophy 2* (Stanford: Stanford University Press, 2004), 129–55; Derrida, "Les pupilles de l'Université. Le principe de raison et l'idée de l'Université," in Derrida, *Du droit à la philosophie* (Paris: Galilée, 1990), 461–98.

The Judeo-Christian, Jean-Luc Nancy

1. The term *historial* echoes Heidegger's notion of authentic historicality, which is what *Dasein* is by its essence. It concerns the fundamental way in which we live our temporality. See Martin Heidegger, *Being and Time*, trans. John Macquarrie and Edward Robinson (New York: Harper and Row, 1962), § 74 "The Basic Constitution of Historicality."—Trans.

2. I will generally translate Nancy's *trait d'union* as "hyphen," which is standard in the translation of Lyotard. When Nancy speaks simply of *trait*, I will use "mark" or, occasionally, "hyphen," according to context.—Trans.

3. In composition, the short or dashed stroke technique is found in the Neo-Impressionism of Georges Seurat and in some of Van Gogh's Seurat-influenced work. Short strokes of contrasting colors create a vibrant light.—Trans.

4. See Émile Benveniste, *Le vocabulaire des institutions indo-européennes*, vol. 1, *Économie, parenté, société* (Paris: Minuit, 1969), 199–202.—Trans.

5. A reference to Jacques Derrida, *The Gift of Death*, trans. David Wills (Chicago: University of Chicago Press, 1996).—Trans.

6. The French *s'y sauver* means to save oneself by dying and escaping one's faith. The French *s'en sauver* means narrowly to escape death. In both

cases, the French verb *sauver* contains a resonance with the signifying universe of Christology and soteriology, which the English "escape" does not convey. — Trans.

7. The paradoxical French reads, "La seule consistence est celle du fini en tant qu'il finit et qu'il se finit." — Trans.

www.ingramcontent.com/pod-product-compliance
Lightning Source LLC
Chambersburg PA
CBHW031236290426
44109CB00012B/314